A Refreshing Moder...
Perennial Problem

Noel Tyl – "Oh, it is so complicated. It is all so important. Yet, how very little time we give to the role of sexual energy in the lives of astrological clients ..."

Glenn Perry – "Problems with sexuality are not simply learned behaviors, but maladies of soul that take us deep into the mystery of human consciousness ..."

Marion D. March – "Health, money, and sex are the three topics closest to most peoples' hearts, and not always in that order; the one that functions the least will become the most urgent of the three ..."

Gina Ceaglio – "While one's personal demons cause torturous pain, they are the fuel feeding the flame of creativity. When we look at the lives of those who produced monumental works, it leaves little doubt ..."

John Townley – "Is sexual fantasy a creative and even desirable escape route or is it a potentially dangerous fountain of thought forms that may damage oneself or others at an astral level ...?"

J. Lee Lehman, Ph.D. – "Homosexuality can tell us a great deal about *all* sexuality ..."

Ted Sharp – "The urge to sexual union is a physical expression of an underlying drive to inner unity. In the true sharing of sexual love between two people, each of them is reborn ..."

Jayj Jacobs – "This article presents a guide to help us to counsel our clients to ascend from okay sex to great sex and to realize the rewards of an elevated, satisfying sexuality ..."

Anthony Louis – "Repressed material (Pluto) is powerful and deserves respect. I have seen cases of inexperienced therapists causing their clients to need hospitalization by digging too deep, too fast into memories of childhood trauma and abuse ..."

B. F. Hammerslough – "What insights, advice and perhaps even inspiration can we provide our clients who suffer from AIDS, and indeed any life-threatening disease ...?"

To Write to the Authors

If you wish to contact the authors or would like more information about this book, please write to the authors in care of Llewellyn Worldwide, and we will forward your request. Both the authors and publisher appreciate hearing from you and learning of your enjoyment of this book and how it has helped you. Llewellyn Worldwide cannot guarantee that every letter written to the authors can be answered, but all will be forwarded. Please write to:

Llewellyn's New Worlds of Mind and Spirit
P.O. Box 64383-K865, St. Paul, MN 55164-0383, U.S.A.
Please enclose a self-addressed, stamped envelope for reply, or $1.00 to cover costs. If outside U.S.A., enclose international postal reply coupon.

Free Catalog from Llewellyn

For more than ninety years Llewellyn has brought its readers knowledge in the fields of metaphysics and human potential. Learn about the newest books in spiritual guidance, natural healing, astrology, occult philosophy, and more. Enjoy book reviews, New Age articles, a calendar of events, plus current advertised products and services. To get your free copy of *Llewellyn's New Worlds*, send your name and address to:

Llewellyn's New Worlds of Mind and Spirit
P.O. Box 64383-K865, St. Paul, MN 55164-0383, U.S.A.

Llewellyn's New World Astrology Series
Book 14

Sexuality in the Horoscope

edited by
Noel Tyl

1994
Llewellyn Publications
St. Paul, Minnesota, 55164-0383, U.S.A.

FIRST EDITION, 1994
First Printing

Photograph by Christopher Wells

Library of Congress Cataloging-in-Publication Data
Sexuality in the horoscope / edited by Noel Tyl.
       p.   cm. — (Llewellyn's new world astrology series: bk. 14)
       Includes bibliographical references.
       ISBN 1-56718-865-6
       1. Astrology and sex. 2. Astrology and psychology. 3. AIDS
(Disease)—Miscellanea. I. Tyl, Noel, 1936–   . II. Series.
  BF1729.S4S48 1994   94-38857
  133.5′864677—dc20   CIP

Llewellyn Publications
A Division of Llewellyn Worldwide, Ltd.
St. Paul, Minnesota 55164-0383, U.S.A.

The New World Astrology Series

This series is designed to give all people who are interested and involved in astrology the latest information on a variety of subjects. Llewellyn has given much thought to the prevailing trends and to the topics that would be most important to our readers.

Future books will include such topics as astrology and sexuality, astrology and counseling, and many other subjects of interest to a wide range of people. This project has evolved because of the lack of information on these subjects and because we wanted to offer our readers the viewpoints of the best experts in each field in one volume.

We anticipate publishing approximately four books per year on varying topics and updating previous editions when new material becomes available. We know this series will fill a gap in your astrological library. Our editor chooses only the best writers and article topics when planning the new books, and we appreciate any feedback from our readers on subjects you would like to see covered.

Llewellyn's New World Astrology Series will be a welcome addition to the novice, student, and professional alike. It will provide introductory as well as advanced information on all the topics listed above—and more.

Enjoy, and feel free to write to Llewellyn with your suggestions or comments.

Other Books in this Series

Spiritual, Metaphysical & New Trends in Modern Astrology

Planets: The Astrological Tools

Financial Astrology

The Houses: Power Places of the Horoscope

The Astrology of the Macrocosm:
New Directions in Mundane Astrology

Astrological Counseling: The Path to Self-Actualization

Intimate Relationships: The Astrology of Attraction

The Web of Relationships: Spiritual, Karmic and Psychological Bonds

How to Use Vocational Astrology for Success in the Workplace

How to Personalize the Outer Planets:
The Astrology of Uranus, Neptune and Pluto

How the Manage the Astrology of Crisis:
Resolution through Astrology

Exploring Consciousness in the Horoscope

Astrology's Special Measurements

Forthcoming

How to Communicate the Horoscope Helpfully

Astrology Looks at History

How to Understand and Use Eastern Systems in Western Astrology

Contents

Introduction: Why Sex?
by Noel Tyl
1

Pluto Pathology: The Dark Side of Human Sexuality
by Glenn Perry
35

Relationship Dynamics and Their Sexual Reality
by Marion March
95

Sexual Energy and Creativity
by Gina Ceaglio
129

Imagination/Fantasy: Sexuality's Escape Valve
by John Townley
161

Delineating Sexuality
by J. Lee Lehman
197

Freeing the Spirit: Getting Beyond Denial
by Ted Sharp
231

Integrating the Sexual Profile for Wholeness
by Jayj Jacobs
271

**Issues of Sexual Repression: The Interface between
Astrology and Psychology**
by Anthony Louis
297

AIDS: An Astro-Medical Perspective
by Bruce Hammerslough
319

Noel Tyl

For over 20 years, Noel Tyl has been one of the most prominent astrologers in the western world. His 17 textbooks, built around the 12-volume *Principles and Practice of Astrology*, were extraordinaily popular throughout the 1970s, teaching astrology with a new and practical sensitivity to modern psychotherapeutic methodology. At the same time, Noel presented lectures and seminars throughout the United States, appearing in practically every metropolitan area and on well over 100 radio and television shows. He also founded and edited *Astrology Now* magazine.

His book *Holistic Astrology: The Analysis of Inner and Outer Environments*, distributed by Llewellyn Publications, has been translated into German and Italian. He is one of astrology's most sought-after lecturers throughout the United States, and his international lectures are very popular throughout Denmark, Norway, South Africa, Germany, and Switzerland, where for the first three World Congresses of Astrology he was a keynote speaker.

Most recently, Noel wrote *Prediction in Astrology* (Llewellyn Publications), a master volume of technique and practice, and has edited Books 9 through 14 of the Llewellyn New World Astrology Series, *How to Use Vocational Astrology*, *How to Personalize the Outer Planets*, *How to Manage the Astrology of Crisis*, *Exploring Consciousness in the Horoscope*, and *Astrology's Special Measurements*. In the spring of 1994, his master opus, *Synthesis and Counseling in Astrology—The Professional Manual* (almost 1,000 pages of analytical technique in practice), was published. Noel is a graduate of Harvard University in psychology and lives in Alexandria, Virginia.

Why Sex?

Noel Tyl

At my fine local bookstore, most of the non-fiction books deal with cooking and travel. The next most numerous are books concerned with female fulfillment, especially sexual fulfillment.

It is safe to say that practically every woman's magazine published in the western world has, in every issue, some article or commentary that deals with sexual fulfillment.

In contrast, my bookstore displays books devoted to male sexuality at a ratio of one to ten those devoted to female, and men's magazines rarely talk about sexual problems, but, instead, depict sexual titillation, conquest, and glory.

Social consciousness is bombarded continuously and erroneously with the suggestion that women are sexually problematic and men are not.

Issuing from this state of affairs is the opinion among many women (and, I dare say, among many frustrated men) that sex is more important for men than it is for women. Of course, this is not the case—it *does* take two to tango—but the erroneous opinion serves a purpose. It works to diminish the importance of sex for women and gives men a self-aggrandized position, free from complicity in the problem itself.

Additionally, especially after marriage when the "search" for fulfillment may have ground to a halt, or settled down to a bored routine, the resulting frustration leads both genders to bother each other less; i.e., women want sex less frequently, men initiate sex less often. This condition pervades American (Western) society, and nourishes many strata of underachievement and misery in our lives. The next step may well be, in heterosocial behavior, that is, that men behave badly, animalistically, and women behave self-sacrificingly, nobly. Finally: women are right, and men are wrong.

It began with Adam, the first of everything human. A man. His heart and mind sent his blood supply throughout his body, including his penis. His senses made contact with the environment. The miracle-promise of procreation cried out for fulfillment, for the necessary "other."

It followed with Eve, the second of everything human. A woman. Her procreative system sent out signals. She and Adam emulated the animal life about them, and we were born.

Immediately, there were problems which religious history has created within complex allegories to teach spiritual doctrine, to control behavior and preserve peace, and to dramatize the existence of the Divine and the schism between our realms. Eve was cast as second, as temptress, as allied with evil. Adam was cast as the seduced, felled by his lust for knowledge. Humans by definition were in bad shape from the very beginning. How difficult this has been throughout socio-religious history.

Indeed, humans did find pleasure in sex, some enjoyment beyond procreation or conquest and submission. These people with very humanized gods saw art, beauty, and divinity in sex. They found pleasure in depicting the human form and recounting tales of togetherness. While poets, painters, and troubadours touched the heart, still the stereotypes prevailed: the man demanded, won, and penetrated, the woman acquiesced, lost, and received.

While psychiatrists and sexologists have only within this century acknowledged the *all-pervasive* energy of sexuality , i.e., the creative process, and measured the appreciation of sex as pleasure in correlation with the increase of intelligence and communication skill, *it has always been so*. Sex has always been more popular among the leaders of society than among the less privileged. With information, the advantaged regulate procreation and increase pleasure; they explore instinct. The less advantaged with less information build the family to help with work and ensure survival; they obey instinct. Among the many, when procreation is finished, pleasure is nowhere in sight. It was never there.

Throughout time, with the constantly reiterated threat of damnation, the churches of the West brought Eden forward: the necessity of procreation and the inconsequence of pleasure. Our primordial drives take cover in fashionable, symbolic forms: anthropologists point out how women paint their lips and blush their cheeks to suggest the vulva and buttocks for all to see, their perfume announcing their heated availability; men stake out their territories and with belligerence and weaponry portray the penis for all to fear, and their smells announce their ubiquitous right. Woman may have one man; men seek many women. The pristine veneer of religious institutions and the celibacy example of some shame us in our animal state.

We play games. We hide nakedness. We lie about feelings. We tend to avoid intimacy. We censor thought, dream, and communication. We feel guilty and even lazy if we spend time giving and receiving pleasure. We suffer within the creative fundament of who we are.

Amid all of this, we live our normal lives. We're told of instincts, expectations of performance, and various outcomes of sexual activities. Society gives us little guidance: we are not taught how to be sexual efficiently. Only in most recent times, within the knowledge of conceptual technologies, has procreation been given any study whatsoever. Medical science and churches have heretofore given us little grace; we have not been allowed to enjoy the expression of sex for pleasure, under penalty of disease, dementia, and/or social dysfunction. And now, except in the socially blessed state of monogamy, sperm is to be avoided at all costs. Confinement of instinct has taken an ultimate form, and the primal energies swirl within.

What are we supposed to do with our feelings, our drives, our imaginations . . . our sexual instincts? Just as a dream takes potentially disruptive stimuli and incorporates them into some mentally manageable "story" to preserve sleep, so our fantasies take our sexual impulses and fabricate some manageable scenario to settle us back into the behavioral routine that preserves peace. It is in dreams and fantasies that we find so much of who we are—what we fear, what we long for.

That we grin (or scowl) and bear it, i.e., the frustration that we accept as "part of life," is not natural. It is a socially evolved way to keep the peace. Armor and plumage have taken different forms now. Worship of the phallus has been transmuted to keeping house, raising children, and putting up with maleness. The male still demands; the woman still receives; "for better or for worse!" The conventional, the conservative, the correct prevail. *Routine protects against the disruption by individuation.*

The enormous energy of selfhood—the thrust and embrace of life to come, the creativity of potential, the pleasure of feeling one's deepest being—goes underground. Men's magazines, books, films, and gossip tell tales in over-sized physical terms commanding the screaming wildness of female need. Women's magazines, books, films, and gossip tell tales of gentleness, trust, cavalier honor, lengthy attention by a tender male; or a worldly and dominant male, lustful, and coercive through the power of love. The expectations built up in our minds and mores are awesomely out of reach. The resulting frustrations inhibit creativity, upset relationships, and, if they are not discharged somehow in reality or fantasy, are turned over to psychiatrists for resolution.

To defend against eons of stereotyping, the roles of male and female in modern Western society have begun to change, most substantially in the last three decades. Women have become more aggressive and men more sensitive. Women's animus is awakened: they demand recognition, respect, and fulfillment. Men's anima is awakened: they are willing to listen.[1]

Oh, it is so complicated. It is all so important. Yet, how very, very little time we give to the role of sexual energy in the lives of

---

1 It is extraordinary that the horoscope can not define male or female. With all the delineation that is possible through our symbologies, one would expect some way to see gender. Perhaps it is that the human is natively androgenous, being of both genders, giving enormous importance to Jung's deductions of animus and anima, the male awareness in the female and the female awareness in the male, respectively. Perhaps this androgyny is presented to us through the classical dual rulerships by Mercury, Venus, Mars, Jupiter, and Saturn of one masculine sign (Earth, Water) and one feminine sign (Fire, Air) each. All of this must certainly be reviewed and assimilated into our study of modern society.

Indeed, the very assignation of genders to the signs and planets in the first place was an extension of man's view of the world (there were few if any female cosmic theorists early in history). After all, Mars, the ruler of Aries (and Pluto) is aggression, force, sex; Venus, the ruler of Taurus (and Libra) is receptive, organizing, relational, aesthetic. Even the very descriptions of these two planets in the preceding sentence assigns power-nouns to Mars and modifying adjectives to Venus.

astrological clients, in the actual horoscopes we embrace to help people help themselves to reach the sun. Is it that our own discomfort with the subject gets in the way? Is it that we are not informed enough to do the subject justice? Is it that we fear being misinterpreted by our clients, jarring them within a tension-wracked area of deepest personal involvement, and incurring their defensiveness?

It is not so difficult in the East. In India, Nepal, Tibet, China, and Japan, sexuality has long been regarded as both an art and a science. Sexuality is worthy of detailed study and practice. It is part of theology. Indeed, as stated unequivocally by scholars, it is the eastern view that no learning is complete without a thorough knowledge of the sexual principles underlying all existence. They see liberation as oriented in a positive spiritual direction, achieving Oneness through sexual intercourse, "the most universally accessible mystical experience."[2]

With clients from the East, when sexuality needs to be discussed, the dialogue is relaxed and flowing. There is no censorship. Sex is part of the good life, not a legacy of complications and fears. Evaluations and understandings of personal involvement in that lifestream are matters of fact. Indeed, in the sexual art of the East, the genitalia of both genders are portrayed as pronounced and out of proportion often, but this is lyrical emphasis rather than dramatic projection of an overstatement born of frustration. Diversity and innovation of sexual expression are depicted routinely. Sex in the East raises no eyebrow.

So we in the West must work through the millennia of Judeo-Christian explanation, through shame and fear of damnation. Through matrices of guilt, we have to find our place on a spectrum between good and evil, right and wrong, approved or disapproved, safe or sorry. If only our western God had a sexual nature.

---

2 *Sexual Secrets; The Alchemy of Ecstacy*, Nik Douglas and Penny Slinger, Destiny Books, New York, 1979.

The Horoscope

The experience of sexuality is complex in its manifestation in life, and in its occurrence in the horoscope. Sexuality involves our states of self-awareness and self-esteem, our capacity for communication, the influence of parental modeling and tutelage, our capacity to express love and to cooperate, and our establishment of relationship with another person who is under the same need pressures and guilt awareness. This brings us from the Ascendant to the 7th House.

Within sexuality expressed in relationship, the Houses 7 through 12 describe the states of self-awareness and self-esteem of the other person. The interaction is deeply dynamic. Indeed, the Houses 7 through 12 have direct correspondences for us on their own, *but the experiences are framed in terms of others' perspectives:* others' monies and estate for the 8th; others' communication, which becomes our learning, the decrees of society's courts, the experience of other locales for the 9th; part of the parental (and in-law) influence in the 10th; friends, love given by others (the fifth of the 7th) in the 11th; and the accumulated interaction with society and other-world, psychical dimensions in the 12th.

The 5th House is the House that echoes the fifth harmonic of the circle, i.e., 360/5=72 degrees, the quintile aspect. The quintile is given *the archetypal symbolism of creativity* because the human form inscribed within the circle can make contact with the circumference at five places: feet, hands, and head. The addition of the head contact emphasizes intelligence, the knowing that plans action, a development out of the the instinctive square aspect, the fourth harmonic, with the human form four-squared within the circle, touching the circumference with only feet and hands.

This archetype of creativity contains the essence of the trine aspect as well; while the House significance is founded on the numerological base of 5, its essence of free-flow is captured within the *third* harmonic (referring to the Elemental Triplicities), i.e., energy manifests most easily, as it should. In the natural distribution of signs, the sign on the 5th House is trine to the sign on the Ascendant: the life-zones of experience of the Ascendant and the 5th House flow easily together, and support one another. Self-awareness and projection extend creatively and smoothly through to the 5th in terms of *putting the self further forward*. This is accomplished through the creation of new life, the extension of ourselves through children. Psychodynamically, it is the experience of giving love.

The 9th House is the fifth House of the 5th, starting at the 5th as a new Ascendant focusing on children, for example, and extending the fifth dynamic even further in terms of creative love given. The 9th House becomes our children's children, our grandchildren. In turn, the fifth dynamic extended from the 9th House brings us again to the Ascendant: our children's children's children. We go forth, we are fruitful, and we multiply. In the natural distribution of signs, the 1st, 5th, and 9th carry the Fire signs of Aries, Leo, and Sagittarius, the archetypal horoscopic of precepts of procreation: self-focus, self-dramatization, self-extension.

The 5th House is the organization center of the procreative matrix: it is love-given, it is children, and it is sex.

Granted, in the natural distribution of signs, Scorpio is the sign given most blatant sexual significance, especially in terms of regeneration and procreation. Much of astrological theory assigns sexuality to the 8th House. But why not include the creation children? Why not any kind of self-expression akin to love?

Perhaps resolution of this theoretical argument is that sexuality is in *both* the 5th and the 8th Houses, and others. Perhaps it is like the conundrum of which parent is in which House of the parental axis. This latter mystery has ceased to mean much in modern times, what with paths to one's profession (10th House) now established independent of parental influence, with the social breakdown of the family structure and the encounter with multiple parent figures, and with the incipience of role reversal between the genders. In the study of sexuality, we must include the values of the other person (the 8th House, the second of the 7th). Sexuality must include the experience of love from someone else, i.e., the 11th, the fifth of the 7th. Indeed, we can not give love from ourselves unless our self-worth is clarified and secure, i.e., our 2nd House, completing the Succedent Grand Cross of Houses.

In other words, we must see sexuality as the dynamic power it is, *based on our relationship with ourselves—the 2nd House—with that beginning extending into sexual preparedness in the 5th*. Then, our sexuality meets the values and preparedness of others' sexuality.

The 11th House, the fifth of our partner, becomes our experience of love received, love hoped for, and our sense of being loveable.

It is no accident that the 2nd House is opposed (is in full awareness of) the 8th, our self-worth and our partner's, and the 5th is opposed the 11th, love given/received. It is no accident that the 2nd is *always* square to the 5th, the 5th square to the 8th, the 8th square to the 11th, the 11th square to the 2nd: *our experience of sexuality has myriad developmental tensions within its purview.* This is how it is supposed to be in the hologram of our horoscope.[3]

What we are dealing with here is the ubiquitous outreach of the process of synthesis: all things are related within the horoscope and within us. Our arbitrary division of the circle into Houses with cusp-lines (and 50-some different systems dividing time and space differently) is simply a device to help us manage so much time and space more easily, to help orient us within the grand circle. Similarly, our arbitrary use of certain "major" planetary aspects more than other "minor" aspects is a way to get on with analysis, i.e., proceeding from the general to the specific, from the more obvious concept to the less.

The basic preparedness for sexual experience, the disposition toward the experience is in the 5th House and, so often, *the kind of sex, the values of sex, or the significance of sex* is in the 8th House. For example, the prostitution of sex is often indicated through aspect and rulership references between the 5th and the 8th House because of that House's significance for sexuality in terms of other people's money (the second of the the 7th), while the 5th House remains the person's basic sexual identity, his or her capacity to give love, to embrace sex in life experience.

Xaviera Hollander

Look at Example #1. This is the horoscope of Xaviera Hollander, the international prostitute and madame, the author of *The Happy Hooker* and several other books, and the sex-guidance columnist for *Penthouse* magazine.[4]

---

3   For a complete development of this thesis applied to the three Grand Crosses of Houses, please see Tyl, *Synthesis & Counseling in Astrology* (Llewellyn Publications, 1994).

4   Hollander herself gave me her birth data during a two-hour long, in-person interview. There are other times published for her birth, but this time of 4:00 A.M. is precisely what she wrote down for me and discussed with me at length.

Hollander's 0 Taurus Ascendant is corroborated amply by her body structure: a stocky woman, not lithe or chic as the courtesan's image is established in our mind, and she became morbidly obese after age 35 or so. Her Ascendant ruler, Venus is highly emphasized conjunct Pluto and square the Ascendant; exactly semisquare her Sun, square her Moon, trine her Mars, sextile her Uranus and very active in midpoint pictures throughout the horoscope.

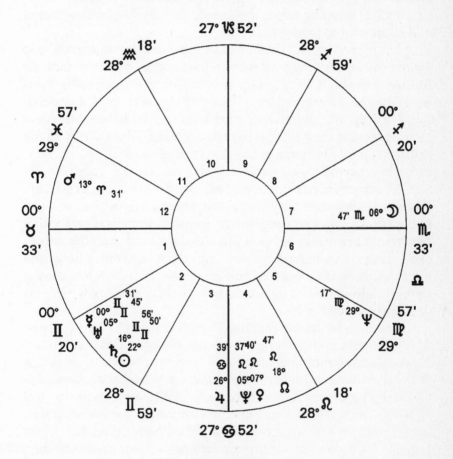

Example 1
Xaviera Hollander
June 15, 1943, 4:00 A.M. JST
Surabaya, Java
112E45 07S15
Placidus Houses

The other aspect groupings are quite clearly delineated: the Mercury-Uranus conjunction in Gemini trines her Neptune (across the signline) which corresponds to her imagination and her writing career, with Mercury ruling her communication 3rd and her work environment 6th, with the Mercury-Uranus conjunction trine her Midheaven. Mercury is the final dispositor of the horoscope. Hollander is an accomplished linguist, speaking six languages fluently. She is a brilliantly engaging conversationalist, and her discourses are replete with sexual references, fantastic psycho-dramatic references, made inoffensive by her charm and command of language.

Saturn is conjunct the Sun in Gemini, and this conjunction is square to Neptune, again a tremendous energy-vector of fantasy. Jupiter is sextile Mercury and sextile Neptune, increasing even more the mental strengths—all things mercurial—and it opposes the Midheaven, channeling again (along with the Mercury-Uranus trine to the Midheaven) her communication ability to the status of an international profession (ruling the 9th).

On a sexual level, we look to the 5th House, ruled by the Sun which is in conjunction with Saturn. This suggests that there is sexual difficulty in development and/or that sex can easily be used as a strategy (often an overcompensation for difficulty). There can be serious purpose involved with the sexual experience. This is particularly important here since Saturn is the ruler of her Midheaven: Hollander's way with sex is directly related to concerns in her early homelife, and sex is Hollander's profession.

The Sun-Saturn conjunction is widely squared Neptune just inside the 5th; and with all the intense focus on Gemini, we can expect that something is other than it seems (Neptune), that it is intensely different, highly individualized. Sexually, Hollander is unabashedly bi-sexual and extremely imaginative in her sexual scenarios, as revealed to me in conversation, in her books, and in her column in *Penthouse* magazine. Nothing is ruled out of her preparedness, her disposition toward sexual experience. To her, sex is a social cause, and she is its champion for individual freedom from confinement.

The 8th House is ruled by Jupiter, and her Jupiter is opposed her Midheaven. As part of her sexual profile, we see the professionalism of the prostitute.

Hollander's sexuality issues from the Venus dominant Ascendant, through the powerfully accentuated 2nd and 3rd of self-awareness and communication for profit, through the 4th with undoubtable roots to her prostitute identity formulated in the early home environment, and into the shining fantasy–5th, through the 6th (Mercury and Venus ruled), and into public relationship through the Moon in Scorpio in the 7th (squared Venus and Pluto, and then into the 8th of others' values. In fact, within Hollander's aspect organization, through tenancy and rulership, the entire horoscope—all Houses—comes together within her extraordinary sexual profile. She lives it well, is helpful to others, and is seriously proud.

Christine Keeler

Example #2 is the horoscope of Christine Keeler, the photo-model call girl prominently involved in the espionage scandal with British Defense Minister John Profumo in the early 1960s. Key in this horoscope is that the Sun in Pisces, ruler of the 5th, is peregrine; i.e., it has no dignity by sign and makes no Ptolemaic aspect with any other planet. The symbolism of the peregrine planet will often dominate the horoscope. Keeler's giving herself up to others is very clear, with the inclination initially introduced by the 12th House group, the absence of any planet in a Cardinal sign, and no square in the horoscope. She could be led by anyone, and she *was* led by the singularly powerful aspect in the horoscope, the angular opposition between Venus and Pluto, with Venus bringing in the 12th House depression-group through the mutual reception between Venus and Uranus.

The 5th House profile then is one of sacrifice, giving oneself over to others for service and support (Pisces), finding some pride in the process (Sun, Leo). There is the suggestion of self-deceiving ideals (a natural defense mechanism) through Mercury's co-rulership of the 5th (and her Ascendant), its conjunction with Venus, both retrograde, and the presence of Neptune (something is other than it seems) in the 5th. Keeler needed to be taken care of. "Friends" took the place of family.

Jupiter is ruler of the 8th and is in her Ascendant exactly trine her Mercury, ruler of her Ascendant and co-ruler of her 5th, in the 10th. Sexually, Keeler did what she was told, and she was paid for it by others (Jupiter also rules the 7th). Undoubtedly,

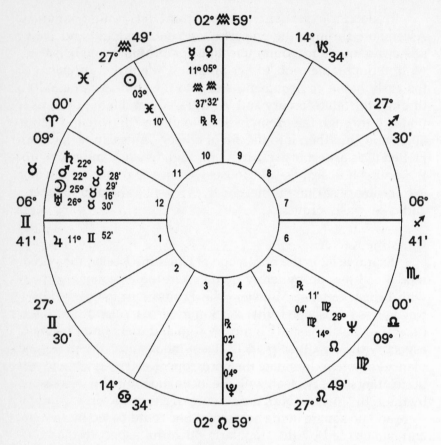

Example 2
Christine Keeler
Feb. 22, 1942, 11:15 A.M. GMD
London, England
00W10 51N30
Placidus Houses

there are serious problems in her cognitive process, with the 12th House group keying the 3rd–9th axis, linked to one of the parents in particular, through Uranus rulership of the 10th, Pluto on the parental axis, and the importance of Mercury.[5]

---

5   The dramatic angularity of Pluto here opposed the Midheaven is part of the profile of prominence established that is very clearly established in astrology. Keeler was a nobody, and, within the Profumo scandal, she became known throughout the world. For a thorough presentation of the profile of prominence, see Tyl, *Synthesis & Counseling in Astrology* (Llewellyn Publications, 1994).

It would be too easy, if you will, to see Venus opposed Pluto, so strongly angular, and deduce "high sex" from this one aspect alone. That analysis would be a flip, irresponsible generalization. This aspect could very well suggest an over-emotional state (perhaps a waste of emotions) within very strong personal problems, especially with Venus ruling Taurus in the 12th, i.e., disposing of the stellium, and ruling Libra on the 6th, illness, emotional illness. What suggests strongly the dimension of sexuality as a means to some kind of personal life-statement is the combination, the synthesis of the wanton passivity suggested by the peregrine Pisces Sun, ruler of the 5th; the Neptune fantasy-element there trine the 12th House group, giving *a veiled outlet to the problems through the 5th House,* through serving friends (Neptune ruling Pisces in the 11th, holding the Sun). Finally, the trine between Jupiter and Mercury links the rulers of the money axis, Keeler's 2nd and the 8th of others' monies, and of course the 7th. Pleasing others raised her self-worth and proved her to be desirable (11th House significance).

Additionally, the retrogradation of the idealization conjunction of Mercury and Venus and the retrogradation of Neptune suggest a second level of significance to all deductions in the horoscope. Prostitution here was a secondary life, as contrasted with Hollander's up-front, full-time dedication to sexuality professionally.

Rosemarie Nitribitt

Example #3 is the horoscope of Rosemarie Nitribitt, a notorious German luxury call girl with a clientele among the politically and financially powerful throughout Europe. She was murdered on November 1, 1957, by a strangler who has never been found.

The organization of this horoscope is astoundingly clear: Venus, ruler of the 5th and the 10th, is in Capricorn (most often a delay in emotional maturation and certainly a coolness or a detachment within emotional expression) opposed Pluto, ruler of the 11th (attention, love received), and this axis is squared by the Moon in Aries (the reigning need to be "numero uno," very important), ruler of the 8th. We need see little more than this to inquire about the sexual profile.

Note as well that the Sun is *also* ruler of the 8th; and Mars-Jupiter are opposed the Sun-Moon midpoint. Mars in Virgo is the mistress (or master) of technique, a kind of passionate chastity or a sexual technician. Finally, see that the 2nd House is highly emphasized: self-worth, money, and its focus involves the rulers of the 5th, 6th, 7th, 8th, and the 2nd itself, Saturn. With the driving Venus-Pluto-Moon T-Square, all Succedent Houses are involved.

Finally, Neptune is peregrine. Something is other than it seems and it pervaded her thinking process (Neptune rules the 3rd; and is being pulled into the 9th). A loss of, or a fabrication, of

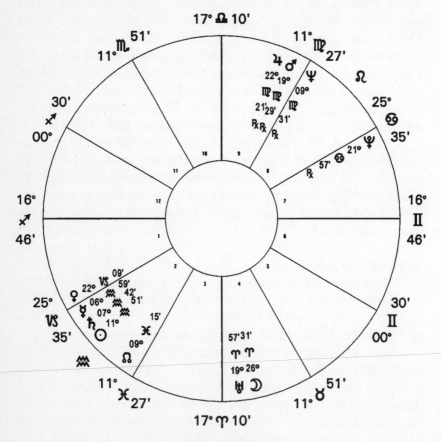

Example 3
Rosemarie Nitribitt
Feb. 1, 1933, 4:45 A.M. CET [Time Suspect]
Frankfurt Am Main, Germany
08E40 50N07
Placidus Houses

an ideal controlled her thinking. The sense of sacrifice that always accompanies Neptune certainly would influence the fundamental development base that brought her into prostitution. She was covert; she went methodically about her business to be unusual, to be important (Sun in Aquarius energizing the Aries Moon), and this Neptunian sense was echoed by the pattern of retrogradation (a second level of concern), the status of the planets above the horizon. Nitribitt had a pathological self-worth anxiety problem that she tried to work out through prostitution. Love missed was money gained.

Lawrence of Arabia

Example #4 is the horoscope of Thomas Edward Lawrence, known as Lawrence of Arabia. Lawrence was an English soldier, archaeologist, and author, but he entered history through his activities in arousing and directing a successful rebellion of the Arabs against the Turks during World War I. His exploits were lionized by a grand film treatment some years ago.

The first impression of this horoscope is certainly other than we would expect; it is compressed, depressed below the horizon. Only the Sun-Moon blend speaks of potential heroism and international exploits with the energies for ego-recognition dramatized—daring and adventure—and lifted to the level where ideals catch fire. This contrast with the weightiness below the horizon is corroborated in Lawrence's life by the fact that he enigmatically fled from his legendary status into obscurity, refusing knighthood, retiring from public life, and even joining the British Air Force as a private, under a pseudonym!

Biographers and historians agree that Lawrence was deeply troubled. His problems manifested within his sex life as well; Lawrence was a homosexual and a masochist of a most dramatic extent.

Two main aspect groups dominate the horoscope: the Moon opposes the Neptune-Pluto conjunction and this axis is squared by Venus in Virgo (a cerebral take-over of the emotions; an intellectualization; a strictness, properness, prissiness); Saturn is conjunct Mercury, the ruler of Lawrence's Ascendant *and* 5th House, with Saturn ruling his 8th. And this most telling conjunction was opposed his Midheaven.

Lawrence's sexuality was cerebrated, his mind came before his body. In fact, the way to his body was *through his mind*, and this approach to his mind would be through discipline, stricture, confinement, punishment.

This analysis is not "automatic," of course: not everyone with Virgo on the cusp of the 5th and Saturn conjunct Mercury, also ruling the Ascendant, is predisposed to masochism sexually. The suggestion for someone else would conceivably be that the sexual profile would be cerebrated, with a very strong sense of

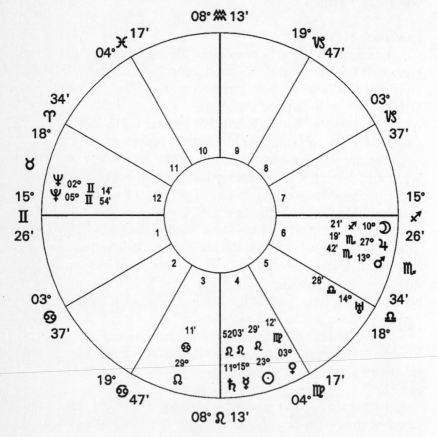

Example 4
Lawrence of Arabia
Aug. 15, 1888, 11:20 P.M. GMT
Tremadoc, Wales GB
04W09 52N56
Placidus Houses

responsibility about sex, an economical way with expressing love, perhaps a slowness in sexual response. But here for Lawrence of Arabia, with his established life-record setting the level of interpretation and with the massive T-Square involved as well, the statements of masochism are securely founded and indeed corroborated.

Going further, we see Mars in Scorpio ruling the 12th and square Mercury-Saturn and the Midheaven; a very powerful excitation and clash of values, hot and cold, private and public, sexual and reserved.

Lawrence was two people; the grandest of heroes (Sun-Moon blend, Sun square Jupiter in Scorpio, a fanatical belief in self; Uranus, ruler of the Midheaven trine the Ascendant as well) and the self-absorbed sexual penitent, apologizing for his grandeur and success. The schism in his life again undoubtedly issued from a problematic home-life (Saturn-Mercury symbolisms opposed the Midheaven; Moon ruling the self-worth 2nd involved with the difficult 12th House conjunction, etc.) which played into his cerebrated natal vulnerabilities to suffer and to be fulfilled in that suffering.

Jeffrey Dahmer, the homosexual serial killer, has Uranus as ruler of the 5th square Venus in Taurus in the 8th. Mercury and the Sun are also in the 8th in Gemini, and Mars in the 6th is semi-square Venus. Obviously, this is a portrait of a sexually intense human being. (See Dahmer's horoscope in Gina Ceaglio's and Glen Perry's chapters in this volume.)

Hugh Hefner's Mars is in Aquarius in his 5th, ruling his 8th, and the Mars is peregrine, running away with much of the personality. (See Ceaglio.)

In these two cases, the 5th and 8th Houses blur into each other. Neither can be analyzed without the other.

Rock star Madonna makes millions marketing her sexuality. Her Mars rules her 8th and is square her Uranus-Sun conjunction, but *Saturn retrograde rules her 5th and is square her Moon.* The real emotional base of Madonna's sexual profile is certainly shown through this Saturn disposition. There are great mother-relationship problems (note her name) and self-worth image problems, which will affect her personal capacity for sexual expression, its significance, its value.

Madonna's predisposition to sex is fundamentally dull, problematic, sullen, and ungratified. On the other hand, the style of sexual expression she has chosen to represent her, to project to the public, to market her identity *in enormous overcompensation,* is certainly shown and acted out by the Mars focus in the 8th, the values established by her public. Additionally, Neptune (something is other than it seems in her personal and public presentations) rules her 7th and squares her Venus, ruler of her self-worth 2nd, the profile of a public sham. (See Madonna's horoscope in John Townley's and Ted Sharp's chapters in this volume.)

At its base, sexuality is a combination of the 5th and the 8th Houses, not one House exclusively in focus over the other.

Planetary Signatures

As the Houses symbolize fields of life experiences, the planets symbolize energies; the needs we have and the behavioral faculties to fulfill them. On the sexual level, the planets speak of the energies involved in the disposition toward and expression of sex. Their roles in the sexual profile are determined *by their placements in the Houses,* especially the 5th and/or the 8th, and *by their rulerships of the Houses,* especially the 5th and/or the 8th.

In short, by tenancy and by rulership, the planets call attention to a particular field of experience and establish a value, a coloration, a distinctive quality for it. Planetary references working together with the Houses is the art of synthesis. In the preceding examples, through planetary placements and rulerships, we have seen very clear House references, especially within the Succedent Grand Cross of Houses, which we can call the Sexual Matrix, and we have been able to bring experiences together through routings of planetary referral. At the same time, our analyses have been strongly influenced by *planetary* placements in signs, in Houses, and in aspect with other planets.

Certain key symbol-concepts articulate potentials within the sexual profile quite reliably. The following are several that are most important to consider.[6]

---

6   These discussions are only a sampling from a full exposition of our sexual orientation to the horoscope. It is excerpted and abbreviated from Tyl, *Synthesis & Counseling in*

1. The Signs

Aries placements show aggression. Venus in Aries often connotes the tease, the testing of the waters through flirting to determine one's personal effect on others. Mars is ultimately aggressive, sex is conquest, and with an intensified Mars complex, for women as well, sex often takes on dimensions to prove oneself, to overcompensate for real or imagined lacks of popularity, attractiveness, or indeed as exploitation (punishment) of the male principle.[7]

Taurus placements suggest the importance of emotional and financial security, of peace and refinement, of self-indulgent awarenesses, of aesthetics and materialism, often directly tied to sex practice. Venus in Taurus connotes faithfulness most often, through thick and thin; the status quo is idealized even under duress. The requirement of comfort and refinement can be important for sexual success.

Gemini and Mercury relate to bi-sexuality, to different sex, to multiple partners, to swiftness in sexual performance. Mars in Gemini increases the nervous demands for sexuality. Uranian aspects to Gemini placements intensify all this.

Cancer can bring a swoon to the expression and actions of love and sexuality. Venus in Cancer suggests a dreamy softness, even an idealization. Mars in Cancer for women suggests the need to rule the roost, and this carries over to the sexual roles and requirements in relationship.

Leo is drama, front and center, on the sexual stage. In extremes, especially through Venus in Leo, there is the possibility of conceit, exhibitionistic tendencies, and conspicuous pampering and indulgence. Mars assumes, demands, pressures, and acquires what it needs. Jupiter in Leo deeply needs recognition and appreciation when configurated at a sexual level. Leo increases the ego-importance of sexual congress.

Virgo brings the mind into sexuality very strongly—for discrimination, for nervous concern, for emotional coolness (Venus), for mastery of technique (Mars), for detailed exactness (Jupiter).

---

7   As with all astrological observances of sensitive development areas, astrology's symbolization acts as a guide to discussion not as an ultimate explanation. The symbolization and our abbreviated descriptive keys of behavioral potentials have within them still other levels of psychodynamic motivation. Life is infinitely more complicated, subtle, and evasive than our language or, indeed, our astrology.

With Neptune emphasized, the fantasy component will be rich in symbolism.

Libra suggests peacefulness, calm, and the abhorrence of tension and worry in matters sexual. Usually there is a keen conspicuous sense of reciprocity in the sex act (Mars) and sometimes a naivete and social flightiness about the sensual with Venus accentuation within Libra. Jupiter involved with Libra constructs can involve an idealization within the deployment of sexual energies.

Scorpio symbolizes intense sexual energy that can be extremely deep in drive and lofty in value, at the same time; the swamp and the heavens. Scorpio dimensions can signify overindulgence, social difficulty, emotional waste, secretiveness, obsession, and, indeed, religious rationalization, especially through Jupiter references to the sign. Additionally, experimentation (akin to research) can be a strong part of the sexual drive, and in many cases diversification can conspicuously include an anal emphasis in sexual practice.

Sagittarius often adds very high standards to sexuality that then can be sacrificed on the stimulating spur of the moment. There can be a flip-flop in sexual values or a history of short-lived ideals. There is speed, even flightiness connected with Sagittarius positions. Mars especially brings the power of opinionation, persuasion, and a certain dimension of situational control into sexual expression.

Capricorn often retards emotional and sexual development. These can be an apparent coldness, a methodical, clock-like way about the sexual process. The paternal influence is so often involved with any difficulties. With Jupiter in relation to Capricorn emphasis, there is the demand that one's authority be acknowledged and respected. This is the sign of the analytical, sexual teacher, or, in stressed complexes, the murky, self-effacing wash-out.

Aquarius is the sign that adds a background of intensification to experiences. With Venus, the emotions become tremendously alive antennae, like litmus papers. With Mars, there can be the inclination to personal eccentricity in sexuality. There is always the sense of individual uniqueness.

Pisces emphasizes receptivity, even self-sacrifice, in the expression of sexuality. The emotions are so very deep with Venus and the energies are so inverted with Mars. Pisces is the energy of the languid sensualist, and, under strong complexities, the willing victim.

2. Significators

With the Sun or Moon in square or opposition with Saturn, Uranus, Neptune, or Pluto, there will usually be some familial component in the upbringing that complicates relationship dynamics in sexual expression (the Moon, the mother; the Sun, the father), especially if the planets involved make reference to the 5th and/or 8th House.

With the ruler(s) of the parental axis (4th–10th) and/or planets in the 4th or 10th under heavy developmental tension by aspect, relating to the 5th or 8th House, there will definitely be some dimension of early-home difficulty involved with the sexual profile, its difficulty in expression, or its idiosynchratic development, and its definite effect on relationships.

When the significator of the 5th House (the planet ruling the House or a major planet in it)[8] in a female horoscope is under high developmental tension (except with Uranus), including retrogradation, the probability is high that there are difficulties with sexual response, most often with orgasmic difficulty in relationship, which is personally frustrating and thoroughly disruptive of many relationship dynamics, sexual and otherwise. *(More about this very important consideration later in this chapter: how it is often offset and treated remedially.)*

When the significator of the 4th House is under high developmental tension, and so is the significator of the 5th, especially if they are within the same tension constructs, one of the parents will usually be a key inhibitor of the client's comfort level with sexuality. If Jupiter is implicated, the core concern will probably be religious.

When Mercury is a significator of the 5th and/or the 8th, talking about sex is very important to arousal, to being alerted to sexual involvement.

Mercury conjunct, square, or opposed Neptune will naturally increase fantasy activity, and that fantasy content as it relates to sexuality will be very important to appreciating needs, assimilating unfinished business in early development, and articulating

---

8 Here in this concern, the 5th House appears empirically to be much more important than the 8th in the female horoscope as the signifying House because of the sensitive role of "giving love" involved with the anxiety, expectations, and reality of relationship dysfunction.

hopes for personal appreciation in the future. The Mercury-Neptune relationship and the Mercury-Venus conjunction carry with them the potentials for idealization, and carry a religious rationale often when Jupiter is involved. See Gemini and Virgo in list category #1 above.

Venus-Pluto aspects (small-orb minor aspects as well, so sensitive is the Venus symbolism) carry with them the potential of extreme emotional involvement in sexuality, on the other side of passion, if you will, in obsessiveness, fixation, or compulsion. Emotionalism can be squandered through activities that have the deepest psychodynamic significance. Venus in a cardinal sign takes on aggression, leadership, a driving nature; in a fixed sign, a rootedness in self-awareness, a narcissistic vector; in a mutable sign, an intensivity of reaction.

Mars-Pluto aspects suggest aggression, the powers of self-assertion, and ego-focus of sexuality, especially Mars in Scorpio and, often, in Taurus. In a male horoscope especially, the significators Mars and Pluto carry with them the dimension of sex for blatant ego reinforcement. These two planets describe the visceral content of sex, come closest to the doing of sex.

Saturn-Venus aspects can introduce a conspicuous age difference (the concomitant psychodynamic identification with parent figures) in relationships, and constrict sexual expression.

Neptune configured in strong aspect with the Sun or the Moon, with Venus or Mercury (see above) bring a sense of suppression to sexuality often, when the 5th and/or the 8th House is involved by rulership or tenancy. If suppression does not fit the general synthesis of the horoscope or the client's reality, Neptune may simply refer to something else than is obvious, i.e., *something is other than it seems* wherever Neptune is located, or where Neptune rules. In the 7th House, the partner is most usually in need of or depends on (co-dependency syndrome is suggested) the person's support, help, leadership. The relationship may be a pretense, a mask, a substitute for some other need complex. In a male horoscope, Neptune strongly keyed to the 5th and/or the 8th and involved in strong, apparently debilitating aspect structure can suggest the possibility of embarrassment and depression about genital size, sexual performance, and, indeed, acute or chronic impotence.

Uranus is intensification, individualization, innovation, adventure. It is critically important when linked with Mercury by strong aspect, elevating the nervous system, which figures prominently in the urgency of the sex drive (and relief to the nervous system through orgasm), especially when linked to the 5th and/or 8th House. When Uranus is in strong aspect with the Sun and significator dynamics involve the 5th and/or the 8th; or with Venus or Mars, intensified or diversified sexual connotations are suggested.

Mars conjunct Neptune or, to a lesser extent, opposed, trine, or square, establishes charisma.

3. Special House Placements

Venus in the 12th House often corresponds to a "private sense of beauty." The aesthetic and emotional needs are privately protected within the accumulation of all that society says one should expect from relationship. The privacy of it all makes sexual fulfillment very difficult. Adjustment of the idealization will be important to freeing up sexual expression. Under heavy accentuation, this Venus position can suggest that sex is ritualized somehow, taken underground, twisted to comply with someone else's demands, i.e., the private sense of beauty—so unattainable—is given up completely.

With Saturn in the 11th, there is a tremendous need for love. This is not a simplistic suggestion: it is a deeply significant core-concern to the person and drives many activities in life development. It opens up a long list of vulnerabilities.

When the significator of the 11th is under high tension, anxiety about one's lovability is almost assured.

When Uranus is in the 11th, the expectation of love and attention is keen and needs to be intensely, demonstratively, and immediately served. The partner must suit these guidelines, or there is no relationship harmony.

Uranus oriental (rising last of all the other planets before the Sun in clockwise motion) suggests adventure and daring as a key to life expression, and will relate obviously to the sexual profile if the clear ties are there to other significators.

Mutual reception establishes a strong tie between two planets that may not be in aspect with each other, or will emphasize two planets that are in aspect. Venus in mutual reception with

Uranus, for example, immediately establishes in our interpretive sense an intensification or creative stylization, or an adventurous twist to expression of the the Venus symbolisms (by definition, Venus will always be in Aquarius, and Uranus will be in either Taurus or Libra). Venus and Saturn in mutual reception (Venus in Capricorn and Saturn in either Taurus or Libra) suggests an important bond within the expression of social, sensual, sexual needs, especially when one or both of these planets signify the 5th or the 8th.

A peregrine planet will probably influence the entire horoscope, including the sexual profile, but focus strongly within the experiences of its House and the House it rules.

FINAL NOTE

It must be repeated that these "keys" are observations of specific, sexual potentials that must find their place *within an orderly discussion of psychosexual development*. They are not for the purpose of entertaining description or prurient investigation, but rather they are intended to guide the appreciation of sexual development as is volunteered corroboratively by the client and framed within the astrologer's awareness of development patterns and structured symbolisms.

Rudolph Valentino

Example #5 is the horoscope of Rudolph Valentino, the silent movie star, dancer, and cult-figure of the 1920s. Valentino was a symbol of male sexuality that, even today, ranks among the most compelling Hollywood images ever produced. This slick gigolo to a film world's female fantasy was homosexual.

Here was a man born in a tiny Italian village, who took Hollywood by storm in his early twenties, captivated the lustful interests of anyone watching films, and was dead at 31; a meteoric rise to world fame and a reputation that lived on beyond the lives of the generations that adored him. Even an opera was written about Valentino; it was premiered by the Washington D.C. and Dallas opera companies in January 1994.

Valentino's popularity potential through his horoscope is seen dramatically in his 0 Libra Ascendant, opposite the Aries Point of

0 Aries, a vital measurement of renown potential researched for half a century by the Uranian School of astrology. (Any 0-degree placement in Cardinal signs of any planet or personal point in the horoscope carries with it the potential of conspicuous public exposure.) Venus, the ruler of the Ascendant, is *peregrine* in Gemini, potentially dominating the horoscope with its symbolism. Immediately, we can be alerted to multiple and diverse potentials within the sexual profile.

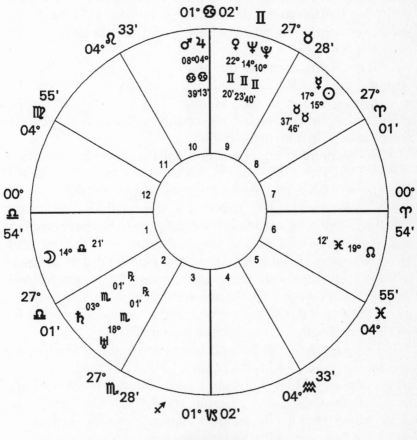

Example 5
Valentino
May 6, 1895, 3:00 P.M. CET
Castellaneta, Italy
16E57 40N38
Placidus Houses

Additionally, the Midheaven is one-degree from square with the Aries Point, with Mars and Jupiter conjunct the MC, square the Ascendant (and the Aries Point) and the Moon in Libra rising: an enormous social thrust for the personality, simply enormous. Note that Venus rules the 9th and is in the 9th, foreign countries (the United States), along with the rare conjunction of Neptune and Pluto, both trine the Moon in the Ascendant.

The flow of popularity in the (silent) communication business (Gemini emphasis; Pluto ruling the 3rd; Neptune, films) is completely free and easy here: there is no square in the horoscope, no tension to get in the way or, indeed, to build deeper substance behind the make-believe world. The horoscope reeks of self-indulgence.

The driving focus of the horoscope is Uranus in Scorpio opposed the Sun-Mercury conjunction in Taurus in the 8th, disposed of by Venus. In fact, Mercury and Venus are in mutual reception, again reinforcing the communication aesthetics that would take Valentino to the public.

In this dominating opposition, the Sun and Mercury are in the 8th and Uranus rules the 5th. We know that the sex profile will energize and intensify Valentino's core energies. Sex will be on his mind continuously. His nervous system will be insistently involved. Any personal anxiety will relate to or be channeled into sexual build-up and release, especially for ego reinforcement. Uranus is oriental, and the daring sheik-of-the-desert image of romantic adventures shown in the movies will become Valentino's personal way as well. Combined with the Venusian outpouring of the rest of the horoscope, this will be sexual magnetism for public consumption . . . without any doubt.

Uranus, ruling the 5th and linked so strongly with the Sun and Mercury and, additionally, the fact that it is retrograde alert us to some second level of significance within sexual interpretation. With the strong, strong Gemini emphasis, led by Venus peregrine, there is little doubt of Valentino's sexual duality: his on-screen heterosexuality and his off-stage homosexual life.

Again, through Saturn retrograde, ruler of the 4th House arm of the parental axis, with Uranus retrograde in the 2nd House of self-worth—also ruled by Venus!—we suspect tough going in relation to his father figure in the early home. Almost assuredly it was some such situation that propelled him out of the home to stardom in a make-believe world far away.[9]

Regular People

When we move away from highly etched examples of prominent people, away from their exposed individualistic sexual profiles, to apply astrology to the lives of "regular people" *we can not leave sex behind*. Regular people experience the same drives, the same upbringing dynamics, the same influence of history, society, education, and, as well, the same problems in relationship that famous people do. At the level of life lived by regular people, sexual needs, expression, diversification, fantasy support or catharsis, problems, and joys abound just as they do for famous people. Astrology, in its holistic service to everyone, must appreciate *their* sexual profile as well.

Orgasmic Response—Let us consider a ubiquitous sexual concern, the difficulty many, many—the majority, as many source references state—women have: orgasmic response in sexual relationship. It is a personal short-fall from aggrandized expectations that hurts deeply privately, and it spawns defensive and over-compensatory behaviors in most other areas of a relationship that can tear apart love and harmony.

The natural need for sexual expression—the exercise of instinct, neuro-muscularity, imagination, and emotions—builds normally just as our bodies grow, as our reproductive systems mature, but it is easily modified or distorted to one degree or another by the teachings of western society filtered through our parents and *their* overlay of sexual frustration and rationalization from *their* parents, etc. As other of our faculties grow along with our sexuality—our intelligence, perception, communication, social interaction, work effort—we encounter controls, interference, adjustment pressures, reinforcements, rewards, and success necessary to our development. In the process of maturation, *frus-*

---

9 Additionally, Valentino had Pluto at the midpoint of Sun/Jupiter; Venus at the midpoint of Jupiter/Pluto; and his Ascendant, on the axis of the Aries Point, square to the midpoint of Venus/Mars! Valentino died on August 23, 1926 in New York City. At death, his Venus and his Moon were once again symbologically dominant: Valentino died of an infected appendix (Venus) and complications from stomach ulcers (Moon and Mars): transiting Saturn had just opposed the Sun and was conjunct his Uranus, transiting Pluto was square the Moon, and SA Neptune, ruler of the 6th, was exactly square the Moon in his Ascendant, ruling his Midheaven.

tration and fulfillment seek out the vulnerabilities we have intrinsically to make their mark, to find a part of us in which they may be retained and become part of who we are.

If we see our parents involved with each other in an unloving, uncivil, or indeed bellicose way, patterned over and over again through outbreaks of anger, upset, coldness, estrangements, abandonment, we must explain it all in some way in our tender growing-up times of discovery. We have to make sense out of the status quo or we are lost. We do not have the conceptualization or verbal skills to understand. Our instincts are to emulate what we see, to assimilate the status quo, through parent modeling. This is why family dysfunction is so regularly repeated one generation to the next; why abused children become abusers; why divorce patterns repeat; why "unfinished business" pushes people to choose repeatedly spouses very like their mothers and fathers.

For example, if security needs are threatened during development, we are going to feel threatened, *who we are* is going to be jeopardized. Our self-worth will be tested as it is being developed. This is especially so *if we are natively vulnerable to self-worth anxiety*, if we are not protected enduringly enough against the onslaught of insecurity.

Astrology sees this particular vulnerability through stress to the significator of the 2nd House, through strong developmental tension with the Sun and/or the Moon (see above, category 2, especially). Defensively, we initially use our mind.

We are in early development, we are threatened, we have our natural vulnerabilities piqued, and we rally to protect ourselves, to justify our existence. Our fantasies construct self-image scenarios: we invent alter-egos in some cases, imaginary playmates; we dream of rescue, "some day my Prince will come." We project conquest, winning, being a champion or victor. Our toys feed those defensive needs. Our crayon drawings and strategies of play show our inner world of understanding and hope. Action heroes and love interests grow in importance in our life. We get out of ourselves to rebuild ourselves. [Under the greatest of abuse, for an extreme example to clarify the norm we are describing, multiple personalities are sometimes created, since the singular identity of self is not able to absorb or explain the pain.]

We know that self-worth is bound to our capacity to give love, to be sexual (the 2nd House is always square to the 5th,

The dynamics of the most common problem in relationship, the female's difficulty with orgasmic response—due to the complexity of the female emotio-sexual idealization, socio-historical residue and continuing pressures, the incompetence and ignorance of the male (and the female, i.e., to help herself), the intrusion of other responsibilities, etc.—can be very subtly shown in the horoscope or, indeed, they can be overridden.

Most simplistically, for example: with Saturn retrograde, ruling the 5th and tensely aspected, our key suggests difficulty in the sexual profile, difficulty anywhere along the spectrum of self-worth development, discovering sexuality, becoming comfortable with it, transferring it into relationships. The woman most certainly will have had to contend with love-neglect from her father in the early home. *How this imploded on her self-worth development and eventually on her extension of self to others is an extremely important deduction for the astrologer to make.* When further difficulty is indicated, further investigation and discussion will be required.

But, the woman may have been able to develop strongly in spite of the early problems, *actually fulfilling the strengthening potential elicited by problems.* This could be shown, for example, by the significator of her self-worth 2nd House in most supportive (i.e., defended, well fortified) aspect elsewhere in the horoscope, and, as well, specific planetary references to sexuality (a Scorpio emphasis, for example; Mars and/or Pluto) which may show themselves to be strong and forthright. In such a case, the astrologer assesses a holistic picture of development. Probably, in such a case, the final outcome of the sexual profile is that the specifications of the relationship have to be just right for everything to "work," and this brings to the foreground of discussion the nature of the ideals projected onto others, how hard is it for those ideals to be met, and so forth.

More complicatedly, a woman has the 5th-11th axis dramatically emphasized. The 8th as well has a singular, powerful sexual reinforcement by planet and aspect. Specifically sexual planetary symbolisms are undeniable. Venus, the ruler of the 5th, is retrograde, involved with the love-given/love-received axis, and is tightly conjoined with Uranus.

This highly intelligent, extremely attractive woman has never been able to maintain a relationship. One marriage lasted only a short time in her youth. While very interested in sex and apparently relatively uninhibited, she has never experienced orgasm in sexual relationship. There is "no problem" in masturbation, according to her, but her solitary technique is *exclusively* through the use of a vibrator. Going deeper with her personal history—her development of sexual awareness—revealed that, from her first experiences as a little girl through her entire life, she had never been stimulated to orgasm by anything but inanimate objects . . . not even by her own person. With this discovery through her consultation with astrology, filled out with full discussion of the dimensions presented in this chapter, the woman gladly made arrangements with a sex therapist for extended consultation to "solve the problem," to resensitize and humanize her sexual, relational system.

Another client of mine, a male, who was born one day earlier than this woman, has basically the same planetary configuration. His birth time has made Uranus the ruler of his 5th, and the Uranus-Venus-retrograde conjunction is in his 8th House. His Venus-retrograde, within this intense conjunction, rules his self-worth 2nd.

This man developed a nervous insecurity in his self-worth profile through a difficult parental interaction time early in his life. In overcompensation—as he readily acknowledged—his boundless energy was devoted to playing the "romantic," being macho, looking for perfection. He is proud to have had 250 female conquests in one particular year and much multiple-partner sex in and out of his marriage.

Of course, in both these cases, much more of the horoscope speaks through the sexual profile, but here in a short description, it is clear to see the intense importance of sex in the social development scheme of each person: the woman developed a response problem within relationships—although she professed that occasional liaisons were indeed fulfilling in other ways—and the man overdid relationships in sexual terms to fulfill other needs in his development. In both cases, the signal of *so much development* was Uranus conjunct Venus in Taurus, with the rulerships specifically channeling intense energies into sexual experience, and the retrogradation of Venus keying *a second level* of developmental concern within it all for both.

Solving the problem begins with getting in touch with one's self, literally and figuratively, before the self can be extended securely to others. Personal sensitization and, specifically, self-stimulation, are the primal beginnings for self-awareness sexually. Every sexual therapy reference on our planet says so. To put it simiplistically, it is the humanization of the solitary response with security, respect, and trust, bringing it into relationship, into the experience of Oneness which transcends self-control factors, coercion factors, and manipulative messages, that gives sexuality its bloom.

Indeed, there are extraordinary variations on sexual expression: homosocial dimensions, fantasy enactment, role-playing into submissive or aggressive directions, multiple sharings, exhibitionism, the elements of danger and adventure, and many more. They all evolve out of developmental circumstances in our early lives, our accumulation of information, the screen of sociometrics upon which our identity is projected, and what we know is possible to fulfill us. Astrology is a means to learning; it is not an end in itself. It is a base upon which to frame questions to start discussion; it is not a collection of answers. And finally, it is the *astrologer* and the *astrologer's knowledge* of life that through astrology's symbolisms illuminates the life we live together with our clients.

This chapter introduces this volume on the management of sexuality in the horoscope and is not the forum for a thorough investigation of the complicated psychodynamic world of sexual development. There are sensitive and authoritative self-help and psychotherapeutic texts in fine bookstores and in libraries covering the subject comprehensively; there are clinical seminars presented by local hospitals and social-help agencies that deal with sexual development, and *this information and knowledge should be part of every astrologer's intelligence.* The outline of classic development scenarios of psychosexual development presented here is valid, and it can help bring astrology once again to this pressing creative dimension in holistic development.

In the sensitive embrace of such a personal area of life experience, I thank you, readers—on behalf of all of us presenting thoughts and experience courageously and sensitively in this volume—for selecting this book and sharing this study with us. We all learn in the process.

Glen Perry

Glenn Perry, Ph.D. is a licensed psychotherapist in private practice in Marin County, California. He has been using astrology as a diagnostic tool since 1974. Glenn received his doctorate from Saybrook Institute in San Francisco. In addition to private practice, he lectures and writes on the application of astrology to the fields of counseling and psychotherapy. He has appeared on radio and television talk shows as a spokesperson for astrology. Antioch College, Union College, and Goddard College have employed him as clinical evaluator and adjunct professor for graduate students attempting to integrate astrology and psychology in their course work.

In 1987 Glenn founded The Association For Astrological Psychology (AAP), a professional organization for psychologists and counselors who are interested in using astrology as a diagnostic tool in ongoing psychotherapeutic work with clients. In addition to serving as president of AAP, he is also the editor-publisher of their official publication, *The Journal of Astro-Psychology*.

His research interests involve the integration of astrology with new paradigm thinking in science and psychology.

# Pluto Pathology: The Dark Side of Human Sexuality

Glenn Perry

S ince Pluto went into Scorpio in 1983, it seems that every variety of sexual ill known to humankind has surfaced in the
media. Daily, we hear about runaway teenage prostitution,
child pornography, the AIDS epidemic, date rape, sexual misconduct in Washington, sexual murder, incest, priests molesting children, children molesting other children; the list seems endless.

The very week that Pluto entered Scorpio, the television
movie *Something About Amelia* was aired, bringing into full public
consciousness the national epidemic of incest. Since then there
has been a veritable avalanche of studies indicating that nearly
one out of every four adults is a survivor of childhood sexual trauma
(Blue, 1985). In his book, *Out of The Shadows*, sex researcher
Patrick Carnes (1983) indicated that one person in 17 is addicted
to sex; not just fond of it, but obsessed by it to the point that it is
destroying his or her life. A case in point was televangelist Jimmy
Swaggart. In 1989, many of us watched Swaggart confess tearful-
ly to an international television audience that demons had possessed his soul and compelled him to have sex with prostitutes.

The dramatic Anita Hill and Clarence Thomas senate investigation in 1991 laid bare the problem of sexual harassment in the
workplace. In 1992, William Kennedy Smith and Mike Tyson educated the public about the prevalence and horrors of rape. We were

also repulsed by the grisly tale of Jeffrey Dahmer, who killed and dismembered his lovers. From *Silence of the Lambs* to the real life story of David Koresh, our nation has been constantly reminded of the disturbing prevalence of sexual perversion, abuse, rape, and misconduct in our communities, and these more sensational cases only serve to distract us from the "everyday" problems of promiscuity, sexual addiction, sexual dysfunction, lack of sexual desire, affairs, and sexual ignorance that plague the general populace.

The argument has been made that these problems have always been with us and we are simply now becoming aware of them. Given Pluto's correspondent transit through Scorpio, there is probably some truth to this. But such a contention only belies the question of *what causes sexual problems?* To date, no one has come up with a grand, unified theory that explains every variant of the enigma. It is generally agreed that the majority of sexual difficulties are learned behaviors that result from certain kinds of experiences. Miseducation and ignorance, childhood sexual trauma, unresolved Oedipal complexes, conditioned response patterns that impair sexual response, and pathological transactions between lovers that create a sexually destructive environment, are but some of the theories that have been advanced by experts. Kaplan (1974) contends that sexual difficulties are caused by a great many factors, and that intervention may be required on several levels. I will not detail in this chapter the various psychological explanations and treatments such a multicausal philosophy offers; rather, my purpose is to explore specifically what *astrology* has to teach us about sexuality.

Astrology offers a unique perspective in that it suggests that *experience itself is the derivative of an inborn psychological disposition* that manifests through the body and environmental events. That is, psyche and matter are mirrors rather than causes of one another. This implies that problems with sexuality are not simply learned behaviors, but maladies of soul that take us deep into the mystery of human consciousness. My goal in this chapter is to explore the Taurus-Scorpio polarity and its planetary representatives, Venus and Pluto. I hope to show that sexual difficulties are symptomatic of deeper, underlying problems that manifest on several different levels simultaneously. To illustrate my ideas, examples will be presented of individuals who have hard aspects between Venus and Pluto.

Let me state at the outset that I do not believe that specific kinds of sexual behaviors, orientations, problems, events, or conflicts can be delineated from the chart without a live individual to provide feedback and confirmation. Certainly there will be hints and suggestions about sexual experiences, but to use astrology to describe or predict a client's sex life is not only irresponsible but destructive, both to the client and to the public's perception of astrologers. First of all, sexuality is a subject of enormous sensitivity; thus the counselor should proceed cautiously. Secondly, it is a subject of great mystery, and should be approached with due humility.

While astrology can be of some value to the counselor in diagnosing and understanding sexual problems, such knowledge must be used judiciously when it comes to interventions. At best we are speculating anyway, for no one can know with certainty exactly how a particular astrological configuration will manifest, or the extent to which a client has already healed problems they might have once had. My own approach is to use the chart as a tool for asking questions and formulating hypotheses in conjunction with information the client volunteers. It is a back and forth movement that can accelerate the diagnostic phase of therapy. Beyond what the client is willing to tell me, however, I keep my opinions to myself.

Taurus and the Need for Sensual Gratification

I want to make it clear that when I talk about a zodiacal sign, I am referring to its archetypal quality; that is, a sign represents some universal principle that is evident both in the world of nature and in the nature of humans. A sign, then, is a singular aspect of the human psyche, and every psyche has all twelve signs operating to varying degrees of emphasis and functionality.

Although traditional astrology associates Scorpio with the sex drive, a good place to start in our efforts to understand sexuality is with Taurus. Scorpio and Taurus are complementary opposites in that one fulfills the other. To understand Scorpio you must first understand Taurus. Individuals who have Taurus prominent in their charts are exemplars of the Taurus archetype in all of us. Like other zodiacal signs, the principle that Taurus represents can be inferred from behavior that is classically Taurean. Any textbook will give you the usual description: Taureans (Taurus energy) are sensuous, attractive, materialistic, concrete, calm, stable, placid, conservative, slow and steady, resistant to change, and possessive. By analyzing these and other Taurean descriptors, we can reduce Taurus to a basic principle, or psychological need. *Taurus represents the need for safety and sensual gratification.* Ultimately, there is no Taurean behavior that cannot be understood in the context of this need.

It may not be immediately apparent that the need for safety and the need for sensual gratification are two faces of the same principle. This becomes more obvious when we look at Taurus from a developmental perspective. I associate zodiacal signs with distinct developmental periods of the human life cycle (Perry, 1989). Aries would be approximately the first 18 months, and Taurus would cover the next two and one-half years. Research in child development indicates that when infants reach about 18 months of age they experience a crisis of sorts; that is, they go through a transition from one perceptual framework to another. Prior to 18 months, infants experience little if any separation between themselves and the outside world. The world, in effect, is their oyster, and infants view themselves as omnipotent. All they have to do is scream or cry and their every need is satisfied. There is no need to exercise any self-control over bodily functions because they are not particularly aware of having a body. An infant's orientation in space and time is limited to "me, here, now." Astrologers can readily see the Aries temperament in this description.

At 18 months, however, the infant suddenly "awakens" to the disturbing realization that there is an objective world peopled with objects that have an existence entirely separate from the infant, and that are not always subject to the infant's control. Piaget (1926) termed this the capacity for *object permanence*, meaning the ability to conceptualize that there are entities that have a reality of their own and that continue to exist even when one cannot see, hear, or feel them.

Since the environment is now perceived to have its own autonomy, *it is no longer predictable;* it can change, it can frustrate, it can intrude, mother can leave and not come back! Out of this awakening to the autonomy of the natural world is born the urgent need to feel that one's own existence is secure. Predictably, infants become very *in*secure at this stage. They are inordinately sensitive to any changes in the environment and require constant reassurance that mother is still there, that she still loves them, and that the world will not suddenly disappear. For an astrologer, it is not difficult to see traces of Taurean behavior in this. Greene (1993), for example, asserts that the famous Taurean loyalty in relationship is based not on abstract moral promises or social codes, but rather on the need to render permanent any situation that provides pleasure, satisfaction, and a sense of security (p. 72).

While the infant's realization that he or she is not omnipotent is disturbing, it need not be overwhelming if the environment is sufficiently stable, predictable, and safe. To help with the transition to this new world-view, toddlers form intense attachments to what Winnicott (1960) called "transitional objects." This is usually some possession, like a Teddy Bear or a favorite blanket, that provides a soothing function for the child and allows him to maintain an illusory sense of control over the objective world. In effect, the concept of "ownership" is born at this stage. Children form various attachments to toys, pets, and things that are distinctly their own. In this, we see the origin of the Taurean tendency to acquire and possess objects.

If development proceeds without major trauma and if the mother is sufficiently available and responsive to her child's need for love and reassurance, the child will eventually develop what Hartman (1952) termed *object constancy*. This occurs at about three years when the child's internalized mental representation of the mother is sufficiently stable and permanent that it can be evoked by the child in the absence of the actual mothering person. With the achievement of object constancy, the child is able to draw upon the mental representation of mother in a way that allows for self-soothing and self-comforting, just as if the mother were present. In an important sense, the mother is present, constantly *inside.* She becomes the ground of the child's love of self. And it is precisely this capacity for self-love that enables the self-concept to remain stable, even in the face of mildly frightening or frustrating experiences. That is, the child is able "to hold on" to a positive self-image despite momentary experiences of pain, because he or she has *internalized* a loving function that previously was provided by the mother.

Prior to this, infants are totally identified with whatever they are experiencing in the moment. If it is a "bad" feeling, then the infant becomes the "bad" self. In effect, an infant cannot have an experience without *becoming the experience.* With the child's emergent capacity for object constancy and self-love, however, he is able to "have" experiences (just as he can "have" possessions) without losing his sense of self. Taurus, then, is this capacity for self-love that allows for a stable and secure sense of identity over time. It is a kind of homeostatic mechanism, its primary function being *to maintain* a self-image that is constant and grounded.

An important corollary to the infant's discovery of an external world is the dawning awareness of its own body. The infant learns, for example, that the body is separate and distinct from other bodies. It can be made to do things, and to hold and possess things, all of which yields a considerable amount of pleasurable sensation. It is precisely the child's capacity to pleasure him- or herself that helps to provide it with a sense of security. To be in physical contact with the mother, or the Teddy Bear, or the ice cream cone, or the bar of soap, anything that can be touched and used for sensual gratification reassures the child that the world is safe and that he or she is an embodied self that is real, solid, and continuous over time. The development of body awareness also allows the child to learn bladder and bowel control. Thus toilet training occurs at this age. Again, the capacity to retain (feces and urine), to hold on, and to possess are distinctly Taurean processes.

A child's uninhibited delight in physical pleasures is paralleled in myths surrounding the goddess Venus, planetary ruler of Taurus. According to Greene (1993), an appropriate term for Venus is "harlot," as the word suggests sexual license and abandon. The temple harlot in ancient times was never a prostitute in the modern sense of the term, but was trained to be a mortal "vessel" for the divine joy and ecstasy of the goddess. "By becoming an embodiment of the divine object of desire and source of pleasure, the temple harlot served as a kind of generator of the creative life force in men, and far from being demeaned by the role, she acquired power and importance through the value placed upon it." (p. 72)

Aphrodite (the corollary to Venus in Greek mythology) is herself the best example of the unbridled, spontaneous sensuality that is characteristic of Taurus. Although married to Hephaistos, she is perennially unfaithful to him, giving herself to any god or hero *she* desires. If a particular god or hero wants Aphrodite, she is unaffected, for it is *her* gratification alone that matters. Aphrodite is not capable of being vulnerable, which is a prerequisite for genuine loving. In fact, she does not so much love as lust. Periodically seized by erotic longing, Aphrodite enchants and seduces her lovers without regard for the consequences. As Greene put it:

> She certainly suffers no insecurities, but expresses absolute power of attraction not because of what she has to offer . . . but because of who she is. She *does* nothing to *be* loved, because she is the essence of the beloved.

In this regard, Venus is self-possessed, her love and pleasure coming from within herself rather than from a god or hero who possesses her. So Venus really symbolizes a quality of absolute self-love and uninhibited sensual pleasure. She can enjoy her body and that of her lover, but does not depend on another for her security. It is not even that Venus necessarily symbolizes sexual pleasure, all myths to the contrary. Sex, in this context, may be regarded as a metaphor for the sensual delights that Venus embodies.

Again, the essence of Taurus is comfort, pleasure, and physical gratification. Venus merely symbolizes how the person goes about wanting things and enjoying them. As ruler of Taurus, Venus is opposed to suffering and vulnerability, which is Scorpio's province. The Taurus goal is merely to content oneself and be happy. Venus is the capacity to indulge oneself in food and drink, in a sensuous massage, a walk in the woods, or lying nude in the sun listening to Mozart. What does Venus want? "Whatever makes *me* happy," she would reply.

Sometimes Venus (and the 2nd House) is associated with "values." But this part of human nature has nothing to do with values in the traditional sense of the term, i.e., one's ethics or moral values. It is instead, the value one places on happiness, and whatever affords that happiness. We might call it material values. This gets back to the idea of valuing whatever gives one pleasure or provides security. The function of Venus is to value and honor whatever it is that one wants in order to feel good. So Venus rules the process of acquiring things, having experiences, or attracting people because of the pleasure and security they afford (which is, in effect, their value).

If Venus/Taurus is integrated and functional, there is no rush, no anxiety about being loved, because love is a state of mind that is internally generated. One glides into relationship at a relaxed pace, unquickened by anxiety. As Greene stated, "She does nothing to be loved, because she is the essence of the beloved." As the partners get to know one another, a basis of trust is established, a Taurean stronghold built to contain the tensions that are inevitably to arise later. This grounding of the relationship in mutual trust takes time and commitment, and is ultimately rooted in the self-security of the individuals involved. It is precisely the Taurean instinct that assures that relationships do not proceed too fast. Taurus requires a slow, cautious approach that enables the individual to take time in learning about the other. This aspect of our nature needs to know that the beloved is safe, stable, and reliable.

It is the capacity for object constancy and its corollary, self-love, that renders Taurus so lovable. The partner is not burdened with any responsibility to provide love, because the Taurus-integrated person already has it. We see this embodied in the relaxed, calm, serene presence of Sun sign Taureans who seem to exude sensuality through every pore. Taurus is voluptuousness wanting to be violated. It is touchable, attractive, earthy, beautiful and therefore desirable. If Scorpio is the lover knocking on the door, Taurus is the one who invites him or her in. If Scorpio is the plow and the seed, Taurus is the fertile field waiting to be plowed. It can not be overstated that Taurus is, first and foremost, committed to the pleasure of one's own body. With Jupiter in Taurus on the Ascendant, Mae West put it best when she purred, "Too much of a good thing can be wonderful."

I have taken much time here to outline the principle of Taurus because it is the foundation of what will later develop into the capacity for sexual enjoyment. Taurus, in effect, is the ground of our being, the source of a stable and secure sense of self—an embodied self—that is firmly rooted in self-love. This is not to imply that safety and security should be the final goal of love, for these will never provide for psychological growth and cannot be sustained indefinitely anyway. The point is, an individual must first be grounded in the pleasurable sensations of his or her own

body before he or she can welcome the exper'
pleasure with someone else. One has to feel
in personal boundaries before one can
boundaries to be penetrated. To "give it up," w
trate and be penetrated, to risk being wounded, w
relinquish control and merge in ecstatic union with the be
this is Scorpio. But if the base security of Taurus is missing or
damaged because of a premature or forced violation of the body,
then the individual will experience tremendous difficulty feeling
safe enough to tolerate the experience of sex.

Scorpio and the Process of Transformation

Again, when I talk about Scorpio I am talking about an archetype
that is embodied in every human being. Individuals with Scorpio
prominent in their charts are merely exemplars of what Scorpio
represents in all of us. Like Taurus, the psychological need of
Scorpio can be inferred from behaviors that are typical of this
sign. We note the penetrating stare, the deep smoldering sexuality, the air of mystery, the passionate intensity. Scorpio is powerful,
provocative, and willing to die for its convictions. It tends to be
crisis-oriented, in that it is innately attracted to conditions of
emergency or transition brought about by irreversible change.
There is, likewise, an attraction to the hidden, the forbidden, and
the dangerous. At its best, Scorpio exposes wrongdoing, roots out
evil, and heals wounds of every sort. Considering all of the above,
it seems that there are three core themes at the heart of Scorpio.
These are (1) **transformation**—death and rebirth, healing, regeneration, renewal, reform; (2) **power**—integrity, intensity, coherence of intention, potency, concentrated force; and (3) **sex**—
fusion, merger, penetration and assimilation, unification, and the
like. Astrologers will readily agree that these themes are typically
associated with Scorpio. I would say, then, that Scorpio represents
the associated needs for sex, power, and transformation. What
may not be clear is how these three processes are interrelated and
interdependent.

To say that Scorpio represents the need for transformation is
to imply something that needs to be transformed, thus a wound,
or injury. Transformation further implies a movement, or evolu-

ı, from the simple to the complex. In chemistry, if two sub-
.ances are put together and there is any kind of reaction, both are
transformed into a third substance that incorporates the two into
a new whole. Likewise, if there is an injury to the body, such as a
diseased or dysfunctional organ, this constitutes a division that
compromises the integrity of the organism. To heal the division is
to eliminate what does not belong and restore the organ to its
proper function—that is, integrate it back into the whole. Transformation, then, is a whole-making process that involves processes of elimination and integration.

On the psychological level, the process is the same. Most
everyone has some aspect of his or her psyche where they feel
wounded, vulnerable, and afraid. Different models refer to this by
various names: complex, shadow, pathogenic belief, trauma, neurosis, the daimonic, the bad self, and the bad object are but a few.
Almost invariably, these wounded parts of the psyche reside in
the unconscious, repressed or dissociated from conscious awareness. Generally, the wound is bound up with some particular
need that has been deemed too dangerous or painful to express.
This could be the need for autonomy, dependency needs, competitive strivings, intimacy, the search for meaning, or the need for
sensual gratification. Somewhere, the individual learned that to
experience this part of one's nature was likely to cause oneself or
others pain. So it remains hidden below the surface of consciousness, and Scorpio, we know, is associated with whatever is hidden or lurking below the surface of things.

Scorpio's attraction to the dark side derives from the impulse
to heal. The healing process, however, invariably involves a certain amount of pain and suffering for the individual who is
wounded. To go into the dark places, to remember the trauma, or
the loss, or the insult, is to confront that part of oneself that is full
of fear and shame. Negative attitudes have to be broken down
and eliminated, painful affects integrated, and the repressed function restored to its rightful place in the overall psychic economy.
All of this is classically Scorpionic.

What, we may ask, is the result of all this suffering and healing? The answer is *power*. Whatever one fears has power. It has
power because it drains energy that would otherwise be available
to the person. Herman (1992), for example, writes that all traumatic experiences share a common similarity of denial and dis-

empowerment. To lift the denial and resolve the fear is *to take back the power that has been lost.* Consider what happens when one is afraid. There is a contraction of the self, a repression that requires a significant expenditure of energy to keep the repressed in place. Jung (1960) called these compacted areas "psychic complexes," which he defined as a magnetic vortex of emotionally charged contents and associated ideas clustered around a central core. A complex constitutes an *image* of a certain psychic situation, e.g., the enjoyment of one's body (Venus/Taurus), that is incompatible with the habitual conscious attitude. The individual, for example, may compensate his fear of bodily pleasure by developing the attitude, "I don't need to be touched or loved—*keep away*." The Venus/Taurus impulse is repressed and behaves, in Jung's words, "like an animated foreign body in the sphere of consciousness" (p. 96). While the complex can be suppressed with an effort of will, it tends to assert itself with a vengeance at first opportunity; perhaps when the individual is stressed, tired, or disinhibited from drugs or alcohol. With a Venus/Taurus complex, this "return of the repressed" might result in inappropriate touching, overindulgence in food or drink, compulsive shopping, and the like. Since Pluto rules Scorpio, we might expect to see this complex symbolized by a Pluto square Venus aspect.

Because these dark areas of the psyche are not consciously recognized, they tend to get projected and identified as residing in someone or something outside the self. In myth and literature, this is symbolized by any entity that embodies evil, e.g., a monster, dragon, devil, demon, or vampire. As symbols of transformation, monsters are Scorpio archetypes. Their common characteristics reveal the essential mechanism of the complex. Monsters are chaos beasts lurking at the interstices of order and inhabiting regions of the unknown. Though the forms and types of monsters are numberless, a single principle underlies a majority of them: a monster is out of place, conforming to no class or violating existing classes. Monsters are mutations, embodiments of new and unfamiliar states.

Take dragons, for example. Perhaps the most widespread monster in myth and folklore, the dragon is said to be born through a mixture of species and its form is always an unlikely compound of apparently disparate and uncombinable parts—the body of a serpent with the scales of a fish; feet, wings, and occasionally the head of a bird; the forelegs of a lion, the ears of a bull, horns of a stag, and so on. Combinations are legion. Likewise, the devil is a hybrid creature—cloven hooves, tail, pointed ears, scales, claws, fangs, and snout. Because monsters embody our fear of transformation, a monster's form merely requires that it be *strange*. It is, in effect, a symbol of what the individual dreads will happen—should he be possessed by the complex that resides in his own unconscious; i.e., he will be transformed into something foreign and monstrous.

Rollo May (1969) points out that it is precisely the repressed instinctual life that constitutes the complex, or what he calls the *daimonic*. "The daimonic is *any natural function which has the power to take over the whole person*" (p. 123). Because the power of the daimonic is bound up with certain memories and needs which are abhorrent to the individual, it can be destructive to the conscious personality in the same way that a monster appears destructive. *When this power goes awry and one element usurps control over the total personality*, we have "daimon possession." Jung referred to this as *enantiodromia*. If one side of a pair of opposites becomes excessively predominant in the personality, it is likely to turn into its contrary, e.g., priests turn into child molesters.[1]

Enantiodromia helps us to understand how daimon possession occurs; in a desperate effort to repress the complex, the individual overcompensates in the opposite direction by identifying with qualities and attributes that are opposed to the nature of the impulse he fears. *Sooner or later, however, the repressed life asserts itself and the conscious personality is abducted into the underworld of the psyche.*

Obviously, the daimonic is not an actual entity but refers to a fundamental, archetypal function of human experience that I associate with Scorpio and its planetary ruler, Pluto. The deteriorated form of this concept, consisting of the belief that we are

---

1 A common characteristic of monsters and devils is that they can transform themselves into anyone or anything. And so can the sexual offender. Witness the mild mannered, soft-spoken Jeffrey Dahmer, or David Koresh, or any of the thousands of rapists, child molesters, and sexual deviants who masquerade as your friendly neighbor, babysitter, or local priest that too late reveal themselves to be yet another variant of the sex drive gone berserk. Devils/monsters almost invariably have a sexual component. The vampire with his erotic blood lust, the dragon to whom must be sacrificed a virgin, and the devil who seduces virgins are obvious examples, all of which represent the eroticization of fear.

taken over by demons flying around equipped with horns, is *a projection of inner experience outward*, reformed into objective reality. May argues that such a conception is specifically damaging to our experience of love and will. "For the destructive activities of the daimonic are only the reverse side of its constructive motivation" (p. 124). In the daimon lies one's vitality, the capacity to open consciously to the power of eros and be transformed. If one represses the daimonic, he or she becomes an accomplice on the side of the destructive possession. To dissolve the power of the daimonic, says May, one must "identify with that which haunts you, not in order to fight it off, but to take it into your self; for it must represent some rejected element in you" (p. 133). To do this is to take back the power that has been projected outward and so restore to oneself the function of what was heretofore repressed. This is empowerment.

The myth of Hercules slaying the Hydra illustrates this principle quite nicely. As one of his twelve labors, Hercules is sent to slay the Lernean Hydra, a serpent-like beast who inhabits a dark cave in a swamp. The nasty Hydra has been preying upon the folk of the countryside. A particularly deadly creature, it has nine snake heads, each of which is equipped with deadly poison fangs. The problem is that no one can kill the Hydra by cutting off its heads, for each severed head sprouts three new ones in return. Hercules makes the mistake of trying to club the Hydra into unconsciousness and then cut off its heads. But this only compounds his difficulty because by attempting to "cut off" the problem, it only grows worse. The heads proliferate and Hercules is about finished. Suddenly, he remembers that Hydras cannot tolerate light. So he drops down to his knees, seizes the Hydra by its legs, and thrusts it up into the sunlight, whereupon it shrivels up and begins to die.

The meaning of this myth is fairly obvious. The serpent, of course, is a primary symbol of Scorpio. Likewise, Scorpio rules dangerous, hidden places like caves. The Hydra is the daimon or complex that is dangerous, precisely because it is repressed into the cave of the unconscious. It preys upon the personality by seeking to subvert and destroy the conscious identity. It can be suppressed temporarily; that is, clubbed into submission, but it cannot be permanently "cut off" because attempts to repress it only cause it to reassert itself with a vengeance (repression, after all, is what started the problem in the first place). The complex proliferates with every effort to sever it from conscious awareness.

The only way the problem *can* be resolved is by humbling oneself, as Hercules did by dropping to his knees, and holding the dark and inferior element of the complex up to the light of consciousness. Once this is done, the complex can be integrated into the personality so that it no longer poses a threat. By such a heroic act, the individual is empowered and transformed. An increase in power accompanies transformation because, with the assimilation of the complex, there is no longer a split in the personality. The energy that was previously bound up in the complex becomes available so that there is a greater coherence of intention, increased unity and integrity, and thus more concentrated force of personality.

But what, one may ask, has this to do with sex? I would argue that sexual problems are really Plutonian problems that have their genesis on a psychological level. This is not to say that sexual trauma, like rape or incest, is not itself the cause of sexual problems. It *can* be. But the insidious effects of trauma are caused by the psychological *aftershocks* of the experience. Such shocks ultimately take up residence in the murky swamps and dark caves of the unconscious, where Hydras are born.

Trauma research has shown that when an organism is faced with an overwhelming external threat against which there is no possibility of escape, there is a tendency to "freeze" or "play dead"—that is, to inhibit or suspend all reaction that would normally be appropriate (Browne, 1990; Herman, 1992). The capacity to suspend or inhibit an overwhelming threatening experience serves the purpose of blocking the threat of internal destabilization. Accordingly, whenever an individual is faced with an overwhelming experience that is sensed as potentially disintegrating, there is the ability to suspend it and "freeze" it in an unassimilated, inchoate form and maintain it in that state indefinitely. This may occur with a singular traumatic experience, like rape or abandonment, or in response to a chronic condition such as growing up with an alcoholic or abusive parent.

The psyche seems to know that to experience the full meaning of the threatening encounter would destroy its core organization. So the encounter is cut off, delayed, dissociated. Also cut off is whatever part of the psyche is associated with the traumatic experience. A child who has been molested, for example, may cut off its connection to its body and need for sensual gratification (Venus/Taurus). This whole area is avoided because it tends to reactivate the original traumatic experience. As such, it constitutes a "dead zone" or "void" in the personality.

Now, just as you cannot cut off the head of a Hydra, the original trauma does not go away, but instead produces the panic attacks, agitation, nightmares, fatigue, emotional blunting, and other clinical phenomena that are associated with Post Traumatic Stress Disorder (PTSD). Just as the Hydra bursts forth from the cave to prey upon innocent folk, *so the daimon bursts forth from the unconscious* in the form of intrusive flashbacks that disrupt conscious functioning. Ultimately, the only way to heal the wound is consciously to "work it through." Generally speaking, this requires giving up control, surrendering to feelings that emerge as the complex is encountered, opening to and embracing the meaning of the experience, eliminating negative attitudes and defenses that were developed to ward off the pain of the original trauma, and integrating the contents of the trauma into consciousness and long-term memory. This is holding the Hydra up to the sunlight. And, as we shall see, it is not dissimilar to what happens during sex.

Sex as a Vehicle and Metaphor for Transformation

Before exploring how sex is both a vehicle and a metaphor for psychological processes of transformation, let us first examine the origins of sex. It may come as a surprise that sexuality was not always a part of life. Neither was death. Sex and death began together. Billions of years before the emergence of plant and animal life, there were single-celled organisms—procaryotes—that could reproduce themselves through cellular division, a process called *mitosis*. These single-celled organisms were made possible by the spontaneous emergence of a self-replicating molecule known as DNA. Because procaryotes could divide and reproduce themselves, they were semi-immortal. In reproduction by asexual cell division, there is no natural death, only forced death. Procaryotes do not die. The dividing cells do not age and they will continue to divide if environmental conditions are favorable.

Eventually, however, the procaryotes overpopulated the planet and stagnated because they depleted the environment of the necessary nutrients for their continued survival. Thus life faced its first crisis. The procaryotes mutated into a new form by producing a molecule called chlorophyll. It was the self-manufacture of chlorophyll that enabled procaryotes to capture solar energy to make their own food, a process known as *photosynthesis*. But photosynthesis produced the planet's first pollutant—oxygen—that accumulated in the atmosphere to the point that it became deadly to the procaryotes. This was life's second crisis. So the procaryotes mutated into yet another form that allowed for the metabolizing of oxygen. This new structure was radically unlike the first, because it involved the joining together of procaryotes to create a totally new form of life—oxygen-metabolizing organisms! With this evolutionary innovation, sex and death began their reign.

These new cellular organisms, called eucaryotes, were too complex to divide, so they had to develop a new way to reproduce. Two tiny creatures called *paramecia* were reputedly the first organisms to mate, the Adam and Eve of the cellular world. As they approached one another, their cell membranes opened and their nuclei moved into a close embrace. Each paramecium exchanged half its genetic material with the other. Then they separated, revitalized. Out of this simple chemical cooperation of primitive bacterial cells we can glimpse the early melding of the rudiments of sex and love.

The ultimate result of genetic exchange was the diversity of plant and animal life, or multicellular organisms. Genetic exchange allowed single-celled creatures to transform themselves into a multiplicity of new organisms. Sex inaugurated phylogenetic evolution, but once organisms developed the capacity for sexual reproduction, they were no longer immortal, and death became a normal event in the life cycle. So sex and death are historical events that entered the process together. The price life paid for the evolution of species (phylogeny) was the devolution of ontogeny, i.e., decay toward death of the individual organism. In Jantsch's (1980) words, "Sexuality can only represent one side of a principle the other side of which is death" (p. 125).

From the above we can draw an important lesson about Scorpio. Each time there was a crisis, it was resolved by the innovation

of some new evolutionary development. Life survived by transforming itself, whenever necessary, into a more complex form.
When single-celled procaryotes were poisoning the environment
with their own waste—oxygen—they fused together to create oxygen-metabolizing multicellular organisms. By developing the
capacity to "take in" rather than "eject out" oxygen, *they embraced
the very thing that threatened to annihilate them.* It is a paradox that
seems to be at the heart of Scorpio. Only by integrating the threatening agent were procaryotes able to evolve into a new life form
and survive. In doing so, they developed the capacity for sexual
reproduction. Sexuality brought about an extraordinary accelera-
tion of evolution and the proliferation of many new life forms, yet
it required the death of the individual organism. From the beginning, sex, death, and transformation were inseparable.

To appreciate how sex can be a metaphor for psychological
processes of transformation, it is useful to outline what happens
during human heterosexual intercourse. To begin, there is a certain amount of foreplay, which I would associate with the Taurus
component of the act. This involves tactile stimulation—sensual
touching, kissing, and caressing—as well as certain sights,
sounds, and smells that contribute to erotic stimulation. All of
these are in the service of pleasuring one another's body and
establishing a proper mood. Most people require a certain minimum of affection and trust before they can engage in satisfactory
sexual encounters. Taurus, of course, represents this need for
affection and trust (safety).

Foreplay eventually leads to penetration, which constitutes
the beginning of the Scorpio phase. As the lovers merge together
in mutual embrace we see a parallel with unicellular organisms
joining together to create a more complex, multicellular being.
Boundaries dissolve as the lovers begin to melt into one another.
This involves a letting go, a voluntary relinquishing of control so
that something deeper takes over and moves through the lovers.
If Taurus is the urge to retain, Scorpio is the urge to release.

As tension mounts, there is a blurring of perceptual ability so
that the lovers are not fully conscious of their own sensations and
physiological responses. They build momentum through pelvic
thrusts and rhythmic undulations, a prelude and analogue to the
culminating vibratory contractions of penis and vagina. With the
approach of orgasm, the entire musculature of the body is taut

from head to toe. The two bodies begin to vibrate together so that they are no longer experienced as material things, separate and distinct, but subsumed in a dancing, pulsating wave form that envelopes both lovers. With orgasm, there is a kind of unitive consciousness as the lovers die in their separate selves and become melded together as one. Psychoanalytic theory has long maintained that coitus and death are emotionally connected, which is why, perhaps, the French call the orgasm, *la petite mort*, or "the little death."[2]

It is paradoxical that, at the peak of sexual gratification, the person does not appear to be experiencing pleasure. Recall that Taurus rules pleasure, whereas its opposite, pain, is ruled by Scorpio. Thus at the climax of sexual excitement, one may bite and scratch, the face contort into a grimace, the body strain and vacantly or shut tightly, the hands grasp, the whole body twitch uncontrollably, and the voice let loose with a muffled cry or loud scream. Far from pleasure, all of this suggests intense suffering and torment, as if one is being wounded. And yet the orgasm is one of the most intense and profoundly satisfying sensations that a human being can experience.

With ejaculation ("throwing out") there is an explosive discharge of accumulated neuromuscular tensions. The male is completely out of control and helpless to stop it. The forcible ejection of spermatic fluid into the woman's vaginal canal is one of intense pleasure, associated with orgasmic throbs and the sensation of spermatic flow.

The vagina is not a passive receptacle for the penis, but an active participant in coitus. Sexual sophisticates have sung the praises of the vagina that eagerly admits, envelopes, and "milks" the penis to a voluptuous climax. Following ejaculation, the sperm swim excitedly into the uterus and up the fallopian tube toward the ovum, the female's egg. If all goes well, a single sperm will penetrate the egg, resulting in fertilization. The sperm adds its twenty-three chromosomes to the twenty-three in the egg, pro-

---

2 It is interesting to note that when a male suffers death by hanging he will ejaculate. In many instances the pants of the condemned would be pulled down just before the hanging so that crowds could witness this event. There has been an alarming rise in accidental deaths of adolescents who purposefully hang themselves in order that they can experience the intense ejaculations that occur as life ebbs from the body. The goal, of course, is to remove the noose before dying.

viding the necessary complement of forty-six for the new human being. In sum, the sperm penetrates the egg, the egg assimilates the sperm, and transformation results. Here again, we see the hallmark of the Scorpio process: penetration, assimilation, transformation. Just as more complex, multicellular organisms evolved from the fusion of unicellular types, so the human child is a mixture of the genetic endowments of the male and female lovers. One could argue that, with every human birth, there is at least the potential, if not the expressed purpose, for an evolutionary advancement of the species.

I have described sexual intercourse and conception at some length because I believe it is an important analogue to what happens in processes of psychological transformation. To establish the basis for this idea further, let us examine briefly how our two lovers come to fall in love, and *why*.

There is reason to believe that people do not fall in love by chance, but in accordance with a specific unconscious plan (Blinder, 1989; Dicks, 1967; Hendrix, 1988; Jung, 1953). The plan seems to be that individuals work out with partners the unconscious conflicts and wounds that derived from earlier important relationships. For this to be effective, it is necessary (1) to select someone who has similar character traits and attitudes as one's parents; and (2) resolve with them whatever unfinished business remains with these parents. The partner, in effect, *functions as a surrogate for the healing of old wounds.*

Jung (1953) provides a useful model for how this process operates. He theorized that the human psyche contained unconscious, autonomous psychic contents representing contrasexual elements of the personality. The *anima* was the psychic representation of the "inner woman" in a man, and the *animus* personified the "inner male" in the woman. According to Jung, the projection of one's anima or animus onto an individual of the opposite sex is responsible for the phenomenon of "falling in love." The particular quality of our relationship with the opposite sex is determined, says Jung, by the degree to which we have integrated the anima or animus. For integration and healing to occur, however, it is necessary to first meet the anima/animus in projected form. Otherwise these figures remain locked in the unconscious and are not "released" to create the struggles that bring with them the potential for a widening of consciousness. In this regard, projections are necessary, for they serve the purpose of bringing the unconscious into view. To integrate the anima/animus part is to develop a wider and deeper conscious perspective.

The anima/animus dichotomy can be "dark" or "light," and most likely contains aspects of both sides in each. The dark anima, for instance, is commonly depicted in film and literature as a *femme fatale* or "fatal attraction" that for various reasons proves destructive to the participants. In many respects, the anima/animus image functions like a complex. It is an erotically charged image of a psychic situation that is split off from the conscious identity and must be integrated if healing/wholeness is to occur.

Animosity in close personal relationships is likely to indicate a particularly problematic or "dark" anima/animus figure. Specific characteristics of the anima/animus serve as compensations for masculine and feminine conscious attitudes respectfully. When the conscious attitude is carried to a negative extreme—e.g., "the macho male," it will tend to produce a corresponding negative attitude through the unconscious, and this split will be reflected in confusion and discord suffered in relationships with members of the opposite sex.

Jung's concept of the anima/animus is similar to the concept of "internal object" in object-relations theory. An internal object is a mental representation, or image, of an actual person that formed from the person's experience with an important figure in childhood, e.g., the mother or father. An internal object exists in relation to a self-representation around some specific need, such as the need for safety and security. Dicks (1967) noted that spouses with marital problems *seem to test each other unconsciously against the role models of earlier love objects with whom they had ambivalent relations.* The hope, or fantasy, is that the spouse will be different from the problematic parent(s). Tensions and misunderstandings occur when "the other fails to play the role of a spouse after the manner of a preconceived model or figure in their fantasy world" (p. 50). Dicks asserts that marital problems are a consequence of mutual projection. Each spouse is perceived as being, to some degree, like one's parent.

> Tensions between marriage partners can result from the disappointment that the partner, after all, plays the marital role like the frustrating parent figure, similarity to whom was denied during courtship. This often collusive discovery leads

to modification of the subject's own role behavior in the direction of regression toward more childish responses to the partner. (p. 62)

The foregoing suggests that marriage is a primary field of manifestation of unresolved earlier object relations. Under ideal conditions, each partner can absorb the regressive needs and problems of the spouse. If these are heightened above tolerable limits, however, there can be an outbreak of stress related symptoms. "Even at this level," says Dicks, "marriage can be seen to act as a natural therapeutic relationship, the partners to some extent suffering themselves to be treated by each other as scapegoats" (p. 66).

Imagine a boy who has Moon conjunct Pluto, with this conjunction squaring Venus. Because the relationship between the boy's parents is riddled with conflict, the mother has appropriated the boy to satisfy her unfulfilled needs for intimacy and companionship. Accordingly, his relationship with his mother is characterized by suffocating control. She is alternately intrusive, manipulative, and seductive. What's worse, she acts hurt or scornful whenever the boy shows interest in a girl his own age. Because of the unnatural closeness between the boy and his mother, the father is jealous. His relationship with his son is strained and distant. Not surprisingly, such a boy may grow up feeling as if his need for love and affection (Venus) is dangerous (Pluto). If he expresses affection to his mother, he feels trapped. She needs him too much. Also, his father becomes angry. But if he expresses affection to a girl his own age, he feels guilty because it threatens and injures his mother. Again, the father is no help because he resents his son, and is not a viable role model for how to be intimate with a woman.

We can speculate that *the boy has internalized an image of woman as needy, controlling, and devouring.* As an adult, he would like to find someone who is just *the opposite* of his mother, a strong and independent woman who respects his need for space, yet who loves him just as passionately as his mother did. In other words, he wants to split off the "bad" qualities of mother/woman and keep the "good" ones. His anima fantasy figure is compensatory to the bad object that has been internalized; it represents only the "light side" of a complex figure.

Suppose our man finds a woman who seems to embody the qualities he is seeking. Dicks would call this "marriage by contrast," or "counter-identification." The idealized partner is chosen in reference to the suffocating, dangerous side of the original object. As Dicks' put it, "The idealized love object is still the same love-object with its badness removed by splitting or denial" (p. 62).

From an astrological perspective, this constitutes a splitting of the Taurus/Scorpio polarity as suggested by the Venus-Pluto square. The pleasurable Venusian qualities of the anima are retained, whereas the painful Plutonian dimension is eliminated. In regard to the phenomenon of "splitting," it is interesting to note that Taurus and Scorpio rule joint processes of retention and elimination. Taurus rules the mouth and throat, which correspond to processes of taking in and retaining. Conversely, Scorpio rules the anus and genitals, which correspond to processes of ejection and elimination. Since Venus and Pluto rule Taurus and Scorpio respectively, it is my hypothesis that difficult aspects between these two planets may be indicative of "splitting." The defense of "splitting" is well known in clinical literature. It is universally present in infants who have not yet achieved object constancy (Taurus). Infants initially experience both self and others in terms of a radical split, "all good" or "all bad," until maturation allows for more sophisticated discrimination. Scharff (1992) describes this process of splitting in terms remarkably similar to the physiological processes ruled by Taurus and Scorpio:

> If an experience is good it is introjected in a psychological mode equivalent to sucking and swallowing. If it is bad it is projected outside into the object in a psychological mode equivalent to spitting out. These alternating modes create potential categories of good/bad, inside/outside, and me/not me. The infant tends to usurp the object's pleasurable qualities and claim them as part of the self and to disown painful qualities and attribute those to the object. (p. 73)

Generally speaking, positive nurturing experiences are conceptualized as "good" object (mother) and "good" self, while negative experiences are organized as "bad" object and "bad" self. In healthy infant development, the child gradually recognizes that both "good" and "bad" aspects of experience are parts of the same person. Other people are neither idealized as "all good," or denigrated as "all bad," but are seen as a mixture of both good and bad parts. The child realizes that this is true for himself as well, allowing for an integrated self-concept and a capacity for ambivalent feelings toward both self and other.

If the child identifies with the good object only, this becomes the basis for later attempts to establish symbiotic relationships with idealized others, alongside a paranoid view of the now separated-out bad mother-world. The bad-self is repressed into the unconscious, and the corresponding bad-object takes up residence in what is perceived as a hostile and threatening environment. This often leads to choosing a partner who initially seems the fulfillment of one's fantasies but quickly turns into one's nightmare. Ironically, the very characteristics of the partner that were the major source of attraction are the same ones that lead to struggle. Again, this is because of the splitting of the light and dark sides of the anima/animus figure.

Recall that the anima/animus is an unconscious aspect of the subject's personality that gets projected. Dicks writes, "Subjects may persecute in their spouses tendencies which originally caused attraction, the partner having been unconsciously perceived as a symbol of 'lost' because repressed aspects of the subject's own personality" (p. 63). In other words, there is a persecution in the partner of denied or repressed parts of the self which are now projected to the partner, even though it seemed to be this "oppositeness" to the ego's conscious self-image that was originally an important part of the attraction for each other.

To provide an example of this process, let us return once again to our friend who has the Moon/Pluto conjunction squaring Venus. Pluto has abducted his Venus and dragged it down into the underworld of his psyche, where it remains imprisoned. This is our psychic complex, the deadly Hydra in the cave. He unconsciously believes that his need for pleasure and intimacy constitutes a "dark and inferior" element of his personality that must be eliminated. He cannot surrender to his need for intimacy with a woman for fear that (1) it will hurt his mother and he will feel guilty (Venus square Moon); and (2) the woman will try to possess and devour him just as his mother did (Venus square Pluto).

Accordingly, his conscious personality compensates the repressed Venus by appearing somewhat arrogant, cold, and invulnerable. Unaware of this conflict, he meets a woman and falls in love despite himself. At first glance, all he sees is the light side of Venus, *which he is projecting;* she is extremely attractive, kind, and affectionate. She loves and adores him.

During courtship, the Hydra slumbers quietly in the cave of unconsciousness so that he does not yet see the "dark" Plutonized Venus he has likewise projected. Eventually, however, the Hydra awakens and our friend begins to notice that his sweet wife is also possessive, needy, and controlling. This is the dark/Pluto side of the Venus complex—the negative anima, or "bad-object." He defends himself against the hated bad-object by withdrawing, spending long hours away at work, and generally avoiding his wife. Predictably, she begins to nag and complain about his lack of availability. He responds by withdrawing further. The pattern escalates and confirms his worst fears that he is about to be devoured.

Ultimately our subject loses all sexual interest in the relationship. His wife spends most of her time with the children while he reverts to his secret, sexual addiction involving excessive masturbation, pornographic literature, and frequent liaisons with prostitutes. With the latter, he acts out sado-masochistic fantasies of domination and submission.

What is happening here and how can it be resolved? While this example may seem extreme, it is actually derived from the case history of a famous person whom I will identify later in this chapter. The process begins with the husband projecting his Venus/Pluto complex into his wife. He utilizes "splitting" during the courtship phase and sees her in an idealized way as the "all good" object—pure, unadulterated Venus. Soon, however, the dark side presents itself and he begins to see her as the needy, suffocating mother/woman, or "all bad" object. In effect, he is trying *to eliminate in himself* this fearful image of a devouring need, so he projects it into his wife. She receives the projection and because of her own vulnerabilities begins to identify with it. *She becomes needy, possessive, and controlling.* Their complementary polarities become rigidly polarized so that the differences that once beguiled and bewitched now become sources of aggravated conflict. They begin to emphasize and exaggerate these differences in ways that feel punishing and antagonistic. They forget what it was that drew them together and lose contact with their earlier feelings of attraction. He withdraws and she pursues at an ever more frantic pace.

As this cyclic pattern escalates, both spouses become increasingly rigid, and their mutual pain builds toward an inevitable climax. Ultimately, there is a huge explosion as both partners release their pent up feelings and toxic emotions. Mutual hostilities may even be punctuated with a resounding "fuck you!" Following this release, there is usually an attempt at reconciliation as the two "work it through" and try to resolve their differences. In the sharing of their pain and in the attempt to understand its basis and origins, there is a potential for healing. If all goes well, a single insight will penetrate one partner's defenses, resulting in psychic fertilization. And this, in turn, may lead to psychological transformation.

The likelihood of marital confrontation resulting in psychological transformation is probably as rare as sexual intercourse resulting in pregnancy. Yet, new life transformation is the ultimate outcome of both processes because at root they are the same. With every crisis, the couple reaches a branch point where they can go into one of two directions. Interestingly, the Chinese figure for "crisis" is comprised of two symbols, one meaning "danger" and the other "opportunity." Just so, with every relationship crisis there is danger that the relationship might end, but also the opportunity for it to change.

The process which leads to change is one of projective identification. The term "projective identification" was originally coined by Melanie Klein (1946) to denote the unconscious process of projecting parts of the self outside the self and into another person and then dealing with the person as though she were characterized by those parts of the self. In the above example, the projected part was the man's Venus, or need for sensual gratification. Terrified of this need, he tries to get rid of it by projecting it into his wife.

His "devouring Venus" is then identified as residing in the wife, that is, she is experienced as embodying that part of himself, whether she happens to be like that or not. Generally, the person being projected into is to some degree "taken over" by the projection without quite knowing it. This is called "introjective identification" and is invariably painful. If, however, she can recognize that she is being perceived in a distorted fashion and is being induced to play the role of the devouring lover, *she can choose to respond differently.* She can "contain" the projection by allowing herself to experience it and by striving to understand it.

Suppose the wife turns to her husband and gently initiates a conversation by saying, "you seem to be afraid that I am going to need you so much that you will lose yourself in the relationship." She then proceeds to share with her husband the pain of her experience and likewise invites him to tell her about his pain. She does not defend herself, nor react with blame, criticism, or advice. She merely contains him and *makes it safe for him to be vulnerable.* If he, too, is able to do this, then the repressed contents of the unconscious in both partners will rise to the surface to be released and transformed.

The planet which seems singularly related to projective identification is Pluto. We know that Pluto has to do with *processes of elimination.* In a simple biological sense, what gets eliminated is whatever the body cannot assimilate, i.e., its waste products—especially feces and urine. To retain these would be poisonous and ultimately destructive. Thus Pluto symbolizes the impulse to eliminate or release whatever is foreign or destructive to the overall integrity of the system. In an analogous sense, there are psychological processes of elimination, too. Any thought, feeling, idea, or impulse which the consciousness of the system deems dangerous and destructive to itself will get eliminated. *The planets to which Pluto is in hard aspect symbolize psychological functions that the individual tries to eliminate.* But where do these functions go? Where *can* they go? One cannot destroy their existence entirely, so they are located outside the self. They are disavowed, expelled, ejected, dismissed, deported, banished, discharged, vomited, spit out, excreted, ejaculated— these are all Plutonian words.

In object-relations theory, projective identification has phallic connotations, whereas introjective identification has vaginal connotations. "Just as the phallus requires the vagina to take it in for purposes of pleasure, bonding, and procreation, and the vagina has to have a penis to encompass in spontaneous, automatic rhythms, so do the processes of introjective and projective identification go together" (Scharff, 1992, p. 289). Some authors attest that influence upon the object in projective identification occurs only if there is an unusually permeable boundary between the projector and the recipient of the projection. This permeability may be in a specific area, such as a complementarity between projector and projectee around the function of Venus. In our example, *the man denies his need for affection while the woman exaggerates hers.* Both are wounded in the same area and are naturally attracted due to complementarity. Accordingly, the man projects his Venus into the woman and she receives and contains it for him. She is naturally permeable to his projection.

When we talk about permeability of boundaries in relation to projection, we are, again, citing an analogy to the anus, urethra, vagina, and penis, all of which are permeable membranes, or openings, which allow for material to pass out of or into the body. Some authors have even cited the similarity between a wound, which is an opening in the membrane of an organism, an "avulsion" or puncture, and the vulva—the external parts of the female genitals—which is similar in appearance to a wound and which also is repeatedly punctured, i.e., by a penis. An avulsion is a tearing asunder, or forcible separation. This, of course, is precisely what occurs when the hymen (maiden head) is broken during first intercourse. There is tearing, pain, bleeding, and the like. So, in a very real sense, the vagina is an area of wounding. To copulate is, originally at least, also to wound. No doubt this is the origin of the word "vulva" which is derived from the Latin *vulnerare* meaning "to wound," and *vulnus*, meaning "wound." To be permeable to a projection, then, is analogous to being penetrated sexually. Both processes require one to be vulnerable, which quite literally means "capable of being wounded."

In summary, *sexual intercourse and projective identification appear to be analogous processes.* In sexual intercourse, the male ejaculates his essence (sperm) into the woman who mixes it with her own essence (egg). The genetic material of the one is combined with the genetic material of the other. The woman contains these contents for a period of time (nine months), then reintroduces the original content (sperm) of the man but in a transformed form, a baby. The child is the transformation of the original projection. This new entity is, hopefully, a more balanced and integrated blend of the best of the two parents. Likewise, in projective identification, the projector ejects that part of himself that needs to be transformed. The receiver of this projection "introjects" its contents and is able to contain and transform them by mixing them with her own awareness. They are then reintroduced to the projector in a form that allows for integration to occur. Ideally this also happens in reverse as the wife projects into the husband, too. The ultimate result is the transformation of both participants who become more balanced and integrated versions of their former selves.

Something like this happens in sex.

The point of this rather long description of sex and projective identification is simply this: *whatever wounds exist psychologically in a person are likely to find their way into that person's sex life.* In their book, *Hidden Bedroom Partners,* Garwood and Hajcak (1987) make this point the cornerstone of their work. "Much of our sexual behavior is motivated by repressed, nonsexual needs which surface and seek satisfaction during sex" (p. 7). It is not simply that sex and projective identification are analogous processes, they are the *same* process occurring on different levels. Sex is both a metaphor for transformation and also a vehicle for it. Projective identification symbolically implies that if a man is to heal his wounds, he has to "make love" to that which is most hated in himself. The same applies to woman. The hated part is experienced first in projected form as the dark side of the anima/animus, but ultimately it must be re-integrated back into the self. This process occurs by means of sexual attraction.

Recall Dicks'(1967) statement that "marriage can be seen to act as a natural therapeutic relationship . . . It is as if each partner was aiming at the restoration of a complete personality through their union" (pp. 64–66). Unknowingly, the person becomes erotically bound to the very thing that is rejected in himself. *To make love to someone who embodies this part is to reintegrate it through identification with the beloved,* leading to renewal and empowerment of the self. This constitutes a kind of death and rebirth. So with sex there is potential death, transformation, and empowerment. Again, this is the essence of Scorpio.

Problems With Integration of Taurus-Scorpio

I have stated that sex is both a metaphor for transformation and also a vehicle for it. Sex itself is a process of transformation, a subset of the larger issue. We see this even in the origins of sex. Life invented sex as a way of resolving an evolutionary crisis. By enabling its existent forms to project into one another and exchange genetic material, unicellular organisms evolved into forces that were progressively more advanced. Here we see how sex is a biological corollary to a psychological process of healing. The implication is plain enough: *a sexual problem may be indicative of a psychological problem occurring on a different level.* The various forms of sexual dysfunction are, in effect, symptomatic of a failure to heal one's psychic wounds.

Properly speaking, Scorpio's contribution to sexuality is emotional and psychological. Scorpio is having sex all the time on an abstract, metaphorical level. By this I mean that sexuality is prefigured in all forms of healing, crisis management, financial transactions, detective work, and various other expressions of Scorpio. Anything that involves penetration, assimilation, and transformation can be a metaphor for sex. It is not until Taurus is brought into the act that sex manifests on a physical level. To have real sexual intercourse requires a body, and the body belongs to Taurus. So sexual intercourse is actually a joining together of Taurus and Scorpio, the physical and the emotional, earth and water.

As mentioned, the difficulties that people have with sexuality are legion, ranging from rape and perversion to simple lack of desire. While it would be naive to suggest that any one thing is the cause of this huge range of problems, I would say that most are related to difficulties integrating the Taurus-Scorpio polarity somewhere in life, somewhere in the horoscope. Because it is an archetypal challenge, all human beings must negotiate it, and the continuum of success/failure is as broad as people are different.

To appreciate the subtle contours of this challenge, let us briefly review the nature of the Taurus-Scorpio polarity. Taurus has to do with object constancy and self-love, which translates into the solid assurance that one is good, loved, and safe, and that one's identity is stable. Scorpio, on the other hand, has to do with crisis and self-transformation, which translates into the need to confront what is "bad" in oneself, heal wounds, take risks, and remain open to change. The dynamic exchange between these two parts of the psyche revolves around themes of safety and risk, pleasure and pain, holding on and letting go, stability and crisis. If Taurus is calm and mellow, Scorpio is anxious and intense. If Taurus rules the mundane world, Scorpio rules the realm of the sacred. Whereas Taurus is soothing, Scorpio is arousing. If Taurus clings to the known, Scorpio opens to the unknown. Taurus is content to pleasure the body, but Scorpio wants to plumb the depths of the soul. Taurus retains, Scorpio releases. How can we reconcile these apparently disparate and uncombinable parts of our nature? Obviously, it is not easy, but, like anything in life, we can learn by examining our mistakes and failures. Let us explore some of the dysfunctional ways that human beings strive to resolve this challenge.

I am going to return to an aspect that we have already examined in the example of our hypothetical couple, that of the Venus-Pluto square. The reason for this is that since Venus rules Taurus and Pluto rules Scorpio, hard aspects between these two planets suggest that the archetypal challenge of integrating the Taurus-Scorpio axis is going to be highlighted by this planetary configuration. There are, of course, other ways this challenge can show up in the chart—planets in Taurus opposing planets in Scorpio, planets in opposition occupying the 2nd and 8th Houses, Pluto in the 2nd, Venus in the 8th, and so on. But Venus square Pluto is a fairly straightforward signature of the challenge, as will be made clear in the case to follow.

Venus square Pluto can manifest in a variety of ways, most of them dramatic, but if one understands the underlying difficulty, then the colorful panoply of symptoms begins to make sense. If I were to summarize the problem in a single phrase, I would simply say *fear of intimacy*. What is it, after all, that Taurus fears? It is loss of safety, security, and the certainty of knowing who one is. And these are almost certainly to be lost the moment one opens oneself to the power of eros. Freud said it best, "never are we so defenseless against suffering as when we love, never so helplessly unhappy as when we have lost our loved object or its love . . ."

It is not simply the fear of losing one's beloved that makes erotic love difficult. More to the point, it is the fear of discovering one's wounds and deficiencies in the process. Erotic love makes one vulnerable. And vulnerability implies a willingness to be pierced by reality, as symbolized by Cupid's arrow that pierces the heart. While affectionate bonding (Taurus) and passionate love (Scorpio) overlap and have many qualities in common, passionate love appears to be characterized by a radical discontinuity with everything that has preceded it. As a consequence, it is one of life's preeminent crucibles for change. Person (1988) asserts that erotic love enacts its role as change-agent in part by giving us a chance to remake the past. "It is not possible to be in love without reinvoking old conflicts, and as they are enacted once again, in a new context, we are provided with another opportunity to resolve them." (p. 350)

When one falls in love, he or she connects deeply with someone and suddenly feels drawn outside of the self into a larger reality. The person is challenged to open up in exactly those places where one is most contracted. This stirs up the pain and confusion of unresolved emotional conflicts and brings the person up against the unseen, unknown elements within. Most people would like to avoid this, yet there is an inevitability about it, just as there is an inevitability to orgasm once a certain point is reached. When a person opens up to the transformative power of love, the desire for the beloved comes together with one's personal "stuff." Then there is ferment, there is alchemy, and there is the possibility for change and renewal. But none of this occurs without a certain amount of pain and suffering.

There is a tendency with Venus square Pluto to avoid the vulnerability that comes with relationship while still trying to have the joys of sexual intimacy. This is at best a compromise, but it can be partially accomplished in a number of ways. Affairs are one variant. If the person is unwilling to confront the problems in his or her relationship and is also unwilling to give up the security the relationship affords, an affair seems a viable compromise. It is, in effect, an "acting out" of the split between the dark and the light sides of the anima/animus figure. One's lover gets all the passion and aliveness—the "good" object—while one's spouse is increasingly seen in a negative light—the "bad" object. Any possibility for real growth is sacrificed because the split prevents one's pain from being communicated in ways that allow for healing.

Another variant is so-called "addictive love," as is made in such books as *Women Who Love Too Much* (Norwood, 1986).

In this case, the person is obsessed with the beloved to the point that it consumes his or her every waking thought. Such love is characterized by an *intensity of feeling* that is easily mistaken for true love, yet is more accurately a measure of the degree of resistance which preceded the loss of control. The person avoids relationship as long as possible for fear of losing all sense of self-value. Once the decision to love is made, it becomes total, all-consuming, out of control, passionate, and potentially destructive. The floodgates open and there is a great surge and outpouring of affectional energy which can carry one away as in a "flood of feeling." This release of affection feels so good that one can easily become addicted to it despite the negative consequences it brings in its wake. The individual cannot terminate/eliminate the toxic relationship, no matter how painful and destructive it becomes, because she or he sees it as one's only source of value.

Preoccupation with the beloved actually serves a defensive function in that the individual does not have to confront the internal wounds that motivated the object choice. With most of the attention going to the beloved, there is little left for introspection. A particularly male version on this theme is the man who "stalks" or is obsessed with some particular woman. He may intrude and harass her to the point of having to be blocked by a legal restraining order. In other instances, the woman may be totally unaware of the man's interest in her. John Hinkley's obsession with Jodie Foster is typical of this type.

Forbidden love is closely related to addictive love. One loves those whose nature is consistent with the distrust of love itself. In other words, if one's internal relationship to "love needs" is that they are dangerous, bad, and must be suppressed, then there is a tendency to fall for people who *embody and reinforce this attitude*, i.e., people who are corrupt, devious, criminals, prostitutes, addicts, convicts, drug dealers, underworld types—in other words, people who are inherently untrustworthy.

I recall an interview with Richard Speck, the man convicted of slashing and choking eight nurses to death in 1966 in one of the most savage crimes of the century. Speck himself was appalled that he received numerous letters in his prison cell every week from women who wanted to correspond with him, visit him, and develop romantic relationships with him. The French have a phrase for this, *amour de la bouche*, "love of the mud." Clearly, love in this context can be perverse and degrading.

Forbidden love could also mean interracial love, or incestuous love, or homosexual love. To love a deviant, as in "social deviant," or to love in what society considers a deviant way, as in homosexuality, may be manifestations of the same process. I am not suggesting that homosexuality is pathological anymore than interracial love is pathological. To suggest that it has no psychological significance, however, would be naive. *The point is that the individual's choice of an object that is socially taboo may reflect an inter-*

nal taboo, fear, or shame associated with loving.[3] There are countless plays and movies that deal with this theme, such as *Thief of Hearts, Two Moon Junction, The Postman Rings Twice,* and *9-1/2 Weeks,* all of which are modern day re-enactments of the ancient myth of Pluto and Persephone. Such stories are eternally captivating because they reflect an archetypal predicament that is endemic to being human. We recognize them instinctively.

Closely associated to forbidden love is dangerous love. We have merely to recall two recent films of Michael Douglas, *Fatal Attraction* and *Basic Instinct,* to get a flavor of what this looks like.[4] Here we have an attraction to people who pose a high risk for negative consequences. These consequences may not be obvious at first, but are implicit, or hidden, in the nature of the person and/or situation. Again, to love dangerously is reflective of the danger the person internally associates with the Venus impulse. The objective situation mirrors the subjective reality.

In such relationships, the probability of betrayal is very high— e.g., the lover may "turn on one" and suddenly become transformed into an adversary, or one partner will lie and exploit the other's trust. Cases of spousal abuse, cheating, theft, and even marital rape typify this process. I had one case of a woman with a Venus-Pluto square who was afraid to leave her abusive husband because she was convinced he would kill her if she did (Perry, 1992). Sometimes the beloved plays the role of tempter, like the serpent in the Garden of Eden. The forbidden fruit may be a dishonest scheme, involvement in drugs, crime, prostitution, weird sex, or anything that has a high potential for destructive consequences. While such involvements are always exciting, they merely substitute for the risk of being vulnerable in a healthy relationship.

---

3   I realize that this is a controversial statement and is likely to arouse the objection that if one feels shame around homosexual love it is due to the fact that our society is homophobic. This undoubtably is true. What the objection fails to address, however, is the significance of the sexual preference quite apart from whether society condemns it. I am suggesting that like any other object orientation, it has meaning.

4   It is always interesting to note how the charts of actors and actresses so often reveal the psychological themes that are "acted out" in the roles they play. Douglas has an opposition between his 8th House Saturn and 2nd House Moon, with both planets forming a T-Square to a Sun-Neptune conjunction in the 11th. The Moon and Saturn are in mutual reception, doubly emphasizing the importance of this aspect and the Houses it occupies. I leave it to the reader to delineate how *Fatal Attraction* and *Basic Instinct* are symbolized by this astrological complex.

A common theme in Venus-Pluto relationships was described by Somerset Maugham in his fictional work, *The Razor's Edge,* where the central character fell in love with a drug addict who eventually committed suicide. Since she was never really available for relationship, one would question why he loved her so deeply. "Passion," explained Maugham, "thrives on impediment."

Recall that Venus/Taurus is the need for safety and security. If one has not developed the capacity for self-love, so that one's security comes from within, then one's ability for tolerating the risks inherent in erotic love will be deficient. There will not be sufficient internal structure to contain the experience. Accordingly, one seeks an external container—an impediment that functions as a homeostatic mechanism that keeps intimacy from becoming too intense. The impediment is like walls, or limits, which make it safe to love since there is always something which prevents it from becoming open-ended and permanent. A good example is the woman who falls in love with someone who is in prison, a situation that is extraordinarily common. The relationship is fine until he gets out and then all hell breaks loose. Some women avoid this problem by marrying men who are serving lifetime sentences. She can visit him in prison, and even have sexual relations, but the walls of the prison serve a containing function not simply for the prisoner, but for the heart of the woman that is imprisoned by her fears. Less dramatic examples that fall into this category are long-distance love affairs, falling in love with someone from another country who has to return soon, or falling for someone who is already married or otherwise in a committed relationship.

Perhaps the most virulent form of the Venus-Pluto square is what I would call abusive love. If Venus is repressed and dysfunctional, the individual is not going to believe that he or she is worthy of love, and if one lacks self-love, one is not going to trust that the partner's love is real. This leads to intensely ambivalent attitudes toward the partner marked by (1) a need to dominate the partner; or (2) an impulse to submit to the partner's dominance. Accordingly, a pattern of dominance and submission ensues with the dominant partner trying to control the submissive one through criticism, withholding of affection, or intimidation. This generally takes the form of telling the partner what to do, what to think, how to act, what to wear, what friends to have, and the like. There is usually a pattern of intense and unreasonable jealousy, possessiveness, checking up on the partner, intrusiveness, threats, or actual acts of violence. In this game, whether you play the dominant or submissive role does not matter. Real intimacy is avoided because neither partner has to be vulnerable in the sense of revealing their deeper fears and insecurities. The goal is merely to assure that the love object will not abandon or betray one.

In the dominant role, the Venus-Pluto person projects his or her "bad-self" into the partner so it appears that *the partner* is unworthy of love and thus deserving of abuse. On the surface, it appears that the dominant partner is trying to change, or heal, the defects of the beloved, but the unconscious strategy is actually to *destroy the partner's self-value so that he or she will not leave.* In the submissive role, the person projects the "bad" persecuting object (usually an abusive parental figure that has been internalized), and thus feels *deserving of abuse.* These processes of projection may go back and forth until the relationship degenerates into an ugly power struggle over who is "good" who is "bad."

It is not difficult to see how the above pattern of interaction can translate into the sexual arena where sado/masochistic fantasies are acted out. In fact, if one looks closely it will be apparent that all versions of the Pluto-Venus dilemma are analogues to the kinds of problems that occur in the sexual arena. Affairs, addictive love, forbidden love, impeded love, and abusive love all tend to be components of what Carnes (1983) defines as sexual addiction. The key component of sexual addiction is shame and deception, and in each of the above categories there is invariably a greater or lesser amount of shame associated with one's object choice.

In sexual addiction, the person overcompensates for their fear of intimacy by engaging in one form or another of compulsive sex. Highly secretive of their behavior, they live in constant fear of being discovered, endanger their careers, their marriages, the welfare of their children, yet feel powerless to stop. Again, this is an "acting out" of an internal state wherein the individual is ashamed and afraid of the need for intimacy. We should not be surprised when Carnes reports that sexual addicts have little self-love (Venus) and are seeking to compensate for an internal deficiency through excessive sex (Pluto). Far from being satisfying, however, their relationships tend to be empty and superficial. They are abusive to their partners and generally have sex with people who are unknown and often unliked.

In those cases, indications that the individual is acting out an unconscious, repressed Venusian impulse is the trance-like mood that precedes the sex act the addict wishes to perform. Sexual acting out becomes ritualized, which serves to intensify and add excitement to the act. The act itself can range from normal heterosexual intercourse to many things less standard—masturbation, a homosexual encounter, exhibitionism, voyeurism, obscene phone calling—even incest, child molesting and rape.[5] Note that in each instance, *the normal vulnerability that accompanies loving is avoided.*

The most dramatic symptoms of the Venus-Pluto square occur in cases of sexual assault and/or perversion, which may be two faces of the same animal. These include incest, pedophilia (love of children, or child molestation), rape, sexual murders, perversions, and prostitution. Again, in each instance, there is the obvious attempt to dominate and control the victim so that the perpetrator avoids entirely any personal vulnerability.

The question inevitably arises as to why hard aspects between Venus-Pluto so often result in the individual becoming a victim of sexual assault. Recall that you can not permanently get rid of an archetype. Repression only renders it more primitive. We can expect, therefore, that if Venus is repressed, it will eventually erupt in some deviant fashion. This may come from within, as in the impulse to violate some sexual taboo, or it may come from without as in cases of sexual assault, molestation, and the like.

---

5 I recall one case involving a married man who was addicted to phone sex. He would call up a 900 number and masturbate while the girl said obscene things to him, yet he was totally impotent with his wife. His chart revealed a close Venus-Pluto quincunx, with Venus being the apex of a T-Square involving a Mars/Moon conjunction in Taurus opposed Neptune in Scorpio. So the Venus-Pluto, Taurus-Scorpio complex was activated several ways.

I had another case involving a married man who had been arrested several times for exhibitionism. He also had Venus in close inconjunct with Pluto. In this case, his Venus was conjunct the Moon and Jupiter in the 12th House with all three planets squaring Neptune in the 8th. He stated that his mother (Moon) was sexually provocative and would demand his help in deceiving the father while she had men over the house for sex. Later as an adult, his own sex life was characterized by secret exhibitionistic acts carried out in shame.

Research indicates that men overwhelmingly are perpetrators of sexual abuse, whereas woman overwhelmingly are victims. Yet, research also indicates that Venus-Pluto contacts occur with the same high frequency in the charts of perpetrators *and* victims.[6]

If Venus is our capacity for self-valuing, then Pluto square Venus suggests a *de*valuing of self, and this is precisely what happens. The devaluation may originate in an actual historical trauma where the individual was exploited or abused by adult caretakers. Later, this will manifest in an impulse to devalue or degrade the self through a relationship of questionable merit. In the female version, the individual sells herself cheaply, as in loving someone who is lowly, base, and mean; or she may actually degrade herself by using sex as a means to obtain money and power, as in prostitution. Promiscuity is yet another variation. The woman projects her self-value onto men and then attempts to obtain love through sexual favors.

The male version of this game often seems to involve the actual exploitation and abuse of woman. Here, the male projects his lack of self-value onto women and degrades them accordingly. Again, however, research indicates that sex offenders are *re-enacting a situation in which they were once themselves victims.* Perpetrators almost universally report having been sexually, physically, or emotionally abused as children. Carnes (1983) puts the figure at 97 percent. According to Stoller (1975), who wrote the book *Perversion: The Erotic Form of Hatred,* the defining attribute in perversion is hostility directed in reality or in fantasy toward one's sex object. At the core of the perverse act, says

---

6 There have been at least two studies linking sexual assault to Venus-Pluto aspects. Davis (1978) reports that after analyzing 31 charts of sexual assault victims she concluded that "Venus is of primary importance. The probabilities of sexual assault dramatically rise if there are discordant aspects between Venus and Pluto" (p. 40). Likewise, Houston (1989) did a statistical analysis of 110 cases of sex murders and found that the frequency of Venus-Pluto aspects occurring on the dates of the murders was far above what could be expected. "A chi square test revealed that the Venus-Pluto major aspects occurred in a non-random way on the dates of occurrence of the stranger-to-stranger sex murders. The result is significant at the 0.01 level. The average percentage of the observed frequencies for the considered 12 years is 26.15 percent, whereas the average percentage of the expected frequencies is 16.71 percent. The range of the observed frequencies is 50 percent, whereas the range of the expected frequencies is 13.7 percent" (p. 24). Reported in Davis, T. P., *Sexual assaults: Pre-identifying Those Vulnerable,* Davis Research Reports, P.O. Box 979, Windermere, Florida 32786, 1978. Also see Houston, L. M., Venus-Pluto aspects on the occurrence dates of sex murders, in *NCGR Research Journal: Astro-Psychological Problems,* Fall 1989, pp. 23–25.

Stoller, is the unconscious attempt to redress an injury, or trauma, that occurred during childhood.

The hostility in perversion takes form in a fantasy of revenge hidden in the actions that make up the perversion and serves to convert childhood trauma to adult triumph. To create the greatest excitement, the perversion must also portray itself as an act of risk-taking. (p. 4)

Stoller found that the perversion was the reliving of an actual historical trauma that affected the child's sense of sexual identity. In the specifics of the perverse act, the past is resolved and the trauma is turned into pleasure, orgasm, and victory. Here again we see the Scorpio theme of empowerment through the resolving of one's fear, except that with perversion there is the need to do the same thing over and over because the trauma that is motivating the perversion remains unconscious. So long as the trauma remains unconscious it can only be "acted out" and never completely healed.

Jeffrey Dahmer

Jeffrey Dahmer may be a typical example. The product of a broken home and himself the victim of childhood sexual molestation by a neighbor boy at age 8, Dahmer was obsessed with manipulation and domination. Those victims that got away later reported to police that Dahmer was fine until they tried to leave. Then he grew panicky. Dahmer reportedly confessed to police that he killed his victims because he wanted to keep them with him. First he would have sex with them, and if he had not already killed them, he would do so immediately following the act. Next he would dismember their bodies and store them in the fridge. Talk about possessive!

Dahmer's chart reveals Venus in Taurus conjunct the Sun in the 8th House, with the Sun forming a close square to Pluto (see Figure 1). While Venus is not itself square to Pluto, it is in Taurus in the Pluto-ruled 8th House. Accordingly, the need for security/sensual gratification is strongly associated with a situation of crisis, wounding, and death (8th House).

Stoller's theory of sexual trauma being at the root of perversion (by which he means *any* sexual act that is motivated by fear and hostility) makes sense in the light of hard aspects between Venus and Pluto. Recall that Venus/Taurus predominantly has to do with concerns that relate directly to late infancy development, approximately 18 months to 4 years, when the child is striving to attain object constancy, self-solidity (body self-image), self-permanence, security, and the like (Perry, 1991). Plutonic disturbances here can undermine the child's sense of safety and emerging sense of self. Rather than attaining assurance of self-permanence, there is the opposite (Scorpio/Pluto) experience of self-annihilation.

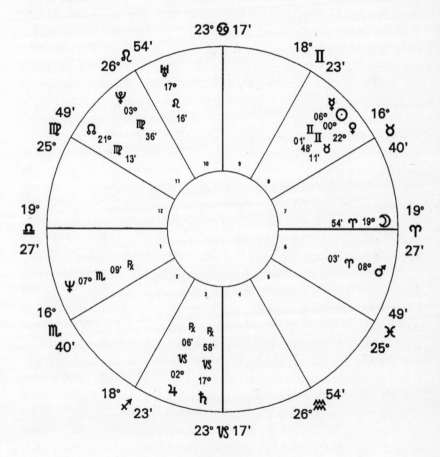

Figure 1
Jeffrey Dahmer
May 21, 1960, 4:34 P.M. CDT
Milwaukee, WI
87W54 43N02
Placidus Houses

The experience of self-annihilation may take the form of what Winnicott (1960) called "maternal impingements"—e.g., mother uses the child to satisfy her own narcissistic needs for love and affection. These maternal impingements are experienced by the child as a terrifying interference with the continuity of his own personal existence. Because the child is appropriated to gratify the narcissistic needs of the parent, the normal parent-child relationship is reversed. While this gives the child considerable power, it also burdens the child with responsibility for the affectional needs of the parent. Such a responsibility is overwhelming and prevents the child from developing a full awareness of his own bodily felt urges. While this is difficult enough, the situation is dramatically worsened if the child is actually seduced, sexually excited, molested, or raped by an older person. Clearly this would constitute a traumatic violation of the child's physical boundaries and sense of security.

I suspect that when Pluto "impinges" upon Venus we have an astrological corollary to sexual assault. To impinge is to encroach or infringe upon, to clash with disruptive impact. Any hard aspects between Pluto and Venus naturally relate to the archetypal opposition between Scorpio and Taurus. Accordingly, when Pluto squares Venus, the implication is that somehow Pluto's energies and demands are violently intruding upon the needs which Venus represents. Pluto symbolizes upheaval, crisis, transition, impermanence, transformation into new states with associated fear and pain, but the need of Venus/Taurus is for sameness, stability, safety, permanence, predictability, comfort, and pleasure. Pluto square Venus may be like an impinging adult who infringes upon the child's needs and appropriates her or him for the adult's own ends, as in cases of child sexual molestation. Such a person would overwhelm the child with his or her own needs, effectively *reversing* (or opposing) the normal adult-child relation. This would be traumatic for the child. It is as if the child is enveloped by a collective force against which he or she is powerless. The child's needs for safety and security are utterly precluded. Just as a child is not equipped to heal the wounds of a dysfunctional parent, so it is unable to channel Pluto into constructive expression. Like an impinging parent, Pluto disrupts and interferes with a child's need to feel safe and loved. In so doing, it impairs and wounds the nascent self which is developing.

Jimmy Swaggart and the Impinging Devil

Previously I cited the man who had Pluto conjunct the Moon squaring Venus. While some of my comments were speculative regarding this individual's family of origin and subsequent marriage, they were not entirely so. The chart example was based on the case of Jimmy Swaggart. Perhaps no one more tragically exemplifies Venus square Pluto than Swaggart (see Figure 2). The preeminent "televangelist," Swaggart was always a firebrand on the subject of moral turpitude, railing against sexual aberrations, adultery, "demon lust," and other diabolical impulses of the human psyche. Then in February 1989, Swaggart was caught by a rival evangelist in the act of paying a prostitute to perform an "obscene act," and later admitted that he had a compulsive fascination with pornography since boyhood.

As part of a Water Grand Trine and the focal point of a T-Cross involving Mars, Venus, Uranus, and the Moon, Pluto is by far the most important planet in Swaggart's chart, and it is the key to understanding his success and downfall. As the psychic complex, or bad-object, Pluto is seldom recognized by the individual as an intrapsychic problem rooted in early childhood experiences. More often it is projected outward as someone or something of malevolent and destructive intent—like the devil.

Swaggart's Pluto is in the 7th House. The 7th House is an area of the not-self, or partner. Its contents describe those qualities which we tend to project onto other people, as well as the way in which we establish intimate relationships in general. Pluto's location there has many permutations for Swaggart. As part of his Grand Trine, its energies are successfully utilized in the service of both his religious beliefs (Jupiter) and his ego, or will (Sun). As the charismatic maestro of high-energy salvation Swaggart had no equal. So long as other people were willing to submit to his need to reform and convert them to Pentecostal Christianity, all went well. But Pluto is also the focal point of an explosive T-Cross. This makes Pluto highly stressed and unstable, giving it a tendency to *overfunction* in ways that frequently turn pathological.

The god Pluto in Greek mythology has degenerated into the devil-concept of Christian theology, and the devil is the dark, worrisome entity that haunted Swaggart's sleeping and waking dreams. I once heard him fervently admonish his congregation,

"Satan hates you. He wants to kill you." In this statement, we see how the devil has become the impinging object in Swaggart's mind. All evil is projected onto the devil, and all good onto Jesus. By implication, other people (7th House) are either "saved" or "damned" and must be treated accordingly. The conception is primitive and exemplifies the ego defense mechanism of "splitting" which is reflected both in Swaggart's horoscope and in his religious beliefs. Pluto in the 7th is Swaggart's hated Satan, as well as his "dark" anima/partner and projected bad-object. Not surprisingly, Swaggart claimed that his sexual indiscretions were due to "demons" trying to possess his soul.

The specifics of Swaggart's demons can be seen from the aspects Pluto forms to other planets. Since it is conjunct the Moon and square both Venus and Uranus in the 4th House, we can reasonably expect that Swaggart's relationship with his mother constitutes one source of his demons (mother = Moon/4th House). Pluto conjunct the Moon images the devouring mother, toward whom there might be unresolved erotic and incestuous feelings, regressive pulls back into the mother's orbit, or intense fear of destructive impulses arising from and toward the object. Note that the Moon is also the focal point of a potentially violent T-Square between Mars in the 10th and Uranus in the 4th, which would seem to support the hypothesis that Swaggart's relationship with his mother involved intensely ambivalent feelings. The opposition to Mars in the 10th (father) from Venus and Uranus in the 4th, as well as the squares to Mars from both the Moon and Pluto, suggest that Swaggart's relationship with his father was equally problematic.[7]

The fact that Pluto is in the 7th House *and* squaring Venus doubly emphasizes the Pluto connection with intimacy, sensuality, and physical pleasure. Pluto's placement in the 7th suggests a fear of intimate encounters and probable power struggles with one's partner. According to one newspaper account, Jimmy and his wife were on the verge of divorce, due to her reluctance to relinquish control of his professional affairs. Swaggart's father allegedly accused her of "stripping Jimmy of his manhood."

---

7 For a detailed analysis of Swaggart's horoscope and family of origin, see my article "The Last Temptation of Jimmy Swaggart" in *The Journal of Astro-Psychology*, Vol. 2, No. 1. Write AAP, 360 Quietwood Drive, San Rafael, CA 94903.

Pluto square Venus in the 4th suggests that the Venus function is associated with a deep, psychic wound. There is likely to be great fear and resistance here—again, quite possibly associated with early trauma involving an attachment to mother (4th House). Due to the pain such experiences engender, they are likely to have been repressed and *the entire Venus function projected*. We do not have to look far to find evidence of Pluto-Venus pathology.

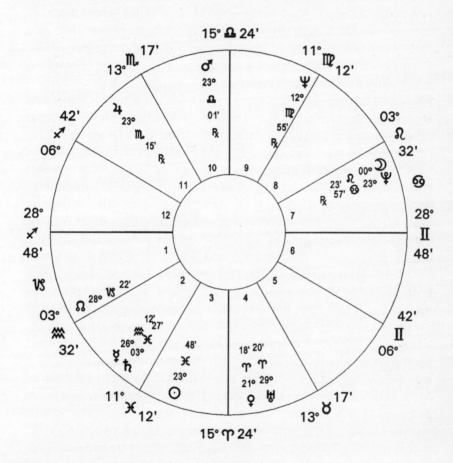

Figure 2
Jimmy Swaggart
Mar. 15, 1935, 1:35 A.M. CST
Ferriday, LA
91W33 31N38
Placidus Houses

A year before his sexual addiction was exposed, Swaggart wrote a 316-page book on sexual arousal, advising his readers to avoid any kind of dancing, even ballroom dancing, because such activities might arouse their sexual passion and lust. He also advised against going to movies, or engaging in mixed public swimming, for the same reason. Masturbation was wrong, he said, because "for the act to be carried out to satisfaction . . . the mind has to dwell on sordid and filthy imagery." These statements exemplify a deep fear of losing control over Venus functions.

As we have seen, this aspect frequently does manifest as a loss of control over sexual impulses, resulting in intense emotional involvements which are perverse and degrading. Swaggart eventually admitted to a compulsive fascination with pornography since boyhood. "Pornography," he once wrote, "titillates and captivates the sickest of the sick and makes them slaves to their own consuming lusts . . . ensnares its victims in a living hell." We now know he was speaking from experience.

Swaggart's tendency toward *amour de la bouche* is a direct consequence of Plutonic repression. His addiction to sex with prostitutes exemplifies how if something *within* the self (e.g., Venus) is subjectively perceived as evil (Pluto), then it can only be experienced externally in a context which reflects the internal association. Love is dragged into the gutter.

With Venus in the 4th and Moon in the 7th, we have double indemnity. Mother's charming, seductive side was probably directed at Jimmy, but I suspect that for her caring and protection Jimmy paid a high price. Moon-Venus contacts in a male horoscope can suggest a confusion between "mother" and "lover." Swaggart might have felt bound to his mother, sensitive to her marital woes, and used by her as a substitute love object. This, of course, would have created Oedipal tensions between Swaggart and his father, who might have viewed Jimmy's overinvolvement with his mother with increasing resentment. Uranus's contribution to this potentially explosive state of affairs would be to destabilize the triangle further. Sudden separations, as in divorce, are quite possible. We know Swaggart's father was married three times. Was Jimmy's mother one of them? If so, did Jimmy feel as if he had taken mother away from father; in effect, replaced him?

If any of this were true, we would expect Swaggart's relationship with his mother to be extremely conflictual. Little boys do not like to be mother's primary love object *because there is no way they can be adequate to the task.* It also interferes with the all-important task of identifying with father. Stoller (1975) points out that a too intense and prolonged intimacy with the mother can result in a flawed sense of maleness. When this occurs, *the child grows up in fear of the feminine,* projecting upon it the power to destroy one's very identity as a male. This sets the stage for perversion, which has at its core hostility toward the love object. It is interesting in this regard to recall Jimmy's father's announcement that Jimmy's wife "stripped him of his manhood." Perhaps she was not the first?

The psychodynamics of perversion are relevant here because we know that Swaggart was in the habit of hiring prostitutes to perform "obscene acts." He was not simply looking for sexual release, but *for a specific fantasy to be played out for his titillation.* One of the prostitutes claimed that Swaggart liked to engage in various sado-masochistic rituals. She alleges that on at least one occasion, Swaggart had her dance naked in front of his car at the edge of a cliff while he sat behind the wheel, revving the engine while masturbating himself to orgasm. In Swaggart's actions, we see a desperate ploy to obtain a sense of power and control over the feared object.

Stoller (1975) has shown that in such ritualized patterns of sex practice, a scenario is created in which are remnants of earlier painful experiences, now redone to make a triumph out of the trauma: the victim becomes the victor. The fear that must be conquered is not some generalized state of oedipal alarm, but an actual historical trauma aimed precisely at one's genitalia or one's gender identity. *The perversion functions as a necessary preserver of potency.* By recreating, in fantasy, the original trauma, the individual transforms fear into pleasure and in so doing takes back the power which was lost. For the sexually damaged person, there is no better way to prove oneself triumphant than to be potent—sexually aroused and ultimately orgasmic—in the presence of the original trauma. This is why I believe that in all dysfunctional expressions of the Venus-Pluto dynamic there is an attempt to avoid the fear that is associated with intimate loving. Swaggart's ritualized intimidation of the prostitute means "I do not need to be afraid of her," thereby making possible the pleasure that would otherwise have been blocked by fear.

Earlier, I mentioned how negative, painful childhood experiences tend to be split off from the conscious ego and remain encapsulated in the unconscious as the "bad-self." The bad-self, in turn, remains fused with the "bad-object," the original source of the trauma. Even if the trauma is not specifically sexual, the function of perversion is to bind into erotic pleasure and potency those unconsciously remembered experiences and their associated feelings of rage and fear. This is why Pluto eroticizes whatever it touches. It sets the stage for an attempt at integration through sexual release. Unfortunately, so long as the original traumatic experiences remain unconscious, the sense of triumph lasts only a short while and must be endlessly repeated.

In Swaggart's tragic tale we see the purposive nature of sexual attraction. If Swaggart's "complex" (bad-self) is his sensual nature, as symbolized in the Venus square to Pluto, then his anima would necessarily be a threatening figure, and it is the projection of a male's anima which *triggers* sexual attraction. A prostitute fits the script. Her dark and forbidden sensuality, with which she is more or less totally identified, is the perfect complement to Swaggart's messianic yearnings. As the "dark" anima, she embodies his own split-off, unidentified sexual needs. The "light" side was undoubtably carried by his wife.

One must go into the dark to heal the split, however. Again, sexuality is purposive in that it binds the individual to that specific opposite which is most needed to bring about growth in consciousness. Perhaps the real lesson of Pluto is that we are erotically bound to that which we most hate within ourselves. Even in perversion, we can see the attempt to integrate the forbidden impulse so that we can become whole and *holy*. It is ironic that the only way for Swaggart to attain the holiness he so earnestly desires is to merge with the object he most despises, the prostitute.

Healing the Taurus-Scorpio Split

While clearly the challenge of integrating the Taurus-Scorpio, Venus-Pluto part of our natures is a formidable one, I would be remiss if I did not include here examples of *successful* transformations, for they abound as well. First, however, let us examine once again the essential nature of the dilemma. People can err on one side or the other of the Taurus-Scorpio axis. If we emphasize the Venus/Taurus side at the expense of Pluto/Scorpio, we end

end up in what Welwood (1990) calls the "bliss trap"—imagining that love is a stairway to heaven that will allow us to leave behind all our fears and limitations:

> The potential distortion here is to imagine that love by itself can solve our problems, provide endless comfort and pleasure, or save us from facing ourselves, our aloneness, our pain, or, ultimately, our death. Becoming too attached to the heavenly side of love leads to rude shocks and disappointments when we inevitably return to earth and have to deal with the real-life challenges of *making a relationship work.* (pp. 54–55)

When partners treat their relationship as a finished *product,* something *to have and possess,* rather than as a living *process* which matures and deepens over time, they will stagnate. If couples try to make their relationship a known quantity that is totally solid, safe, and subordinated to Taurean needs for security, then they lose any possibility for growth and change. If partners collude to play everything safe and avoid entirely the fear and pain of their union, the relationship will soon become boring, monotonous, stale, predictable, and stultifying. In short, *life demands that we evolve.*

We can, however, err on the Scorpio-Pluto side as well. This occurs when Venus is sacrificed in the pursuit of Plutonian risk and excitement. Relationships are characterized by secrecy and shame, furtive encounters with strangers met in bars, premature intimacy with people we do not really know or even like, affairs, betrayal, domination, and abuse. Taurean attachments are avoided and pain is circumvented, since one cannot suffer the loss of something he never had. When the Taurus-Venus side is integrated, there is foreplay, there is a slow, gradual process of getting to know one another. In a word there is *vulnerability.* But if one fears intimacy, this process arouses too much anxiety and will tend to be abruptly terminated. In its stead there is usually an erotic "come-on," a manipulative ploy designed to trick, pressure, or seduce. The quicker the "score," the more rapid the resolution of the fear ineradicably associated with intimacy. Sexual harassment, sexual abuse, perversions, and rape are its more severe expressions, but fear of intimacy can also subtly manifest in the sexual dysfunction of the average couple—premature ejaculation and orgasmic dysfunction being common examples. Kaplan (1974) writes that some people are so conflicted about their erotic needs that they actively *discourage their partners from stimulating them effectively*:

> Patients who avoid effective sexual expression because of the anxiety such feelings mobilize tend to focus on genital stimulation and on the orgasm and are apt to neglect the sensual potential of the rest of the body and of non-orgasmic eroticism. Orgasm produces relief because the anxiety-provoking sexual situation is thus terminated. (p. 124)

I believe that the key to resolving the Taurus-Scorpio challenge lies in the concept of vulnerability. During the process of development, the individual invariably forms various attachments. These can be to things, to beliefs, to occupations, or to people. These Taurean attachments define the boundaries of what is known and familiar; they provide comfort and security.

On the other hand, living also exposes one to the risk of being injured. This can be an actual childhood trauma, or merely the shame associated with expressing some natural part of oneself that was forbidden, for various reasons, by one's family. These painful psychic wounds establish the boundary of what is strange and unknown; they arouse distress and fear. Clearly this is Scorpio. Growth involves penetrating the boundaries of the strange, confronting one's psychic wounds, and integrating them into what is known and familiar, thus expanding the boundaries of the self. In the process, old attachments are sacrificed and the self dies, only to be reborn in a new, more complex version of itself. Person (1988) drives the point home:

> Because of the identification with the beloved that always occurs in passionate love, love often demands a significant reordering of values and priorities. In love the self is exposed to new risks that may result in enlarged possibilities. We are emboldened to cross internal psychological boundaries and defy taboos both internal and external, liberating us from ourselves and the strictures of habit and defense, the deformities of earlier unhappy experience and inhibitions. Under the sway of love, we may feel the impetus to begin new phases of life, initiate new projects and undertake new responsibilities. We may even feel born again, as love rewrites the narrative of our lives through its own compelling force. (p. 350)

The point is that passionate love provides both the incentive and the feedback that is required for personal transformation. Not only do we need the beloved to mirror back to us what we cannot see in ourselves, but it is precisely our attachment to the beloved (Taurus) that motivates us to endure the trials and tests of erotic love (Scorpio). There needs to be stability in a healthy relationship, but not so much that growth is stunted. There needs also to be risk, but no so much that the individual becomes subject to abuse. *The middle ground between the two is a tender, vulnerable space that must be approached with an exquisite balance of caution and courage.* It is only here, at the borders of the known and the unknown, that change can occur. It is only in the sharing of one's pain, and in the experience of having it contained and understood by a loving other, that real intimacy and real healing is possible. This opens the door to sexual arousal that is deep, transformative, and ultimately empowering.

On a metaphorical level, this process is illustrated in what writers call the "key moment" or "key event" that occurs in every good story. This is the turning point that brings into focus all previous events and imbues them with meaning. It occurs in response to crisis and constitutes a moment of illumination that unlocks or releases the total meaning of the story. Usually the "key moment" involves the surfacing of a painful truth that was previously hidden or unclear. It is invariably a moment of intense feeling. Similarly, in relationships, the "key moment" is a *sharing of the wound*, that moment when one or both participants reveals or acknowledges some secret hurt or pain that damaged their capacity to trust and to love. The unconscious comes into view and is offered up to the beloved in hopes that it can be healed. Ideally, it is received and felt by the beloved, understood and contained, and then given back transformed by the process of having been shared. In this moment, erotic love is awakened and the natural consequence of this awakening is sexual union. In a way, it has already been attained. Just as in literature the "key moment" leads to the "climax" of the story—the decisive episode that reveals the success or failure of the adventure at a physical level—so in a relationship the "key moment" leads to the "climax" that occurs when true love is consummated in sexual union.

This suggests that in a healthy relationship, processes of projective and introjective identification must necessarily precede sexual union. There is a movement from the subtle to the gross. First there is a mental and emotional union, and *then* a physical one. It is interesting to meditate on the concept of "true" love. Perhaps love is "true" *when truth comes out*, when the individuals involved are willing to risk sharing their most vulnerable and heretofore hidden wounds, the deepest truth of their souls.

In myth, this is slaying the dragon; the lover is willing to die for his beloved. The symbolism here is that passionate love requires us *to sacrifice our attachments to identifications that limit and constrict;* we must go into the cave of the unconscious and confront our deepest fear in order to resolve the soul's divisions and so transform ourselves into a more unified state. If this process of natural healing is blocked, however, one's willingness to die for the beloved may devolve into an impulse to destroy the beloved.

All of which implies that a certain amount of fear and hostility is natural in sexual intimacy. It is well-established that there are marked physiological similarities between fear and sexual arousal (rapid heartbeat, rapid respiration, and adrenaline rush). I recall a study at Providence Veterans' Hospital in Rhode Island where sexually normal men and women were shown erotic film clips immediately after viewing some anxiety-provoking scenes (automobile accidents and grisly segments of Alfred Hitchcock thrillers). A control group was shown the same erotic film clips but without the anxiety-provoking scenes. The result was that subjects were more aroused by the terror-then-sex sequence than by the X-rated scenario alone. The explanation was that the erotic is especially titillating *when it provides relief to an underlying anxiety.* Perhaps this is why sex and violence are so often paired in popular films.

Stoller (1975) questions whether powerful sexual excitement can ever exist without hostility also being present. Such hostility may be minimal, repressed, distorted by reaction formation, attenuated, or overt as in the pathological cases. Yet, in virtually all sexual excitement some unconscious hostility may be essential.

One must understand that hostility is simply the surface manifestation of fear, or wounding. If someone bumps up against a deep wound on the surface of one's skin, a natural response is anger: "Ow! Watch out!" Likewise, when the beloved bumps up against a psychic wound, as he or she inevitably will, a certain amount of anger is generated. Anger serves a protective or defensive function. It is no doubt significant that the cry of the wounded is so often, "Fuck you!" We can begin to see the metaphorical significance of these words, *for it is precisely where we are wounded that erotic energy is generated.* Both literally and figuratively, we need to have sex "here," but not too roughly, or we are apt to return the insult with the above invective, for this is where we are most tender.

The most important difference between perverse and "normal" sexuality may simply be the degree of hostility that is bound or released in the sexual activity. "If hostility could be totally lifted out of sexual excitement there would be no perversions," says Stoller, "but how much loving sexuality would be possible?" (p. 89). In both perversion and "normal sexuality," there is a common theme: as the sexual act unfolds, there is an unconscious fantasy of surmounting fear. Inside sexual excitement are desires—conscious and unconscious—to heal some past trauma or frustration. The sexual act serves to transform childhood wounds into adult triumph. We can reasonably conclude, therefore, that the evolutionary purpose of sexuality is for the transformation of fear and pain into love and pleasure.

That this is possible even for those with difficult aspects between Pluto and Venus is absolutely certain. In fact, it may be that the ultimate manifestation of Venus-Pluto contacts is to become a "wounded healer" in the area of the body and sexuality. I have mentioned that so long as one's wounding remains unconscious there is a compulsion to repeatedly act it out in dysfunctional ways, with relief being fleeting at best. It follows that if one is to become truly healed one must become *aware* of how one is wounded and how this wound manifests in the body, in the emotions, and in the mind. Again, the key is *awareness.* Again, there is no better arena in which to develop that awareness than intimate relationship.

One couple who exemplifies this process is Debbie and Carlos Rosas. Frontrunners in the field of mind/body integration, the Rosas have been happily married for 8 years. Debbie has Venus in the 10th opposed to Pluto in the 4th to less than one degree of orb. Her husband, Carlos, has Pluto in the 7th sextile Venus in the 5th, within three degrees. Both are internationally renowned "movement healers" and co-founders of the NIA technique (Non-Impact Aerobics), a mind-body approach to holistic fitness that grew out of their own healing experience.[8] NIA incorporates elements of martial arts, akido, yoga, somatics, and sacred dance. In the aerobics field, it constitutes a revolutionary new stand—"one that calls for the kind of self-respect and self-determination that gives people back their inherent power to change, to take charge of their own well-being; one that honors the unique body structure of each of us and elicits the truest, most evocative expression of our emotional bodies moving in unison with our physical bodies" (Rosas, 1987, p. 13). Unlike traditional jump-aerobics, the NIA technique focuses on connecting the body to the emotions. Accordingly, it is a deeper, more interior form of exercise fueled by drums, rhythms and pulsating movements. The Rosas state that NIA provides for total body fitness, but also allows participants to discover the "feeling body" and "integrate the pelvis."

It is not difficult to see how the Venus-Pluto dynamic is implicit in the NIA technique. NIA focuses on healing the split between the body (Venus/Taurus) and the emotions (Pluto/Scorpio), leading to an opening of the pelvis and culminating in self-empowerment. Recall that when Jimmy Swaggart admonished his followers to avoid any kind of dancing because it might "arouse their sexual passion and lust," it was precisely this opening of the pelvic region that he feared. Yet, this is what we all *have* to do, for every human being is challenged to integrate the Taurus-Scorpio axis in one form or another. On their brochure, the Rosas make this explicit:

> If we are to learn, we must embody the experience, bridging the gap between psyche and soma. We must begin to observe that which is subtle, unseen, yet felt. Adapting to, readapting and recreating our inner and outer selves into a new reality that will bridge the gap creating "feeling" and "thinking" beings.

While a dysfunctional Venus-Pluto aspect can sink to the absolute lowest form of sexuality, it can rise to the highest as well. In the Rosas' partnership, we get a glimpse of the power and beauty that can emerge out of the Venus-Pluto dynamic. Just as

---

8   The Rosas have a third partner that forms the triad of the NIA corporation. Significantly, she has Venus conjunct the Ascendent forming an *exact* square to Pluto in the 9th. She is an incredibly healthy, vibrant, and spectacularly beautiful woman who, like the Rosas, is a "movement healer" and teacher of mind-body fitness.

NIA incorporates sacred dance into its exercise regime, so marriage is itself a sacred dance. Welwood (1990), for example, writes that love between man and woman presents a "sacred challenge—to go beyond the single-minded pursuit of purely personal gratifications [Venus] and tap into larger, universal energies at work in life as a whole [Pluto]" (p. 58). Relationship is a sacred path in that it helps us to discover what is most essential and real—the mysteries, depths, and heights of human experience.

It is precisely the hard aspects between Venus and Pluto that compel the individual to heal the split between body and soul, psyche and soma.

This can entail a passionate commitment to the deepest truth of one's being and to the beloved as well. Tompkins (1989) captures the essence of this:

> At best, Venus-Pluto relationships may be painful simply because the individual does insist on real relationship and refuses to pretend that whatever problems do exist aren't actually there. This unflinching courage and honesty can indeed raise the art of relating to a completely different level. It is surely Venus-Pluto people who really can transform themselves and their partners from frogs into princes and princesses. (p. 197)

Perhaps the best example of Venus-Pluto love is embodied in the figure of Christ. According to orthodox Christian doctrine, Jesus sacrificed his life for the sins of humankind. In so doing, he redeemed humanity and provided us with the gift of eternal life, i.e., humans could die and be reborn in heaven. Each individual must decide for himself as to the literal truth of this doctrine, but I tend to see such stories metaphorically. The redemptive love of Christ has great power because of his willingness to die for the beloved (humanity). Just so, if a man is willing to die for his beloved, that is, radically change himself in the process of loving, then ultimately he attains wholeness —oneness with all life and the Universe (heaven). Jesus was a saviour in the sense that he provided a model for what every person has to do—die and be reborn that she may become whole, which, after all, is what "holy" means.

It is not surprising that the story of Jesus Christ held such power for Jimmy Swaggart. His mistake, I believe, was in projecting all healing power onto the figure of Christ, and all destructive power onto the figure of Satan. While the healing power of prayer is well-established, in the final analysis each individual must take responsibility for his own healing. Swaggart could not do this. Instead, he "acted out" his wound, locating both its cause (Satan) and its solution (Jesus) outside of himself.

This is what we do when we split the anima/animus figure into a dark and light side. First we attach ourselves to a partner by seeing only the loved aspects of the anima/animus figure. Then when problems arise, we try to rid ourselves of the pain by locating its source in the beloved as well. We initially want our lover to be our savior, but later turn him or her into our devil. Again, the problem lies in the failure to be vulnerable. Self-empowerment means taking responsibility for one's own healing through a willingness to reveal one's pain and shame. This requires a remembering and a sharing of the dark places; it requires a determination to die so that one's capacity to love may be reborn. "Love can thus be seen as a paradigm for any profound realignment of personality and values, such as those that occur in the great religious conversion experiences" (Person, 1988, p. 350).

One thing is certain, sex cannot be burdened with the task of carrying our wounds indefinitely. As mentioned earlier, Garwood and Hajcak (1987) contend that "a great deal of our sexual behavior is motivated by repressed or hidden nonsexual needs" (p. vii). These nonsexual needs can influence and control sexual behavior. In effect, the individual tries to satisfy various needs through sexuality—the need for security, nurturance, intimacy, power, anger, self-esteem, and the like. I suspect that to identify these needs, one merely has to look at what planets occupy the 8th House, what House Pluto occupies, and what planets Pluto aspects and disposits. The point is that when nonsexual needs intrude, sex loses much of its joy and satisfaction because it is burdened by having to satisfy needs that go beyond its province. My contention is that only by bringing these hidden, repressed needs to the surface and *sharing them with the lover* are they prevented from handicapping sexual enjoyment.

It is precisely the sharing of the wound and its related affect—the anger, the loneliness, the insecurity, the fear of failure, the confusion—that makes healthy sex possible. *Loss of genuine passion is the price one pays for the failure to be vulnerable.* Then one has to substitute bogus risks—affairs, new partners, kinky sex, perversions, unavailable or dangerous love objects—in a desperate attempt to capture the excitement that healthy sex naturally provides. Again, *sex takes place on several levels.* If there is not first a sharing of the wound—the key moment—then sex has to bind the wound; the injury is "acted out" in a sexual context and thus remains unconscious. Sex on this level can never be completely satisfying.

In the final analysis, whom we attract and the specific challenges the relationship provides will always present opportunities for healing, but it is up to each individual to risk the pain that true love entails. The most erotic thing we can do is share our pain. Never are humans so lovable as when they are willing to be vulnerable, for it arouses the most deep and personal response in the recipient of the sharing. The lover is given reason to hope that he, too, can still be loved if his secrets are revealed.

I once had a girlfriend ask me to divulge to her my most secret sexual fantasy, something I had never shared with anyone before. I knew immediately what it was, but had always been too ashamed to admit it. She agreed that she would share hers as well. Once told, the erotic energy was at a feverish pitch and our lovemaking was much deeper and more intense than usual. Only later did I realize that at the heart of both our fantasies was a wound from childhood that had been eroticized. In the telling of the fantasy, the wound was a bit less tender than it had been.

References

Blinder, M. *Choosing Lovers*. Macomb, IL: Glenbridge Publishing, Ltd., 1989.

Blue, E. S. *Secret Survivors: Uncovering Incest and Its Aftereffects in Women*. New York: John Wiley & Sons, Inc., 1990.

Browne, I. *Psychological Trauma, or Unexperienced Experience*. Revision, Vol. 12, No. 4, 3–10, 1990.

Carnes, P. *Out of the Shadows: Understanding Sexual Addiction*. Minneapolis, MN: Compcare Publications, 1983.

Dicks, H. V. *Marital Tensions*. New York: Basic Books, 1967.

Greene, L. *The Great Harlot: The Mythology and Psychology of Venus*. In L. Greene & H. Sasportas (Eds.), *The Inner Planets: Building Blocks of Personal Reality*. York Beach, ME: Samuel Weiser, Inc., 1993.

Garwood, M., & Hajcak, F. *Hidden Bedroom Partners*. San Diego, CA: Libra Publishers, 1987.

Hartman, H. "The Mutual Influences in the Development of Ego and Id." In *Essays on Ego Psychology*. New York: International University Press, pp. 155–182, 1952.

Hendrix, H. *Getting the Love You Want*. New York: Harper & Row, 1988.

Herman, J. L. *Trauma and Recovery*. New York: Basic Books, 1992.

Jantsch, E. *The Self-Organizing Universe*. New York: Pergamon Press, 1980.

Jung, C. G. Two essays on analytical psychology. *Collected Works*, Vol. 7, Bollingen Series XX. New York: Pantheon, 1953.

Jung, C. G. The structure and dynamics of the psyche. *Collected Works*, Vol. 8, Bollingen Series XX. New York: Pantheon,1960.

Kaplan, H. D. *The New Sex Therapy*. New York: Bruner/Mazel, 1974.

Klein, M. Notes on some schizoid mechanism, 1946.

International Journal of Psycho-Analysis 27: 99–100.

May, R. *Love and Will*. New York: W. W. Morton & Company, 1969.

Norwood, R. *Women Who Love Too Much*. Los Angeles: Jeremy Tarcher, Inc., 1986.

Perry, G. "Psychopathology of the zodiac." *Journal of Astro-Psychology*, Vol. 2, No. 3, 1–6, 1989.

_____. "Sun square Pluto: Aspect of the false self." *Journal of Astro–Psychology*, Vol. 4, No. 4, 1–10, 1991.

_____. "Astrological correlations in a case of spousal abuse." *Journal of Astro-Psychology,* Vol. 5, No. 4, 9–12, 1992.

Person, E. S. *Dreams of Love and Fateful Encounters.* New York: W. W. Norton & Company, 1988.

Piaget, J. *The Language and Thought of the Child.* New York: Harcourt, Brace, 1926.

Rosas, C, & Rosas, D. *Non-Impact Aerobics.* New York: Avon Books, 1987.

Scharff, J. *Projective and Introjective Identification and the Use of the Therapist's Self.* Northvale, NJ: Jason Aronson, 1992.

Stoller, R. *Perversion: The Erotic Form of Hatred.* New York: Pantheon Books, 1975.

Tompkins, S. *Aspects in Astrology: A Comprehensive Guide to Interpretation.* Longmead, England: Element Books, 1989.

Welwood, J. Intimate relationship as path. *The Journal of Transpersonal Psychology,* Vol. 22, No. 1, 51–58, 1990.

Winnicott, D. W. "The theory of the parent–infant relationship" (1960). In *The Maturational Processes and the Facilitating Environment,* pp. 73–81. London: Hogarth Press, 1975.

Marion D. March

Born in Germany, raised and schooled in Switzerland, Marion came to the United States in 1941 and acted in films and on the stage. A teacher and professional astrologer since 1970 with a large international clientele, Marion speaks five languages and is a popular lecturer all over the world, as well as a writer for magazines here and abroad.

With Joan McEvers, in 1975 she founded Aquarius Workshops, a school of astrology whose magazine *Aspects* is still one of the most respected in the astrological community. Together they wrote the best selling five-volume series *The Only Way to . . . Learn Astrology, The Only Way to . . . Learn About Tomorrow and The Only Way to . . . Learn About Relationships* as well as *Astrology: Old Theme, New Thoughts*. The books have been translated into Spanish, Yugoslav, Czech, Portuguese and Japanese.

Marion's service to the astrological community includes: Coordinator for UAC '86 (United Astrology Congress) and '92, UAC '89 Program and assistant coordinator, four years AFAN Steering Committee, President of Aquarius Workshops, and editor of *Aspects* magazine. Together with Joan McEvers she is the recipient of the 1989 Regulus award for Education and PAI 1990 annual award. In 1992 she received the Regulus Community Service award. Marion has also been active in forming and promoting ARC, a worldwide computer link for astrologers. She lives in Encino, California.

Relationship Dynamics and Their Sexual Reality

Marion March

Sex lies at the root of life and we can never learn to reverence life until we know how to understand sex.

—Havelock Ellis

"Sex Holds Clues to Mysteries of the Mind" proclaims the latest article, one of many in the media on the eternal subject of Sex. From Freud to Kinsey, from "True Love" stories to pornography, from sexual repression to sexual revolution, from the sexual free-for-all to AIDS-inspired conservatism, sexuality remains one of the prime keys to understanding human drives, as well as human fears and inhibitions.

In 1981, Anna Freud observed that the world her celebrated father had explored seethed with sexual repression; but that, the sexual revolution notwithstanding, sexuality is still intensely private and remains the key to understanding personality disorders. Why necessarily "disorders?" Why can't we just enjoy sex for the pleasure of it?

Bishop Fulton J. Sheen may have provided an answer when he said: "Sex has become one of the most discussed subjects of modern times. The Victorians pretended it did not exist; the moderns pretend that nothing else exists." Young or old, rich or poor, single or married,if we do not have an active sex life, we may feel we're missing out, we're not participating fully, life is passing us by.

More Is Better

But what constitutes an active sex life? Is it a numbers game played in the locker room? "Hey you, how many babes did you sleep with this week? Can't match Magic Johnson yet? Too bad!" Or is it a teenager's whispered intimacy to her best friend that she's scared of being called chicken for not participating in the latest "sleeping bag" marathon, a high school game that counts how many "guys" you can have intercourse with in one night.

I live in the Los Angeles area where supposedly "everything goes," where morals are seemingly at a low ebb due to the amoral influence of motion pictures, yet the Magic Johnson remark was overheard in an adult locker room in a gym near Seattle, considered to be a nice northwestern family town. The sleeping bag marathon was a yearly pregraduation ritual that went undetected for six years in a posh school on Long Island, New York. In other words, the need to prove ourselves sexually is all-pervasive and, by now, a world-wide phenomenon.

Of course, nowhere does the pendulum swing as far as in our basically puritan country. In most European countries, "making love" is accepted as a normal, run-of-the-mill activity. You eat, you sleep, you make love, but much has changed in the United States, Canada, New Zealand and Australia, those English speaking countries where women have won nearly equal status (meaning they now have even more work to do than before) and as "equals" will often be the ones to ask for a date.

This new role, seen as aggressive by a large percentage of men, has left them in a quandary. Such roles as the initiator, the strong one, the money earner, the predominant sex, were accepted by males as theirs by habit, heritage and, nearly, law. Now with their world turned topsy turvy, they are not only allowed to, but are supposed to, show their tender nature in such areas as fathering; yet must sublimate formerly accepted sexual advances and act as though that mini-skirt does not turn them on. Then, to add insult to injury, while they assume a nonchalant air, this new female breed will ask them out to lunch! It's enough to drive an old-fashioned man crazy!

Does Age Make a Difference?

Age is one clue to today's mixed behavior. The older you are, the harder it is to get used to a sea change. The old-fashioned gentleman will continue to give a lady his seat on the bus and open doors for her. He will send her roses before asking her for a date and often he may turn out to be a great lover who cares as much about her pleasure as his.

The Yuppie generation seems to have the most trouble; they are caught in two worlds, brought up one way and now finding their behavior passé at the ripe age of 40. A disgruntled 41-year-old client recently told me that his fiancée had the gall to suggest that he might also want to relocate, since *she* had been offered a management job in another city. That really undid his male ego.

On the other hand, a 44-year-old, just-divorced female client expressed her utter amazement that "the nice widower I met on the cruise expects me to pay my own airfare when I come up to visit him next week!"

The young generation seems to compensate for a blurring of gender difference by the lack of tenderness or gentleness with each other. Everything seems to be very "cool" and matter of fact, or, as social-commentary author Allan Bloom states: "This is just 'behavior' (as in 'animal behavior'), not emotion and yearning structured by some great tradition, cultural or artistic."

The young tend to fall into two categories: more or most is best, versus let's postpone the whole thing for a few more years. I have never seen as many sexually uncommitted high school graduates as I have in the last seven or eight years, especially among the boys. It is not because of AIDS, but because of a general malaise—not feeling sure enough of their own masculinity to face the strong females of today.

Anytime there is a major change in behavior patterns, and the sexual revolution most certainly qualifies, it takes many years to see the final results. We are still changing, and the last word has not been spoken. What we harmlessly thought of as more sexual freedom, the experts blame for an increase of homosexuality, a rise in violence, including the battered-wife syndrome and more frequent break-ups of families.

What is the Real Cause?

Did the the so-called sexual revolution cause all these problems? What about Western Europe where the sexual mores have always been much freer? They too are experiencing an increase of crime, of divorces. *Le plus ça change, le plus c'est la même chose* says a well known French proverb, "the more things change, the more they are the same." The Marquis de Sade committed his "vicious and unnatural sexual crimes" (words used in MacMillan's *Everyman's Encyclopedia*), for which he was imprisoned, at the end of the 18th century. The word "Sadism" stems from his sexual acts, perpetrated long before our quasi-sexual rebellion.

My serious, Capricorn grandfather, born in 1861, and his bourgeois-looking wife shared a *ménage a trois* for more than 20 years! I called their friend "uncle" and totally accepted the fact that "uncle" was always there. Only as I grew up did I question my mother, and when I got into astrology, I realized that my simple-looking grandmother had a stellium in Aries, including Venus trine Uranus in the 5th House, Mars in Taurus and Scorpio on the cusp of the 8th House, a very sexual chart!

My grandfather had Virgo rising, Saturn conjunct Jupiter in the 1st House, quincunx Venus in Aquarius. Venus was involved in a T-square with Mars in Scorpio and the MC in Taurus. His Sun and Moon were in Capricorn in the 5th House. A lot of sexual needs here too, but also sexual insecurities. I presume that when he met sweet-looking Grandma, he felt very macho and protective. When he got to know her better, he probably realized that the time needed to pursue his professional ambitions, combined with the fact that his sex drive was not always in high gear, might not be enough for her. Divorce was not in vogue in those days; holding a family together was. Being European, as well as a practical Capricorn with a detached Venus in Aquarius, he probably reasoned that a threesome might be safer and more fun for all. It most likely was, since it lasted until my grandmother died.

As Gertrude Stein said "A rose is a rose is a rose," so we should acknowledge that sex is sex is sex, regardless in which century, which country, or on which continent.

Childhood Traumas

Whether it affected my grandparents at the turn of the 19th century, or a couple today, if there are sexual problems or difficulties, they often stem from childhood experiences or traumas. Psychiatrists and psychologists spend hours digging the terrain they call the patient's memory, until hidden events emerge to explain a potential predicament. Uncovering a childhood trauma can reveal the key to what may prevent someone from having a satisfying emotional relationship. But sometimes it isn't even an event, it may just be a hovering anxiety, like being less loved by a parent than is a sibling. At times, the parents' relationship to each other is so close that a child feels unwanted or unneeded. Maybe a parent dies and leaves the child with an unresolved feeling of abandonment.

I have two clients who spent years in therapy until they realized that part of their inability to have a fulfilling one-to-one relationship stemmed from the fact that their respective parents separated after each of them had been punished for some minor childhood offense; in their young minds, the two events had been simultaneous and therefore *causal;* it meant that the separation was *their* fault. This feeling of guilt prevented them from allowing themselves closeness with another human being.

As astrologers, we are all very familiar with the importance of childhood development and are lucky to have a roadmap called the horoscope to show us the many ways a client could have gone, as well as a questioning mind to ask which way he or she did go.

My Credentials

Since sex is so all-encompassing, and my topic covers more than just the astrological approach, I owe you an explanation of where I come from. I've been into astrology since 1965, and a professional astrologer since 1970. I have a fairly large clientele in the Los Angeles area and many additional clients in other American cities, in a number of European countries, especially England, Switzerland, France, and Germany, as well as a few in Canada, New Zealand, and South America.

Though I have taken some psychology and counseling courses, I am *not* a licensed therapist and would never presume to do their work. I am blessed with a lot of common sense, an analytical mind, and a love of people; but most of all, I am fortunate to work closely with a psychiatrist and a psychologist. The former provides me with birth data of his clients, and we discuss potential problems that might arise in the near future or whatever I discover from my careful perusal of their horoscopes. He will consult me particularly in those cases where he suspects suicidal tendencies, and usually keeps me abreast of happenings. This interaction has taught me a lot over the years.

The psychologist sends me many of her patients when she feels that they have reached a plateau and somehow can not break through or, more often than not, can not seem to remember parts of their childhood. I get all necessary information from the client directly. We tape the astrological consultation (as I always do) and they (my client and the psychologist) work with the tape in their future sessions.

This is of course an ideal situation, since I can discuss anything and everything, open wounds without worrying, knowing that the client is in capable hands. The psychologist in turn keeps me well informed and many of her patients become regular clients of mine. I can not tell you how much I have learned, thanks to her input. She, in turn, assures me that I have shortened many of her sessions by half, and enabled her to get to the bottom of her patients' problems in record time. We've been good for each other, and that is the best of all possible worlds.

Sexual or Moral Judgment

Whether you work with others or alone, if you want to help people understand their own strengths and weaknesses, successes and failures, you have to accept them as they are. That includes their looks, even if they are not as well-groomed as you expect them to be; their behavior, even if it does not live up to the way you were raised; their religion, even if it is not yours; and their morals, as different from yours as they may be. The latter is not always easy, especially if their sexual patterns are decidedly foreign to you.

Health, money, and sex are the three topics closest to most people's hearts, and not always in that order; *the one that functions the least will become the most urgent of the three.* If, as an astrologer, you can not handle a frank sexual discussion, your help for the client may be limited. Of course, those of us who believe in the synchronicity of the universe know that we only attract those clients whom we *can* help.

My European upbringing in a very avant-garde town, my association with the psychiatrist and psychologist, as well as my Sun in Aquarius, have enabled me to accept anything that comes my way, as long as it is between two consenting adults. I have reserved moral judgment, but have offered suggestions based on individual horoscopes or on desired results when integrating two horoscopes.

Following here are interesting case histories that have come my way which show how one person's sexual needs affect his or her partner, how one's sexual reality can change a relationship for better or worse, how one individual's hang-up can overcome or resolve another's inhibition in a good scenario or kill the relationship in a bad one.

Bernard and Linda

Bernard is a brilliant director and producer who started as a set designer in Europe. Though "making it" in Hollywood is tough, his creativity and obvious artistic talents helped him to an early breakthrough, and success was assured from then on. His private life seemed every bit as trouble-free as his professional one. He married a cool and collected looking American beauty named Linda. She started as his assistant when he was still designing sets, but as he advanced into directing and producing, she retired to have children.

They built a wonderful house on top of a hill overlooking the Pacific Ocean; her greatest pride was her garden that always sprouted some new, never-before-seen tropical wonder. His love and joy were his children and two collies, friendly, yet big enough to fight off the coyotes that came calling many nights. Friends said Bernard should have been an actor, since he loved being the center of attention, especially at parties. The "ragsheets" never had a detrimental story about him; if anything, they used him as an example of how a clean-cut family can survive in Hollywood.

However, what you see is not always what you get. Bernard retired in 1985 at age 60. Making films had become too hectic. What once was an artistic and creative undertaking, "was now a money machine spitting out box-office hits without regard of content" (his words). In order to bring a picture in on time, the crew was pushed into 16-hour days, even though overtime cost more than extra days would have. It all made no sense anymore, so he decided to sit in his beautiful study and finally write the books he always wanted to write. The children had long since flown the nest, were married and had children of their own. Linda led a busy life of community concerns; nobody would disturb him.

Book one was a horrendous struggle. Nobody wanted to copy his scribbled yellow pad notes. When he finally laboriously typed a manuscript, no publisher would accept anything that was not on a computer disc. Learning to work a computer was a nightmare and made him feel old and stupid. When the book was finally published, it was not the success he had expected, and a follow-up volume would be an ego trip rather than an eagerly awaited work.

Considered an excellent speaker and much in demand while still in the business, he was now asked to lecture once or twice a year at best, while his wife was in great demand and had gathered two awards for her charitable activities. The phone rang often, but was rarely for him. By 1987 a deep depression had set in, and Bernard went into counseling, first alone, and then for some sessions with Linda, who was threatening a separation if he did not stop insulting her in private and public; calling her a whore, forbidding her to see certain people, and spending their money on worthless investments, to the point where she was afraid she would be left penniless within a few years.

How could an idyllic marriage deteriorate to such an extent? Bernard, with his Leo Ascendant, was able to project a dramatic and showy personality with an air of insouciance and bravura. Neptune conjunct the Ascendant permitted him to display many personalities, a chameleon-like quality that allowed him to turn on the charm and charisma at will and fool others as well as himself into believing anything. This ability to wrap his persona (the Ascendant) into a variety of packages suited his private, 4th House Scorpio Sun to a tee.

His professional face did not reveal the inner man either. With Taurus on the MC and Venus conjunct Jupiter in Capricorn in the 5th House, he portrays well the ambitious and hard-working (Capricorn) man, artistic and creative (5th House), generous and full of big ideas (conjunction with Jupiter), intense in what he does (opposition to Pluto) and disciplined in his métier (sextile to Saturn). Yet concealed behind this talented facade is a very private individual (Sun in Scorpio in the 4th), not totally clear as to who he is or wants to be (Sun's only aspect is a square to Neptune).

Emotionally, he is able to detach when necessary, especially in his work milieu (Moon in Aquarius in the 6th House), yet very self-protective and emotionally unsure (Saturn in 4th square the Moon), possibly due to feeling unloved by his parents or not loved as much as his siblings. Bernard has two brothers, one older, one younger, and as is often the case with a middle child who has little to differentiate himself from his other siblings, he felt that the parents preferred the older brother and coddled the younger one, leaving him "stranded to fend for himself" (his words).

His sexual hunger is impressive; Scorpios can be very impassioned and sensuous. Saturn, so near the Sun also in Scorpio, though not conjunct, can often lead to some form of overcompensation. Most erotic of all is Mars in Scorpio, making no planetary aspects, which frequently can denote a wish to burn the candle at both ends. A 5th House Venus, in love with love, conjunct Jupiter who wants to embellish everything, are both signs pointing to someone who needs an active sex life. Add to that an 8th House Uranus stirring his mind-set and nervous sys-

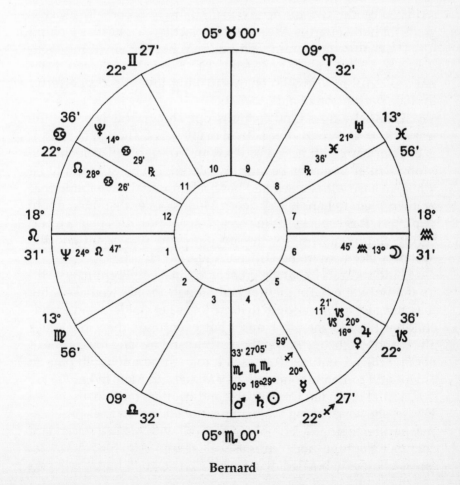

Bernard

tem (square Mercury), and you have the pleasure-seeking exper-
imenter par excellence.

How does Linda fit into this? In a partner or one-to-one
relationship, Bernard, with Aquarius on his 7th House cusp and
its ruler, Uranus, in Pisces in the 8th, is looking for an independent, not run-of-the-mill type female (Aquarius). She should be
sensual (ruler Uranus in the 8th), yet sensitive to his needs
(Uranus in Pisces). She should be organized (Uranus trine Saturn) and able to compete intellectually with him (Aquarius *per
se*, also Uranus square Mercury). With Uranus part of a Yod (Sextile Jupiter, both quincunx the Ascendant) the 7th House cusp,
mirroring the wife, becomes the "boomerang" point of the yod,
so when Bernard cannot make the necessary adjustments
required by the two quincunxes, Linda may become the scape-
goat. Yet her Aquarius Ascendant is exactly what he was looking
for. That, plus the Sun in Gemini, give her the air of independ-
ence and intellect he was seeking. Her Sun in the 5th would signal a playful nature who enjoys making love, fitting perfectly
into his perception of a partner.

What else does Linda's horoscope show? This is one of the
least "hung-up" charts I've seen in many years. Though her Moon
is in Capricorn, at times considered an "up-tight" placement, the
Moon's ruler Saturn is beautifully placed, enabling Linda to be
totally at ease with herself and her background. I have found that
women seem to handle Capricorn Moons better than men do. In
this chart, it is especially welcome, since it provides balance and
earthy common sense for the airy Sun and Ascendant and the
Moon's placement in the 11th, an Aquarian House.

Linda admits to having great emotional equilibrium, with little if anything ever bothering her enough for her to make a big
fuss. She also acknowledges that she loves her children and grandchildren (Sun in the 5th House) but even more than that, she's
always adored being wooed (Sun in 5th) and making love is one of
her favorite adventures. (Intense Pluto in the amorous 5th plus an
ardent and romantic conjunction of Venus and Mars in Leo).

With Leo on her Descendant, and its ruler, the Sun, in the 5th
House, she was looking for an impassioned and at times provocative partner. Bernard certainly fit that bill with his Leo Ascendant
conjunct Neptune, and Venus as well as Jupiter in his 5th House.
She was quickly bowled over by his charm, good looks, and per-

suasive personality. They not only worked well together, but in her words, "had fantastic sex from day one." His European background and training surely helped, as did having Uranus, that imaginative planet that always relishes doing what's different, in the 8th House of sexual enjoyment.

So what went wrong? Linda is one of those women who can have multiple orgasms during intercourse and the longer the partner can hold back his orgasm, the more enjoyment Linda can have. Of course, there are many other ways that Linda can climax, and six to seven orgasms in one sexual session were not unusual for her. In the beginning, this was most exciting and arousing for Bernard, and they could not keep their hands off each other. As

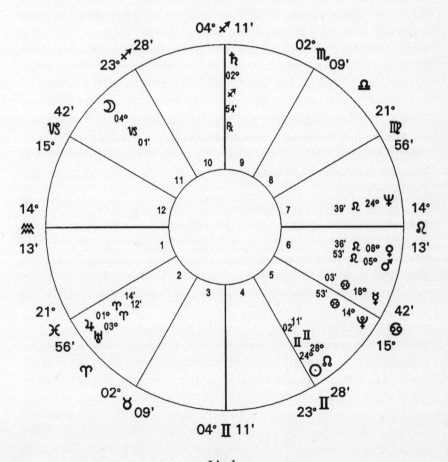

Linda

the years went by, Bernard started flirting with other young women, then he began making audacious sexual overtures in front of Linda, to the point of her great exasperation. Then he tried to convince her that they could have a fabulous time if she would agree to get involved with a few other people. Though taken aback at first, Bernard's seductive imagination persuaded her. He carefully drew her into an invisible net and trapped her, never realizing that he had really trapped himself.

This all happened around the time of his male midlife crisis when, astrologically speaking, transiting Neptune squared its natal position, but also conjuncted his Sun. Transiting Saturn had just reached its zenith, conjunct the Midheaven. If that were not enough, the Solar Arc directed Sun opposed Pluto which rules it, while SA Pluto squared the Sun—a stunning amount of intense eroticism and sensual appetite. The SA Moon, by now in Pisces, trined the Sun, while SA Mars had just left the conjunction with Mercury, producing much energy to communicate verbally, such as convincing Linda; and physically, by exploring new territories.

First he brought in a young girl he had ogled for a while and they had a few threesomes. Then he picked a man he thought would be a good lover for Linda and they had foursomes that might involve a whole out-of-town, week-end trip. Always the producer, he would manage the *mise en scène* wherever it might take place.

If he decided that they should each have twosomes with their respective lovers, who changed often, he would pick the hotel or motel and would decide at what time they had to finish in order to drive home together. Although she confirms that she thoroughly enjoyed the various sexual encounters he staged, she was sure she was doing it for *his* sake, so that he could pursue his lusty yearnings.

He was sure he was writing the perfect scenario for the perfect open marriage. Sex and fun for all parties involved. No bad conscience, no lies, no threats, no blackmail—just pure enjoyment. He felt it was the optimal solution to prevent divorce, so often the typical dissolution of Hollywood marriages.

That was, of course, part of the trap. Sexual familiarity can bring on boredom; by midlife, other partners often look more exciting than one's own . . . but that was only part of Bernard's problem. The old tapes of inadequacy, of not being worthy of parental love (seen astrologically by the Saturn/Moon square), started nagging at him. Now, the fear of inadequacy had taken on sexual overtones. Instead of realizing that he might be afraid of not satisfying his wife, whom he viewed as erotically very needy with her multiple orgasmic capacity, he tried to reassure himself by first pursuing, then catching and, best of all, satisfying other women. To alleviate his guilt completely, he had to make sure that Linda also received pleasure and satisfaction. By staging three-somes and foursomes, he not only satisfied an inclination to voyeurism, but as well his need to stay in control, to supervise, to direct the action, and to give Linda some "fun" (his word).

The perfect plan was really an intricately woven web. The more complex the scenarios, the harder it became to stay in control. As time went by, doubts set in. As his professional life waned and his retirement plans fizzled, doubts became obsessions. He accused Linda of having a much better time with other men than with him. When she suggested they drop the whole thing, that she was really getting too old for these games, he accused her of having affairs behind his back. By then, he was sure that she probably had slept with every Tom, Dick, and Harry before they got married; that she had cheated on him long before he suggested an open marriage; that she was indeed a nymphomaniac. The once-beautiful web had become a frightening trap.

By 1985, when Bernard retired, his Progressed Ascendant had just changed signs, from hard-working Virgo to Libra, the sign that more than any other loves the "joy of doing nothing," and the Sun had just changed into 0 Aquarius. Bernard was truly ready for some changes, but the universe had a few tough ones in store for him.

Between 1985 and 1987 his Secondary Progressed Saturn had reached 24 Scorpio 35, exactly squaring his natal Neptune; secondary Venus was at 24 Aquarius, the three forming a difficult T-square, involving areas of early inadequacy (Saturn) as well as work issues (Saturn rules the 6th House), provinces of creativity as well as illusion (Neptune) and sex (Neptune rules the 8th House); added to this challenging equation is an unrealistic (Neptune) attitude toward love (Venus) and a grappling with issues of status (Venus rules the MC) and the question of how to express this inner turmoil (Venus also rules the 3rd House). By 1987, the secondary Moon in Taurus was ready to complete the T-square and make it a fixed Grand Cross. With the addition of the emotional lunar challenges, Bernard's inner pain was more than he could handle and his deep cry for help became audible.

Astrologically, many other aspects had developed. By Solar Arc direction, Mercury and Uranus, at 24 Aquarius and Taurus respectively, were now forming a T-square with natal Neptune, heightening the previously discussed feelings of confusion (Neptune), inability to express them (Mercury), yet awareness (Uranus) that something was amiss. SA Jupiter, mirroring optimism as well as exaggeration, was quincunx Neptune, calling for adjustments, especially in sexual matters, since SA Jupiter was in the 8th House and Neptune rules it.

SA Venus had also reached the 8th House, first quincunx the Ascendant, repeating the above message of adjustments about love and sex, only personalizing it even more, since the aspect involves the Ascendant. This same Venus trined Saturn, sextiled Jupiter and conjuncted Uranus while squaring Mercury. Love, status, communication, and sex matters all came to the fore and demanded attention. Many other astrological indicators, especially by direction and transit, added to Bernard's discomfort and confusion, with transiting Pluto riding herd on natal Mars opposition the MC, surely one of the most formidable ones for him to handle.

By 1988, some of the venom had been spit out. Bernard was able to resume a civil tone toward Linda, and eventually admitted that he was the instigator and had enticed her. He started doing volunteer work, particularly enjoyed working with young people, and even had fun holding story-telling sessions at the public library. Early in 1990, when transiting Saturn, ruler of his 6th House of work, conjuncted his natal Venus, ruler of his 10th House of career and status, he started a totally new professional life when a prestigious university engaged him to teach film-making in general and directing in particular. He jumped at the opportunity and has been a changed man ever since. He is so happy in what he does that he easily weathered Pluto's transit to his natal Saturn, square his natal Ascendant. At this writing (July 1993), he seems to be handling the square to Neptune quite well.

Sexually, he has toned down considerably. He does not seem to feel pressured or intimidated by Linda's ability to enjoy herself; he just accepts it. I am not sure if it is age, being more at peace with himself, a fear of AIDS, or the combination of all three, that has brought about the cessation of chasing pretty women. Linda, usually the unflappable one, seems to carry the most scars from this experience. She cannot quite forget all his accusations, and her confidence in Bernard's veracity and love is precarious. Her outside life is pretty much unchanged: she still looks stunning and is socially as much in demand as always. Whereas before, Bernard could do no wrong, she now finds much to criticize and therefore avoids spending too much time alone with him. In her eyes, he is still "fragile" (her word) and she does not want to be the one who "sets him off again." Although the marriage functions, it will never be the same; something has gone out of it and I doubt it can ever be rekindled.

By 1990 Linda's Sun had progressed to 24 Leo, conjunct her own and Bernard's Neptune. Her Ascendant by secondary progression was at 24 Taurus, all interwoven with Bernard's fixed T-Square/Grand Cross developed through directions and progressions. Progressed Mercury at 5 Leo was conjunct her natal Mars, squaring Bernard's natal Mars/MC opposition. Progressed Venus at 24 Virgo had just reached a square to her natal Sun and to add mayhem to an already difficult situation, the progressed Moon at 2 Aries had just conjuncted Jupiter and Uranus.

Linda's Solar Arc Mars at 4 Libra in the 8th House of sex , was square her Moon—which can be very emotional and physically depleting. SA Pluto, now in her 7th House of partnerships, was quincunx her Ascendant, calling for some intense modifications in her behavior and attitudes. Her SA Moon at 2 Pisces square natal Saturn probably denoted the heavy emotional burden she had to carry during the time of Bernard's insulting remarks. Thankfully, SA Saturn at 1 Aquarius sextiled its natal position as well as the Jupiter/Uranus conjunction, reflecting her ability to keep her head above water.

In observing life, working with professional counselors and using synastry in my astrological practice, one thing becomes very clear: *sex is one of the determining factors of whether a relationship will succeed or not;* more so than financial ups and downs, disputes about values or tastes, and even involvement with mothers-in-law or other relatives. It is not just a question of sexual compatibility, nor the desired frequency, which may vary between partners; *it is the invisible net created as an expression of per-*

sonal problems into which one partner pulls the other, that so often suf-focates both. Sometimes, but not always, with help, a couple can extricate themselves from this web before it is too late.

Magda (aka Grit) and Jan

Magda was a friend before she became a client. I met her in 1956 on one of my frequent trips back to Switzerland. Her husband had died the year before and she was trying to rebuild some kind of life. Though nearly 60 years old, she was a snip of a thing who, from a distance, looked no older than 20 years. All of five feet tall, weighing under 100 pounds, she had a figure like a young boy: no hips, a small bosom, and long, slender limbs. She

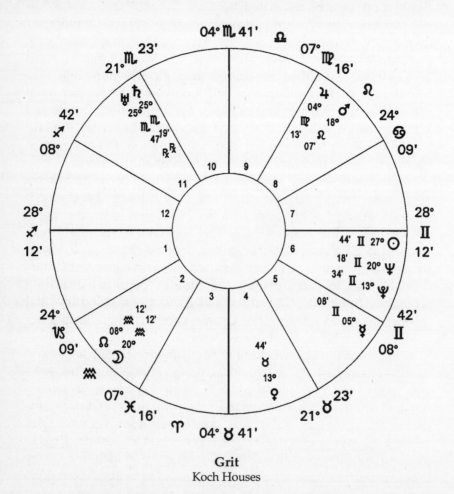

Grit
Koch Houses

drove a small convertible Italian racing car, definitely meant for a younger person. It suited her just fine, in fact the more contradictions she could conjure up, the happier she was.

She hated her name, Magda, and preferred to be called "Grit," her nickname. Grit and I hit it off immediately, easily understood when you look at our horoscopes. Grit was born June 18, 1897 at 8:27 pm MET in Berlin, Schönberg, Germany, 13E22–52N28. Grit's Moon is exactly conjunct my Sun! I was present the day she met Jan, the man who became the second love of her life.

As he tells the story: "A mutual friend had suggested I contact this widow to help finish translating some of the books her now-deceased husband had been working on. I called her, and we

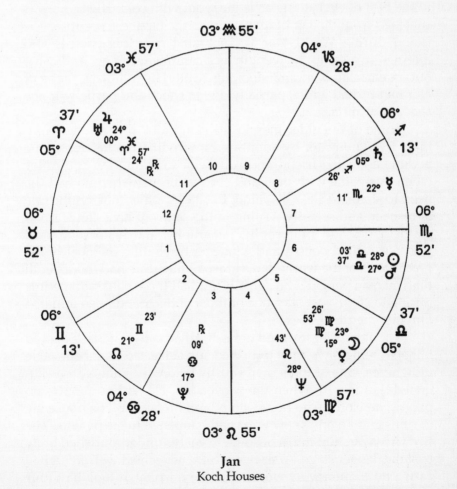

Jan
Koch Houses

made a date to meet at 3 P.M. in a cafe on the square. I would recognize her by a red flower she would wear or carry. A bit appre-
hensive, I arrived early and silently wondered where an elderly
lady would put a red flower. Punctually at 3 P.M., this red convertible comes speeding along, brakes squeal and out jumps this
young girl in very high heels wearing an enormous straw-hat
with a bunch of red carnations. Well, to make a long story short,
we met and I fell wildly in love with her."

Jan's data: October 22, 1927 at 6:45 pm Java Time (-7.5) Ban-
dung, Java 107E36–6S54

Jan's life had been tumultuous. Though not yet 29 years old,
his hair was totally white. Raised in Java by Dutch parents, used
to the best of everything as is the wont with colonialists, he was
snatched from the lap of luxury when the Japanese occupied the
island during World War II. Separated from his parents and
interned in a camp, he went in as a carefree teen-ager and came
out an emaciated, strange-looking adult. His full black mane of
hair had turned white, partially due to shock and partially to the
lack of nutrition.

Some of the older men in the camp took pity on the seemingly lost youngster by adopting him in different fashions. One
became a trusted friend and counselor to whom Jan could flee
when overcome with pain and sorrow, or just when he had the
need to share, to clear his mind, to talk. Another took on the role
of teacher, and secretly writing in the sands of Java, Jan learned
mathematics and philosophy, geography, and history. A third
prisoner recited poetry, and whatever he could remember of the
great books of the world. Jan's grasp of literature had more depth
than many a person who actually studied these books. Sometime
during his four-year stay, one or more of his friends also initiated
him into the rites of sex.

Though never tortured himself, Jan saw two of his "adopted
fathers" being physically punished and subjected to unbelievable
indignities. One of them died shortly before the country was liberated. Jan was 18 when the war ended. He had no money, no
papers, no clothes, no possessions, and no family. His house lay
in ruins and no one knew what had happened to his parents. The
Red Cross put him into a hospital to get his undernourished body
past the danger stage. After two weeks, he seemed well enough to
earn a bit of money by working in the hospital. It took him four

months to gain weight, to experience normal digestion, and save enough money for a trip to Holland to try to find his parents, but he never found them. As he discovered much later, they had been in another camp; his father had died and his mother was near death when the Japanese left Java. Some friends flew her to Amsterdam where she had been operated on. By the time Jan's search brought him to Holland, his mother was on her way back to Java to look for him.

To earn money he took all kinds of odd jobs; while working in a bookstore he met a Dutch professor of Far Eastern religions who was also a writer, resided in India, and needed a secretary. Jan eagerly accepted the job. Like most Dutchmen, Jan spoke five languages fluently; learning Sanskrit would not present a hurdle. While in India he also learned about Eastern religions and philosophies, and became a devoted follower of Vedanta. He accepted as fact that he probably was homosexual and his relationship with the professor became much more involved than just employer and secretary.

In 1952 the professor died, leaving Jan as his sole heir. He returned to Europe and finally found his mother, who was aghast that her cuddly little boy had become a gaunt-looking stranger, a man filled with ideas totally alien to her way of thinking. The relationship was cool and strained. Jan earned a degree at university and also managed to have the professor's books published. Now he was looking for other metaphysical works to edit and publish, which led to his meeting with Grit.

Jan's horoscope mirrors a sensual being. Libra loves to be in love, and Jan's Sun is there, conjunct Mars, representing sexual drive, though in Libra it tends to express itself in a gentler and more suave manner than one might expect from Mars in general. With sensuous Taurus on the Ascendant, his tactile sense was highly developed. Venus, in cool and collected Virgo, rules both Taurus and Libra, and is in the romantic and amorous 5th House, sextile Pluto, intensifying the Venusian characteristics—offsetting some of the provocative energy, at least on the outside.

Venus in Virgo gathers additional emphasis with the Moon also in Virgo; emotionally, Jan likes to feel virtuous and proper, a luxury he may not always be permitted with the Moon opposite overstated Jupiter and nonconformist Uranus. The Jupiter/Uranus conjunction is involved in a yod, quincunx the Sun/Mars conjunction as well as Neptune. Therefore Jupiter, ruler of the 8th House of sexual performance and drives, reflects certain adjustments Jan might make in his sexual conduct, while Uranus implies his need to perform in an unorthodox way. Saturn at the cusp of the 8th House often implies frustration and can manifest as general doubt of sexual ability, which may lead to overcompensation or abstinence, depending on other aspects in the horoscope as well as free will.

Jan chose a bit of both. While he was young, he just went along with what others seemed to want of him, first at home, then in the camp and later in India. He was very much at ease with men, especially the ones who treated him with love rather than lust, who appealed to his sense of touch rather than imposing their masculine thrust. He had seen a few women who had appealed to him, but he really did not want to be the initiator, especially in an area where he felt slightly unsure and ill at ease. After the professor's death, he opted for abstinence, partially to mourn his dead friend, to some degree for religious reasons, but also to prove his inner strength and self-discipline. Yet if the truth be known, he really hadn't met anyone who seemed important enough to get involved with, until Grit came along.

She was old enough to satisfy an unfulfilled yearning for his mother; her figure was boyish enough to gratify his homosexual leanings; she was cute looking and had the charm to accommodate his Libran need for attractiveness and refinement, and she was exotic enough to please his prominent Jupiter/Uranus conjunction.

Astrologically speaking, it was nice that Grit's Sun at 27 Gemini trined his Sun/Mars while her Ascendant sextiled it. Her Ascendant trine Jan's Neptune probably served as a seductive magnet; so did Jan's North Node at 20 Gemini partile conjunction to Grit's Neptune and trine her Sun. Their Venuses, at 14 Taurus and 16 Virgo respectively, trined each other, an automatic mutual attraction and feeling of warmth, while Jan's Mercury at 22 Scorpio, though widely, filled Grit's natal T-square of Moon opposite Mars, both square Venus.

It has been my experience that *the filling of a T-square by another's planet is a formidable enticement which can work like a magnet,* inexorably drawing one in; whether happily or not depends on other aspects in the two horoscopes, as well as free will. Jan's

Mercury is rather well-aspected natally and its 7th Hc
tion indicates a basic need for partners or people to relate to, ιι
use as sounding boards. Since it rules his 2nd and 5th Houses of
self-worth and love, communicating with a loved one can be
exactly what he needs to develop his own values and creativity.

Grit had a bit more difficulty since her focal planet, Venus,
formed only squares to the Moon and Mars and had no easy outlets. Jan's Mercury fell into her 11th House, not far from her Sat-
urn/Uranus conjunction. What might her friends (11th House)
think of her showing up with a man 30 years her junior? Even if he
only looked 20 years younger! The Uranian part of her nature,
strongly emphasized with an Aquarian Moon and Uranus in accidental dignity in the 11th House, said: "Who cares as long as we
get along and enjoy each other." The Saturnian side was more cautious, especially since in 1956 her secondary progressed MC was at
0 Capricorn and her standing in the community did matter to her.

They came up with the perfect solution. They each kept their
own residences; Grit in Switzerland, Jan first in Holland and later
in Italy. He lived with her a few months, she with him another
few; in between they lived alone or they traveled together. Grit's
husband had fulfilled some of her 5th and 8th House needs well.
The Moon which rules the 8th is in her 2nd House; he had left her
all the money (8th House = partner's resources) she needed to feel
secure (2nd House). Her Venus-ruled 5th House was involved
with the 8th through the Venus T-square to the Moon and Mars.

Grit's and her husband's 33-year marriage had been loving
and intellectually fulfilling (Mercury in Gemini in the 5th desires
love mixed with some cerebral activity, especially when it squares
Jupiter in the 8th House), but he had not always lived up to her
Mars in Leo 8th House needs, especially in the last 10 years when
romance had faded as his health became delicate. Jan's Neptune
in Leo, falling into her 8th House, felt romantic as well as beguil-
ing, just what she didn't want or need at this time in her life.

How could Jan, so far only introduced to homosexuality, fall
in love with a woman? Of course, she represented the mother
image, replacing the real mother he now was at odds with, not
only because she was 30 years older, but also, as mentioned earlier, because his Mercury, ruling his 5th House, filled her T-
square, involving her Moon and Venus, the two female
archetypes. Jan's Moon, illustrative of *his* anima or the female

within him, was in his 5th House of love. It probably helped that Grit's Ascendant at 28 Sagittarius occupies his 8th House of sexual attraction and performance and that her Moon falls into his 10th House of status; there is nothing wrong with being accepted in certain "upper crust" circles. Jan's Sagittarian 8th House needs could find fulfillment in various ways, as indicated by ruler Jupiter conjunct Uranus. Homosexuality, not always accepted as run-of-the-mill sex, fits the bill; so does sexual intimacy with a much older woman.

I question whether either was the solution to his previously discussed yod, but I know that these two helped each other, loved each other and lived in relative happiness for 15 years, until 1971 when Grit asked me to look at their charts. She thought he might be tiring of her and have found someone else, whether a man or a woman.

By then, Jan's Solar Arc directed Uranus (planet of the unexpected and unusual) was beginning to trine his natal Venus (planet of love and affairs of the heart) in the 5th House, while SA Venus itself was now at 0 Scorpio. The secondary Venus at 26 Libra 15 was within one degree of natal Mars (planet of carnal desire). Mercury, ruler of his natal 5th House of fun and games, having been retrograde for 20 years, had now progressed to 24 Scorpio, exactly trine natal Jupiter, ruler of his 8th House of sex; these were just a few of the progressed and directed aspects that stood out. Transiting Neptune was hovering around 4 Sagittarius, ready to enter Jan's 8th House while transiting Jupiter was about to follow suit. In the meantime, transiting Pluto had opposed natal Uranus and transiting Saturn opposed its own position from the 2nd to the 8th House.

He had met a young Frenchman, spaced out on drugs, whom he first helped to overcome his addiction and then converted to Vedanta. Jacques became a disciple, only to soon overtake the "master." "You've become lazy and spoiled," he would scold Jan. "Luxury and fun have beguiled you. The food for your stomach assumes more importance than the food for your soul. Your religious stance is a sham. You are using the words but have forgotten the meaning behind them."

Poor Jan—what might have been a little fling or 8th House dalliance turned out to be a turning point in his life—there was an 8th House regeneration, and Grit became the guilty party. It was *her* fault that he had lost his way. *She* had seduced him into a lifestyle that had alienated him from his religious habits. After all, she was the older one and should have made sure that he meditated each day, that he rose early enough to greet the sun. Was it his fault that her bed was warmer and more inviting than the cold terrace at 5 A.M.? Of course not!

Despite her still-youthful looks, Grit was a wise woman. She quickly understood what was happening and knew that Jan's and her relationship could never be the same again. She decided that she had lived a wonderful life with two exciting men and that it was time to bow out. She shared her decision with me in March of 1972. By April, she had developed a serious stomach ailment which hospitalized her. In August, her doctors operated. The operation was successful, but Grit died in November of 1972. I saw her twice that year. She was totally at peace. Jan was beating his breast and moaning that he had brought on her illness. He never left her side after she came home from the hospital, and carried her in his arms both literally and figuratively. When she died, Jupiter, ruler of her Ascendant or physical body, by Solar Arc direction was filling her natal T-Square by opposing Venus. Transiting Jupiter was trining natal Jupiter. The progressed Moon, ruling her natal 8th House, was at 17 Scorpio, also filling her natal T-Square. Transiting Saturn at 20 Gemini was conjunct natal Neptune, and with transiting Uranus at 20 Libra was forming an Air Grand Trine with her natal Moon at 20 Aquarius. She was at peace.

Jan was devastated. Now Jacques was in charge. He convinced Jan to return to India; to make an Ashram out of his inherited property; to live the life of an ascetic. Occasionally, I still hear from Jan. He reconciled with his mother, but rarely saw her. She died a few years ago. Despite Jacques' admonitions, he now feels that his real "growing-up" years were those spent with Grit; that it was thanks to her that he learned to understand both the anima and animus within, which in turn enabled him to define the higher consciousness he was looking for. "She is the one who brought me nearer to my God, my Atman" he wrote in one of his letters to me, "only I did not know it and never could tell her . . ."

Does sex between two people have to be debauched, strange, or off-key to be meaningful in a relationship? Is sexual reality only "real" when those involved become aware of it because it is different, doesn't work, or has gone stale? Do we take everything for granted while it works well and only pay attention when it blows up in our faces?

Adultery, to Jane Austen, for example, held tremendous human repercussion. Adultery today is . . . self-expression! When Elizabeth Taylor and Richard Burton began their legendary affair, the Vatican denounced the couple, since both were married to others at the time, for "erotic vagrancy." Recently, when two famous Hollywood stars openly admitted to an affair, though one of them was married, the papers referred to it as "tempestuous *affaires du coeur*" (affairs of the heart); although, to the best of my knowledge, the heart had little to do with it. After all, one person's perversion is another person's pleasure!

With so much emphasis on sex all around us, so much attention paid to the pornographic and scandalous side of sex, it becomes harder and harder to have a relationship, especially a marriage, where a man and woman meet, fall in love, make love, get married and live happy and satisfying lives together for many years. Although my files still contain many couples who lead everyday types of existences, the cases I recalled when writing this chapter were not the easy ones, the ones asking for a yearly update or when to buy a new house.

What immediately came to mind was the man who married five times until he came to grips with his homosexual tendencies and needs; the fairly frequent occurrence of males who have become impotent with their wives, yet perform beautifully with their paramours; the man who could never have an erection with anyone he loved, only with whores, because he had never forgiven his mother for dying and his father for placing him in an orphanage. These and more are, of course, fascinating studies of aberrant cases, which are engrossing to read, but would mislead you into thinking that those types of sexual inter-relations are more important than the so-called conventional sexual life experienced by countless committed couples. The following is one of them.

Lorraine and Jeff

Lorraine came from a prim and proper family where manners, behavior, and morals all played an important role—so did living up to the neighbors' standards, wearing the right clothes with the right labels. She is the middle child of three daughters and grew up convinced that her sisters were more beautiful, more intelligent, and more desirable.

Capricorn rising often has the tendenc
especially if the ruler, Saturn, is conjunct Nep
always see herself or certain situations clearly
(p. 120), Saturn also squares Uranus, indi
quently experiences inner turmoil between h
do another's bidding, versus a wish to break free anu u ...
thing. Last but not least, Saturn forms a wide square to the
Ascendant which it rules, resulting in a tension-producing T-
square (with Uranus).

Lorraine's Venus has no planetary aspects, often describing a
person who needs constant reassurance of being loved and cher-
ished; especially since, in her case, it is in Cancer. She was able to
hide many of her feelings of inadequacy behind an air of compo-
sure, as well as bravura (Sun conjunct Moon and Pluto in Leo).
She was a meticulous dresser and watched her figure like a hawk.
During her university years she shared an apartment with three
other girls. Her sisters and roommates all made fun of her
because she was still a virgin at the ripe old age of 20. Nobody
knew that she was anorexic, that her menstrual cycle had disappeared, and, as well, any sexual desires.

As luck had it, a knee twisted while skiing, sending her to
the doctor and a general check-up. The ensuing psychological and
physical therapies came in time to prevent any permanent damage. Lorraine had to recognize that there was a compulsive side to
her nature which she would have to combat much of her life. (Sun
and Moon conjunct Pluto, all in proud Leo in the fixed, Scorpionic
8th House).

In 1974 her roommate, Kathy, introduced her brother Jeff to
Lorraine. Jeff had just returned home from his legal studies and
was anxiously awaiting the verdict of whether he had passed the
Bar exams. How does the storyline go? "They met, they fell in
love, and lived happily ever after?" Well, nearly . . .

Jeff was a nice-looking young man, sensitive and gentle in
appearance and demeanor, with a romantic bent that really
appealed to Lorraine. (Well-mannered Libra rising, ruler Venus in
romantic Pisces in the 5th House). Though an ardent and rather
experienced lover, (Libra rising, Sun and Moon in sensuous Taurus, Venus in the 5th House trine exuberant Jupiter), Jeff was
intrigued by a 21-year old-virgin. His patient and gentlemanly
approach was just what Lorraine needed to bolster her confi-

ce. With Taurus on the cusp of her 5th House of love affairs, ne was looking for a man reflecting some of those Taurean qualities, and Jeff's Sun and Moon in Taurus fit the bill. Her sexual needs with Leo on the cusp of her 8th House and Mars in Leo, responded well to his Mars in Aries.

Lorraine is a fairly erotic woman, once aroused and liberated, as is usually the case with the Sun and the Moon both in the 8th House (and, especially with Pluto in the 8th House as well). Jeff is not only a good lover, concerned about his partner's needs being fulfilled (Sun and Moon in the 7th House, a well-aspected Venus) but he is also imaginative in his sexual explorations and performance (resourceful Uranus in the 8th House). Variety and

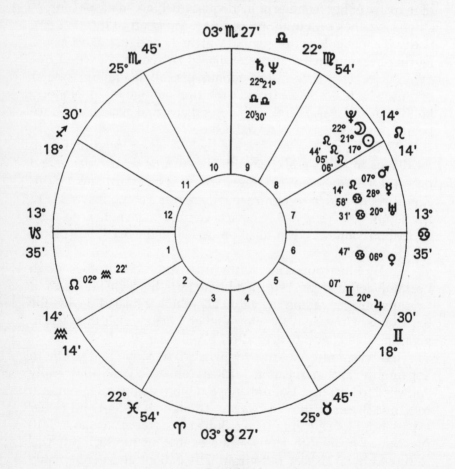

Lorraine

versatility in the everyday intercourse of any long-time relationship can make the difference between staying together out of habit or truly looking forward to the next new sexual fantasy.

Lorraine and Jeff married in 1975. They have two lovely children born in 1978 and 1981. His career took off like a meteor; they bought a beautiful home, sent the children to the best schools, owned a chalet in the Sierras and lived the good, yuppie life. During the Reagan years, when everything boomed, his law firm, where he was now a partner, was bought up by a conglomerate. The buy-out paid a handsome sum and they asked him to stay on and handle some of the corporate legal matters. In 1991, when the economy started to slow down and lawyers became too plentiful,

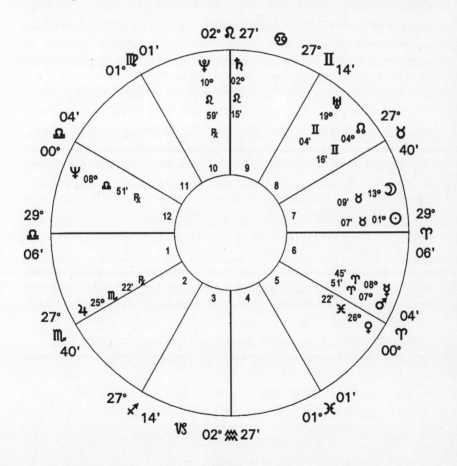

Jeff

his firm let 70 of 100 lawyers go—including him. Though they had saved some money, it was quickly spent for the children's schooling and their rather expensive life-style.

Love and family were a deep bond to help Lorraine weather the storm, one especially hard for her to handle, since living a certain way, being part of a certain group of people, buying at certain stores, were still all-important matters to her. (Ambitious, conformist Capricorn rising, Sun and Moon in regal Leo.) But sex played a big role too. As she told me when I saw her for an update in August 1992: "He can drive me crazy when he tries to push some of the blame for our money troubles on me (Jeff's Moon [wife] in the 7th House, his Sun also there square Saturn [not ready to accept the responsibility), but he is such a great husband and father and a wonderful lover. I'll never find another mate who seems to know my every erotic wish and desire. I'm sure we've had as many fights as other normal couples, but not all of them have such fun ways of making up!"

In September 1991, when Jeff was fired, his Secondary Progressed Moon had just reached 1 Capricorn, trine his Sun, and ready to quincunx Saturn and the MC. A few adjustments and some reorganization of his life in general were called for. Solar Arc Jupiter at 8 Capricorn, ruling his directed Ascendant, squared Mars which is conjunct Mercury in Aries as well as Neptune in Libra, forming a powerful T-Square. Venus, his natal chart and Sun ruler, at 8 Taurus, was quincunx Neptune and approaching a square to Pluto, well describing the sense of utter frustration and not knowing where to turn.

His directed Moon at 25 Gemini quincunxed natal Jupiter reflecting more indecision and emotional *angst*. SA Uranus not only squared his natal Sun, but conjuncted natal Saturn and MC: no solid ground was left under his feet; only the unexpected to look forward to. The *coup de grace* was delivered by transiting Saturn at 0 Aquarius filling his natal T-Square. These were indeed tough times for Jeff.

Interestingly, Lorraine's Secondary Progressed Moon in September 1991 was at 2 Capricorn, conjunct Jeff's progressed Moon. But in her horoscope, this did not make any aspects. Only later did it oppose Venus, quincunx Mars and finally conjunct the Ascendant in July 1992. Her Venus at 21 Leo conjuncted her Moon, certainly an emotional period, but not necessarily difficult, except that one is never sure how a natally unaspected planet will act when thrust into an aspect with another planet.

By Solar Arc, Lorraine's Ascendant was at 20 Aquarius, quincunx its ruler, Uranus in her 7th House of partners. It also applied to an opposition of the Moon and then Pluto, as well as a quincunx to Saturn and Neptune forming a heavy-duty yod. Thankfully, this Ascendant trined natal Jupiter, allowing for some optimism along the way. SA Venus at 13 Leo quincunxed her Ascendant while Mercury at 15 Leo trined it. Many changes were called for, some very intense and deep, with Pluto at 29 Virgo ready to change signs, Saturn to follow suit the next year, and Venus about to move from the 7th to the 8th House.

Lorraine went to work, something she probably should have done long before, as symbolized by her 6th House Jupiter and Venus (what you enjoy and love to do). Jeff found an interesting new job on May 3, 1993 when transiting Mars, ruler of his 6th House of work, conjuncted his Saturn/Mc while Secondary Progressed Mars conjuncted his natal Moon. Transiting Saturn at 29 Aquarius trined his Ascendant and of course transiting Pluto at 24 Scorpio was playing catch-up with his natal Jupiter. Transiting Venus, his natal chart ruler, was at nearly 7 Aries on May 3rd, conjunct his natal Mars, possibly giving his personality that extra special something he needed to sell himself.

Would Lorraine have stayed with Jeff through thick and thin, in these days of quick and easy divorces, *if their sexual interplay had not been so good?* Probably yes, since they had children to see through school and college, were family oriented and shared many tastes; but sex and money are the two leading causes of divorce and separation. You better understand each other well in one area or the other. Here's another example of how a romantic love relationship can cope with problems.

Arturo and Laura

Arturo (born in South America) was a wonderful looking 6'4" hunk of a man. Outgoing (Aries Sun/Mercury), charming and suave (Pisces rising), and always ready to court the ladies (Venus in Taurus, Pluto in the 5th House), he had little trouble in getting them to do his bidding, whether for a harmless flirtation, a one-night-stand, or a steaming affair. After a slow start in the United States, he finally made good inroads in the booming real estate market in California, especially between 1983 and 1988.

At work, he met Laura and they fell in love. She was in the throes of a divorce.

For a while it was a *sub-rosa* affair, pretty hot and heavy, with her fiery Leo Sun in the 5th House conjunct Pluto, ruler of her 8th House of sex. Her Venus conjunct Mars and Neptune, and all three in amorous Libra, made this a romantic, impassioned, and memorable liaison—enough so that, in 1987, Arturo left his wife of 25 years and moved in with Laura and her 9 year-old son.

At first, life was nothing but bliss. Money came rolling in. Laura was a hard worker who enjoyed what she was doing (Aries

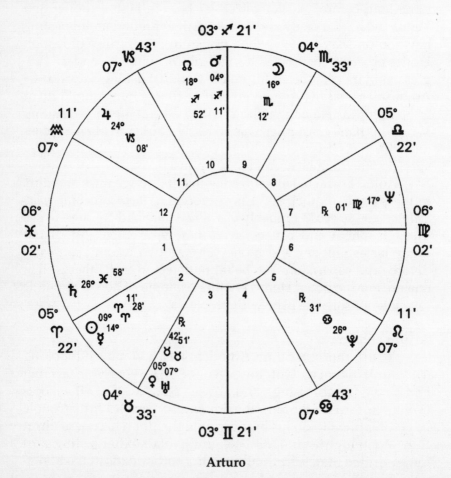

Arturo

Ascendant, ruler Mars in the 6th House of work with Venus, Neptune and Jupiter). She also needed the money, since her ex-husband sent a limited amount of child support and she was adamant about having her son attend a good private school. Arturo did well too, though the eagerness to go to work seemed to fade now that he could see Laura at home. In fact, many mornings she would be off early while he lazed around and strolled into at the office around 11 A.M. or noon. She also was not too happy that, as many South Americans can be, he was utterly useless around the house, hopeless at marketing, never made his bed; and his cooking ability extended to boiling water for coffee . . . but he was wonderful with the boy, which Laura appreciated, and he was especially wonderful in bed.

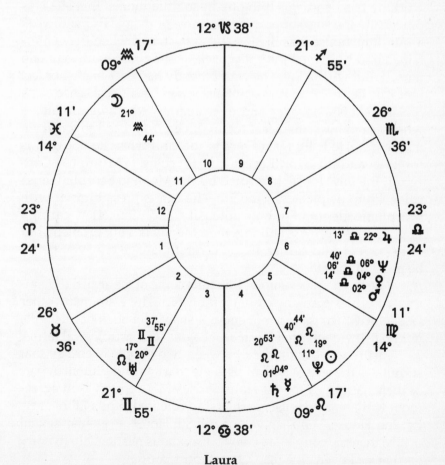

Laura

As time went on, the "me and mine" orientation of Aries started coming to the fore. The less work there was, the more Arturo slipped into his ego mode. With Pisces rising, so under-standing and sensitive in the beginning, he became self-pitying, and with the Ascendant ruler Neptune in the 7th House in Virgo, the pedestal on which Arturo had placed Laura began to crum-ble. Instead of praising her sales ability as he had at first, he now accused her of trying to show him up by listing and selling more houses than he did. His formerly optimistic career approach and forward-looking ideas (Mars in Sagittarius conjunct the MC) now took on tones of braggadocio.

At times, Laura felt she should just throw him out and start all over. He was not holding up his part of the bargain; he was not working hard and was bringing in so little money that she was practically the sole support for the three of them. His handiwork around the house was inadequate at best, and when they enter-tained and he played the *grand seigneur* she could hardly contain herself. But what a lover he was! Nobody had ever made her feel that way before. And it was not just sex in its crassest sense.

As she stated over and over again: "When we are alone, when I'm in his arms, I feel totally loved from head to toe, from inside out. He truly makes *love* to me, and when he does, all is forgiven and it is worth every effort it costs!" (Arturo has Can-cer on the 5th House, it is ruled by the Moon in Scorpio whose ruler, Pluto, is placed in the 5th—he can express himself with Scorpionic depth, Plutonic intensity and Cancerian caring.) Laura and Arturo are still together. Money is a big problem, but not sex. As I said earlier, if you cannot manage one, you better be good in the *other!*

The foregoing examples illustrate some of the sexual dynam-ics that can exist in any close relationship. There are many other facets for which there is not enough space in a book of this type, nor really evidence that it can be recognized in astrological terms.

Just remember that sex between two people is energy that stimulates the senses and arouses the Martian and Plutonian part of their natures. If the 1st House, Aries-Mars energy is in agree-ment with the 7th House, partnership-oriented Venus-Libra ener-gy; 2nd House, Venusian values and 8th House, Plutonian sexual needs; then the couple can enjoy harmonious relationship dynam-ics that will overcome many, if not most, hurdles.

For example: Does it matter which way you reach an orgasm? Is the so-called "missionary" intercourse position better than others or, better said, does it really matter who's on top? Must there be an orgasm, or can some fun foreplay provide the needed sensual satisfaction? Does a couple always have to "make love" or can one gratify the other being a whore one day and a lady the next, a stud today and a gentleman tomorrow? Can a sexually very active person be satisfied with less, but very rewarding, sex? I think the answer to all these questions is "Yes."

Gina Ceaglio

Gina Ceaglio is a professional astrologer, counselor, teacher, writer, and lecturer with more than 25 years experience. She established the Academy of Astrological Studies in San Diego, California in 1970, the first school to offer a two-year curriculum with post-graduate work in astrological counseling. She regularly lectures at seminars, symposia, and conferences nationally and internationally, and has an extensive private counseling practice.

Her company, Pegasus Tapes, distributes audio-cassettes on astrological, psychological, and mythological themes by astrology's most renowned speakers. Very active in the astrological community, she is the founder of the San Diego Astrological Society, a member of NCGR, served three terms on the Steering Committee of AFAN, is a past Vice President and Director of ISAR, the coordinator of UAC '89, and on the planning committee for UAC '92 and UAC '95.

Sexual Energy and Creativity

Gina Ceaglio

"Life is the childhood of our immortality," said Goethe,[1] one of the greatest thinkers of modern times, and, according to William James,[2] the American philosopher, "The greatest use of life is to spend it for something that will outlast it." It is our passionate desire for immortality that drives us to replicate ourselves in human form, creating children to keep a measure of our spark alive after we depart. That same consuming passion to leave behind a footprint, some memorable contribution that will survive our death, is what fans the flame of our creativity.

Since recorded time, the greatest minds and wisest philosophers have told us that sexual energy is creativity in its purest, most primordial form. In psychoanalytic terms, sexual energy is defined as *Libido, the instinctual craving or drive behind all human activities.* Traditional theory states that *all human beings are born with instinctual drives that are constantly active, even though a person is usually not conscious of being driven in this way.* Hindu philosophy and religion refer to a life-power called *Kundalini* that lies coiled like a serpent around the gonads at the base of the spine

---

1 Johann Wolfgang von Goethe: August 28, 1749–March 22, 1832.

2 William James: January 11, 1842–August 26, 1910. Son of philosopher, Henry James Sr. and brother of novelist, Henry James.

and can be aroused by Yogic practices to achieve *Samadhi*, a state of ecstasy and bliss. Tantric Yoga, practiced in Tibetan Buddhism, teaches ritual techniques to arouse one's dormant psychophysical powers by the physical and mental use of sexual forces.

The correlation of sexual energy with creativity is most vividly described in the Kabbalah:[3] *In order for a creation to be possible there must first be a contraction, a concentration of all energies at a center. Then, an expansion must occur; the gathered energies must be sent forth in concentrated form as a ray or beam of energy.* It would be difficult to find a more lucid description of the sex act itself. In fact, the vital connection between sexual energy and creativity is so well acknowledged that in 1934, at age 69, William Butler Yeats,[4] perhaps the greatest English language poet of the twentieth century, underwent the Steinach operation, a procedure that stimulates the production of sexual hormones, which he believed would rejuvenate his flagging creativity.

That concept brings several questions to mind. If something needs rejuvenation, it infers an ailing or depleted state. Does that mean that by limiting our physical sex activity we might conserve our sexual energy and increase our creativity? Is that the reason athletes refrain from sex before a sports event, and does it increase their physical strength or their creativity or both? Does dissipating our sexual reserves in multiple libidinous encounters put a drain on our creative reservoir and, if so, will a celibate be more creative than a Don Juan? Can the Kundalini serpent lose its vigor and die, or are we born with a bottomless well of sexual energy that remains forever full, continually replenishing itself? Again, perhaps the Kabbalah answers those questions best:

> Polarity is the principle that runs through the whole of creation and is, in fact, the basis of manifestation . . . *the creative is pure energy, limitless and tireless* . . . (and) when it acts upon the receptive, its energy is gathered up and set to work.

So the answer to all those questions seems to lie less in the amplitude of our sexual energy than the potency of our power to

---

3   Kabbalah: Hebrew word for tradition, originally designated the legal tradition of Judaism and later applied to the Jewish mystical tradition. Based on Old Testament revelation, interpreted with the aid of hermeneutic techniques.

4   William Butler Yeats, born in Ireland on June 13, 1865, died January 28, 1939.

direct it to a receptacle, a receiver, an outlet. Creativity is a dual, not a singular process; just as the sex act, for supreme fulfillment, needs two to tango.

If sexual energy is common to the human condition, possessed by all, so then creativity is innate—our natural birthright. Certainly, what makes each of us unique is our milieu, our sphere of interest, our chosen method of expression and the amount of energy we focus behind it. It appears that where there is such a driving force for individual expression that it hints of obsession, the end result can be creation that survives the test of time.

While the power that drives our self-expression is sexual in origin, some of what we produce may not be overtly sexual in content, but much of it is. Dating back to the 5th and 4th Centuries B.C., ancient Greek culture produced vase painting and ordinary household articles like jars and pots decorated with depictions of a wide range of explicit sex acts, both homosexual and heterosexual. Modern excavations of the Roman cities of Pompeii and Herculaneum, buried by Mount Vesuvius' eruption in A.D. 79, disclosed wall paintings and phallic art, including earrings and amulets molded in phallic shape.

Greek and Roman literature that survived Christian censorship are often explicitly sexual, such as the Songs of Catullus, the poems in Ovid's *Art of Love* and Petronius's *Satyricon* (first century A.D.). Christianity, with its mistrust of the body, did what it could to destroy surviving ancient examples, but the rediscovery of ancient learning in the Renaissance led to widespread imitation of the classical models. The paintings and sculptures of nudes by Titian, Rubens, Bernini and many others have obvious sexual qualities.

Booksellers in the 19th century invented the term *erotica*, derived from Eros, the Greek god of physical desire, to lend respectability to items that might be seized by the police. Works with artistic, social, or historical value are deemed erotica; worthless ones are pornography, and, until the twentieth Century, written works that treated sex explicitly were relegated to the pornographic underground. The distinction between erotica and pornography is chiefly a Western issue, and tastes change with time. In the twentieth century, such distinctions broke down, and numerous modern novels, including James Joyce's *Ulysses* (1922), D. H. Lawrence's *Lady Chatterly's Lover* (1928), and Vladimir Nabokov's *Lolita* (1955), considered pornographic when they first appeared, were later judged to be erotic. Now a burgeoning industry of erotica has developed in all art forms: in fiction, Henry Miller; in film, Bernardo Bertolucci's *Last Tango In Paris*; in dance, Martha Graham's erotic choreography; in photography, Robert Mapplethorpe, whose homoerotic 1989 and 1990 exhibitions caused much controversy. Displaying one's own sexuality as an art form has been prominent in every culture, from Salome's[5] dance of the seven veils to current sexually explicit movies and magazines.

As astrologers we will find evidence of sexual energy and creativity in everyone's chart, since it is an integral part of the human condition. Where do we look and what factors must we consider in defining the *motivation*, the *extent*, and projected *direction* of sexually energized creativity? What sets the famous contributors to our cultural legacy apart from those of us who bring our energetic style to creating a business procedure, a family meal, or simply performing pedestrian routines with élan and creative flair?

First, referring to the Yogic *Kundalini* and psychiatry's *Libido* as sexual energy, we know that to be Aries' Mars and Scorpio's Pluto. The Kabbalah's teaching that polarity is the principle that runs through the whole of creation—*the creative acting on the receptive*—calls to mind archetypal images of completion: in Jungian terms, the animus and anima; in astrological circuitry, sign and planet gender—male/female, positive/negative electrodes. In element relationship, it is Fire and Air acting on Earth and Water that completes the circle of creativity. Astrologically, we are talking squares, semisquares, quincunxes, and sesquiquadrates, so *creativity must have the energy of these aspects to manifest.*

I would expect to find these configurations with Mars in the charts of renowned creative persons, and, in those whose fame has become immortalized, I would expect to find Pluto aspected as well. Scorpio's Pluto, with its symbology of the Phoenix rising from the ashes of its death to be transformed and reborn, is to me the perfect image of immortality. The Greek myth of Demeter's daughter Core also is a wonderfully descriptive metaphor. The maiden Core was abducted by Hades (Pluto) and taken to the underworld (death), but allowed to return as Persephone (reborn)

---

5   Salome, daughter of Herodias, asked for and received the head of John the Baptist as a reward for her dance. (Mark 6:14–29).

to enjoy life for a while each year, and a year to the gods may be a lifetime to us mortals.

When we're interpreting and measuring the power of a desire or need, we must also take into account Jung's principle of *shadow*. He describes shadow as "emotionally charged ideas, impulses, or concepts usually originating in childhood, that are partly or wholly repressed in the personal unconscious and can function as repression, compensation, or projection." To some degree, every sign holds the archetypal shadow of its opposite sign; Libra is shadow to Aries and Aries to Libra, Scorpio is shadow to Taurus and Taurus to Scorpio, Leo is shadow to Aquarius and Aquarius to Leo, and so on. However, *much more power is given to shadow when there are no planets in an element, or only one planet (singleton) there*. The person has little or no conscious contact with the archetypal nature of the element and cannot "own" it, *but unconsciously feels a great need for its qualities*. Therefore, it is strongly emphasized and manifests by over-compensation or projection onto other people. "That's not me, it's you!"

In the creative sense, an author might project shadow to the protagonist in a novel; a composer might make it the theme of a musical composition; a dancer might embody it in choreography and style; an artist might render it in a painting. Squares and oppositions in the chart are similar indicators of the potential for denial, repression, compensation, or projection, and often find outlets in creative expression, be it nice or nasty. Indeed, were Josef Mengele, the chief medical officer at Auschwitz concentration camp, who sought to create blue eyes from brown, or Jeffrey Dahmer, whose creative use of sexual energy resulted in such heinous crimes, any less creative than a masterful Michelangelo preserving in stone his idealized concept of the human form? A sobering thought.

While one's personal demons cause torturous pain, raising havoc in one's life, particularly with interpersonal and social relationships, *they are the fuel feeding the flame of creativity*. When we look at the lives of those who produced monumental works, it leaves little doubt. Consider Edgar Allen Poe, Vincent van Gogh, Toulouse-Lautrec, Stephen Foster, or Jack London, to name only a few. Their personal lives were a shambles, but while their internal torment ultimately caused their physical deaths, their works became immortal. One wonders if somehow they could have been rid of their demons, might not "adjusted mediocrity" have set in, destroying their creative genius? I suspect Theodore Dreis-er[6] was right when he wrote:

> Art is the stored honey of the human soul,
> gathered on wings of misery and travail.

Perhaps the message to astrologers is, "love your squares, T-Crosses, oppositions, dynamic conjunctions, semisquares, sesqui-quadrates and quincunxes, for they are the source of your highest creative potential." In this same stream of thought, we must ask ourselves how great is the service we give to a client if we counsel them to avoid discomfort, challenge, pain?

I have selected ten charts of people from various fields of creative expression who have made a significant impact on our world or tapped into the well-spring of artistic expression and appreciably enriched the flow. You will recall that I mentioned before which planets, signs, and configurations we might expect to find in a chart with which to correlate sexual energy and creativity with astrological symbolism. To reiterate: Mars and Pluto appear to describe both sexual energy and the creative process, with a powerful Pluto driving obsessively against all odds to achieve immortality.

Normally, we astrologers think of Scorpio and the 8th House for sex, Leo and the 5th House for creative self-expression, so placements in those signs and houses (with a dash of Venus for romance) might be expected, right? Well, let's see. Five of my ten examples have 5th or 8th House placements, but only one of the ten has a dynamic relationship between Mars or Pluto and Venus. However, *every one of the ten has Mars or Pluto (often both) angular and/or in high energy aspect to personal planets.* Frequently it is one of the Lights (Sun or Moon), Mercury, Jupiter, or Saturn that is involved, and often the configuration will include the transpersonal planets, Uranus and Neptune. I wondered if, in some mysterious way, I had chosen only those people with this phenomenon, so, in addition to the charts printed here for interpretation, I selected at random the following list of famous creative people to check out the Mars/Pluto signature. Source is "A" or "B" Data from Lois Rodden's *American Book of Charts.*

---

6   Theodore Dreiser, 1871–1945, was the leading American exponent of literary Natural-ism, best known as the author of *An American Tragedy.*

VINCENT VAN GOGH (artist), Pluto-Mars-Neptune conjunction square Mercury.

MICHELANGELO (artist and sculptor), Mars conjunction Sun opposition Pluto.

PAUL GAUGUIN (artist), Pluto conjunction Uranus square Jupiter. Mars at the midpoint of Sun square Moon.

YEHUDI MENUHIN (violinist), Mars angular (conjunct IC), square Saturn. Pluto angular (conjunct Descendant).

HENRI MATISSE (artist), Pluto angular conjunct Jupiter, Mars opposition Mercury and Uranus.

JOHN LENNON (musician), Pluto angular (conjunct Midheaven) opposed Moon square Mercury.

WILLIAM BUTLER YEATS (poet and dramatist), T-Cross with Mars angular opposed Moon, both square Pluto and Venus.

ORSON WELLES (director, producer, writer, actor), Pluto angular conjunct Saturn.

SIDNEY POITIER (actor, director), Pluto angular square Uranus. Mars conjunct Saturn.

GEORGE BERNARD SHAW (novelist, dramatist), T-Cross Pluto opposed Mars square Sun–Venus.

CLAUDE DEBUSSY (musician, composer), Pluto conjunct Midheaven. Mars square Moon.

LENNY BRUCE (stand-up comic/satirist), T-Cross Pluto angular opposed Jupiter square Mars–Sun.

GEORGE LUCAS (movie producer-director), T-Cross Pluto angular opposed Moon square Mercury–Venus.

Now, does this mean that if a client comes to you with Mars or Pluto angular, conjunct, opposition or square other planets that your client is or will be a creative genius? No. *There is no way we can tell from a chart what anyone will do with the potential implied.* You will see, when we compare similar potentials in famous and infamous charts, that how each person will deal with internal conflicts and direct pain outward can not be fathomed from the chart alone. We must have dialogue with a client face to face if we hope to discover where the person is in the process of unfolding to conscious individuation. However, within the chart and the province of astrology are the internal struggles and possible outlets for one's sexual energy and creativity.

First, let's look at a few women whose overt sexuality was their primary claim to fame.

Mae West

Mae West was a legend in American entertainment for more than 50 years. She began in burlesque, then wrote her own plays and became famous on Broadway for her quick wit, double entendres, and exaggerated sexiness, for which she was briefly jailed on charges of obscenity. She then moved on to Hollywood and worldwide fame where she wrote her own screenplays, always portraying herself as a brassy seductress. Even at age 84, with her sexiness and inimitable style still intact, she starred in "Sextette" and her written memoirs, *Goodness Had Nothing To Do With It*, is a classic.

Her angular 10th House Pluto surely indicates intense sexual energy and creative drive put on world display and, in the Air sign Gemini, she did it with tantalizing humor and plutonian innuendo. The trine to Mars in Aquarius adds the daring, shocking, inventive flair and provides a wide open channel for her lusty sensuality to transmit to her audience, totally unedited. Angular Neptune is conjunct Pluto, lending a seductive, chameleon quality to her sexy public image, and both are in tight, dynamic square to Mercury, deepening her intellect and intensifying her imagination. With the cleverness of Gemini (Pluto-Neptune) tied to the skill and precision of Virgo (Mercury), you get a vivid translation of these energies into her written and spoken style. Also, notice that the square completes the creative thrust of Pluto-Neptune in Air (Masculine) by acting on the receptive Mercury in Earth (Feminine).

With these measurements and, as well, such a strong Ego identity (Sun in the 1st House, sextile Moon, trine Jupiter), we might question the unconscious inner turmoil that would erupt into the outward creative process; we might wonder what was buried in her unconscious that she found hard to deal with. One configuration that helps us is her Moon square Saturn, suggesting an emotionally deprived child who grew up feeling inadequate, unworthy of love, and fearful of rejection. Her creation of an erotic, voluptuous femme fatale, totally irresistible to men, could certainly be seen as a marvelous compensating mechanism!

Then, the Pluto-Neptune conjunction presents a powerful dichotomy in needs: Pluto signifies strength and mastery; Neptune signifies weakness and impotence. Here they are bundled together in conflict, in and of themselves. Their message is: "I have to be strong, but I fear I'm weak. I must have mastery over myself and all of my environment, but I fear I'm impotent." Or: "I must be compassionate but I fear I'm cruel. I must be a savior, but I fear I am a destroyer." And square Mercury in Virgo: "I must display a penetrating intellect, perfect in every way, and if my

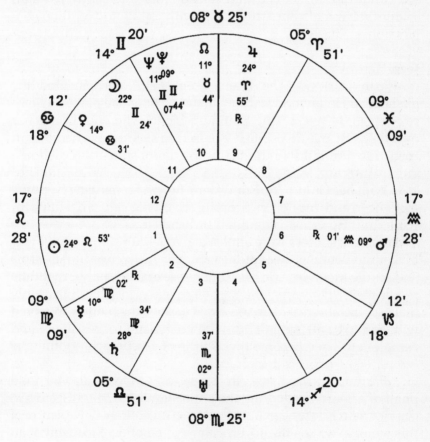

Chart 1
Mae West
Aug. 17, 1892, 4:35 A.M. EST
Brooklyn, NY
73W56 40N38
Placidus Houses

mind is confused or my speech risque, I will disappear (Neptune) or die (Pluto)."

How much easier to give the power, the sensitivity, the words, to a fictitious person who is not me! And when we look at the characters Mae West created, we see sexy, seductive heroines in full command, with power and control, clever penetrating minds, and sardonic, cutting repartee, contained within a softly feminine exterior. In her private life, after one very brief marriage, she selected macho males, usually much younger than she, whom she could dazzle, seduce, and control. [See interesting parallels within Valentino's horoscope, also with the Pluto-Neptune conjunction, p. 25.—Ed.]

Jean Harlow

Jean Harlow, "The Blond Bombshell," encapsulated the glamour of Hollywood stardom in the 1930s as she played a lusty, sex-driven, wise-cracking platinum blond who could hold her own with any man. Despite her on-screen success, she had a short tragic life, fraught with problems in relationships, and died of a kidney infection at age 26.

With her Grand Trine in Water—Sun in Pisces trine Neptune in Cancer and Jupiter in Scorpio, involving her 6th House of work, 10th House of recognition and 2nd House of money—fame and material success were almost a given. With smoldering Pluto in Gemini conjunct her Midheaven, trine Mercury in Aquarius and sextile Moon in Aries, her intense sexuality easily caught the public's eye. However, the so-called "easy" aspects can imply malaise, the absence of creative drive, since the planets involved will tend to be all Yang or Yin with no dynamic of resistance and completion. They become the aspects of acceptance—nothing is wrong, so no effort is demanded.

Fortunately that same 7th House Aries Moon is also the focal point of a T-Cross, squaring the opposition from Mars-Uranus in Capricorn to Neptune in Cancer. We get an entirely new picture of this woman: we see the anger, pain, and emotional torment of an inner child who felt betrayed, abused, and abandoned. Also, notice her Aries Venus in the 7th House, describing an ardent desire to be loved by significant others; it makes no major aspects to any planet, so she feels disconnected from pleasure, isolated and alone. As an adult, she unconsciously expected those kinds of treatment from people she loved and it was validated by one failed marriage and a second husband who committed suicide. What better proof of abandonment? Perhaps her ultimate betrayal, if the story is true, was by her mother, who let her die with her illness undiagnosed or attended by a physician, because medical help was against her (the mother's) religion.

Yet during Harlow's brief life, *struggling with that inner pain was the thrust driving her creativity;* Mars in feminine Earth was completed through Moon in masculine Fire, which in turn found its outlet

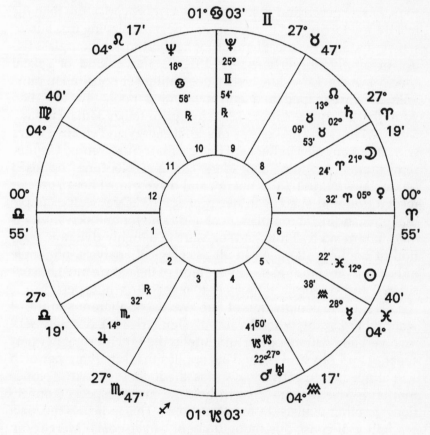

Chart 2
Jean Harlow
Mar. 3, 1911, 7:40 P.M. CST
Kansas City, MO
94W34 390N05
Placidus Houses

in the feminine Water of her 10th House Neptune. She compensated for her unconscious self-image of helplessness, unlovability, and victimization by projecting to the world a sexy, independent, tough, self-sufficient (Mars-Uranus) siren (Neptune) with inner vulnerability (Moon). In fact, she often played the rough "bad" girl from the wrong side of the tracks, who had a soft heart of gold.

Jayne Mansfield

At one time, Jayne Mansfield was being groomed by her film studio to become the new Marilyn Monroe, but in imitating Monroe's looks, speech and gestures, she was more caricature than the real thing, starring in "B" Movies and never achieving true superstar status. She was most famous for her bosom, her hourglass figure of ample proportions (40"-18"-36") and a kind of sexual "sticky sweetness" evidenced by decorating her house all in pink, with a heart-shaped bed and swimming pool. She too died young, in an automobile accident just prior to her 34th birthday.

Certainly she had plenty of sexual energy and creative drive with Pluto angular in her 1st House square Sun, Venus, Uranus, semisquare Neptune, and Mars conjunct Neptune, opposed Moon. So why didn't this energy and drive propel her to greater recognition and success in her profession? Here is an example that outstanding accomplishment and fame for one's creativity is not guaranteed by Pluto and/or Mars in a highly dynamic position or configuration. As in all astrological analysis, no single indicator ever stands alone. Every facet of the nature must be considered and synthesized together to reveal the whole person.

The triple conjunction of Sun, Venus, and Uranus in the "I want what I want, when I want it" sign Aries is extremely self-involved and square powerful Pluto in the 1st House of her personality and physical body. This implies that satisfying her own sexual needs in creative ways took the highest priority. Notice that both Mercury and Saturn hold no major aspects (connections) to other planets (human functions). This indicates the inaccessibility of conscious thought about career goals (Mercury in 10th House) to structure a plan, and the discipline (Saturn) to move beyond personal satisfactions. It's interesting to note that she expressed her ego (Sun) individuality (Uranus) and pleasure principle (Venus) by using her sexual energy (Pluto) to create children (Venus ruling the 5th), which is supported by maternal, nur-

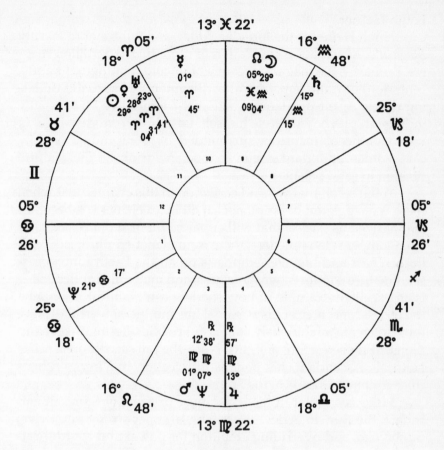

Chart 3
Jayne Mansfield
Apr. 19, 1933, 9:11 A.M. EST
Bryn Mawr, PA
75W18 40N01
Placidus Houses

turing Cancer rising. Unlike other sexy sirens of that time, she bore five children by three different husbands.

Now let's look at a couple of gentlemen: one whose commercialization of sex brought him fame, and another whose personal sexual appeal was the most significant factor in his unprecedented worldwide acclaim—Hugh Hefner and Elvis Presley.

Hugh Hefner

Hugh Hefner is the founder, editor, and publisher of *Playboy Magazine,* which has a circulation of more than 3.5 million readers. Primarily, the magazine features full-color photographs and a centerfold of nude females, called Playmates, in sexually titillating poses. A self-proclaimed hedonist, Hefner lived a sensually indulgent, playboy lifestyle himself, until his recent marriage. In his magnificent mansion, surrounded by voluptuous, scantily clad women, abundant epicurean food and drink, he "held court" dressed in satin pajamas.

You'll recall that we said earlier on in this chapter that when there is a singleton or no planets at all in an element, it becomes emphasized as *shadow* that will either be repressed, projected, or over-compensated for. Here, there is no planet-emphasized Earth in the chart and his over-emphasis on all the Earth functions—sex, creature comforts, sensuousness, and material gratification—is an excellent example of how shadow can manifest. It became the obsessive center of his personal life and the powerful driving force to create a fabulously successful public offering that champions all those earthly delights. Note, the only Earth presence is Hefner's Ascendant, his personal projection in Virgo, with its ruler conjunct Uranus in the 7th!

Pluto is angular in his 10th House of worldly achievement, square the Sun in Aries, describing a super-strong sex drive, macho ego, and overriding ambition for power and control. Saturn in Scorpio is the focal point of a Fixed T-Cross, square both Neptune in Leo and Jupiter in Aquarius. The outlet of energy generated within a T-Cross is opposite the focal point, so here it is aimed at his Taurus (Aha!) 9th House of publishing. He projected his personal struggle with setting boundaries on carnal objectives (Saturn in Scorpio) so as not to violate his spiritual faith (Neptune) and intellectualized values (Jupiter), by creating a publication that glorified sex and the female form, and how graphically his Moon in Pisces trine Pluto in Cancer describes his portrayal of women in the public arena as objects to be both adored and covetously desired!

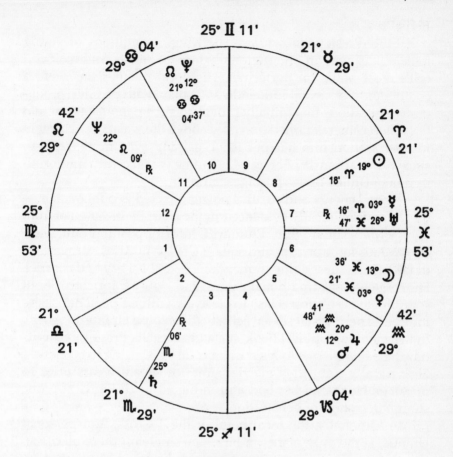

Chart 4
Hugh Hefner
Apr. 9, 1926, 4:20 P.M. CST
Chicago, IL
87W39 41N51
Placidus Houses

Elvis Presley

Elvis Presley, known as "The King" to millions of young female fans, was an internationally famous singer, and rock and roll's most powerful performer. His vocal mannerisms were a combination of sexual innuendo and sneer, with physically suggestive gyrations that initially provoked such parental alarm that television cameras filmed him only above the waist. The cult that formed around him has persisted, gaining even more strength since his death in 1977 at age 42, and he was recently immortalized on a United States postage stamp.

Sexual energy and creative power directed to public achievement are dramatically evidenced in the chart by his angular 10th House Mars square Sun. Pluto in Cancer opposition Sun, Mercury, Venus in Capricorn and square Uranus in Aries, form a Cardinal T-Cross, describing tremendous sexual energy and conflict. His conventional, traditional values (2nd House Capricorn) about sex (8th House Cancer) clash explosively with his personal desire for free, experimental sexual activity (5th House Uranus in Aries). In her autobiographical book, his wife, Priscilla Presley, recounts how he paid homage to his puritan code by refusing to take away her virginity until they married. Yet, for several years prior to marriage he shared her bed and indulged in all kinds of erotic stimulation short of penetration.

Additionally, the focal point of the T-Cross, transpersonal Uranus, is the only planet in Fire. The singleton there places an unconscious emphasis on issues surrounding the Fire functions— libido, passion, enthusiasm, *joie de vivre*, vigor and hope. The feeling of being denied these qualities becomes melancholy, and we surely see evidence of that in the intimate accounts of his life. The T-Cross is let out to the Libran 11th House and we can assume he was compensating for feeling a lack of these functions in his own conscious nature by surrounding himself with a continuous entourage of energetic young males to draw fire from. Also, there is a probable factor of projection involved here: let the on-stage personality engage in that wildly kinetic, outrageously sexy performance and I will avoid feeling the Cancer-Capricorn guilt on a personal level.

We can look to the T-Cross and singleton fiery Uranus as well for Presley's irresponsible, erratic handling of firearms. He is reported to have been obsessed with guns, frequently brandishing a weapon, violently threatening close allies, and shooting out TV sets. Perhaps the TV was symbolic of his projected on-stage image, about which he felt overpowering guilt, and his repressed anger and rage spontaneously (Uranus) erupted from the deep caverns of his unconscious to annihilate it (Pluto). Certainly, we get a picture of a complex and troubled young man whose sexually related conflicts spawned exceptional creativity.

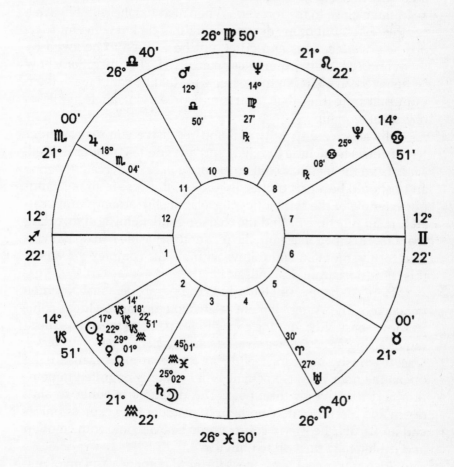

Chart 5
Elvis Presley
Jan. 8, 1935, 4:35 A.M. CST
Tupelo, MS
88W42 34N15
Placidus Houses

Now let's take a look at a macabre case where sexual energy and creativity took a ghastly, perverted road to immortalized infamy—Jeffrey Dahmer.

Jeffrey Dahmer

Recently, a horrified public went into shock hearing the grisly reports that Jeffrey Dahmer had murdered numerous young men and engaged in ritualistic cannibalism after their deaths "to keep them close to me forever." When arrested, he calmly gave a complete account of his deeds, saying that he knew his murderous acts were callous and cruel, but he wanted to be loved by them and sensually experience their physical beauty. Somehow he believed, in a kind of messianic way, that he could make them immortal by eating their hearts and preserving their skulls as objects of worship.

His acts were so truly evil and repulsive you may wonder why I chose to include his chart and ask you to consider it. Well, aside from the fact that I felt an example of sexual creativity gone awry should be a part of this discussion, this case is an outstanding example of the symbiotic interrelationship among complicated human functions. I find the chart so challenging and revealing that I feel justified in asking the reader to set aside personal revulsion for the moment and follow with me the complex threads of this intricate astrological mosaic.

Here we have a singleton in Water—transpersonal Neptune in Scorpio. The Water element relates to emotion, feelings, compassion, sensitivity, and the capacity for pain, so when it is missing or a singleton, *feelings seem frightening and without boundaries.* Unconsciously, he fears feeling anything at all, because if he opens the door even a crack, he will be totally engulfed in emotion and dissolve or disappear. The dynamic is either to shut down and feel absolutely nothing (remember how expressionless and implacable he was in court?), or to be overcome with emotion and hysterically float off to oblivion.

Also, notice that Neptune is the focal point of a Yod involving Mars in Aries sextile Mercury in Gemini, which imposes watery, ephemeral Neptune on his sexual desires and cognitive reasoning process. This inclines me to believe him when he said he felt fearful, impotent, confused, and inadequate in normal sexual situations. Of course, taking drugs will anesthetize the fear, allowing the feelings full sway, and, according to his confession, that's what he did, to himself as well as to his victims. He admitted he had to be drunk before he could select a victim, then, because he didn't want them to feel any pain, he drugged them before conducting his sexual rituals and murderous fantasies; and isn't it interesting that the ploy he used to lure them to his apartment was to pose for photographs, another Neptune-ruled activity?

His Sun in the 8th House conjunct Mercury, square Pluto describes a powerful libido and creative drive, a subjective ego,

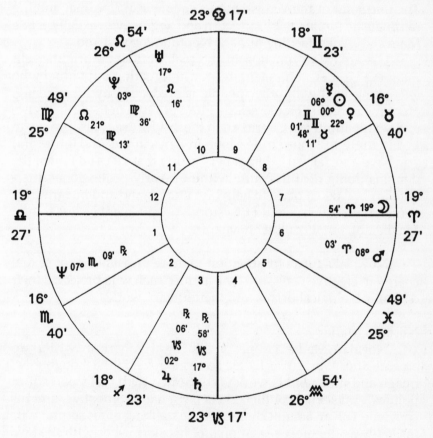

Chart 6
Jeffrey Dahmer
May 21, 1960, 4:34 P.M. CDT
Milwaukee, WI
87W54 43N02
Placidus Houses

concerned primarily with himself, and mental preoccupation with sex and death. The midpoint of that square is 17° of Cardinal signs, so Saturn at 17° Capricorn conjunct his IC combines with the Sun and Mercury-Pluto, and suggests traumatic (probably violent) early experiences with a male parental figure. The violence (Pluto) and cruelty (Saturn) are a part of his own nature that he can't accept in himself, and are cloaked in that Neptunian sensitivity to pain, which he also fears. His 8th House Venus in Taurus desperately wants to enjoy all the sensual pleasures, and square Uranus in Leo, he created inventive, dramatic scenarios to bring it about. The midpoint of the Venus-Uranus square is 4° Cardinal, pulling in ritualistic Jupiter at 2° Capricorn and aggressive, sexually active Mars at 8° Aries, feeding into the Neptune-focused Yod.

His ability to function in the real world as a bright, well-mannered, quiet, competent, responsible, caring individual who gets along well with other people is evidenced by Libra rising, Neptune in the 1st House sextile Pluto in Virgo in the 11th House, and sextile Jupiter in Capricorn in the 3rd House. Add Uranus in Leo in the 10th House trine Moon in Aries in the 7th House, and you have a socialized external personality that gives no hint of the demons doing deathly battle within. If early professional intervention had taken place to help him understand and integrate his agonizing conflicts, would this story's denouement be less tragic? Maybe not, but it couldn't have hurt.

Now, let's turn our attention to more pleasant use of sexual energy in creative ways and look at three men who projected their dynamic biological drives into their literary works.

Norman Mailer

Norman Mailer is one of the finest American writers to emerge after World War II. He seems to revel in the "tough guy" image and much of his work is concerned with violence, radical politics, and sexual conflict. He is personally combative, and his conviction on an assault charge for the stabbing of his second wife in 1960 was the most sensational of his skirmishes with the law. Mailer won the Pulitzer Prize and National Book Award for *Armies of the Night*, published in 1968. His best known novel is probably *The Naked And The Dead*, which grew out of his combat experience in the Pacific, and is considered among the finest of modern war novels.

Much of his success has depended equally on his brilliance as an essayist and journalist. His published collections deal with a wide range of issues, from boxing to politics to race relations. Among them are *The Presidential Papers* (1963), *Cannibals and Christians* (1966), and *Pieces and Pontifications* (1982). *The Prisoner Of Sex* (1971), is a personal response to the feminist movement, and *The Executioner's Song* (1979) is his novelistic treatment of the execution of Gary Gilmore in Provo, Utah. Although he has not yet achieved his goal of "making a revolution in the conscious-

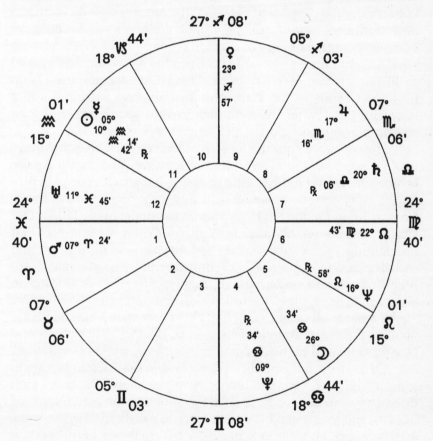

Chart 7
Norman Mailer
Jan. 31, 1923, 9:05 A.M. EST
Long Beach, NJ
74W09 39N41
Placidus Houses

ness of our times," his works are powerful representations of his singular, apocalyptic vision of Americans and their world.

First of all, both planets indicating sexual energy and creativity are angular and square to one another: Mars in Aries in the conscious 1st House square Pluto in Cancer in the subconscious 4th. This high-tension dynamic describes his pugnacious personality, his overt sex drive, and activism to deal with inner life-death issues of transformation. It's a struggle that builds frustration and repressed rage, either erupting in personal violence or projected to attacking the sins of others. Obviously, he has experienced both. Without a channel of escape, if the Mars and Pluto were just projected back and forth, he might simply have become an extremely angry, destructive man, perhaps not even knowing what angered him. The sextile between his Aries Mars rising and his Aquarian Sun-Mercury in the 11th House and the trine from Pluto to Uranus in the 12th, provides an easy avenue for that powerful Fire/Water steam to flow toward social, humanitarian concerns in ego-conscious, intellectual ways.

However, without the tension of his Fixed T-Cross in Aquarius-Leo-Scorpio, (Sun opposition Neptune, and both square Jupiter), he would not have the irritating impetus he needs to produce a *tangible* body of work. Notice that the focal point of the T-Cross is Jupiter in the 8th House and it has outlet in his Taurus 2nd House of material, physical resolutions. When we interpret that unrelenting T-Cross, we see his life-force-purpose of freedom and equality (Sun in Aquarius) is in conflict with messianic rule (Neptune in Leo), and underhanded, manipulative justice (Jupiter in Scorpio). What a vividly explicit description of his *Armies of the Night,* a personal narrative of the 1967 peace march on the Pentagon, his *Pieces and Pontifications* in 1982, dealing with politics and race relations and his black-comic masterpiece, *An American Dream!*

Of course, all the qualities described in the T-Cross belong to him as well. His Aquarian tendency to "let all men be free—then do as I say," to believe he is a savior, showing the way (Neptune in Leo), and to use exploitive influence to satisfy his own sensual, earthly needs, (Jupiter in Scorpio), is his challenge of integration and individuation. We also need to mention here that, in addition to the outlet of the T-Square pointing to Taurus, *he has no planets in Earth.* You will recall that missing Earth emphasizes, by repression, compensation, or projection, issues around the body—sexuality, sensuality, the pleasure centers, and material rewards.

Now let's look at his 5th House Moon in Cancer opposed his 11th House Mercury in Aquarius and square his 7th House Saturn in Libra. This configuration not only describes his lean and mean literary style, but also indicates another highly charged dynamic. It tells us that his subconscious feelings (Moon) of emotional deprivation (Saturn) are translated intellectually (Mercury) to "I must earn love by my deeds, it will not be given unconditionally and if my performance doesn't measure up to other people's expectations (Saturn in Libra), I'll be rejected." It is a potent prod for achievement, but his unconscious impulses for nonconformity (Moon sesquiquadrate Uranus in the 12th) can defeat the very goal that it engenders. Undoubtedly, it's a constant source of inner pain and nagging fear, but like all our so-called difficult aspects, it's a burr-under-the-saddle he can not ignore. It continually pressures him to create works that will bring him love and approval.

Ernest Hemingway

Ernest Hemingway, 1899-1961, was the American writer considered to be one of the most influential authors of the first half of the 20th century. He was awarded the Nobel Prize for literature in 1954 and created a distinguished body of prose, much of which was based on his own adventurous life. Kept from the armed forces in World War I by deficient eyesight, he volunteered as a Red Cross ambulance driver in Italy, an experience that later was to become the theme and locale of one of his most successful novels, *A Farewell To Arms* (1929). After working as a journalist and foreign correspondent for various newspapers, he settled in Paris and launched his career as a serious writer. His first volume of short stories displayed a laconic prose style, a blend of realism and romanticism, that became the hallmark of all of his writing.

His memorable novel, *The Sun Also Rises*, based on his experiences in Paris and Pamplona, was an immediate success. It solidified his reputation and made him a leader of the so-called "lost generation." With the publication of *Men Without Women, The Killers, Winner Take Nothing, The Fifth Column* and *Death in the Afternoon*, his fame extended worldwide. *The Snows of Kilimanjaro* and *The Short Happy Life of Francis Macomber* were based on his adventures as a big-game hunter in Africa, and his service as a war correspondent in the Spanish Civil War led to his most ambitious novel, *For Whom The Bell Tolls*, in 1941.

An estate outside Havana, Cuba became his residence for 20 years and after the United States entered World War II, believe it or not, he armed his cabin cruiser and spent two years hunting German submarines in the Caribbean! As a war correspondent in 1944, he followed the Fourth Infantry Division and joined in the liberation of Paris. In 1950, he published *Across the River and Into the Trees* and, in 1953, was awarded the Pulitzer Prize for *The Old Man and the Sea*. Hemingway left Cuba in 1960 for his home in Ketchum, Idaho and, on July 2nd 1961, he put a shotgun in his mouth and pulled the trigger.

His chart shows the same angular emphasis on personal machismo, aggressive sexual energy, and creative drive as did Norman Mailer's, however there is a major and highly significant difference. Here the 1st House Mars in Virgo is the focal point of a powerful T-Cross with 10th House Pluto in Gemini and 4th House Saturn in Sagittarius. There is mental preoccupation and possible obsession with violence (Pluto-Gemini), aggression, (Mars-Virgo) and ritualistic cruelty (Saturn-Sagittarius), concerning sex, life, and death. He experienced all those qualities in himself, testing his survival instincts by living on the edge in daring exploits, tempting death in wars, confronting wild beasts on safari or in the streets of Pamplona, and being orgasmicly enthralled with ritualistic death at bull fights. The outlet for that accumulation of bombastic energy is in the 7th Piscean House, and I feel sure it was projected onto his four marriages. We also see a kind of mythical, "knights of the roundtable" camaraderie in the relationship he set up with his male counterparts, where he was "Papa" instead of King Arthur, but it was in his creative imagination and writing laconic prose with an arresting blend of realism with romanticism that he is immortalized.

Now, notice that his conscious sexual desires (Mars rising) are squared by transpersonal Neptune, suggesting an unconscious, yet always active (Neptune angular), uneasy concern with crippling weakness. It is an attack on his Martian virility and, given his overwhelming admiration of power and strength, unimaginable to accept as his own. So he projected that shadow to the protagonists in his novels, many of whom were either sexually impotent, as in *The Sun Also Rises*, or helpless against the powerful forces of nature, as in *The Old Man and the Sea*, or tragic victims, like the Spanish people in *For Whom The Bell Tolls*.

The published accounts of Hemingway's final years assign mental deterioration and paranoid fears as causes for his suicide. I think we also can consider the possibility that it might have been his inability to accept the gut-wrenching (Pluto) reality (Saturn) of his own sexual impotence and vanishing virility (Mars-Neptune) that persuaded him to finally give up on life. Certainly his choice of a shotgun, with its phallic symbology, as the vehicle for his demise was completely in character.

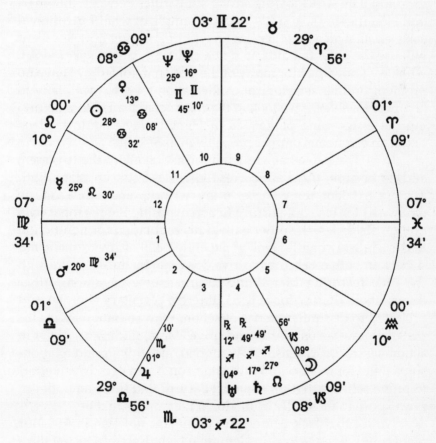

Chart 8
Ernest Hemingway
Jul 21, 1899, 8:00 A.M. CST
Oak Park, IL
87W47 41N53
Placidus Houses

Jack Anderson

Jack Anderson is a hard-hitting investigative reporter-journalist, whose muckraking articles and columns arguably have great impact throughout America. He is a true crusader, with a bombastic lecturing style, and a kind of missionary zeal for fighting injustice. Famous for exposing corruption, denouncing wrongdoers who have betrayed the public trust, and revealing top-secret government reports, his writing and manner are straightforward and brusque.

You'll be struck by the strong similarities between this chart and Hemingway's, and it's a good example of what I mentioned early on, that an astrologer has no way of knowing how the client will use the potential indicated in a chart. Of course, *after the fact*, when we know the biography of the person involved, we have no problem finding astrological confirmation for what we know to be true. However, if we look at the chart "cold," a T-Cross involving the exact same planets as in Hemingway's could lead us down an erroneous path of probable manifestation.

In this case, we have much information about the two men, and, to be sure, there are correspondences between them. Both possess a talent for concise, pithy writing, and while one is renowned for his soul-stirring fiction exposing the personal pain of life's struggles, the other gained his reputation for non-fiction that is a brashly painful look at the underbelly of government and society. In both cases, the creative drive can be traced to the high dynamic featuring Mars-Pluto-Saturn. However, among other things, their T-Cross focus is on different planetary energies and projected to dissimilar arenas of action. With Hemingway, it's his personal, raw sexual desire and drive (Mars) finding an outlet in action-set stories of sensitive, wounded, individuals and relationships (7th House Pisces). With Anderson it's an ego-driven effort to prove self-worth (Sun conjunct Saturn) that finds an outlet in raw exposé to forcefully bring down the powers that be.

Notice that Jack Anderson's dominant function is Air, four planets in Libra and one in Gemini, which describes his intellectual detachment and objectivity. His singleton planet in Fire accounts for the over-emphasis on evangelistic zeal (Neptune in Leo quincunx Mars), and his singleton planet in Earth is his aggressive attack (Mars) on authority and government (Capricorn). Pluto and Mars, the planets of sexual energy and creativity, are in angular opposition spanning his Ascendant-Descendant axis. They form the explosive T-Cross to his Sun conjunct Saturn, angular in the 4th House and the focus of his T-Cross. Pluto rising describes his potent sex drive and the need for personal power and control, opposition Mars in Capricorn suggests hostility toward authority, peers, and limiting boundaries, square Sun conjunct Saturn in Libra is his need for approval (Libra) to preserve (Saturn) his ego (Sun).

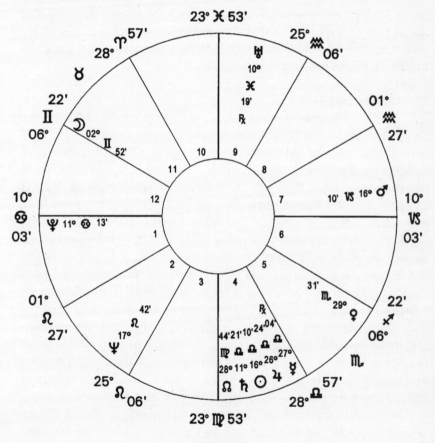

Chart 9
Jack Anderson
Oct. 9, 1922 10:18 P.M. PST
Long Beach, CA
118W11 33N46
Placidus Houses

The midpoint of his Sun-Mars square is 1° Sagittarius (or 1°of any other Mutable sign) and the midpoint of his Sun-Pluto square is 28° Leo (or 28° of any other Fixed sign), so his *Moon-Venus opposition falls directly on those midpoints.* This means his emotional security (Moon) and pleasure fulfillment (Venus) needs are inexorably tied in to his Pluto-Mars-Sun T-Cross and creative drive. Figuring out how, like Caesar's wife, to stay above reproach, gain approval, and feel emotionally secure, while pursuing his own sexual desires, pleasure, and power needs, is the conundrum he must constantly try to solve. Probably, we will never know just how he deals internally with these struggles, but it's apparent that his compulsion to dig-up-the-dirt, uncovering transgressions of people in high places, is a marvelous, ventilating mechanism for him that benefits us all.

Suzanne Somers

Here's a multi-talented actress whose portrayal of the sexy dumb-blond in the television series, *Three's Company* in 1977 brought her worldwide fame. However, her attempt to pressure the producers for an exorbitantly high salary increase resulted in her dismissal from the show. Subsequently she sang and danced in her own Las Vegas show that received lukewarm approval, starred in two TV series that fizzled out, wrote several collections of poetry and a book detailing her abusive family life. Numerous appearances on talk shows publicizing the book kept her in the public eye, and recently she scored a huge commercial success merchandising her physical fitness invention, *Thigh Master*™. Currently she is starring in the television sit-com *Step By Step*.

With planetary emphasis in Earth missing, and Venus holding only one minor aspect (sesquiquadrate Moon), there is an over-emphasis on the Aphrodite principle of tantalizing sexuality, on the physical body, sensual delights and all the lovely things of the material world. We see it operating in all her career endeavors: her television roles, her Vegas show, her body-molding fitness device (Sagittarius, thighs!) and her disastrous bid for a salary boost. With her Moon in Cancer square Sun in Libra, she feels her conscious ego demands and her inner needs conflict, so pursuing one seems to negate or deny the other. Her Moon is also widely square to Neptune in Libra, indicating an unrealistic expectation of the kind or amount of unconditional love she needs to feel emotionally secure. Reality never measures up to unreasonable anticipations, so she is constantly disappointed and sees herself as the victim who will always be betrayed. By unconsciously creating no-win circumstances to validate that view, she perpetuates the image and her "losing streak," beginning with the *Three's Company* fiasco, rather typical of that syndrome.

However, the dogged determination with which she pursues her goal, despite repeated setbacks and rejections, is evidenced by

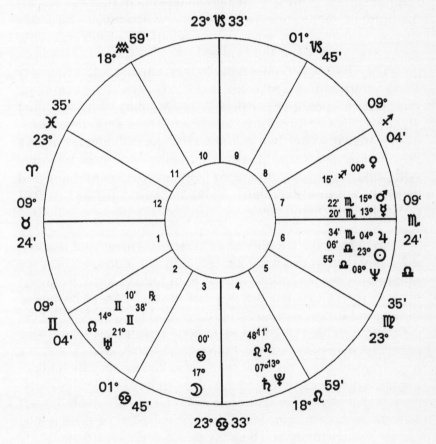

Chart 10
Suzanne Somers
Oct. 16, 1946 6:11 P.M. PST
San Mateo, CA
122W19 37N34
Placidus Houses

her five planets in Fixed signs. This is a relentless gutsy lady who never gives up—a tough survivor in every sense of the word. The power-packed square between Mars conjunct Mercury in Scorpio and Pluto conjunct Saturn in Leo, is eloquent testimony to her sexual energy and creative drive. Mars in the 7th House tells us she seeks out worthy opponents and challenging situations to defend herself against (square Saturn) and overcome (Pluto); an exercise that sharpens her creative skills and gives her self-confidence a boost. But she can get over-confident and self-important (Jupiter square Saturn), extremely independent (Uranus sesquiquadrate Jupiter, semisquare Saturn), and *overestimate her power* (Jupiter square Pluto) when she goes out on a limb regarding finance (Uranus in the 2nd House).

The challenge represented by her angular Mars-Mercury Pluto-Saturn square is to realize that it isn't aggressive, manipulative "others," peers, or partners (Mars, Mercury) who block her vigorous drive (Saturn, Pluto) to succeed. Those attributes of frustration are within her own nature and call for fulfilling her desires by coupling her keen, penetrating intellect and bold initiative with self-discipline, a structured plan and persevering effort. It certainly appears that she is getting a better handle on that process of integration now.

So, what have we learned about sexual energy and creativity? I have submitted they are one and the same: a quest for immortality by replicating ourselves in human form, or giving birth to works that will survive our death. I believe Mars and Pluto graphically describe that process, and we have found these planets prominent in charts of famous creative persons. To be sure, this overview is not a thorough research project, and we might reasonably expect that charts of *un*known persons containing these dynamics will be found. The primary implication, however, is that *when other astrological indicators are present to support vigorous application of the Mars/Pluto dynamic*, that person's sexual energy and creativity will be pronounced and gain attention.

For decades, I've tried to convince students (and anyone else who will listen) that squares, T-Crosses, semisquares, quincunxes and sesquiquadrates are *the best aspects you can have*. We know projection is endemic to the square configuration, that we have difficulty owning up to the characteristics the planets represent.

However, the "it's not me, it's you!" syndrome, so apparent in our early life, is a marvelous way to recognize ourselves through others if we will silently ask, "what is there in *me* that sees that in *you?*" Since we can't relate to anything we haven't experienced, it is the best psych-yourself-out tool I know of.

The revered Grand Trine is static, a closed system that goes nowhere, but the T-Cross, square, quincunx, sesquiquadrate, and semisquare get you off your duff to let you know that you're alive. These are aspects that complete the circuit of creativity with the interchange between the masculine-active and feminine-receptive signs and, as this investigation has shown us, *the T-Cross may be the very best of all!* It supplies a crucible for concentrating energy, then points the way for its deliverance.

> In wisdom and understanding we have the archetypal Positive and Negative ... It is from these primary pairs ... that the Pillars of the Universe spring, between which is woven the web of Manifestation.
>
> —Kabbalah (B.C. 12007–700? A.D.)

John Townley

John Townley has a long history of innovative approaches to astrology, beginning with his introduction of the now-standard composite chart technique in his book *The Composite Chart*, in 1973. Since then, he has pioneered various techniques for astrological cycle analysis in several books on the subject, and he also wrote the enduring text on sexual astrology, *Planets In Love*. He is currently completing a forthcoming book on relationships which will combine synastry, composite, and other chart-combination techniques in a large-scale overview on the subject.

He is also the editor of the Renaissance Latin track of Project Hindsight, which is engaged in translating all known historical astrological texts into English, and is the co-author with Robert Schmidt of a book about "synchronicity," inventor Paul Kammerer's theories about the structure of reality, which impact strongly on the creation of a tangible, physical basis for astrology within the context of broad scientific theory.

Outside of astrological affairs, John is a well-known maritime music historian, preservationist, performer, record producer, and recording studio designer. He has produced 13 albums of historical music and regularly performs at museums and festivals across the United States and Europe.

 # Imagination/ Fantasy: Sexuality's Escape Valve

John Townley and friends

When Noel Tyl first asked me to do an article on this subject, I was somewhat at an impasse as to how to treat it. Everybody knows that when you can't get the sex you need you channel it off into fantasy—otherwise you would explode, endocrinologically speaking. Mother Nature has already provided a channel for it, in case you might be too repressed to fantasize by yourself, and it's called a wet dream, unless, of course, you are extremely skilled in rechannelling your sex drive into other areas of life: work, service, prayer, art. Some say that is a higher form of expressing sexuality—others say it's just chickening out.

But all of this is obvious, and well-covered by others in the areas of psychology, sexology, sociology, religion, and elsewhere. How would one treat the subject astrologically in a way which would not be a slavish astrological reinterpretation of what, let us say, psychology has already pronounced? This is a sin astrologers regularly commit in a variety of areas, and one to be avoided if astrology is to be respected as having something to say of itself. This is why I cringe, for instance, at the term "Jungian astrologer." Let's divide Jung up into signs and houses and say it's ours and siphon off a little legitimacy (such as Jung has to offer) in the process. Spare me.

There are legitimate structural approaches one might take to the subject which are solely astrological, and although they make a universal framework on which to look at sex and fantasy in the horoscope, they add more technique than depth to the subject, and in some cases border on the trivial. But let us scan them, for a start.

Sexually speaking, it is useful to divide the chart up into planetary pairs male and female, yang and yin, active and responsive, at different levels of internal and external development. These would be:

Sun/Moon. The primary emissive and reflective energies. These represent the innermost driving energies of the child (and later the adult/child) and are general and non-specific in nature. They are totally dominant in early childhood (birth to age four or five) and rule the "I give/I receive" focus then, and serve as its underpinnings through the rest of life.

Mars/Venus. This is sexuality as it develops hormonally in middle childhood (from about age five or six to puberty—for details, see any of the works of definitive sexologist and researcher, Dr. John Money). This is where real sex-play rehearsal begins, and it is where lasting fundamental sexual predelictions, normal and/or unusual, have their origin.

Jupiter/Saturn. This represents the social structure of sexuality, where sexuality is molded from without by the rules and regulations governing it in the context of the individual's environment, and generally begins at puberty. It is the "yes" and "no" codes by which the individual learns about expected and allowed conduct in matters sexual.

Uranus/Neptune. This might be called the "spiritual" side of sexuality, and certainly marks the use of physical sexuality to gain other, though not necessarily higher, goals. It generally comes into play in early adulthood, and it is what allows sexual energy to be channeled into other areas or to refine itself into something clearer and more developed than the raw physical energy of Mars/Venus. Some might say it is a higher "octave" of these, but again, the word "higher" may be improvidently used here, as afflictions by these outer planets can cause channeling into sex crimes which, to the perpetrator, may seem like mystical acts—a feeling generally lost upon the victim and the rest of society.

Mercury/Pluto. These are a sexual odd couple, as they are not considered particularly male or female, yet they are critical in sexual implementation and do work as opposites. It is said that the primary sexual organ is the brain, and so Mercury is certainly the ultimate architect of all fantasies and their structure, whereas the other planets just give impetus and design direction. The ultimate experience of sexuality, however, is the wash-away of the individual personality in the ultimate orgasm (which ideally, after much practice, should be the raising of the kundalini). Hence the French term *la petite mort* for the orgasm. Mercury builds, Pluto washes away—kind of like building a sand castle that goes off on the next big wave. On a large scale, one might envision one's life as the ultimate fantasy, and death as the final orgasm. People with dominant outer planets, for better or for worse, often see it just that way.

Thus, as far as sexual expression goes, the horoscope represents the varied interplay between these male and female aspects in easy or harsh aspect, colored by the signs and manifested in the houses. Sun square Pluto, for instance, gives a great subconscious fear of death to the primary male energy (whether it be a male or female nativity), which results in a need *for control to stave off destruction*—a difficult pairing, indeed, and one with a dark but not very specific fantasy life. Mercury conjunct Neptune gives lots of imagination, though not necessarily the will or ability to make it reality.

Throughout, the usual rules may be followed, such as when a difficult aspect is present, looking to a supportive one to channel the blocked energies—e.g., with a Mars square Venus (opportunity and desire don't seem to coincide), look to a supportive aspect to either planet for a solution. Pretty standard stuff.

One might also look for the types of signatures that make people fantasize and suggest a fertile imagination, sexual or otherwise. Here, Mercury is of course critical, as it provides the structure for anything that comes to mind. A Mercury in the 12th House stressed by Saturn may eliminate fantasy (and even dreams) entirely. A well-posited Mercury trine the Moon can make for a flow of fantasy and dreams. Where outer planets are absent in the pattern, the fantasies will run toward the "normal" or mundane. *Where outer planets are involved, the more unusual, both in a positive and negative sense, fantasies will be,* as they are literally more "advanced," whatever path they are on, even when simply channelled elsewhere.

The nature of the aspect also has a story to tell, as a quintile (72°) brings great creativity and timing to quickly turn fantasy into reality, whereas a septile may take much longer to implement, as it requires that everything be in place before anything can begin. Noniles (40°) are merry and jocular, whereas 11ths (32°44′) are hostile and frustrated. The 13th, my favorite (27°42′), is eccentric and unusual—one step beyond normality, often just for the sake of it, and into unknown territory—sometimes offering the greatest rewards or the greatest dangers, the lot of all explorers.

And last, but certainly not least, is the manifestation (or lack of it) of sexual fantasy *between partners* in real life. This is often depicted by the composite chart which, if it is a tangle of conflicts, may show fantasies at cross-purposes, which either get manifested to the distress of both or are entirely repressed at the equal cost of frustration. If the composite is favorable, on the other hand, difficulties at the individual level may find solution in the partnership, and the frustrated fantasies of each may be able to open up and bear fruit in the company of the other.

If there is one thing that is easy to forget about fantasy, it is that it is *not* reality. When we speak of making fantasy into reality, we describe an ongoing, cyclical process, whether it is sexual or applies in any other aspect of life. "Is that all there is to it?" is so often the response to the fulfilled dream, whether it is a sexual scenario finally played out or success in career finally attained. Your dreams precede you and always will, so it is important to savor what you have, as well as what you would like to have, or else fantasy becomes a prison of ever-disappointed expectation. Appreciate the present, but dream on and move on—*and so the present will move with you.*

In the real world—in which the individual and natal horoscope function—there is another element which drives fantasy, and that is *deprivation.* In this we come a bit closer to our original title, which is sexual imagination and fantasy as escape valve. The less we have of what we would like, the more we dream about it and model it in our minds. Those fortunate enough to be born with Venus conjunct Mars, unless it is extremely stressed, can be active sexually any time and any way they want, so they don't tend to have rich fantasy lives. Those who can't (say Venus conjunct Saturn), are likely to spend a lot more time fantasizing about what they would like to do and with whom they would like to do it. It has been a common theme in popular psychology that fantasy is a healthy way to take up the sexual energies that can't be released in real life, and the last 20 years has seen a virtual subset of the publishing industry devoted to exploring sexual fantasy and its various possibilities, from simple quiet dreaming to phone and computer network sex. The idea is that it's harmless and is, indeed, an "escape valve" for sexual frustration.

But is it? Both right-wing fundamentalist Christian groups and radical feminists have stated that the wrong kind of fantasy (especially the pornography which expresses it) simply breeds and foments sex crimes and wrong thinking about women and sex. Is there anything to this? There may be, but not necessarily on the level at which these folks express it.

To explore these issues further, I recently organized a forum on the subject of this article at an astrological retreat near the lovely mountain town of Polanica, in Poland. Panelists included astrologers from Poland and Denmark, who had a lot to say on the subject (more than there is room for here), as did the audience. They had a more spiritual and esoteric view of the issues, and quickly dispensed with the technical end and went directly to grappling with the sometimes contradictory spiritual implications of the subject, though not without a ready sense of humor. Here follow highlights of the lovely, sunny morning of Monday, July 5, 1993.

Dramatis Personae:

Margot Graham—Sociologist and philosopher at Warsaw University. Astrologer for over fifteen years and acknowledged leader of the Warsaw astrological community.

Toben Hansen—Danish psychotherapist and esoteric astrologer, based in Copenhagen.

Andrias Dahlmann—Tai Chi teacher, researcher into the psychology of dreams, New Age festival organizer in Copenhagen, Denmark.

Majka Wasislewska—Warsaw astrologer, abstract painter, and interior designer.

Mieczyslaw Zietek—Warsaw horticulturalist, politician, astrological computer program designer, 15 years with the Psychotronic Society.

John Townley, moderator—American astrological author, musician, historian.

JT: Well, I guess we could probably start off just trying to think of what fantasy is as opposed to reality, where this might be especially found in a horoscope, and what it might be subject to as time goes by. Some people report, for instance, having no fantasies at all while others *live* in a fantasy world. Some people go from living in a fantasy world to not thinking about it at all from time to time. So I throw it open to the panel, what kind of person, astrologically speaking, would have a rich fantasy life?

AD: One with many planets in water, and have the ability to imagine pictures.

MG: I think Neptune is very important to fantasy, all the more since Neptune is thought to be the higher octave of Venus. So if we have a person who is not very well-developed, if we have Venus ruling his emotional life, we can say that with further spiritual growth or development, *Neptune seems to replace Venus in a way*. So Venus is then left to other things, while fantasy in general and the transformation of erotic fantasies will be ruled by Neptune, if this role is taken over by Neptune, and this can be even devoid of physical associations. It could be just an interest in art or in music, in mysticism. There could be a sublimation of all these erotic needs, desires, interests. So Venus and Neptune are very important—I think even more important than Mars, because Mars only personifies our drive on a purely physical level.

Venus is emotions, and Neptune as a higher octave is able to idealize, to sublimate all these things and make it possible to leave these things without the need to have them realized on the physical plane. This is especially true of people who are in the process of developing spiritually. Of course, if somebody is not trying to develop spiritually, it would have a totally different effect. It could have a negative effect giving these people great illusions and an inclination to cheat, to lead people astray, to be very dishonest.

JT: Hold that thought. Torben, any thoughts?

TH: Yes. To supplement what was already said, I think I'll touch upon the way to distinguish a little between men and women who are entering the world of spiritual development. I agree completely with Margot on that aspect of the connection between Venus and Neptune. Venus is more or less the creative thought process with the mind and Neptune the more all-inclusive love aspect which might help us transform our fantasies. That is a way of realizing them. It depends on if you want—and now I speak in a tantric, psychological way—really to transmute or sublimate these energies, which is the vertical process of using the energy, or if you want to express the energy via some kind of thoughts, words, or actions, which is the more horizontal way of doing it.

Really experienced tantric psychologists in Denmark distinguish between men and women. The female energy system is more round and able to carry on and sublimate the energy. It's a solar-plexus focus and heart connection. The male energy is more focused within the hara chakra and the physical center at the base of the spine. Venus here relates more to an active way of using this energy. It takes the active role, in fact, in the beginning of the spiritual development, but later on, both sexes become able to integrate what we call their anima or animus.

Let me give you an example to make it more simple. When every man here is able to act more like a woman or perhaps take many different female roles into his life, then his heart will awaken, so it's not only head and hara and base of spine chakra, and the other way around for the woman. For the woman, the sexual aspect as related to fantasy is dependent upon a more active way, a more masculine way of behaving. Fantasy might be the first level, visualization, creative thinking and then going on to direct action within the sexual act. So here comes the connection again between head and body—for women it's very important to put the body into things, to act it out. So I hope this gives that very important psychological distinction between the processes of man and woman.

JT: Well, I guess in a sort of very grossly American way that's saying that men should feel it a little bit more and women should do it a little bit more. Something we all devoutly hope! Mieczyslaw, what do you have to contribute to this?

MZ: Everything that has been said so far has been theoretical, and not necessarily practical. When you're younger, it's easier to talk about practical aspects. One is more eager to. From a theoretical side, I haven't really thought about the roles of man or woman. I was more interested to know how it is in the chart,how these things look in people who are interested in their own sex, how it is related to their chart.

JT: That's fine. Majka, on the subject?

MW: As far as fantasy and astrology are concerned, I think I would choose Mars as a starting point in all this and look at its position and how it is aspected, how it is related to water signs and all the rest in the chart. Its connection to the whole is very important, in my opinion. Also, its relationship to the 8th House: if there is a Neptunian, watery 8th House, then in my opinion it might have its potential in this area. So depending on how it is connected with the rest, we might get these creative fantasies which could create beautiful connections between the head and the rest of the body, the sky, and the earth; or with afflictions, it could be something destructive which would be, you know, going round inside there [confused], and you won't know what's going on.

JT: Well, I would agree very much with Majka about the Mars aspect, for practical and physiological reasons. Mars is directly associated with testosterone, which is the main hormone associated with physical sexual arousal in both men and women, and I think the levels of that are extremely important in determining whether a fantasy by itself becomes a sexual fantasy, or just drifts off into thinking about beautiful things in the woods or some such. Especially important are its particular aspects to Mercury and to Pluto, I think, where Pluto, of course, is another aspect of sexuality, a very *forceful* aspect of sexuality. I think Torben has something to say about that.

TH: I think that gives us a very good way to connect those two dimensions, because I see Pluto/Mars representing the personality level, both of them related to Venus. But then in the process of transforming/transmuting the sexuality in the latest stages of spiritual development, *there* Neptune comes in and represents the higher self, the soul, which is kind of like the whale that swallows the personality. And Uranus is important here too: Uranus' esoteric astrological teachings represent the higher chakra and can be transferred also to the heart and even the chakra of the brow.

To make this more concrete, I think it would be good to relate it to our own experience—and I wouldn't talk about this if I hadn't been through this process. Now remember, I speak from the more or less male point of view, but I've been working as a psychotherapist also with a woman going through these same transformations.

Taking my own experience first, I have a very strong sexuality and also a very strong imagination; I was very aware of this during my spiritual development. Take, for instance, my sexual activities in connection with my masturbation fantasies. There I can see very much this Pluto/Mars thing reflected, always combined with Venus; but later on, in the process of transforming and creating higher fantasies, sublimating, it was different.

For example, I've had some experience of years of celibacy where I could follow very closely how hard it was to carry all that sexual energy and use it in a constructive way. You will probably experience a great inner pressure, which might lead you to all kinds of strange actions and fantasies, and running away from yourself when feeling strong attraction to somebody—but it is in fact an important step for the yogi to try and press the energy through the system and see what comes out of it; in other words, to raise the kundalini. But I can say from my experience that this will only be properly done when you have experienced *enough normal sexual life* and maybe have reached a kind of emptiness, a feeling that this doesn't really give me enough.

JT: I would reply very quickly to that—particularly addressing Pluto/Mars and the idea of forcing, as hatha yoga does, the kundalini. There is within sexuality, both in fantasy, and if you're very careful, in reality, a kind of a left-hand path, which for those who are risk-takers involves all kinds of sexuality which go to the extreme. In a horoscope, people who are more likely to do this would have hard aspects from the *outer* planets to Mars and Venus. We're talking about practices which include sadomasochism, but also many others that physically and emotionally push those involved to the limits of tolerance. This type of sex has recently been much trivialized by the likes of Madonna, and now that it is out in the open eases the tremendous fear we had of it before. But it nevertheless is an area which has been around and in action for many thousands of years.

Pushing yourself physically and sexually to an extreme, like the flagellants of the Middle Ages, at the least induces a trance-like state and certainly an altered level of consciousness. In the ideal application, it actually kicks the kundalini into action. The danger of it is, of course, that if you're not ready for that and the kundalini ascends on slightly the wrong path, then you could be in some serious physical and psychological trouble. But depending on your personal inclination, it's a trade-off between years of meditation and months of action. Not recommended for everybody. However, people should be aware that *a large percentage of fantasies recorded by psychologists have a very strong element of force within them* which reflects in most people, symbolically speaking I guess, *the pressure of the kundalini sitting down at the bottom chakra pushing like mad trying to get up.* Freud's original ideas very much reflect that concept, although he was probably unaware of the concept of the kundalini.

MG: So these psychiatrists, they have that quality in themselves?

JT: No doubt, but I was simply outlining the types of fantasies people have. The element of force is quite strong in both men and women, stronger in men naturally. But maybe we should direct ourselves to some of the implications, not just the analysis of the thing itself.

There are two questions I would like to bring up that perhaps might not be so frequently asked in America, but would certainly be asked here, where I think the attitude, if not practice, towards sexuality is a bit more advanced than in the United States. The first is fairly obvious and that comes from viewing fantasy as a kind of visualization. Now, from way back in the United States, to cite a very physical and commercial example, in the books of Andrew Carnegie and in various other more new age teachings, *visualization is the way to make something come true.* If you believe a visualization, that a fantasy is something that actually has the power of making something come true, *do you not at the point begin to have social responsibility for what you are fantasizing.* This I think goes to the heart of the issue, though no one has said this openly. This is why many people are against pornography, because they believe it to be the stimulus to fantasies *that will come true* and they either don't like the specific content of the pornography or fantasy or they would just as soon have sex eliminated totally. *Is there a responsibility? Should you censor your fantasies?* Andreas has something to say here.

AD: After having been in a relationship for seven years, I was obsessed, a slave to this woman. After the relationship, I decided to be on my own. While getting into esoteric things, I visualized that I was together with this old girlfriend. I visualized I was together with her while I was masturbating and I started wondering if *this energy could reach her.* I had read that those pictures that you visualize stay in your aura in the room but I felt that it was wrong somehow. Also, the energy disappeared and I fell asleep, so I presume it traveled elsewhere. Still, I couldn't repress my loss and that I wanted to have physical contact, but now instead of visualizing I think nice thoughts or do some action to redirect the energy.

MG: For twelve years now, I have been intensely interested in Theosophy and esoteric teachings, and to me it's clear that *thoughts act like objects* and, as we are responsible for our needs and for our words, we are responsible also for our thoughts. These thought forms are like radio waves that flow and can be intercepted. So thinking is the same as action on a different level, on a different, less physical, level of action. So all yoga recommends learning to control one's thinking—so for me, what you've said is absolutely clear.

JT: But it's not obvious to a lot of other people.

MG: Nevertheless, thinking *is* like action. We are responsible for our thoughts. Our thoughts are like waves. Clairvoyants, people who see the aura, see the thought-forms physically because they are subtle matter, matter which the machines, the apparatus, the equipment that we have invented so far is unable to register, although slowly science is beginning to learn to register what all sensitive clairvoyant people see very easiy. So thinking and fantasies and even wishes and uncontrolled thoughts *may be harmful.* It's good to remember that.

It's not easy in the beginning to control one's thinking and to know what should be thought. We can not tell somebody from without, don't do this, don't think in this way, because that would be nineteenth-century Victorian suppression of the interest in sexuality, and thus a limitation. It must come from within. So what Torben said is appropriate, that one should go cover the *entire* path of life—who knows what should be discarded, at which level we are working. Because the fully developed person is one who has all the chakras developed, if we use this terminology, and we can say he's a full human being, so this example of these flagellants that you mention is a negative one, because they were *suppressing* their desires. They wanted to live in an ideal world. But one covers it all if one develops the whole way.

For instance, in India it is thought that until one reaches 21 years of age one develops physically as a person, from 20-40 one has to set up a family and have children, and then the next 20 years, until 60, one should make provisions for the children and give them some security. When he/she has done that, at around 60 he should take his walking stick and with a begging bowl, a large bowl, go away and live for purely spiritual purposes. One cannot impose on young people, tell them to absolutely abstain from interest in sex, because that's very bad. It's like in Pandora's box: you lock energy in it, so every time there is some slip, there's no full control and this demon can jump out of the box, so it's good to go through the full development. *Everything is necessary at any specific stage of development.* We cannot say that the higher chakras are better than lower chakras because for these higher chakras to develop fully, first the lower chakras have to be developed fully.

JT: By that plan, I think I've probably reached about the age of 18. Further comments! Malgosia has a question.

Malgosia Szyszkowska (from audience): I think that I would recommend that everybody have all types of fantasies and not to be afraid of it or think of it as something that should be or shouldn't be done. This picture that appears to us as fantasy shows us what we have inside of us so, if we try to protect ourselves against it, *we know nothing about ourselves.* It is not that our fantasy is realized immediately—that I want that guy and I immediately get him. I have to want that and pursue it: *I have to feed my fantasy additionally, and that depends on my will*—I create this picture, then this picture starts living when I give my energy to it. But I can say "No, thank you very much. I have this picture, but no thanks," and then nothing will happen. That person is free, he can observe himself within, but he doesn't have to follow after each of his pictures, each of the visualizations that he creates.

MW: She's saying that we should fantasize on the loose and quietly, because this is the only way for us to get to know ourselves, find ourselves again, and that any censorship is like a break, it makes us distance ourselves from ourselves. So thanks to these observations, we are later able to do something with it, but that's a separate thing. First we have to have this brief fantasy to begin with.

JT: Well, it's interesting to me that we have two seemingly, but not necessarily, opposite views. One has been the current one in the material world, if I can say that, where it is believed fantasy would be a way of getting to know yourself better. On the other hand, if fantasies are thought-forms, as Theosophy believes, suppose in my fantasies late at night I choose for Majka to appear in my dreams while physically she doesn't want anything to do with me. Yet, she doesn't have any control over it, because it's my fantasy—am I an astral rapist? How do we reconcile these two opinions?

TH: As far as I can see, they are *not opposites*, but they may represent *different stages of consciousness*. Scientifically speaking, in the first stage of our consciousness, after having taken on incarnation as souls, we represent the consciousness of polarity and from that state of consciousness we develop into the next state of consciousness which is the state of supplementerism, where we supply each other, like yin/yang. Here is what the Tibetans call the Chi-kai psychology, the psychology of dynamics starts, and this is our way to an even higher state expressed as affinity/unity.

Here we might say that the general man or woman would benefit from using *all kinds of imagination*, mirroring themselves in the outer world, in the concrete reality. Then later on comes the realization of what this mental process, those emotions and actions, have built up; what we call karma of violence or, of course, the positive aspect of karma, those energies which come back as blessings because you did something good. Here we can include the teachings of Jesus when he was enlightened by the Christ: he reformed the Jewish teachings, and this for the Jew in every one of us, the Jew representing the personality, to become more like the Christ, who is the sole principal for all of us. *When we reproduce thought forms, they determine our actions.* So the positive thinker always produces thought forms knowing that they will materialize. You throw that thought form out of your own space into the aura of someone else.

JT: So, the answer to this question would appear to be that yes, that in some esoteric fashion, I am indeed a serial rapist, and so are many of us.

TH: Yes, and here I want to give a more inclusive Buddhist version of this, because Christianity has told us *not* to do this! But Buddha was more wise. He taught us *the consequences* of this process and then he told us to do as we like, *but to take those consequences*—and he even gave us techniques to get in control of those energies, and that is primarily the esoteric, tantric Buddhist teachings of today. There are people who work with dreams, polarization, meditation, exercises, visualizations, psychodrama and also the Jungian way of using combined Gestalt technique and archetypical integration.

MG: I am absolutely in accord with Torben, and I would like to illustrate. Let's imagine that each of us is like a TV transmitter station, so each of us sends out a personal program, and it's always possible that somebody will intercept the program and receive it. For instance, in the case of drastic films with scenes with sex or violence, as a rule there is a concern in normal television broadcasting not to have them watched by children, or by teenagers. Sometimes, for this reason they are shown after 10 P.M. It is the same with the "programs" that *we* transmit, so it's our responsibility. Additionally, the present bad state the world is in is *the consequence of the bad state of people.*

It is said that that energy from higher planes is descending to lower planes in order to improve the condition the world is in. If we change the thinking, we should change the consciousness—if, for instance, we have more people thinking in a constructive, positive way they will be sending good thoughts, good wishes, and their television program, so to speak, will be full of good, of love, of calm, serenity. This will become precipitated to the lower planes which will receive this energy, and it will then manifest itself on the physical plane. It is the hope that, in this way, the New Age, the Aquarian Age, will start on earth. Because absolutely nobody can do this work for us; we must do it ourselves.

People have a great responsibility for what is happening on earth because, as we are developing our higher minds, we are able to receive all kinds of inspiration from spiritual levels and transmute this energy to bring it down to lower planes, to the world of other life forms which are less developed—say, to animals, to plants, minerals. So the New Age can only begin by the change in consciousness, by good positive thinking. And this is in all spheres. This is like a physical law, so it's not wishful thinking only; it's the principle on which the world functions. It applies to everything.

JT: Before we wrap this up, I would like to get back to the practical here. Like Mieczyslaw, I tend to favor something you can immediately take action on. Everybody here seems to agree that when you throw these thoughts out, they hit people. I want to know how do the likes of Majka and Malgosia protect themselves from folks like me? Psychic self-defense is what we're talking about. Somebody give me a couple of immediately practical things of how you do it.

MW: But everyone might not necessarily *want* to protect themselves! The thoughts might be very nice, if they're not too aggressive!

JT: But what about when they *do* want to protect themselves? I hope you are all flinging fantasy-thoughts at me like mad. Not all of you may feel the same way in reverse, however.

Irena Haszczynska (from the audience): Coming back to what Margot says, she said that there is time in life for everything, but there are situations when, in a way, we overlook our time and then maybe in all spheres of life, if we're talking about sex and sexual fantasy and one is in a situation of unfulfillment, one has missed one's time or something. Should we mobilize all our forces to make up for this loss, if it's possible and there are opportunities for it? Am I supposed to keep in my mind all the time that time flies, that my time has gone by, that it's over?

JT: Your time is never over.

IH: Or maybe acclimate myself; but the older I get, the younger I get in every way, so maybe there is *still* time for me.

IH: And then coming back to this positive thinking. Thoughts flow away and they come back, so is this Tao philosophy that this Gestalt method be responsible for thoughts, for words, for yourself? Take the moment as it is. Do not analyze. Do not think, *but experience*. So how can we reconcile it all, because these are contradictions that each of us comes up against; and it is the same with fantasy. We can have good fantasies and bad fantasies. We see how much violence there is in the world, and all the people who have those dark emotions and who liberate them inside. But perhaps their alter ego may restrict them in some way—yet they do throw these fantasies out, though fantasies can be good or bad. It depends on what imagination people have. *It's very difficult to be responsible for one's thoughts.*

MW: But one *must* fantasize in order to learn about one's self.

Audience member: Margot spoke about controlling one's thinking; that it is very important and very wise. I'm a Catholic, but in this case I like the Buddhist position in this. It's more difficult, because it's much harder to do something and then accept the consequences of your deeds than just to stop, refrain from doing anything because it's forbidden. We talked about men's fantasies, they have this one real concrete woman and she causes men to fantasize about her. In the young girl, these fantasies are very often connected not with one concrete male. Rather, they are very broad, symbolic.

JT: But last, and definitely least, you cannot do a television program like this in America if you were talking about sexuality, and particularly talking about violent sexuality, without giving advice to young women whether they should carry mace or stun guns or learn karate. Is there (I know there is), perhaps a quick way you could describe, an easy psychic or *spiritual* method to protect yourself. Put yourself in a cocoon of light, something like that. Back to the practical here.

From audience: You just have to try to be in harmony. You shouldn't try to protect yourself from thinking.

JT: OK, that's one method. Another method?

TH: I stick to that method of using all the means presented here.

TH: You see, as far as I can see, it would be wise really to know one's self. Know one's limits, the weak aspects of one's self, and strengthen them. For one woman, it might be very valuable to learn feminist self-defense, not necessarily violent, but to integrate her masculine aspect—being able to use her voice, showing bodily force and power, using courage. It can be used in many other connections and that's a good thing, too, but that's only one thing.

The other one, which is recommended by many, is that of using visualization techniques of either an egg or cocoon, maybe calling for spiritual guides, archangels, or using the pentagram, the blue pentagram in your aura, but this is as far as my teachers go. This is only one step, because as you reach your higher state of consciousness you will always be able to absorb the energy from others and then transform that into something positive when anybody throws any thought forms toward you. Don't think you are able to do that yet already, but it might be possible. What Christ says, in his very new teachings, given by Alice Bailey and the Tibetan disciples, which are really both the teachings of Buddha and a renewed reformation of the Christian teachings, is that *the greatest protection is love,* to expand your radiation through the heart of the seven rays. Understanding and love. This will protect you.

JT: This is getting down to the nitty gritty. I have two more comments that are dying to be made here.

AD: You talk about knowing yourself all the time, so you know what you want, and you are sending the signals out consciously. You are saying that resistance makes persistence; if you suppress something it comes to the fore, so if you're open to anyone's sexual fantasy, if they get to you, it's your fault. Perhaps it's more for women; how do they dress, *physical, physical.* Do you women want to be a fantasy object or not? (MS: Sometimes yes, sometimes no.) (MW: It's more important how we undress—it's best to be undressed!)

MG: There is a science of victimology, and it is said that the victim attracts her/its oppressor. Very often there are these people who are liable to be raped, who act in a provocative way. I wanted to say about dressing, this is a great problem of our culture because the entire fashion production, the best couturieres, the best artists, they all exert themselves to dress women in the most attractive way. So this works against what we're talking about.

Of course, in the past, women felt that they were sex objects, only body, only this outer shell. Now they have revolted, rebelled, and they have found their own role to play, but fashion nevertheless is baring the breast, the buttocks, the legs so there is this contradiction. But here we can look for help in what is happening in primitive cultures. For instance, for the Blacks in parts of Africa where it's very hot and everybody runs around naked, *men don't react at all* when they see an undressed woman. They only start, their lust is awakened, when they see a woman who is covered!

JT: This is an argument for global warming, folks!

MG: But then the same conclusion comes from married life. So I think that at present when women walk around more undressed than 100 years ago, men have fewer fantasies. That's bad. The man doesn't have to try to guess what her calf is like, or her shoulder or arm, because it's all on display. So that's one thing.

And the other thing is this realization of karma. The fact that certain people become the victims of rape may perhaps be necessary for these victims to learn the results of their own earlier, perhaps violent deeds, maybe very similar actions in previous incarnations. So it is reasonable that the victim and the person who is her oppressor have this karmic relationship between them.

So this is again a Buddhist approach here: that there is no good, no evil on a higher level, but *everything is necessary for evolution*; we have to learn the consequences of evil. I value very much Ole Nidal's teachings—he is also a Danish fellow from Copenhagen who says that if on the level N something is evil or bad, perhaps on a level N+1 it is necessary and good. So in fact, we cannot really divide things into good and bad. *Everything depends on the viewpoint*, on the perspective. So everything can be good if we are open and ready to develop, to draw conclusions, to learn and be ready to change so that we don't enter the river twice, the same river, to repeat our mistakes. So everything is necessary and needed. Everything can serve good.

Going Forward

Although our Polish forum on fantasy and sexuality explored potential aspects of the subject that might not have been brought up elsewhere, it also ended with a dichotomy of opinion that requires further exploration to resolve. The solution may be simply to move to a higher level of approach, as Torben Hansen suggested, in order to transcend the apparent conflict.

At the end, the question remained: is sexual fantasy a creative and even desirable escape route that allows us both to release sexual tension and explore the possibilities of our sexuality by intellectual modeling, or is it a potentially dangerous fountain of thought forms that may damage oneself or victimize others at some kind of astral level? Modern psychology tends to espouse the former opinion (intellectual modeling), while both traditional and New Age Western spiritual opinion tends to promote the later (potential hurt). Furthermore, how does astrology fit into all of this, and can it be of any help in understanding the matter?

It is often the case that when issues polarize, as in this case, both sides are trying to prop up an intellectual illusion. What really needs to be done is to stand back and find a larger view that includes the essential elements of both, but which transcends their differences *and thereby unites them*. That is the essence of how new paradigms, scientific or otherwise, develop. Here, this may be done, first, by undercutting some of the artificially-installed props.

That is easy to do in the case of the spiritual side, since further exploration of theosophical work on thought forms makes the previous opinions expressed seem a bit simplistic and alarmist. In order to do anyone serious astral harm with thought projection, you must be *very* focused and send your astral missiles with great force and accuracy to their targets. That takes considerable spiritual training and skill. Unlike the story of the sorcerer's apprentice, you don't accidentally pull the trigger on an astral howitzer by saying the wrong spell (or having the wrong fantasy) and thereby wind up blowing up your neighbor. In the real world of spiritual technology (not an oxymoron, honest), *an unskilled magician is not a magician at all*. This is particularly the case in using sexual fantasy for experimental modeling and self-exploration, since anyone doing that is by definition *not* focused, and is trying to become so.

The worst effect most persons' fantasies are likely to produce is some local astral pollution—although if enough people are doing that, the air up there could get hard to breathe, which is a well-taken part of Margot Graham's point. If there *is* a danger here, it might more likely be suffocating in one's own smoke-filled room, so to speak. Yet, as Andreas pointed out, after masturbatory orgasm, the spiritual smoke dissipates and you can go to sleep.

On the other hand, someone with highly-developed spiritual skills and evil intent can indeed rain down misfortune on others from the astral plane. I have seen it happen, and it is something you need some serious protective skills to deflect. Nevertheless, it is a relative rarity (acquiring spiritual skills tends to shift the individual away from intentional hostility), and it effectively falls entirely outside the realm of this discussion, which is the usefulness (or lack of it) of sexual fantasy in general.

The political and traditional religious versions of this subject run in parallel; if you think of this sort of stuff, you might go and do it, God forbid. Rather than summoning up the image of thought-forms, this approach suggests that *thought causes action* and those who imagine sexual acts of whatever kind are more likely to commit them. Although cosmetically different than the so-called spiritual argument, this approach also places sexuality *firmly in the area of the mind,* almost as if sex would never happen if no one told you about it (this goes back to the Adam and Eve myth, among others). Yet, it is also easy to dismiss much of this view as imaginary, since more sexually open and permissive cultures such as Holland or Sweden tend to have many fewer problems with sexuality than do more restrictive cultures like Japan, or those in transition, such as the United States. Nevertheless, it is quite true that if you don't ever even think about it, you're less likely to do it!

The psychological side of the argument also has some vulnerable props, subject to removal in the same fashion, i.e., by exploring in greater depth what is known about *the psychological realities of sexual fantasy.* The presumption has been made, as is often done at the level of popular psychology, that *fantasies can somehow resolve sexual problems,* and by indulging in them you may better understand yourself and know how to behave when it comes to doing the real thing. It is as if you can pick and choose, based on self-created fantasy, what you're really going to like doing in the real world when you get the chance. It is as if you can try them all out in your mind and then say "No thank you" or "I'll try that," to the reality version when it presents itself.

A concrete example comes to mind of a female client of mine who had often fantasized herself being gang-raped (the ultimate "fantasy" for females, if you believe neo-feminist sexual philosopher Camille Paglia). When she finally rounded up eight men to live it out with, she discovered that they were not all perfectly in tune with her fantasy of how it should proceed. (How could they be?) That, combined with the sheer physical arduousness of the event (something usually overlooked in fantasy), turned the occasion into a traumatic nightmare that ruined both sex and fantasy for her afterward.

The results of turning fantasy into reality don't have to be disappointing because they are disastrous. They can be disappointing because they are just plain boring. The very self-consciousness and self-control necessary to carry it off, as well as the distraction of the inevitable unanticipated impedimentary details, as often as not make the participants wonder what they ever thought would be so good about this anyway. So you managed to bring it off safely and without a hitch—so what?

The prevalence of this kind of experience makes it necessary to rethink the concept of fantasy *as something of which we are in charge*, something we can willfully pursue and explore, and thus get a better understanding of ourselves and a better grip on our psyches. In the last few decades, it was fashionable in psychology circles to say that the primary human sex organ is the brain, and therefore if we get hold of our sexual concepts, notions, and fantasies, we've got it all in the bag. Along with this theory went the idea that, for instance, most cases of impotence and sexual dysfunction were of psychological origin, and therapy of the sort Masters and Johnson pioneered during the 1970s would be the answer to most sexual problems.

Recently, however, the preponderance of medical opinion on the subject has made a serious reversal, thanks to better understanding of complex hormonal processes, and it is now believed that most impotence and sexual dysfunction are of *physiological* origin and are treatable on a somatic level, rather than a psychological one. Whereas we had previously put Mercury in charge of the whole subject, quite contrary to traditional astrological feeling, now it is beginning to be recognized that sexuality is part of a *whole-body process* that includes the mind, but is not restricted to it, or necessarily ruled by it.

Thus, when we think of fantasy, whether deeply repressed or openly explored, as something we can (or should) control and utilize for our own ends, perhaps we are looking at an illusion. Perhaps we are not looking here at the mainstream of human sexuality, but *at an ancillary result of something deeper going on inside.*

Further indications that this might be the case come from the fact that fantasies tend *to recur and repeat themselves,* as if they are trying to lead somewhere, but never quite get there, no matter how much you manipulate them. When you do successfully live them out, they simply take new forms and lead you further along the path to who knows where. It is as if there is something *deeper you are looking for,* but somehow can not reach.

Dr. John Money, probably the world's leading theoretician in sexual psychology, paints just this picture throughout his many works on paraphilia, which is sexual fantasy carried to its extreme, where specific fetishes and other than "normal" expressions of sexuality become essential for any sexual satisfaction at all. He traces these to the construction of "lovemaps" during middle childhood, where the child senses from external (mostly adult) input that sexuality is essentially taboo and thus becomes blocked from natural expression of it. *However, because the pressure for expression remains, the child builds an alternate set of rules* that allows sexuality to find an outlet while circumventing the official taboos, thus allowing a circumspect "triumph" over the "tragedy" of repression.

That the repressive adult world actually respects and encourages such unnecessary and bizarre maneuvers is pointed up by laws that allow depiction of all sorts of bondage, whipping, and other "deviant" behavior, but forbid the portrayal of ordinary genital penetration. How clear a message! That S/M should be the most common of these expressions is even more logical, once this premise is accepted, as when you are tied up and helpless, *you no longer have control of, or blame for, what you are doing—and you're getting punished for it, to boot!*

This, logically, is where astrology comes into the picture, as if there is one thing a horoscope is good for, it is for spotting these sort of *energy blockages*. Hard aspects, and especially conjunctions of the Sun, Moon, and inner planets to Saturn and the outer planets are most typical of the syndrome. When these occur, it is often an indication that sexuality is blocked from easy, "normal" expression and *must find another channel of expression,* sometimes in paraphilia or fantasy alone, sometimes through sublimation into totally non-sexual areas such as work, family, or religion.

Saturn conjunct Venus, for instance, holds down and frustrates desire, either through lack of opportunity for expression or negative sexual experience, *thus raising the level of desire while thwarting it at the same time.* The result? Often a storm of fantasies that for the moment serve to release the pressure, without addressing the cause. Like Andreas said, you can go to sleep—but it comes back the next day. Whether the blockage is external (simple unavailability for the exchange of energies between two persons that makes up the essence of sexual expression), or internal (ingrained inhibitions preventing full expression when there is opportunity for it), the result can be similar: a rich fantasy life which becomes a complex and variegated substitute for an otherwise simple and desirable reality.

A good simile might be that of a rushing rapids, where the natural flow of a river has been blocked. The water gets through eventually, but in the process creates a miasma of rainbow-producing spray, a colorful mist of illusion surrounding its troublesome course. Not until the rocks are finally worn away, which does occur in time (rivers have a lot more of it than we do), does the course run true and peacefully again.

Since we don't have eons of time to spend on restoring our balance (well, perhaps we do in a cosmic sense, but not in one lifetime), what can be done to recognize and correct the situation? Here we may very much come back to what Torben Hansen was advising about working on better expression of all the energy centers in the body. Men more often have lots of expression of all of the energy centers in the body. Men more often have lots of expression in the lower two, but get blocked at the heart, which they need consciously to develop. Women tend to have plenty of heart and emotion, but turn off the lower two. Thus, neither gender is whole, but one has the potential of helping the other become restored to balance.

The horoscope can be of use in spotting where the blockages lie (Pluto-Sun troubles, for instance likely concern the heart chakra, as fear and power are associated with the inability to open the heart), directly according to planetary associations with the different centers. (See chakra discussion and diagram later in this chapter.)

Fantasy falls properly into the picture, then, not as an end in itself or even a major tool of change, but as an accompaniment to and symptom of deeper, ongoing sexual evolution. The necessary Mercury element (which provides the details) can be a significant factor in providing partners with something specific to do and with which to embellish their sexual communication, but the caution is to avoid letting the fantasy become an end in itself, the ultimate expression of which is paraphilia, which isolates rather than unites a person with the inner process of sexuality.

In the end, sexual fantasy may be seen as a two-edged sword. It can be used effectively for modeling potential experience, but it cannot always predict the actual results (as my hapless client discovered). It can provide endlessly different forms of amusement, but it can also distract from focusing on the real work that needs to be done inside. Total lack of it can leave you without a real-life path to follow, while too much of it can totally obscure your vision of the path you need to establish. Certainly repression of it, no matter how bizarre or politically or morally incorrect it may seem, brings you to a dead halt, because you are refusing to acknowledge the symptoms of a deeper and inexorable need. Astrological analysis may help us get a better fix on our fantasies, just as our fantasies may suggest to us the nature of the sexual pressures that spawn them, but only a union of all the physical, emotional, and intellectual expressions of our minds and bodies will ultimately serve to get us where we want to be.

Fantasy, like its ruler Neptune, is what is imagined but can not be, an evergreen promise and hope, but *always* in reality different than expected. Ultimately, clear and definitive action in the real physical world (Uranus) is the resolving factor, and imagination and contemplation are its servants. In the realm of sexuality, perhaps this may be a lesson of the current watershed (in so many ways) Uranus/Neptune conjunction. What-is determines what-might-be, and what-might-be, what-can and will-be, and on . . .

So upon final inspection, we step up to the Buddhist point of view as suggested in our forum: each of us has a path, sexual and otherwise, to follow, and for each of us it is different. We can not force it along, or stop it. Nor can we take a short cut by adopting someone else's path. No matter what direction it leads us, it is ours, and we must live it, love it, and rejoice in it. How ever it presents itself along the way, whether seemingly good or bad, real or illusion, we must go to the heart of the fire, i.e., embrace it and take responsibility for it as we grow. *It* is us, just as *we* are.

Harmonic Aspects

All astrologers are familiar with the traditional Ptolomaic aspects (conjunction, sextile, square, trine, opposition) and usually the more recently used semi-sextile and quincunx. I have regularly used aspects which come from dividing the circle into 5ths, 7ths, 9ths, 11ths, and 13ths, often called "harmonic" aspects. John Addey's pioneering work on harmonic charts during the 1970s brought these aspects into greater usage. Exactly what they mean and how important they are is still a matter to be decided, even among those who use these aspects regularly, so here is my personal approach, based on the theory and structure of the number combinations involved, and sustained by observation in practice (anecdotal evidence, as some might call experience).

The 5th part of the circle (quintile): 72°, 144°. This is an aspect with some age and tradition behind it, having been used for quite a while. It is generally associated with natural "talent," though of what kind is not always made clear. In fact, it has to do with the ability to spot and utilize proportion in either time or space or both. Frequent in the charts of musicians, artists, architects, orators, and others who depend on a good sense of time or proportion for success. This can be for good or ill, as for instance the chart of Hitler is riddled with 5ths and their double, 10ths: certainly he was the most talented and compelling orator of the 20th century, he was an aspiring architect, and the timing of his decisions was impeccable, despite the way he used it. This quality is likely derived from mathematical applications of the number five itself, from which *phi*, the Golden Section, is derived. Its formula is $phi = [\sqrt{5}-1]/2$, or 0.6180339, and it is the universal proportion of growth within the biological kingdom. It is the proportion of your elbow to your overall arm, your navel to your whole frame, seashell and pinecone spiral length and count from level to level, leaf positioning in vines, and so on; much-used in all forms of art in architecture, since those are at least, in part, imitations of life.

The 7th part of the circle (septile): 51°26', 102°51', 154°17'. This aspect is not so much in use, though it has had some popularity. It appears to represent a kind of large-scale, universal outlook on the applications of the planets so attached. It is an ability (indeed, an insistence) to see the Big Picture instead of getting hung up in the details or in only one part of the story. This has a lot of mythological background. As in most Western and much Eastern scripture and secular beliefs, the number seven is associated with completion: the seven days of creation (and thus, the days of the week), the seven heavens, seven archangels, seven pillars of wisdom, seven colors of the rainbow, seven visible planets, seven chakras, seven deadly sins, and so forth. It does, indeed, seem to lend *a broad scope of vision* in the planetary areas involved in any given horoscope.

The 9th part of the circle (nonile): 40°, 80°, 160° (120° coincides with trine). This aspect is fundamental in Hindu astrology, but peripheral in the West. It is, in my experience, the ultimate "nice person" aspect, of which the quintessential bleeding heart liberal must be entirely constructed. It indicates sympathy, generosity, humanitarianism, and general good will, although it does not always translate this into assertive action. You want friends? Get some of these aspects.

The 11th part of the circle: 32°44', 65°27', 98°11', 130°55', 163°38'. This is a really rough aspect, and wholly unused among traditional astrologers. It doesn't even have a formal name. There is a lot of Biblical symbolism concerning the number 11 itself, and all of it has to do with insufficiency, frustration, and incompletion, a situation that just falls short of the more whole and complete number 12. It also seems to be a somewhat revolutionary number, as it expresses dissatisfaction with the status quo and fuels a need to overthrow it. Oddly, in numerology it is called the number of the World Savior, but that may also have overtones of overthrow. Remembering what Christ did to the money-changers gives us a hint. Also His statement, "Think not that I came to send peace on earth: I came not to send peace but a sword. For I am come to set a man at variance with his father, and the daughter against her mother, and the daughter-in-law against her mother-in-law." (Matthew 10:34–35). Troublesome stuff—okay if you're the Son of

God, but hard to handle as a mere mortal. The Ayatollah Khomeini's chart was loaded with 11th part aspects.

The 13th part of the circle: 27°42′, 55°23′, 83°05′, 110°46′, 138°28′, 166°09′. This is one step beyond the natural twelve, and folks with a lot of this tend to be one step beyond, indeed. It is an aspect of the eccentric, the adventurer, the person who decides to travel the road less taken or forge out into the woods when the road ends. Sexually, it can be rather kinky (until, of course, kinks become mainstream, and thus boring), and it may lead to great adventure or simply to a useless backwater or cul-de-sac. Some paths are less-traveled for good reason, but there is always interest and amusement here, if nothing else. Those traveling in pastures beyond the pale should take appropriate cautions concerning both the perils of the unknown and those who don't feel comfortable with the unusual.

Although these are the main extra fractions of the circle I use for aspects, it would seem logical to use more, for structural reasons. Many of the higher, finer aspects are mutual multiples of larger ones (deciles, for instance, being half of quintiles), but there are still some prime numbers to be reckoned with, such as 17, 19, 23, 29, 31, and so on. I have found 17 and 19 to be sort of "upper octaves" of 11 and 13, or at least similar in some ways. For the rest, seek out Addey's work for clues.

Astrology and the Chakras

It is one thing to point to astrology as a way to analyze blockages or imbalances in the flow of energy through the chakras, the seven energy centers of the human body/spirit complex. It is another to figure out exactly how to do it, as there has been little published on the connection between astrology and the chakras, despite their obvious, if little commented-upon, connection.

The most prolific comment on the subject which I have come upon is in a small book called *Understanding the Chakras*, by Peter Rendel (Aquarian/Thorsons, Harper/Collins, 1974 and 1990). His treatment of the chakras and their symbolism is very astrological, at least on the surface, but also rather contradictory (see illustration). He neatly assigns planetary rulerships to the lower six chakras according to Ptolemy's sign/planet rulership scheme. It leaves out, however, both the three outer planets and also the crown chakra. Similarly, he assigns triplicities and quadruplicities to the upper three and lower four chakras, so that each sign gets both a higher and lower chakra affiliation (this time the crown chakra gets included).

In both cases, however, many of the resulting associations are counterintuitive or contradictory. Mars, for instance, is said to rule the solar chakra, which is associated with the stomach and therefore also lunar. Venus is given association with the heart chakra, yet Sun and Leo are traditionally associated with the heart and its energy. Perhaps his very neat structural assignments are better on paper than in real life, or perhaps it is all too esoteric for me to understand (like Alice Bailey). It is my feeling that some real hands-on research by astrologers who also are therapeutic touch practitioners is in order to really straighten this out.

Nevertheless, it is easy to make some educated guesses as to possible associations which allow some practical application of astrology to the spotting of blockages.

Root chakra—this is associated with the spinal column and kidneys, and so has Saturnian overtones. It is also where the kundalini rests, the most powerful force in the body, and thus perhaps Pluto.

Sacral chakra—associated with the gonads, and thus perhaps Pluto/Scorpio, but also (according to Leadbetter) the area for absorption of solar prana and the swelling of bodily energy, so perhaps Jupiter or Sun.

Solar chakra—stomach, liver, gall bladder, nervous system. This would seem to be associated with a primarily reactive planet (hardly Mars as Rendel suggests). If the term "gut reaction" is a good key phrase for this chakra, likely the Moon.

Heart chakra—properly, I should think, the Sun and Leo, though Venus is involved here as well.

Throat chakra—bronchial and vocal apparatus, lungs, alimentary canal. This could be Mercury for its communication potential but also Venus (traditionally Taurus and throat) for its role in ingestion.

Brow chakra—lower brain, left eye, ears, nose, nervous system. This ought to be Mercury, but Uranus might apply as well, as this is a point for clarity of perception.

Crown chakra—upper brain, right eye (these physical assignations, as those mentioned for the other chakras, are from the very practical work on therapeutic touch, *Hands Of Light*, by Barbara Ann Brennan, Bantam 1988). Also Mercury, but maybe a little Uranus and Neptune thrown in. This is the gateway to the cosmos when the kundalini rises. Also perhaps Sun/Moon,

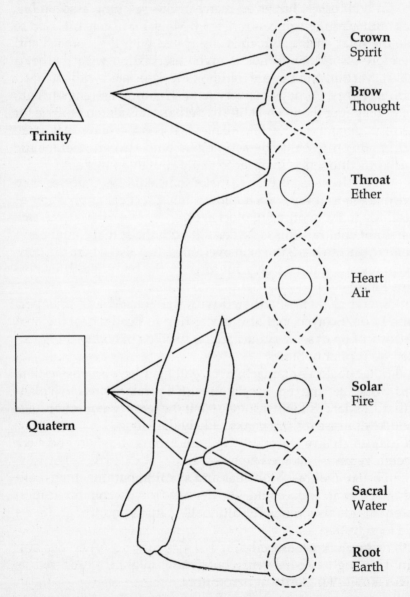

as these two are usually depicted in this place in most Tibetan statuary.

Confusing? Yes and no. More research would make all this much more exact, yet you can still get a ball-park feel for it: Sun-Pluto troubles pit the sex drive against the heart. Mercury-Neptune puts it all up top and can disconnect proper lower functions. Moon-Uranus pits upper and middle chakras against each other or means blocks in both.

Chart 1 — Madonna

One of the problems of writing about sexual astrology, as it is with sexual research in general, is that sex is generally a private matter and those whose example charts you use usually prefer to remain anonymous. Thus, the reader has to take the writer's word for it that the nativity in question actually exists and its owner has the sexual predelictions alleged in the analysis.

This is increasingly less of a problem since sex has become more open, and here we have a nativity (source: Lois Rodden, from Madonna's parents) where the native's sexuality and fantasies are not only known but broadly advertised. For all the criticisms about Madonna's style from the sexual far right to the far left, without question she has been an overwhelming influence on coming generations to let sex and fantasy out into the open and to believe it is all right to do so, no matter what the fantasy content.

To do so, and even commercialize on it in the process, took both moral courage, and skillful and determined business acumen that one cannot help but admire, however one may judge the music, aesthetics, or politics. In a way, particularly with bondage and S/M, she has brought the fantasy so far into reality as to make it banal and ho-hum and make the rest of us (well, some of the rest of us) ready to move on to some other, as yet unarticulated and unfulfilled, fantasy. This is okay, in that it lets it into the open and makes it okay for the rest of us, but also not so okay, as it can be too easy to pass over the powerful inner meaning of her fantasies and move along without seeing where it is actually meant to lead, which has by and large been the case.

But to the chart. It features a strong Mercury, necessary for articulation of fantasy, conjunct the Ascendant. It is also conjunct Pluto, so the forces of structure and dissolution, so essential to sexual fantasy (and reality), are right up front. In fact, Moon, Sun,

Pluto, and Mercury are in a tangle, indeed, with Sun/Moon = Pluto, Moon/Pluto = Mercury. Sun is strongly reinforced by Saturn (trine), giving strength and confidence. Jupiter is conjunct Neptune, lending burgeoning imagination and a certain religious fervor (this is often called the "high priest" aspect). Neptune is quincunx the MC, forcing this side of her into the public eye. Venus square Neptune makes for uncertainty of desire, and the need to keep seeking to find it. As Uranus = Sun/Venus, it will be in the unusual and outspoken where she will try to express it.

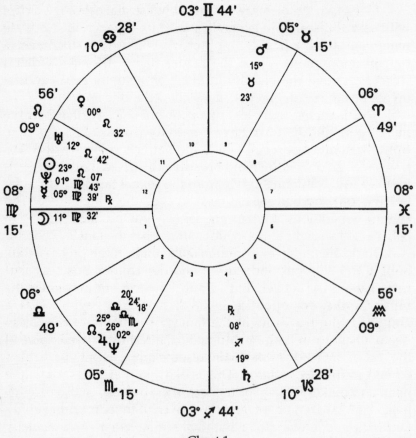

Chart 1
Madonna
Aug. 16, 1958, 7:05 A.M. EST
Bay City, MI
43N36 83W53
Koch Houses

Uranus rising ahead of the Sun adds to the iconoclastic nature of her inner drive.

The chart is very water-shy, with only Neptune in water, where it was for her whole generation. This shows in the campy, artificiality of her sex persona, much like that of a drag queen—an elaborate outer construction trying to create real inner feelings by appearing to already have more than plenty of them. The weight of the whole chart taken together focuses around the Pluto-Sun-Uranus area in the 12th, shocking and compulsive sexuality from the most perilous house of the soul.

The finer aspects fill out the picture. The Jupiter-Uranus quintile shows explosive, yet precision timing, always leaping on to the next move—the perfect reflection of her music and stage show (the 5th harmonic is integrally associated with proportion in space and time, the number five being the root of phi, the golden section, remember). Septiles of Saturn, Mercury, and Jupiter along with the Moon and Neptune display an ability to see an overview, the big picture, where both fantasy and business are concerned. 11ths of Sun-Mars and Moon-Saturn show her notable impatience with incompetence and a certain inclination to project her own failings on others. Eccentric 13ths of Venus-Saturn (desire in chains), Mercury-Mars (sharp tongue), and Jupiter-Pluto (oddly compulsive ambition) fill out a chart remarkably consistent with her well-documented public and private image.

Many share multiple chart features with Madonna, and may share much of her desires and fantasies, sexual and otherwise. Yet she has made a crusade and a career of it, self-obsessed with her inner vision to the last. One last observation may shed some light on this, namely the degree of her Sun. Both Marc Edmund Jones and Dane Rudhyar agree the 24th degree of Leo is a degree of inner mission and blind determination to follow this path to outer destiny. T. E. Lawrence and Napoleon Bonaparte both had Sun in this degree. All three share these qualities, and along with them a unique and driven sexuality as well.

Chart 2 — Zip Koon

Chart 2 represents a well-known graphic illustrator of S/M fantasies, so it may be said that sexual fantasy is his business. This man is overflowing with the salient measurements in his sexual profile. Sun and Venus oppose Neptune, Moon squares Uranus, and Saturn squares Pluto. A real tight set of tie-ups. This might make for a very internalized situation, with little outward expression, except for the lack of earth which un-anchors this man to be an adventurer, however tightly-wound. Furthermore, there is a network of Mars-Moon-Mercury-Neptune in the 11th aspect and Mars-Sun-Venus in the 13th, putting this personality beyond the ordinary and into an area of strong expression of internal complexities of both troublesome and unusual nature. Furthermore,

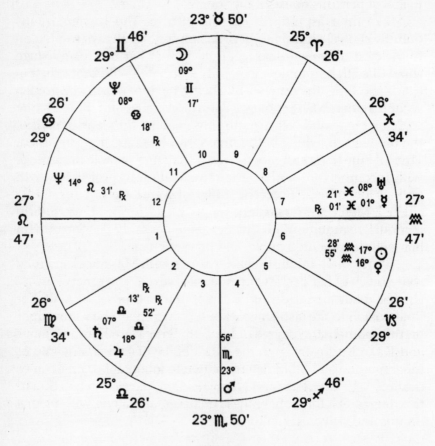

Chart 2
Zip Koon
Feb. 6, 1922, 6:30 P.M. CST
Sheridan, AR
34N18 92W24
Koch Houses

the midpoint structure of Pluto = Venus/Mars and Moon/Jupiter = Neptune-Venus axis clearly is the stuff of which S/M fantasies are made.

What is interesting about this chart is that this man progressed from primarily a homosexual orientation in the early 1970s, to one which (at least in artistic expression) is primarily heterosexual of late. The S/M theme remains the same, as well as an artistic streak (despite the lack of 5ths, as anyone looking at his artwork would recognize!). The chart is a tangle of blockages which need to be overcome, in the process of which a plethora of imaginary images are generated, expressing and developing the underlying emotional and sexual situation.

Chart 3 — "Big Bert"

This early light of the Eulenspiegel Society (an international S/M liberation group) is gay, dominant, and into heavy-leather boot scenes, i.e., while wearing engineer's boots, he likes to step on his partner. Even a casual inspection of the chart shows that quincunxes from Neptune and from Pluto are the aspect focuses of the chart, with a strong Pisces element (feet!). Bert is actually a fairly laid-back, philosophical personality, quite accepting of his unusual situation, with Mars-Jupiter, Sun-Uranus, and Moon-Venus all in septiles. The oft-present 11th is there with Venus-Pluto in an harmonic opposition (22nd) to Venus-Saturn-Uranus, as is the 13th (Mars-Saturn). Midpoints as well show up outer-planet tangles: Moon = Mercury/Uranus, Uranus = Moon/Saturn.

Both charts 2 and 3 show the typical hard aspects involving outer and inner planets, which typifies unusual sexuality and *likely odd blockages* and "Byzantine" pathways between chakras. It should be noted, however, that these kind of aspects, however convoluted, do not necessarily indicate a high degree of fantasy or unusual sexual expression. The same symbolisms of the planets involved may also be interpreted as entirely *non*-sexual and thus interpreted in another light: for example, a child born and a ship launched at the same instance, a block apart (hospital next to shipyard). Remember, without astrological symbolism, we can't mix apples with oranges. Also, even in the case of two persons born at virtually the same instant and close together (as with twins), the "butterfly effect," so loved by chaos theorists, has great application, as the individual input of life, from instant to instant, detail by detail, leads into radically diverging pathways of physical and even emotional expression, despite the restraining and containing overall astrological factors involved. Herein lies the talent of the consulting astrologer, *using technical analysis mixed with intuitive observation*, to see whether the aspects with which we have been dealing have primarily sexual application, or have greater influence elsewhere.

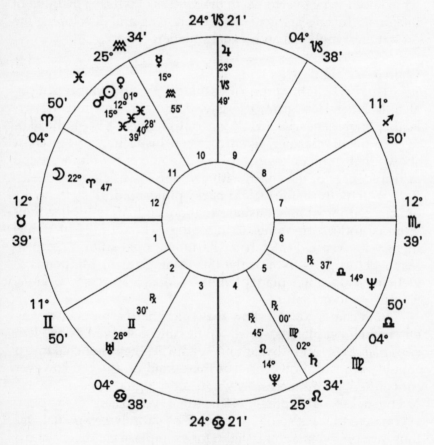

Chart 3
"Big Bert"
Mar. 3, 1949, 8:57 A.M. EST
New York, NY
40N43 74W00
Koch Houses

Some Recommended Reading

Brennan, Barbara Ann. *Hands Of Light*. Bantam, 1988.

Bullough, Verne. *Sexual Variation In Society and History*. Wiley, 1976.

Marcus, Maria. *A Taste For Pain, On Masochism and Female Sexuality*. St. Martin's Press, 1981.

Money, John. *Lovemaps*. Irvington Publishers, 1986.

_____. *Love and Lovesickness*. Johns Hopkins Press, 1980.

Weinberg, Thomas and Kamel, G. W. Levi, editors. *S and M, Studies In Sadomasochism*. Prometheus Books, 1983.

Reik, Theodore. *Masochism in Sex and Society*. Pyramid Books, 1941.

Rendel, Peter, *Understanding The Chakras*. Harper/Collins, 1979.

Schimmel, Annemarie. *The Mystery Of Numbers*. Oxford Univ. Press, 1993.

Tennov, Dorothy. *Love and Limerance: The Experience Of Being In Love*. Stein and Day, 1979.

Varley, Desmond. *Seven, The Number Of Creation*. G. Bell & Sons, 1976.

J. Lee Lehman

J. Lee Lehman (Ph.D., Rutgers University) is Research Director for the National Council for Geocosmic Research. Her books, to date, are *The Ultimate Asteroid Book* (1988), *Essential Dignities* (1989), and *The Book of Rulerships* (1992). She is the head of the Classical Studies in Horary Course and is the Corporate Treasurer for the United Astrology Congress, Inc.

Her published articles have included statistical studies of homosexuality and term rulerships; and historical work on classical techniques, including the Part of Fortune, reception, Almutens, horary, natural rulerships, and Solstice Points.

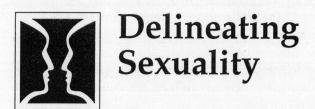

Delineating Sexuality

J. Lee Lehman

> Using astrology
> I can easily measure the stars;
> Yet intimate as I am with her soft body,
> I cannot fathom the depth of her love.
>
> —Sixth Dalai Lama[1]

Homosexuality can tell us a great deal about *all* sexuality. Why? Homosexual behavior has been known since ancient times. In some societies, such as ancient Greece and feudal Japan where the martial arts have flourished, male homosexuality was even encouraged. In the same societies, female homosexuality was also common. The anti-sexual tendencies of the Christian founding fathers resulted in the suppression of *all* forms of nonreproductive sex, until the breakdown of Christian hegemony over Western thought. Parallel developments may be observed in Buddhism, with puritanical sects roundly condemning homosexuality, as well as any other recreational sex.

Those societies that have difficulty with sexual morality have even more difficulty with homosexuality. Thus, we can use the tolerance of homosexuality as a measure for the sexual tolerance of the society in general.

---

1   c.f. Stevens, p. 79.

A word about terminology. I am using the term "homosexual" generically: i.e., I am applying it to both sexes. I could, of course, choose to say "lesbians and gay men" throughout. But I won't. The term originally applied to both sexes, and in my opinion, it still should.

Whatever the favored causative principles—genetic, behavioral, or both—what are the primary differences which distinguish homosexuality from heterosexuality, apart from the obvious issue of the gender of the partner? In modern Western society, there are three differences: homosexuals cannot marry, homosexuals cannot have children through their homosexual relationships, and homosexuals are discriminated against to a greater or lesser degree.

Even these cultural differences are disappearing in modern Western society, since not all heterosexuals *choose* to marry, and *choose* to have children. Many heterosexuals are also discriminated against, albeit seldom for their sexual preferences.

While grand philosophical statements could be made on the subject of choice, I think the point is clear. To a large extent, it is possible to deal with homosexual people (or astrological clients, within our context) by playing spin-the-pronoun.

The real differences mentioned above boil down to one basic fact in practice: much of the homosexual experience requires conscious consideration and adaptation concerning sexual behavior that many heterosexuals take for granted. In other words, if you are programmed by society to marry and have children, you don't have to think about it. If part of that program is to get divorced frequently, then you may get a divorce without much mental or physical effort.

The child often recognizes at an early age which side of the gender coin he or she prefers. This is apart from any same-sex infatuation, which is a fairly common stage among pre-adolescents. So, if no one tells you, the proto-homosexual, about homosexuality when you are growing up, then you have to find it, and discover how to do it for yourself. You must create this portion of yourself *de novo*, without recourse to the sexual mythology available to heterosexuals.

In practice, most homosexuals who are successful in finding the homosexual subculture then adopt a position of conformity within it; everyone wants "to belong," after all. This has the advantage of minimizing the need for conscious thought. Much as it has become fashionable to extol the virtues of free will, *if people really exercised it that often astrologers would be out of business!*

One more point: people tend to idealize their own culture and assume that this is the way life always was, and the way it *should* be. This assumption is especially dangerous in the realm of sexuality. Technological improvements in contraception and abortion in the nineteenth and twentieth centuries have radically redefined sexual lifestyles, but this is not necessarily the most profound change in sexual practice during our history.

We do well to remember in our era where marriage or partnership is idealized as a universal condition, that *this has not always been so.* The Catholic idealization of celibacy grew out of philosophical roots in profoundly anti-materialist Stoicism and Gnosticism. This ideal of celibacy in turn grew into rabid misogyny, as women were blamed for men's inability to control themselves. A parallel development occurred in the more puritan sects of Buddhism (c.f., Ranke-Heinemann & Stevens).

While the Church may have extolled, the great unwashed mainly ignored. Strange as it may seem, marriage was not considered universal, or necessarily preferable. In the Feudal system, universal marriage was not desired. Only the oldest son was encouraged to marry, because otherwise it would split the patrimony too much. (Interestingly, it was advantageous to marry off all one's daughters, because their husbands' families then became natural allies in all the inevitable feuds.)

The religious approach was different. By this time, a celibate (in theory, if not in practice) clergy was running things. The sacraments were not defined until the 12th Century, and marriage was only grudgingly included, for the reason that marriage conferred no grace; it was only a bulwark against sin. The strategy of the clergy—who could not prevent their parishioners from marrying—was to encourage them to strive toward the ideal of celibacy in *other* ways. The foremost method used to achieve these aims was to ban sex on the myriad feast days, during the entire forty days of Lent, and if that were not enough, several days prior to receiving communion.[2]

---

2 There is evidence that one of the results of these restrictions was that many people ceased to take communion except at Christmas and Easter, which were both preceded by sexless periods anyway.

Interestingly, there is one tantalizing astrological correlation with this. The sign Scorpio is somewhat reviled because of its alleged sexual drive. If we follow the genesis of the person with Sun in Scorpio, conception would typically occur with the Sun in Aquarius: late January to February. This period—Candlemas in the Ancient System—was always considered a time for prayer and fasting, for Druids and Christians alike. Lent frequently encompassed part of it as well. The belief was prevalent that the sins of the father were visited on the children. If so, wouldn't the depraved sin of the fathers having sex at a "fallow" (Aquarius) time then be visited on the (Scorpio) offspring in the form of alleged sexual depravity? A pagan Roman Empire author such as Firmicus could be much gentler on Scorpios than many moderns, despite his lurid depictions of the means of death to be endured by sign and house.

The first consideration in any discussion of sexuality should be the person, regardless of gender or sexual preference. Sexuality is merely one facet of our interactions with other people. How can we begin to understand our relations with others if we do not understand ourselves?

When we delineate a sexual relationship, it is best to begin by considering the fundamental components of any sexual encounter: first each person as an individual, and then the relationship formed by those individuals. For simplicity's sake, I shall only be considering one-on-one pairings; there is no evidence to suggest that menages-à-trois or -à-quatres are any more common among gays than among straights. My approach to delineation is neo-Renaissance: primarily my methods date from the 17th Century or earlier, with some modern considerations (like the Outer Planets) thrown in. I have also included modern chart types, such as composite and time-space charts.

Case One: Is She, or Isn't She?
A Metaphor for Dysfunction

A client contacted me several years ago for a reading about his wife. While they had been married for over thirty years, and had children, his wife had never had an orgasm. He contacted me because he knew of my expertise about homosexuality, and wanted to know if I could explain why his wife didn't climax:

perhaps she was a lesbian?[3]

Sexual preference is not easy to read clearly in a chart from the standpoint of heterosexuality/homosexuality (see below for a discussion of why I say this). *What is clearer is the individual's personal sexual adaptations.* From that, certain inferences may be made.

To consider one's approach to sexuality—or anything else— we should begin with the Ascendant. All issues of self are, at heart, matters of the 1st House. The ruler of the Libra Ascendant is Venus, but the alternate ruler, the Almuten,[4] is Saturn. Venus is in Capricorn in the 4th House. Venus' condition is weak. She has no particular dignity in Capricorn, thus peregrine.[5] Since Venus is also a natural ruler of sex (the sex organs, specifically) and fertility,[6] this particular Venus[7] is at sea: this woman does not feel completely at home with her sexuality. The closest planetary aspect that Venus makes is a quincunx with Neptune: she is quite capable of living in a fantasy world. Venus in Capricorn can be very rutty or very prim, depending on the cultural environment as well as astrological factors such as aspect patterns.

Saturn as Almuten of the 1st House is probably telling us less about her sexuality than about her whole life. Saturn is in detriment in Leo in the 11th House, but in mutual reception with the Sun. Saturn is also opposite Uranus. She values friendship. Her affections are strong. But this is not an indication of sexual interest *per se*.

---

3   The reader may wonder if this question raises ethical issues because my client was asking for information about someone else, based on her chart. I chose to go ahead and read for him because I felt that the question was a variant on whether the dysfunction of his wife was his fault, or a result of something more general.

4   The Almuten is the planet which owns the greatest number of essential dignities for that degree of the zodiac. In classical astrology, there were five essential dignities: rulership, exaltation, triplicity, term, and face. Saturn is both the exaltation and term ruler of 3° Libra: this gives it primacy over Venus. For further information on how to calculate Almutens, and on essential dignities in general, see Lehman (1989) or Lehman (1993).

5   The term *peregrine* classically means lacking all five essential dignities. In addition, in some interpretations, it also is not in mutual reception by sign and exaltation. In this example, Saturn rules Capricorn, Mars is exalted there, the triplicity ruler is the Moon, the term ruler is Mercury, and the face ruler is also the Moon. A peregrine planet in horary means damaged goods; in natal it represents an exile: a stranger in a strange land.

6   c.f., Dariot, page 23; Lilly, page 247; etc. Rulership references are collected in Lehman (1992) (b).

7   Venus traditionally ruled fertility *and* the genitals, male and female. Beyond its specific house rulerships given here, the pair of Venus and Mars should be understood to refer to sexuality and that which needs to be done to make it happen.

The Wife's Moon is Void-of-Course in Virgo. Virgo, like the other Earth signs, has a naturalistic approach to sex. However, a Moon in Virgo does not define herself to any great degree as a sexual being.

The mythological connection with Virgo is to Ceres. Ceres was not married. Her daughter Kore/Persephone was extremely important to her, but the sex necessary to beget Persephone was not. The male gods were almost shadow figures to her. They were of no primal importance, except to the degree that their actions affected her, as when Hades/Pluto stole Persephone from her.

This issue of non-identification with the act of sex—and the identity of the sperm-bearer—goes to the heart of the earlier

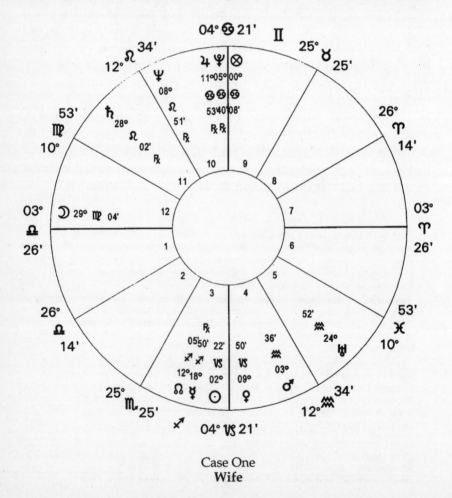

Case One
Wife

meaning of the word "virgin," as in Vestal Virgin. The historical meaning was of an unattached (unmarried) woman, not a woman who had never had sex. The Sacred Prostitute was part of the same fertility milieu as Ceres. The Sacred Prostitute had sex with many men, as a religious and cultural rite. Again, the Prostitute had no interest in the identity of the individual men with whom she fornicated. The Moon in Virgo woman is not necessarily—or even usually—promiscuous. However, any morality associated with sex is not coming from the Moon placement! She feels that her own self-worth is dependent on what she accomplishes in the world, just as Ceres had her duty in the fields.

Virgos (and Earth signs in general) are very sensitive to touch: as such the orgasmic cycle may prove to be too intense for her. Alternately, if the sexual encounter is not to her liking, she may just dissociate. Because Mercury rules Virgo as well as being exalted there, the Moon in Virgo person is likely to be quite curious, and this is what leads to experimentation in the early (mercurial) stage of adulthood or late adolescence.

The fact that her Moon is Void-of-Course brings another element into play: the Void-of-Course planet is more detached by definition, *since it has finished its relations to the other planets.* Virgo is quite capable of being detached anyway—especially when compared to the other Earth signs. By detaching herself emotionally during the act of sex, she is quite capable of preventing or bypassing the orgasmic cycle, whether consciously or not.

Consider this placement within the context of the rest of her chart. With the Sun in Capricorn she has a pragmatic approach to life in general that is quite in tune with her emotional makeup. Given the fact that the Sun is opposite Pluto, power dynamics— and the fear of powerlessness—is of primary concern to her. She may be terrified of anything which would make her appear to, or actually, lose control. Abandoning herself to the throes of orgasmic ecstasy could fall in this realm. This Sun-Pluto opposition is especially accentuated by its angularity from the 10th House to the 3rd House.[8] However, with Libra Rising, the issue of partnership is magnified for her. Partnership becomes important to her, and yet, emotionally, she is incapable of *merging* with the partner.

---

8 While the Sun is in the 3rd House, it is within 5° of the IC. In the classical system, any planet this close to an angle is considered angular.

She can go through the motions, but there is a core which is untouched.

Mars in Aquarius has dignity only through its mutual reception by term. Mars in an air sign is rather detached. In Saturn's sign, Mars' sexual ardor is lessened, especially as the Native gets older.

The wife's absence of orgasms is easy to explain without even referring to the husband's chart. There is indication that the absence of climax is a result of her own psychological predisposition, and not because of the relationship with him.

Here the question of homosexuality was really a metaphor for another question: why didn't she seem to enjoy sex, at least with her husband? The husband, a Gemini (and who but a Gemini would have found all this out, anyway?), could not imagine that his wife simply could not enjoy sex. To him, lesbian tendencies on her part seemed an easier explanation than a low sex drive.

The alert reader has no doubt noticed that in the delineation above, there was not one mention of the 8th House. This is because I am using classical methods: there is no evidence that the 8th House was used for sexuality in the way that modern astrology does.[9] There is one intriguing temptation to attribute sex to the 8th House: one wonders how much the linguistic history of referring to orgasm as the "little death" somehow caused one to link the House of Death to the House of Little Death.

The topic of sex and sexuality raises most of the dangerous issues that confront us concerning our personalities. One of the issues which often receives short shrift astrologically is *planetary emphasis in signs of opposite gender from the gender of the person:* in other words, men with heavy placements in female signs, and women with heavy placements in male signs.

Historically, this was one of the undertone accusations concerning homosexuals: that gay men are effeminate and lesbians are masculine. Thus, we might expect a cross-gender emphasis by

---

9 The modern usage comes from equating planet with sign and with house. There are only two classical instances where some degree of equation was done: city and country rulerships, and parts of the body. Thus, there were some referrals to the 8th House for the genitals, but this was not used outside of medical astrology. Traditionally, the 8th House ruled the spouse's portion, death, inheritance other than titles and property, and the opponent's second in a duel.

sign with prominent planets. This does not happen in practice, at least as far as sexual preference is concerned.

Because our culture has a male bias, this phenomenon is easier to study in men. A "masculine" woman is understandable, because she is striving to be "human," at least by the definitions of a male-identified culture. Thus, many women have endured the questionable compliment, "you think like a man." An effeminate man, on the other hand, is truly out of luck. We can trace this loathing of the effeminate back to Ancient Rome and earlier. In Rome, homosexuality was not frowned upon, *as long as the man was the "active" partner.* If he was the "inserter," he was fine. If he was the "insertee," he was less than a man, and therefore loathsome. Men developed what we would now label an obsession around the proper behavior of *real* men, and this obsession is with us to this day.

Since anything which can look feminine is therefore suspect, *let's examine sexuality in men dominated by feminine signs.* To overstate the argument, I have selected two men, both involved with sado-masochism, but from very different perspectives.

Case Two: A Kinky Homophobe

Don is heterosexual. He has been married twice, and has a daughter. His last divorce was over ten years ago, and he has dated extensively since. He has successfully run a small business which he recently sold, and he now works part time in a professional capacity.

Don has been obsessed with pornography since high school. He has also had a long-standing interest in "swinging," before, during, between, and after his marriages. However, in those multiple sex-partner situations, he *never* got involved in anything homosexual. In one-on-one sexual encounters, his penchant is for the flavor of sexual behavior known as bondage and discipline (B & D), always as the dominator. Furthermore, he engages in tying women up with or *without* their consent. Many of us would call this rape, not B & D. Curiously, despite the fact that heterosexual porn frequently shows pseudo-lesbian interludes (presumably so the man can fantasize about getting both women), Don cannot bring himself to utter the word "lesbian," despite an otherwise stellar vocabulary.

Don is a double Cancer, Sun and Ascendant, with Venus in Cancer as well. He has the typical male Sun in Cancer syndrome: women find him very easy to talk to. Often women find men with the Sun in Cancer to be very good listeners. They believe that he is being sympathetic. Whether he is in fact sympathetic is basically dependent on his Moon. Don's Moon in Libra is rather detached, so the sympathy is appearance only.

There is a further component to the syndrome. Conflicted Cancer men observe that women prefer their company, and then see whether they can manipulate them to get what they want. This is in contrast to men with Sun in Scorpio or Pisces. In these two signs, the personality differences between men and women of the same Sun sign do not seem as pronounced. This may be because Cancer is ruled by the Moon, the quintessential female planet, while Scorpio is ruled by Mars and Pisces by Jupiter, both male planets. The average macho-indoctrinated male in our society would therefore find the other two water signs less foreign or threatening.

Don's angular Sun is conjunct Pluto, surely a start at an explanation for his interest in B & D. This is accentuated because the Sun-Pluto conjunction is square his Moon-Uranus opposition; quite an explosive T-square. The very term, "bondage and discipline," exudes Saturn, and his Saturn is his most dignified planet, in the 8th House, in Aquarius, and, most significantly, unaspected, except for an inconjunct[10] to Venus in the 12th House. Thus, the only release for the energy of this very strong Saturn is Venus; sex and women. Venus' position in the 12th House may refer to the bedroom, but it is also imprisonment. With his Mars there as well, his sexual proclivities seem truly drawn in that direction, into confinement.

There is one other sexual interpretation for his T-square. One of the generally agreed upon natural rulerships of Uranus is electrical equipment. We can easily extrapolate this to technology, or gadgetry in general. With the involvement of both Lights in the T-square with Uranus, Don is a gadget freak in every way imaginable. How about sex toys? How about high-tech porn?

---

10 In Lehman (1992 (a) I discuss which quincunxes should also be called inconjunct, based on Ptolemy's work. To summarize, all quincunx or semi-sextile pairs which include a fixed sign are also inconjunct. Inconjunct quincunxes and semi-sextiles are more difficult to handle than pairs which are not inconjunct.

With Mars in Gemini, the written or spoken word is important in his display of passion, thus the linkage to porn. His Mercury, however, is in Leo and peregrine while his Sun is in mute Cancer. Despite his intelligence and education, he finds it difficult to express himself verbally. [Recall footnote 5, p. 203.—Ed.]

I had mentioned earlier that the classical linkage of the 8th House to sex was really a medical one. In his case, while his Saturn is strong by sign, it is also retrograde. For years he has had an undiagnosable penile discharge. Since it has not been diagnosed, it cannot be treated.

In Don's case, his own fears about his masculinity have been transformed into a literal attempt to dominate women. The natal

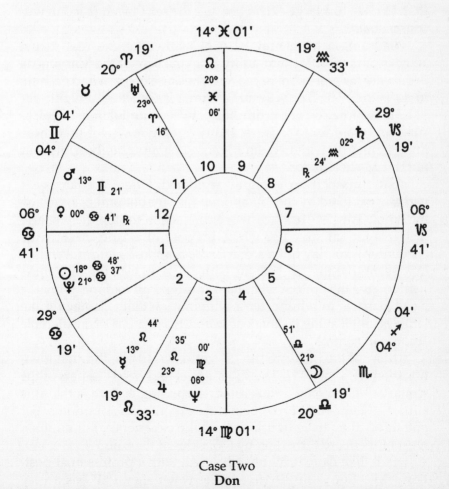

Case Two
Don

chart shows sexual dynamics too strong to be ignored in the delineation of any relationship he might have.

Case Three: New York's Finest

Back in the days before AIDS decimated the gay male community, things were a little wilder. In the mid-seventies I met Phil, who was one of New York's finest—but not in the police sense of the term.

Phil was one of New York's best "tops," a term applied to the "Sadist" half of the sado-masochistic pair. Phil is also gay. The world of sado-masochists may seem terribly kinky to the uninitiated, but I would argue that Phil's sex life is actually *far* less kinky than Don's—to a large extent because the sex Phil engaged in was consensual.

Sado-masochism may be a misnomer for the real sexual activity of the S & M community. The practices of the Marquis de Sade were far more similar to Don's, because consent had nothing to do with it. The S & M sexual community practices a highly ritualized exploration of the fine line between humiliation and pleasure, and pain and pleasure. Many people may feel that these lines should be widened, and ignored as much as possible, but not S & M aficionados.

Sado-masochism is highly regulated. Often, the fantasy is verbally explored by the "S" and the "M" (or bottom) prior to acting it out. The "M" has a code word or action to stop the scenario if it gets too intense. The whole purpose of a sado-masochistic encounter is to play out a scene *for the masochist's benefit*. While it may seem that the "S" gets the better deal, in fact, the top works hard to give the bottom what he wants. As Phil told me, it takes a lot of practice to administer a whipping without damaging the kidneys, nor leaving permanent scars. This requires a considerable amount of control.

Most of the pleasure the "S" gets is vicarious, through identification with the "M". The "S" may get "serviced" as part of the scenario, but he may not. Another surprising feature is that it is almost essential that tops begin their experiences as bottoms. For one thing, they have to understand the experience. For another, most of them are turned on by *both* sides of the coin.

Phil, like Don, is highly educated, with a professional position. Phil's Sun is in Pisces, another water sign. Phil has a very tight Moon-Pluto aspect: a trine, unlike Don's Moon-Pluto square. Phil's Pluto is right at his Midheaven, easily the most elevated planet in the chart. This trine shows the (self) control that Phil must exercise in pleasuring his partners. One wonders how well Don can perform with his square.

Phil's Mercury at 29° Pisces is in detriment, fall, and peregrine, a very weak Mercury. In any case, the Pisces-Aries cusp is a fascinating transition point. Natives with personal planets at both 29° Pisces and 0° Aries may be highly promiscuous, because these are two rather extreme energies to try to balance. Often, there is much experimentation along the way.

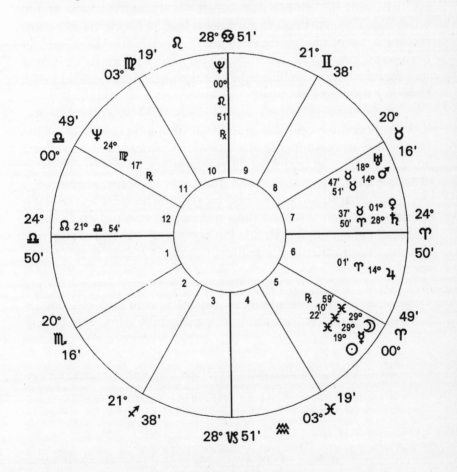

Case Three
Phil

Phil's Mercury is opposite Neptune, which gives him a rich fantasy life. This is no doubt important in identifying with his "bottom."

Phil's Venus and Mars are both in Taurus, again, feminine signs. His Venus is square Pluto. Despite this, he maintains excellent friendships with women, although he doesn't sleep with them. His Venus is conjunct Saturn out-of-sign, and Saturn is also square Pluto, again, out-of-sign. We have already observed Saturn's involvement with B & D, an involvement we should surely expect in S & M as well.

Phil has dealt with the challenges of his feminine sign planets by turning his sexuality upside down: by taking a walk on the wild side. This has been so successful that he functions in a completely conventional manner in every other realm. Don has not been so successful: he has allowed his need to dominate women to infect the rest of his life. Apparently, Don's idea of wild is too tame to purge his demons.

If we proceed beyond the individual issues represented by the natal chart to relationship itself, we are presented with several added levels of complexity. First, there are now *two* charts to examine and delineate. Second, there are cross-currents between those two charts, as represented by such techniques as synastry, composite,[11] or the Davison time-space relationship chart.[12] Third, there are the events that define the beginning and end of the relationship, not to mention significant changes within the relationship over time.

What is the moment of a relationship? This is essentially the same issue that all electional, mundane, and horary astrologers face. In electional work, when does a business come into being?

---

11 The composite chart, also called the midpoint chart, is created by calculating the midpoint of each planetary pair: e.g., the two people's Suns, Moons, etc. These midpoint planets are then placed in a chart that is produced by computing a midpoint Midheaven, and then calculating the rest of the house cusps for the latitude of the relationship. The primary reference for this system is Hand (1975) [and John Townley, *The Composite Chart*, 1973.—Ed.].

12 The Davison chart is produced by calculating the midpoint in time and space between the two birth charts. Then, a chart is calculated for that date, time, and location. The primary reference is Davison (1977). When the composite and relationship charts are compared, the mean Nodes will be identical, the Midheavens within a couple of degrees, and the Suns will be within a couple of minutes.

Similarly, what is the "first breath" of the relationship? Does the time of first meeting tell the eventual outcome of the relationship, i.e., whether the two people *can* have a sexual relationship, or whether they *will* have a sexual relationship? We will explore these issues in our final example.

One point: when showing astrological delineations as examples, it is actually preferable to use *un*successful relationships, or people who are to some extent dysfunctional. For one thing, the warts make the reading more interesting! In a relationship delineation for publication, it is helpful to know the end-point. The only time one can truly state that "they lived happily ever after" is if at least one of the parties is dead! An unfortunate side-effect of the use of eventually unsuccessful relationships is that it implies that most relationships are *also* unsuccessful.

Case Four: a Sexual Relationship

Linda and Ann both had been in a number of relationships before they encountered each other. They have since moved on to others after this one was over.

Both are Scorpios. Both are writers. Linda is also an artist. With all this Scorpio lying about, we shall have an opportunity to evaluate the relative merits of Mars as ruler of Scorpio versus Pluto.

Linda is a double Scorpio. Eroticism has been one of the major themes of her art. There are three other recurring themes: race, physical disability, and family relationships, mainly involving her mother.

In classical delineation, the mother is represented by the 10th House, given here by the Sun, ruler of the 10th, and Jupiter in the 10th. The Sun is conjunct the Ascendant, so her mother looms large. As for her other artistic themes, one could make a good case for Saturn (in Gemini) ruling both race and physical disability. I would be comfortable in assigning all oppressed people in a particular society to a Saturn rulership, but would hope the subjects of oppression diminish over time!

Mars rules the Scorpio Ascendant (classically), and Mars is conjunct Saturn.

To view Linda's sex life, we turn to the Ascendant, Sun, Moon, Venus, and Mars. The Ascendant and the Sun are conjunct, from the 12th House side. Like many 12th House Suns, Linda seems shy publicly, although with Leo on the MC she is perfectly comfortable in the spotlight. The Sun is within 5° of the Ascendant, so of course it should be considered angular. This angularity means she is more outgoing than many 12th House Sun types. Her Venus and Mars are square, both in Mercury-ruled signs. She not only enjoys talking about sex, and talking during sex, but drawing or photographing it! Her Sun is also square Pluto; she was raped in her teens.

Linda's Moon is peregrine and in its detriment in the 3rd House, but conjunct the Part of Fortune. Writing has become an effective and lucrative method of exploring and expressing her feelings. A strong theme of emotional pain pervades her work

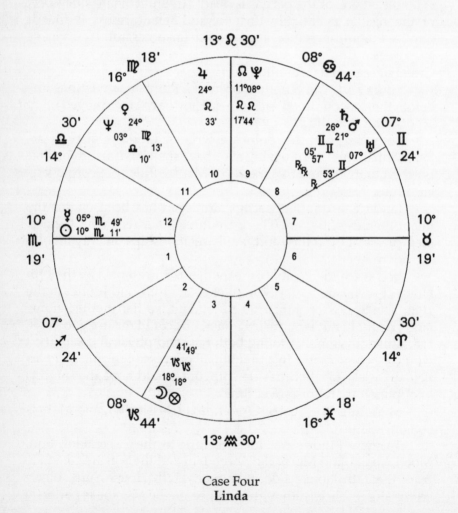

Case Four
Linda

and she has attained a measure of success and reputation within the lesbian subculture. While she lives frugally, the financial rewards have enabled her to support herself.

Now we'll look at Ann's horoscope: Ann's Ascendant is co-ruled (Almuten) by Venus and Saturn. Her Venus is within 5° of the Ascendant from the 12th, an angular placement. It is dignified in Libra, conjunct Jupiter, semi-sextile the Moon and trine Uranus. Jupiter rules her 3rd, and hence, her writing. Her Jupiter is in a mutual reception *by exaltation* with Saturn. Her Saturn is not strong in the sign of Cancer and is in a tight trine to Mercury in the 2nd. Mercury rules her 9th and 12th Houses.

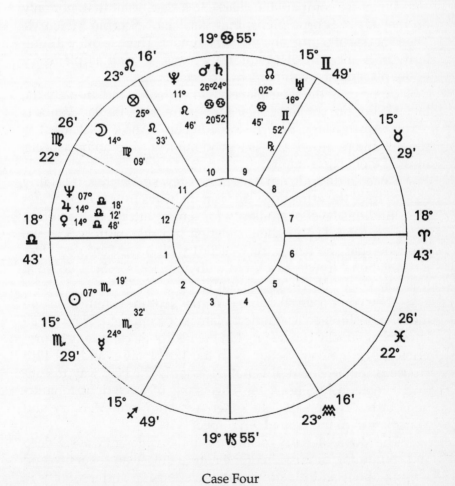

Case Four
Ann

Ann's Moon in Virgo, in the 11th and ruling the 8th and 10th (by exaltation), has many of the features of the wife in Case One: an extreme sensitivity to touch. Ann also has Sun square Pluto, indicating that her sexual appetite can also take a walk on the wild side.

Mars rules her Sun, and Mars is conjunct Saturn. Mars rules or co-rules the 2nd and 7th Houses. While Mars has some dignity in Cancer, there is a tendency for the Mars in Cancer native to get what she wants less by getting it herself than by getting others to get it for her. The conjunction with Saturn puts a damper on Mars' ardor.

When we compare the charts, it is significant that, not only do they share Scorpio Suns, they also share Scorpio Mercurys. Their modes of expression are very similar. There is quite a similarity of planets in distribution by signs, as well as planetary house placements within the two charts.

Comparing the same planets that we look at individually, the lovers' Suns are conjunct, their Moons are trine, Linda's Venus is sextile Ann's Mars, Saturn and Mercury. Ann's Ascendant is square Linda's Moon. This is a good number of common aspects, most of them harmonious.

Since Linda and Ann have quite a few similarities, it is fairly easy to trace the attraction. This is not always true! Often, water signs find this level of similarity to be more attractive than other signs may. Linda's previous relationship was with a Scorpio, showing that she had a track record with other Scorpios. (Her next relationship was to a Virgo with no planets in Scorpio, so at least she wasn't obsessive about it!)

Their composite chart has a Venus-Neptune conjunction and the relationship had a significant fantasy component. Now we all know that fantasy can be great in the bedroom, especially appropriate since the conjunction is in the 12th House, and the 12th House is the bedroom. It is not necessarily the best way to conduct a relationship, however. This is one of three tight conjunctions in the composite. The other two are Moon-Mercury and Mars-Saturn in the 1st and 9th respectively.

The Moon-Mercury manifested in two different ways: a deep and continuing discussion of the nature of lesbian sexuality, and writing about and illustrating the relationship and sexuality in general. During the time they were together, a number of erotic anthologies from the female perspective began to appear. Both contributed to publications of this sort, mostly through works of fantasy. Mercury is the natural ruler of writing. Jupiter, ruler of the Composite 3rd House is in Virgo, disposed by Mercury. The 11th House includes dreams[13] and hopes, so it is germane that many of the works they produced were fictional.

The two planets that show distancing in any relationship are Saturn and Pluto, so we can safely say that the third conjunction,

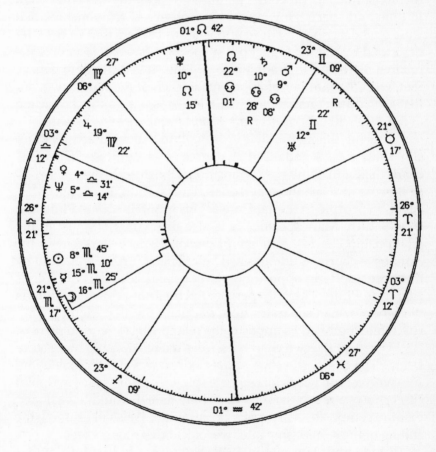

Case Four
Linda & Ann

---

13 11th House dreams are secular. Religious dreams and visions are 9th House matters.

Mars-Saturn, was not so positive in manifestation. The conjunction of Mars and Saturn produced a need for separate *working* space. Unfortunately, what began as separate space for creative purposes became separate brooding spaces when the relationship began to unravel.

Before considering the Davison time-space relationship chart, I want to state my opinion about these two methods of chart comparison. Of course, both of them are twentieth century developments. I have to admit to an aesthetic preference for the relationship chart (to come) because it represents an actual point in time and space. However, I have observed relationships that were well described by the composite, and others that were better described by the relationship. I suspect we have an issue like the relative merits of different house systems. It is difficult to believe that, with the number of adherents to each of the house systems, that each doesn't have some merit. Perhaps part of the dimension of our free will is *to choose our systemic frequencies of resonance.*

Bearing this in mind, it is difficult to believe that a relationship with the Ascendant at 29 degrees of a sign (see "Davison" chart) is not in some way "transitional" instead of "permanent." In this case we see three personal planets—Sun, Mars, and Mercury—in Scorpio in the 1st House. This group is square Pluto and trine Saturn. Mars specifically is also inconjunct Uranus. In the relationship chart, the theme of personal space—present in the composite chart—is emphasized here. This is further enhanced by the close applying opposition of Venus and Uranus, with Venus also trine Pluto. The only personal planet not aspecting Pluto is the Moon, which separates from a square. But that Moon in Taurus, while dignified, is opposite the relationship's Scorpio planets.

Which of the two charts describes the relationship more accurately? The composite chart shows a dreamy, yet intense relationship with certain needs for separate space. The time-space midpoint chart shows a much darker side. At the time, I would have hoped that the composite chart was more accurate! We shall examine the ending of the relationship after we look at two more charts.

Linda and Ann met in 1979. They went to bed for the first time two days later. The relationship lasted until 1984.

But what is the moment of their relationship? When does it begin? Is a sexual relationship fated, given that the appropriate components necessary for a sexual relationship were present? To answer these questions, we must study event charts or horaries that are specific to the *whens* of their relationship: when they met, when they first had sex, when they moved in together, or similar events.

We can study the Time of Meeting chart essentially in several ways: either as a chart by itself, or in relation to Linda and Ann's natal charts, or in a comparison with their relationship/composite maps.

Let us begin with the Time of Meeting as a chart apart from the specific protagonists. The Time of Meeting chart (p. 219) has 0 degrees rising, the ruling Moon at 0 degrees, and Mercury at 0 degrees. This time clearly shows a beginning. The chart-ruling

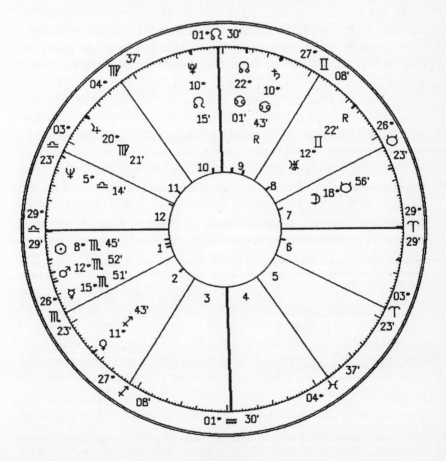

Case Four
Linda & Ann

Moon is conjunct the Descendant, the angle of partnership. The Moon is in detriment and peregrine, meaning she is too weak to produce an ultimately satisfying relationship.[14] The next aspect of the Moon is to Fortuna, a sextile, in 3°, then a trine to Saturn in 7°, followed by a square to Mars in 8°.

The method of interpreting an event chart is given in Dorotheus.[15] We may assign the 1st House to the initiator of the meeting, and the 7th House to the other party. Note that the 7th House is given to the other party, not because we are interested in considering if the two of them will go to bed. At the time of meeting, the other person is always the 7th House: the other party. There are two exceptions: the first is relationships by blood or marriage; the second is if the two people meet professionally, such as meeting a prospective boss or real estate agent for the first time.

Linda was the initiator of the action: she was the one who traveled to the site where they met. Linda's significator was the Moon; Ann's was Saturn. As mentioned, the Moon comes to trine Saturn: the two people "come together." Saturn is retrograde: in a classical delineation, *a retrograde planet brings things about suddenly*. This relationship was sudden; the sexual component began two days later.

But why sexual? When someone meets someone else "personally," that is, not for business reasons, they can become friends, lovers, or committed lovers. The 5th House rules *les amours* in the words of 16th Century author Claude Dariot: love affairs. The co-Almutens of the 5th House are Venus and Saturn, plus the two planets posited there, Uranus and Pluto. We're

---

14 In horary, a peregrine planet represents damaged goods. I would be tempted to call this relationship "damaged" or "flawed" from the beginning. Sometimes, however, a peregrine planet is simply one that wanders around too much to produce a concerted or consistent action. ["Peregrine" *classically* does not consider aspects; see footnote 5, p. 201.—Ed.]

15 Dorotheus of Sidon, First Century A.D., wrote a manual which simultaneously discusses horary, electional, and event interpretation using House rulerships that would look completely familiar to the modern horary astrologer. For example, he used the 1st House as the buyer, the 7th House as the seller, and the 10th House as the price in real estate questions. However, it is clear that he preferred to use a chart for an event which had already happened instead of a horary about it *if a time for the event was known*. In any case, the method of delineation was the same, no matter the chart, except for one thing. In horary, the 1st House always represents the Querent, the person asking the question. In event or electional, the 1st House generally represents the person(s) initiating the action. This has carried down to us in the use of the 1st House for the challenger in contest delineation.

already using Saturn as the 7th House ruler, so we examine Venus. The Moon does eventually sextile Venus, but after a lot of other things have happened: they would only have an affair *if nothing else happens with any of the other aspects which happen first*.

As for the 11th, the best ruler would be the Sun, (exhalted) Almuten of the 11th and located in the 11th. The Moon comes to square the Sun eventually too: they can only become friends *later*, and with difficulty, given the nature of the square.

Obviously, not every 7th House relationship is necessarily a long-term lover type. They could also be open enemies! (And isn't

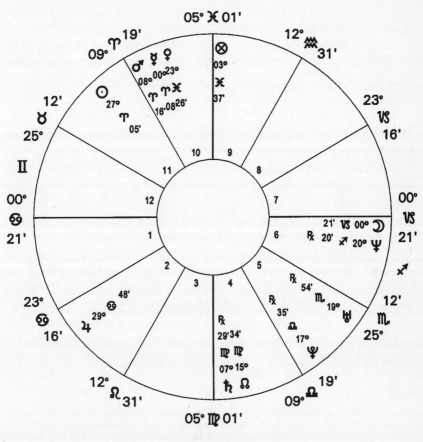

Case Four
**Linda & Ann
Meeting**

it fascinating that the same house rules those two types!) The 7th House also in effect rules acquaintances, because it is the default house whenever two people are considered. And of course, there is always the question of whether the parties are available for a sexual relationship.

We know that Linda and Ann were available for a sexual relationship—and then some! They described the time of meeting after the fact as a time when they *knew* they would become involved sexually: they essentially locked onto it, and the moment when it happened sexually was simply when it became feasible. That moment occurred two days later.

The First Sex chart[16] does not show all the hallmarks of the beginning of the relationship the way the Time of Meeting chart does: although Ascendant ruler Jupiter had moved from 29° Cancer to 0° Leo. The Descendant ruler is Mercury, and Mercury is 2° (two days!) past the trine to Jupiter. Their sense of the relationship was that the sex was inevitable from the time they met two days previously: it was a foregone conclusion.

Venus was dignified in the 3rd House, but void-of-course. Mars was likewise dignified in Aries. This was quite a successful sexual encounter in the sense that both parties were satisfied with the outcome, and became lovers for four years—a fairly long time in terms of their own past histories. Both Mars and the 7th House ruler Mercury were in the 4th House, the generic house for the end-of-the-matter. Mars was in mutual reception by exaltation with Jupiter in Leo, the Ascendant ruler.

And while we contemplate the end-of-the-matter, let us also consider the end of the relationship. In this type of interpretation, the more precise terminology would be death of the relationship. The use of the 4th House as end-of-the-matter is really a *provisional end,* more than in the sense of the outcome of the event. The outcome was that they got together and had a relationship. But it wasn't permanent.

---

16 I am often asked what to use for the timing of the First Sex chart! The possibilities boggle the mind! Curiously, I have found that many people, even nonastrologers, intuitively notice a particular point during the sexual courtship where sex becomes inevitable. Whether this is when they make out on the couch, or arrive in the bedroom, or even climax, varies by individual. My policy is to ask the person when she or he felt the sexual encounter begin, or at least when during that time the pair knew that they were going to conjoin, as it were.

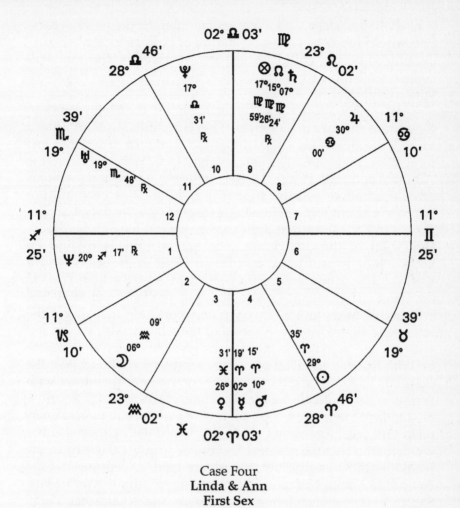

Case Four
Linda & Ann
First Sex

The death of the relationship is thus an 8th House matter relative to either of these two event charts. In the Time of Meeting chart (p. 219), the 8th House is ruled (Almuten) by Mars (exhalted in Capricorn). Mars is moving to an opposition of retrograde Pluto. That certainly sounds like destruction! The degree difference is 9; therefore, I would predict that the relationship could not last more than nine years.[17] Because Pluto is *retrograde*, the ending

---

17 Pluto is in the 5th House, and thus succedent, while Mars was in the 10th House. Both are in cardinal signs. While cardinal and angular placements usually speak to shorter time intervals, I was considering this as far as the *longest possible* relationship.

is likely to be *sudden*, and likely sooner than the degree of separation would indicate. Given the nature of Pluto, a violent or catastrophic outcome could ensue. Saturn, ruler of the 8th, will conjoin the Node in 8°. Both are mutable and cadent, so this translates to eight years.

As further support in the meeting chart, the Moon comes to the square of Mars in 8 degrees. This is another stressful aspect: these three combined suggest that the relationship will not last more than eight years. The first sex chart (p. 221) has Jupiter as the Almuten of the 8th House, located in the 8th. This is not giving us any information, because Jupiter is right at 0° of Leo, and not approaching anything of interest, except a weak semi-sextile with Saturn in 7.5°. Since that didn't work, we can look at the Moon, sign ruler of the 8th House. The old standby is to find an approaching aspect between the 8th House significator and a malefic. The Moon inconjoins Saturn in a year's time (i.e., 1° applying). That would be stressful, but probably not fatal. She will sextile Mars in 4°. Thus, we may conclude that this is the lower end figure for the duration of the relationship. We are left with a range from four to eight years, given the two charts together. With Mars in the First Sex Chart representing the trigger, the reason is likely to be either a quarrel or a sexual encounter with someone else; both are classic Mars interpretations.

In fact, the relationship ended with a physically violent quarrel in 1984 precipitated by Linda going to bed with someone else, a woman who became her next lover after Ann. At the time of the break-up, transiting Jupiter was square Linda's Neptune and the composite Venus-Neptune, Mars was approaching Ann's Mars, Saturn was conjunct Linda's Ascendant and square her Pluto, Venus was square the relationship Moon, and finally *Pluto, at 29° of Libra, was conjunct the relationship Ascendant* ("Davison," page 219).

A Causation Interlude

In the examples given, I've said nothing about astrological indicators of homosexuality. There is a reason: *there are none!* Many astrologers *think* they have found astrological significators because they rely on their own chart collections without considering that each of us draws people to us through the lens of her or his own natal chart.

In practice, this means that astrologers who have difficulty with homosexuality will draw homosexual clients who have difficulty with their own homosexuality! Astrologers who believe that all homosexual men are "effeminate" will get effeminate gay men as their clients. Astrologers who are completely accepting of homosexuality will draw a cross section of homosexuals as broad as the cross section of heterosexuals.

The astrological theories which have been developed cluster around three explanations, including: 1) severe "affliction" of inner planets by outer ones, usually Uranus, or sometimes Neptune in the case of lesbians; 2) "affliction" of Moon and Venus in a man, and one assumes Sun and Mars in lesbians; and 3) stress on the alleged houses of sexuality and/or relationship and karma (i.e., 5th, 7th, 8th or 12th).

The earliest and most common theory, Uranus afflictions, was championed by Karl Guenther Heimsoth in 1928. Unfortunately, his training as a Freudian made him interested in latent tendencies: his 34 illustrating cases included *no* practicing homosexuals! Because of this—that Heimsoth gets to pick who is homosexual rather that relying on the documented behavior of his "subjects"—his theory can be dismissed out of hand for inadequate documentation. However, the total absurdity of his methodology has not prevented many popularizers from picking up and broadcasting it to the point that many astrologers accept it today without question.

Methodology aside, Heimsoth's theory is difficult to test because his criterion was "affliction." With three outer planets to play with, and two to four inner ones, it is almost always possible to find *some* affliction to explain the chart in front of you. Unfortunately, most astrological theories of "causation"—be it of bunions or sexual preference—are worded so vaguely that they are next to useless. They can neither be tested nor rigorously applied.

I tested theories by Ebertin, Jerndal, Henderson, Ryan, Darling and Oliver, Jansky and Nauman, and van Dam using samples of gay men from my files, as well as obtaining the Jansky-Nauman data to ascertain the validity of their results.[18] Rather than rehash the statistics here, I will simply state the conclusions: *none of the theories held up.* Some were rejected on theoretical grounds: i.e., the models were so flawed that they could be rejected out-of-hand. These rejected models included Jansky/

Nauman, Darling/Oliver, Ryan, and Ebertin. Other theories—such as Jerndal's and van Dam's—simply are not supported by moderate to large data sets.

How does one explain these discrepancies? One problem is sampling and experimental design, but that is not the only problem. I would like to consider the rationale behind these particular theories, and, unfortunately, most theories for *any* behavior proposed by astrologers.

In each of the astrological models given, the assumption is that homosexuality results from a disruption of the "normal" patterns of functioning. It may be by a rebellion against normal patterns (Uranus), breakdown of opposite sex attraction (Sun-Mars or Moon-Venus), or stress concerning the expression of sexuality (5th, 7th or 8th house conflicts). In each of these cases homosexuality is viewed by heterosexuals in essentially negative terms: either fear/loathing of the opposite sex, or inability to function within "normal" sexual channels. However, many gays experience "coming out" (identifying as homosexual for the first time) as a *positive* process; frequently by falling head-over-heels in love with a person of the same sex and then coming to terms with what that means.

According to *The Gay Report*, a study of several thousand lesbians and gay men, 87 percent of the lesbians and 66 percent of the gay men had had heterosexual sex; 55 percent of the lesbians and 36 percent of the gay men felt negatively about heterosexual sex. Clearly, a large number of gays do not in fact feel negatively about heterosexual relationships. These results confirm the findings of Kinsey and associates, who concluded that *sexual preference is best expressed as a spectrum, not an either/or condition.*

It would appear that any study on homosexuality is incomplete without realizing that for many gays, homosexuality represents a positive choice and experience. Astrologers, like psychologists, have been more used to cataloging their *problems.* In most empirical research, the most crucial step is framing the proper question. I submit that the question, "How do you tell a homosexual?" is no more useful than "How do you tell a heterosexual?" In either case, one gets bogged down in retroactive

---

18 c.f., Lehman (1980) and Lehman (1976). Full descriptions of the nature of these theories, as well as their statistical and other problems are given, especially in 1980.

analysis—always with 20/20 hindsight—of no use whatsoever to the client. Homosexuals do not usually visit astrologers to be told they are gay, or to discuss the causes of their homosexuality. They come for the same reasons everyone else does.

Sex and the Projection Principle

In my work with lesbians, I have encountered no aspect, no house location, no ruler which is present in all cases, or even most cases. One observation I can make is that most lesbians I have studied are not using Moon-Venus or Sun-Mars combinations in the way that conventional astrological theories suggest that they would. However, the same is true of my straight female clients. Considering the change in western family patterns over the centuries since these astrological forms were set down, this is hardly surprising. Unfortunately, there has been an insidious change in the interpretation of many of the classical methods as a result of the influence of psychological models in astrology.

If we study the delineation methods in practice in the 17th century and the few centuries previous to that, the system was to address "questions of the 1st House," "questions of the 2nd House," and so forth. Whether the Native was male or female, the 7th House represented the marriage partner. In the case of marriages in men's charts, the wife was also signified by Moon and Venus. In the case of marriages in women's charts, the husband was also signified by Sun and Mars. Of course, homosexuality was not mentioned since the church considered it a sin. In those days, the purpose of marriage was to produce offspring and gain financial advantage, and homosexuals generally married the opposite sex like everyone else.

These multiple significators were used to judge specific questions: how many spouses, would the Native marry for money, who would rule the roost, would the wife be faithful (of course, the reverse was not considered), would the wife be a virgin (again, not discussed for men), would the pair love each other, who would love the other more, would they argue or quarrel frequently, and ultimately, who would die first.

It was common to give a physical description of the prospective spouse, usually shown by the dignities of the Descendant and the ruler of the Descendant, either as sign ruler or Almuten.

How much could the sstrologer actually say about the spouse? With luck, he[19] could get the marks and moles, the financial status, and so forth. But the twentieth century astrologer in effect goes much further, but without claiming to do so.

The source of the change has been the integration of the psychological concept of *projection* into astrological delineation. And what was the change? Originally, Mars and the Sun were natural rulers of men in a woman's chart. In the twentieth Century, astrologers changed this to mean that women *project* their Sun and Mars energy. The difference is this. In a classical reading, Sun and Mars could be used as Significators of men *if the issue being discussed was an issue of men,* for example, the issue of marriage in the woman's life. The Sun and Mars would still be delineated *as her planets and energy* when this issue did not involve men in her life. For example, the calculation of the Hyleg or Alchocoden[20] was identical between men and women. There was no hint that a Sun- or Mars-ruled house would be interpreted any differently in a woman's chart than would a Moon- or Venus-ruled one.

The psychologically-based projection method of delineation is the assumption that women project their Sun energy onto others *regardless of whether the issue involves men or not.* What had been a specific use of natural rulers became a blanket statement about *all* uses of that planet. Thus, the Sun and Mars become almost vestigial except through projection: a woman without a man has nowhere to project all this energy, and thus, she is truly incomplete.This is why in these examples, I have taken the simpler and earlier approach of using Venus and Mars as delineators of sexuality. *Both* women and men use *both* planets. Do people project onto others? Of course, but the process is not as simple as giving up two planets!

---

19 And it would have been he, of course!

20 Feeling a little weak in the Alchocoden? The Hyleg was the giver of life, generally the Sun, Moon, or Ascendant, with the calculation requiring that the Hyleg be in particular house areas and beginning with the Sun or the Moon depending on whether it was a day or night birth. The Alchocoden, or giver of years, was the Almuten of the Hyleg. It was used in determining the expected length of life.

The Moment of the Relationship

What is a sexual relationship astrologically? It is an affair of the 1st and 7th or 1st and 5th Houses, played out to a large extent through the rulers of those houses and the natural relationship significators Venus and Mars.

How do we delineate it? We begin with the natal charts and see how capable the parties are of sustaining any kind of relationship in the first place. We can then compare the two charts, and see how they function together. Finally, there are significant "moments" to a relationship; those nexus times when the relationship begins or changes. In a heterosexual context, the marriage chart may be one of those times. But in all relationships, there is the time of meeting, and in the case of sexual relationships, the time of first sex.

It is virtually impossible to imagine all the different things that people get out of relationships, or what the many rationales are for getting into a relationship in the first place. It is far simpler to delineate what the true purpose of a relationship is, rather than whether this particular relationship is sexual, platonic, or nonexistent.

The delineation of the death of a relationship has many of the same difficulties as the delineation of actual physical death, but with fewer perceived moral issues! Astrologers who choose to criticize classical methods often do so because they are uncomfortable with the ancient inclusion of information and timing on the Native's death, and the death of the Native's parents, children, and spouses. Beyond our society's basic aversion to discussing death at all, there is the very real observation that the longevity of people in the late twentieth century is better than that of people in the seventeenth century, and yet *when death occurs the aspects are similar or the same!*

Most modern classicists would respond by saying that "death" aspects really represent crisis periods. They are physical crises: health problems in the case of natal, or events in the case of a relationship. In other words, these are not crises of mental anguish, or boredom, or mental stress. They occur in the material world. Do they spell doom for the Native or relationship? Not necessarily, but they must be overcome to survive.

When I delineated this relationship to Linda at the time of its inception, I did not discuss the possible death of the relationship. She didn't ask; I didn't volunteer.

The end of the relationship fell during the period between that predicted from the Time of Meeting chart and the First Sex chart. It did not fall exactly at the time given by either chart. The transits told the story. I mentioned previously the transits at the time of the break-up. While gratifying astrologically, again, I would not have felt comfortable predicting that *that time* was necessarily the death of the relationship, and not just a garden variety stress point. But transiting Pluto to the relationship Ascendant provided more stress than the relationship could handle.

So when is the moment of a relationship? To a large extent, it is when the participants say so. We may presume that certain moments, like Time of Meeting, or First Sex, Engagement, or Marriage, are probably charged periods for the protagonists. Different people view these moments with differing priorities, and the astrologer does not have access to each person's internal thoughts! The best the astrologer can do is to find which chart(s) describe the relationship best, describe the parties best, and describe the events of the relationship best. Then, read that chart. If none of the possible relationship charts works, go back to natal and synastry.

Any valid chart must tell the story. If the chart doesn't do it, consider using a different chart. Happy hunting!

References

Dariot, Claude. 1558/1990. *Introduction au Jugement des Astres suivie d'un Traité des élections propres pour le commencement des choses.* Adapted to modern French by Chantal Etienne. Pardés: Puiseaux.

Dariot, Claudius. *A Brief and Most Easy Introduction to the Astrological Judgment of the Stars, whereby Every Man may with Small Labor give Answers to any Question Demanded.* (1583) Translated by Fabian Wither. London: Thomas Pursfoote. Issaquah, WA: Just Us & Associates, reprint, 1992.

Dariot, Claudius. 1653. *Dariotus Redivivus, or a Briefe Introduction conducing to the Judgment of the Stars, wherein the whole Art of Judiciall Astrologie is briefly and plainly Delivered.* Translated by Fabian Wither, enlarged and adorned by N[athaniel] S[park]. London: Printed for Andrew King.

Darling, H. F. and Ruth Hale Oliver. *Astropsychiatry.* Lakemont, GA: C.S.A. Press, 1973.

Davison, Ronald. *Synastry.* New York: ASI, 1977.

Duby, Georges, ed. *A History of Private Life. Revelations of the Medieval World.* Cambridge, MA: Harvard Belknap, 1988.

Hand, Robert. *Planets in Composite.* West Chester: Whitford Press, 1975.

Heimsoth, Karl Guenther. *Homosexuality in the Horoscope.* Tempe, AZ: AFA, 1928.

Jansky, Robert and Eileen Nauman. 1979. Cited by Joseph Goodavage in *Mercury Hour* #22:26.

Jay, Karla and Allen Young. *The Gay Report.* New York: Summit, 1979.

Jerndal, Jens. "Male homosexuality in the birth chart." *CAO Times* 3(4):21–22, 1978.

_____. 1980. "Energy structures of homosexuality and some observations on statistics in astrology." *CAO Times* 4(2):14–16.

Kinsey, A. C. et al. *Sexual Behavior in the Human Male.* Philadelphia: W. B. Saunders, 1948.

Kinsey, A.C. et al. *Sexual Behavior in the Human Female.* Philadelphia: W. B. Saunders, 1953.

Lehman, J. Lee. "Predicting Homosexuality from the horoscope." *CAO Times* 4(3): 10–13, 1980.

_____. "Predicting homosexuality from the horoscope: A Review. "*NCGR Journal,* Winter 1986/1987: 51–57.

_____. *Essential Dignities.* West Chester, PA: Whitford Press, 1989.

_____. "When a Quincunx is not inconjunct." *Aspects* 17(2): 7–14, 1992(a).

_____. *The Book of Rulerships.* West Chester, PA: Whitford Press, 1992(b).

_____. "Old tricks for new horaries." *NCGR Journal,* Winter 1992–1993: 13–21.

Lilly, William. *Christian Astrology.* (1647) London: Regulus, reprinted 1985.

Nauman, E. Cited by J. F. Goodavage, *Mercury Hour* #22: 26, 1979.

Ryan, Anne. *Planets in Mutual Reception.* So. Euclid, OH: House of Astrology, Inc., 1980.

Ranke-Heinemann, Uta. *Eunuchs for the Kingdom of Heaven.* Translated by Peter Heinegg. New York: Doubleday, 1990.

Sidonius, Dorotheus. *Carmen Astrologicum,* translated by David Pingree. Leipzig: B. G. Teubner Verlagsgesellschaft, 1976.

van Dam, Wm. *Astrology and Homosexuality.* York Beach: Weiser, 1985.

Stevens, John. *Lust for Enlightenment.* Boston: Shambhala, 1990.

Watters, Barbara. 1971. *Sex and the Outer Planets.* Washington, DC: Valhalla, 1971.

Ted Sharp

Ted Sharp has been a professional astrologer for over 20 years. He was a pioneer in Past-Life Therapy, working since 1972 both individually and with groups across America. He has hosted his own radio talk show and appeared on many different TV shows, as well as writing articles on astrology and Past-Life Therapy for a variety of publications. With his wife, Content Hagen, MSW, LCSW, Ted consults in Change Management and conducts various twelve-step training, educational, and therapeutic programs in the Baltimore-Washington, D.C. area.

An honors graduate of the University of Tennessee and former USAF officer, Ted lived for almost 20 years in Virginia Beach, Virginia, and was most active as an organizer of weekend astrological seminars. He now resides in Ellicott City, Maryland.

Freeing the Spirit: Getting Beyond Denial

Ted Sharp

Freeing the spirit! No brief chapter can begin to do justice to a subject so fascinating and so profound in its implications for each of us. What follows is a sketch of some pertinent topics, some horoscope examples of persons who dedicated themselves to spiritual growth, and others who are cultural icons, who mirror the great current need for emotional healing in Western society. I have also included some important practical steps for getting beyond denial to emotional healing.

Freeing the spirit or the liberation of the soul, is the primary goal of all the refined systems of Eastern spiritual technology. In the most spiritually advanced times of ancient Egypt and various other times and places of high spiritual awareness in the panorama of human history, great teachers have helped willing and diligent students make great progress toward this goal of freeing the spirit. Most Westerners who are serious about real spiritual growth usually end up adopting an Eastern approach or "guru," or some variation thereof.

Can we do it here and now? Does astrology have a part to play? Do relatively recent findings concerning the prevalence of addiction in Western society, the rise of Twelve Step recovery models, and new female/male perspectives on cultural evolution provide important clues? To each question I believe the answer is "Yes."

Spiritual Growth Model

In the beginning all was Light and oneness with God or the Source. With the creation of the material world came the archetypal division into yang/yin, positive and negative, day and night, male and female, etc. This is why sex as we think of it makes the world go 'round.

According to the Ancient Wisdom teachings all humans have several bodies—spiritual, mental, emotional and physical—with only the physical being visible to most. The connecting points between the bodies, which are called the endocrine glands in modern medicine, are the physical analog to the spiritual bodies' chakras, Sanskrit for wheels or discs, described by sensitives as whirling vortices of energy.

Traditionally, there are seven chakras through which all life energies work. These chakras range, more or less in linear form, along the human spinal column. The energy moves from the base or sex chakra to the crown chakra through which ultimate spiritual enlightenment occurs. Taken as a whole the experiences provided through these chakras constitute all mankind's individual and collective experience.

Although this seems like a very simple process according to the Wisdom Teachings, it takes an average soul many lifetimes in this three-dimensional material world to achieve the ultimate spiritual goal of oneness with God or the Source. While a full discussion of reincarnation—the concept of many lifetimes in which to experience, learn, and grow—is beyond the scope of this article, reincarnation is an essential part of the spiritual liberation process. The central idea is that we have many bodies, many experiences in different times, places, and races, all designed to help us learn and grow as both students and teachers.

That is because in our learning process we have developed attachments, perhaps numbered in the millions, in many lives in the material world. Since all attachments are at first fear-based, we have to learn to dissolve these fears with love. Again, we state in a few words what can take humans many lifetimes, some say many thousands, to achieve.

There is an old Hindu story to illustrate the time the average soul takes to achieve unity with the Source. Imagine a bird with a scarf in its beak flying over the Himalayan mountains. As the bird passes the top of the highest mountains, the scarf lightly brushes the peak. The time it would take the bird and the scarf to wear the mountain range down to a flat plain is the time it takes the average soul to achieve ultimate spiritual liberation.

Are you ready now to shortcut this process on earth? As you might expect, you are not the first to have this thought when confronted with this scenario.

According to the great teachers, man cannot in one human life pass through all seven stages from the lowest level of human consciousness to the highest state of universal consciousness because his nervous system could not tolerate the vast difference in tension or vibration rate. It takes usually many lifetimes to cover the lower chakras or levels of experience or gradually to increase the resistance of the nervous system.

From the middle level or 4th chakra at which he is spiritually awakened, a devoted spiritual seeker may, if he wishes, progress consciously to the highest level in a single lifetime. Of course, the Masters caution that this progress requires great dedication, and *the concentrated use of the sexual energy present in the body* as fuel for spiritual enlightenment is highly preferred, if not essential.

Throughout many millennia, some of the highest spiritual teachers have devised schools or temples of initiation or places where humans could shortcut the spiritual growth process of overcoming fear with love. They devised training and tests which concentrated the experiences normally spread across many human lifetimes into the short span of a single lifetime. However, the very greatest teachers of recorded history have sought to bring truth and enlightenment directly to the masses and not concentrate merely on a favored few living in a time and place where temples of initiation exist.

For those living in the East, which historically has had a more extensive spiritual tradition, the great role model for spiritual growth and enlightenment has been the venerable Buddha with his Eight Fold Path. Although the Jews look to Abraham and Moses and await the coming of the Messiah, and the Muslims look to Mohammed, for the majority of Westerners Jesus the Christ has historically been the greatest spiritual role model.

It seems that the greatest teachers have successfully tried to refine the essence of the spiritual teachings. Although there is some controversy about whether or not the existing four gospels of the

New Testament contain all of Jesus' recorded teachings, He would appear to have summarized all the ancient teachings in a relatively few sentences. More importantly, His example as a role model for spiritual growth has inspired millions over the centuries, especially in the West. Let us take an astrological look at Jesus.

Jesus of Nazareth

The putative, and, I believe, highly probable, horoscope of Jesus of Nazareth, as thoroughly and compellingly researched by the late Hawaiian astrologer, Don "Moby Dick" Jacobs, is stunning, almost overwhelming in its concentration, focus, and challenge. Jacobs himself called it: "the neatest and most compact, most concentrated and focused horoscope I have ever seen!" We will not attempt to discuss it in depth, but mainly focus on the chart's indicated potential for personality transformation and liberating the spirit.

Jesus' mission would seem to be that of a teacher who made his teaching unforgettable by living it so completely. Note the extremely heavy emphasis in the 3rd House, the almost limitless potential for psychic sensitivity promised by the five trines from the Sun, Moon, Uranus, Jupiter and Saturn all conjunct in Pisces in the 3rd House of communication, learning and teaching to their dispositor, Neptune in Scorpio in the 11th House. With these five 3rd House placements under high developmental tension and awareness from an opposed retrograde Pluto in Virgo in the 9th, this man had an overwhelming need to travel, learn, teach, and communicate a transformational philosophy with powerful conviction based on direct psychic perceptions.

With this Neptune placement in the 11th House, his life wish or dream was to teach and model the ultimate transforming power of divine love to triumph even over the most appalling and humiliating public execution by world authorities. Ultimately he could proclaim: "I and my Father are one."

Having Mercury ruler of the Midheaven in Aquarius and Jupiter, the Ascendant ruler, most closely conjunct Uranus, His message was revolutionary to entrenched, oppressive authority both secular and religious. The revolutionary truth he taught and embodied so dramatically and powerfully was the evolutionary necessity for each of us to strive to personally express universal love and compassion in all our thoughts and actions.

Significantly, the six oppositions in Jesus' chart all involved the planets symbolizing the will, Mars and Pluto, with both placed in the southern hemisphere. Mars symbolizes the lower will and Pluto the Higher Spiritual will. They and Neptune are retrograde, indicating some unfinished matters in the unconscious still to be resolved involving total trust and surrender to God the Father (note Sun, Moon, and Saturn opposing the MC) and the willingness to act in accordance with beliefs based on psychic perception and inner guidance. [More information about Jacobs' studies of Jesus: The Joshua Foundation, Mill Valley, CA.—Ed.]

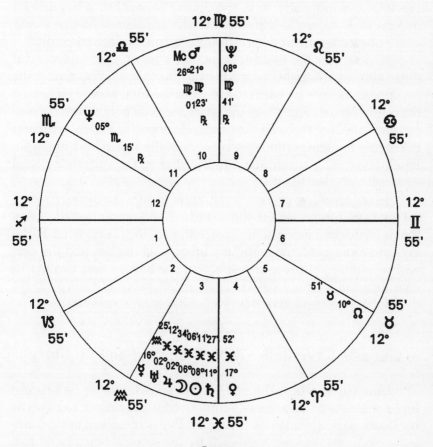

Jesus
March 1, 0007 B.C., 1:21 A.M.
Bethlehem, Judea
Equal Houses

The five oppositions to Pluto from the Pisces planets in the 3rd House indicate the incredible high conscious and subconscious nervous tension, resistance and awareness involving the knowing, teaching, and living out such a clearly perceived transformational philosophy. Jesus saw clearly, clairvoyantly, but he was mostly communicating with people who saw "through a glass darkly."

He was born on a New Moon in Pisces in the dawn of the Piscean Age and the symbol of his followers was the fish. His message of universal love (Love God with all your heart and soul and love your neighbor as yourself) and liberation of the soul through seeking unity with the Source seems but a vague and unattainable dream to many today who are enmeshed in a world of chaotic materialism where "ignorant armies clash by night."

If we credit the psychic source of Edgar Cayce and several other ancient independent traditions, the soul who became Jesus had previous lives on earth (Cayce said the total was 30 including the one as Jesus). This gives the chart a special poignancy. He was not just tiptoeing through the tulips. He, too, had to deal with and overcome the temptations and snares of the world and the flesh. Finally he totally surrendered to the Higher, thus achieving total triumph over death.

Jesus' teaching and demonstration of self-sacrificing universal love and forgiveness is still so radical and revolutionary today that it is honored more in the breach than in the observance. However, no other personage nor any other teaching has had the pervasive, subtle yet profound effect on the history and destiny of countless millions of lives as has this man, Jesus. His life portrays the highest expression of the symbolic Neptune potential.

Genesis Revisited—A New Look at an Old Story

The individual who achieves cosmic consciousness has recaptured the state of awareness symbolized brilliantly in Genesis as the Garden of Eden. It was lost when Eve (symbolical of predominate emotion) was overpowered by the serpent (earthly animal sexual energy), causing Adam (predominate reason) also to succumb. According to Cayce, the soul that was Jesus had its first human incarnation as Adam.

The tree of the knowledge of good and evil is symbolic of the human spinal column and the nervous system with its network of nerves and its enmeshment in the phenomenal world of duality via the five senses. (Note that astrologically Gemini, a dual sign, rules the nervous system and the basic mental acquisition of sensational form-world knowledge.)

The forbidden fruit in the center of the Garden was the apple (symbolic of the brute, animalistic sexual energies which tie man to Earth). Tightening the symbolic focus, we can also see how the whole Adam and Eve legend symbolizes one individual human soul becoming enmeshed in a physical body.

Thus the "knowledge of good and evil," promised to Eve by the "serpent" refers to the experience of suffering in duality and illusion to which man, imprisoned in the identity of mortal flesh, is heir. Falling into delusion, through the misuse of his feeling and reason—or Adam-and-Eve consciousness—man relinquishes his right to remain in the Edenic perfect state of unity. In light of this understanding, each of us has then the personal responsibility for restoring his archetypal parents (dual yin-yang, animus-anima nature) to a unified harmony or Edenic consciousness.

The condition of being human is thus expressed very basically in sexuality. Adam, the original androgyne, saw the animals of the Earth, and desired to be like them, desired to be split into male and female. With the "fall" ["realityization"?—Ed.] of Adam and Eve, time (Saturn) and history began. For in gaining sexuality, there was no other way of experiencing ultimate redemption save through the knowledge of good and evil, the ultimate tension of polarity giving rise, in time, to the synthesis that is spiritual rebirth.

Lighting the Human Christmas Tree

Since the practice of yoga—whatever its form—has as its goal the transmutation of base sexual energy into the gold of conscious unity with the Source of all life, let us examine the actual dynamics of spiritual growth a bit more specifically.

Yogis of various backgrounds teach us that consciousness may be likened to an FM band on a radio receiver. If one tunes the receiver to one station, he receives only the information of one reality, one level of existence. However, multidimensional man through the alchemical transformation of the sexual energy which binds him to the physical plane of sex, time, and death (Eros, Chronos and Thanatos, respectively), is able, by a disciplined application of will, to tune his consciousness to a different station on the FM band and discover worlds *beyond matter* in the limitless realm of spirit.

In yoga, the cerebrospinal system is the FM band, and the chakras or spiritual centers along the spine symbolize the various stations or levels of cosmic information into which we may tune. They etherically or spiritually correspond to the physical endocrine glandular system and, as stated above, are the points at which the mental, the spiritual, the emotional, and the physical bodies are joined.

After visiting symbolically (or literally like Mohammed) the seven heavens or universes representing the seven presently known chakras, the spiritual explorer returns to his physical body, now transformed by the process of spiritual adventuring, in possession of a new, cosmically attuned nervous system and a cosmic awareness with which to expedite his evolutionary process in human form. Again this is a process which the Ancient Wisdom tells us normally takes lifetimes.

Thus is accomplished man's ultimate mission on earth: the spiritualization of materiality and the redemption of the physical form-world through the mastery of sexual energy. In a philosophical sense, Eden is regained!

The underlying truths which form the basis for physical matter-reality seem always to be clairvoyantly glimpsed by the creative artist long before they are validated by the pedantic scientist. In this special awareness, the artist is ever the harbinger of times to come.

In "Little Giddings" from his *Four Quartets*, T. S. Eliot eloquently describes the same journey to rebirth which science is just now beginning hesitantly to validate physiologically and psychologically:

> We shall not cease from exploration
> And the end of our exploring
> Will be to arrive where we started
> And to know the place for the first time . . .
> When the tongues of flame are in-folded
> Into the crowned knot of fire
> And the fire and the rose are one.

Yogis would label the union of the fire and the rose as the marriage of Kundalini (the fire of sexual energy) and the thousand-petaled lotus (the crown chakra).

The purpose of yoga is union of the seemingly diverse aspects of man's multidimensional being into one whole spiritual entity. Matter is transformed into spirit, and thus man's evolution is stepped up to another level. Then is the Fall reversed. Symbolically, semen instead of being expended outwardly, flows in pranic form up the spinal column (now the vagina) and is planted in the brain (womb) to fertilize the spiritual birth of a divine child. Thus the individual becomes both male and female in this intense and ecstatic moment of transcendent illumination. The human Christmas tree is lit. The crowning herald star of divine birth illuminates the entire nervous system. Joy to the World, the Lord is born! Let Heaven and Nature sing!

So the next time you see a meditating Yogi who really knows his stuff with his eyeballs rolled up and his lips curled into a blissful smile of nirbikapal samadhi—the highest state of consciousness—you are witnessing a man who is publicly having a continuous interior orgasm. Joyous energy released in an interior union of this nature, in comparison to the best physical orgasm you ever had, is like comparing an atomic bomb to a firecracker, or an oceanic tidal wave to a bathtub ripple. Or, at least, that is what all the great spiritual teachers tell us.

This perspective puts the potential of meditation into a whole new light. This is why the mind is the greatest erogenous zone. This is how saints do it!

The Astrological Reflection of Sexual Energy

With this overview of the basic growth-tension-to-unity which is the sexual urge in all men and women, how may the art-science of astrology help to illuminate each person's loving use of his creative sexual energy to move more directly toward the goal of cosmic consciousness?

Astrologically, of course, sex is a function of one's whole horoscope. No aspect of human existence can be viewed as entirely separate from the whole, and no other separate aspect of our human identity is more basically intertwined throughout every facet of earthly physical existence than is the dimension of sexuality. The writhing serpent of Biblical Genesis continues to bedevil and bewitch mankind, the outcast from Eden, until AdamEve awakens from suffering's thralldom and joyously disciplines this aspect of consciousness.

The Sun as ruler of Leo and the 5th House indicates the steady radiance of creative energy which may be invested in a spontaneous, playful way in everything from children to the stock market to recreational pursuits of all types, from love affairs to vacations. It is basically a potential dramatic outpouring of energy to light up and lift up, a joy in being, an instructional entertainment which seeks appreciation, the creative capacity to express the ultimate personal power of love. *Challenging aspects to the Sun indicate that the basic life force has been misused or abused and needs to be rebuilt.*

If the Sun, 5th House, and Leo key the potential capacity for giving love, Mars is the urge to fulfill primal desire through the physical application of energy, the lower will, aggression. It was Adam's desiring to be split like the animals into sexual polarity which led to his banishment from Eden.

The force of will can cut and separate, or knit and heal, if Mars (fission) is controlled to operate in service to the higher spiritual will symbolized by Pluto (fusion), co-ruler with Mars of Aries and Scorpio. Mars and Pluto at the Ascendant or the point of eternal dawn are symbolic indicators, not only of physical birth (Adam's fall is recapitulated in each successive new-born babe), but also spiritual rebirth, through the fusing, transforming, resurrecting energy of the higher spiritual will (Pluto).

As we have noted in the horoscope of Jesus, the Mars-Pluto relationship is *vital to the process of redirecting the primal sexual energy of desire into mastery over forms of spiritual energy.*

The impulsive dynamic energy thrust and active desire of Mars must be alchemically transmuted by the astrological element of fire at the Ascendant, as controlled by the highest expression of Pluto. Anything that does not support spiritual growth is eliminated. Only the essence is lifted in a process of cleansing release. Indeed, a rebirth! Man is a soul who wears a body. *To awaken from spiritual amnesia is to awaken from physical bondage.*

Venus is the principle of attraction, succinctly expressed universally as *like attracts like. Venus then functions as the mirror which reflects ourselves back to ourselves from others.* We magnetically and inevitably attract throughout life, from birth to death and beyond, persons and environments that reflect our virtues and our vices.

An important message is contained in the Venusian ruler-ship of Taurus and Libra. Taurus and the 2nd House are psycho-logically the index of the personal consolidation of self-value and self-possession while Libra and the 7th House indicate the poten-tial degree of balanced, reciprocal mutual love sharing with an intimate equal in relationship. Obviously, we can only recognize, share, and relate the priceless gift of love with another *to the degree to which we enjoy and identify it within ourselves.*

Whereas challenging aspects with Mars show where the will has been applied in service to purely personal desires or rashly, impulsively used to dominate physically, the difficult condition withVenus denotes the short-circuiting of the flow of the energies of love in equal relationship and a probable lack of self-esteem.

The Moon depicts the past-accumulated sensory input resulting from interaction with the environment of planet earth, and is the indicator of the prime personality need which must be positively fulfilled so emotional responses may be channeled cre-atively and constructively.

For better or worse, the Moon keys largely automatic habit patterns. Depending on placement and aspects, the Moon is high-ly significant in healthy sexual functioning and spiritual growth efforts. Its condition astrologically reveals *to what degree you are potentially a prisoner of the past.* Challenging aspects to the Moon may indicate difficulties with the anima and the emotional body. It is an inescapable fact of life in Western culture that practically every single individual needs emotional healing as a key part of a spiritual growth program.

As consciousness expands in spiritual growth, one must sooner or later gain total control of these unconscious response patterns, predominant in personality form (Eve) so that the emo-tional nature is completely disciplined to reflect fully and perfect-ly the radiant source of life energy symbolized by the Sun.

Needless to say, this is much more easily talked about than accomplished in the seemingly trivial details of day-to-day living. It requires much more than a casual discipline and in no way involves a repression of energy, but rather a positive expression of emotional energy. This repression/expression principle is not widely comprehended, and is often misunderstood in application to spiritual advancement.

No one should take vows of celibacy unless they are sure they have reached a level of spiritual growth where there is no thought of feeling of sacrifice because they are using the sexual energy to open the higher chakras and stimulate the endocrine glands associated with them. Abstinence is an option for more rapid spiritual growth, not an absolute requirement.

The Ascendant is of paramount importance to us all because it is the point of physical birth and spiritual rebirth. The positive qualities of the rising sign are what we are seeking to make a part of our soul's evolutionary pattern in the present lifetime. This is the prime point of integration, where all the disparate conflicts expressed elsewhere in the horoscope come to resolution, fulfillment, and ultimate transformation. The sexual polarity is here fused to unity. Here is symbolically the daily dawning of the Sun's light and the yearly return of the Sun's illumination and rebirth at its point of astrological exaltation. This is the alpha-omega-alpha.

At physical birth, Aries says, "I am." At spiritual rebirth, Aries proclaims "I Am That I Am"; the total definition of the spiritually awakened.

Since this is the point of the ultimate spiritual rebirth of the male-female, the spiritual androgyne, it is fittingly ruled esoterically by Mercury, which is neither positive nor negative, but a carrier of the message. Exoterically, Mercury conveys the five senses and builds intellectual awareness and theoretical approaches to distinguish the inner from the outer, but dealing with duality ultimately breeds separateness, anxiety, worry. As proper spiritual rebirth is experienced, the whole network of communications is attuned to a gradual admission of input from worlds which vibrate at a higher rate than the physical form-world.

The mental, consciousness computer—partly temporal, partly eternal—is then the exalted agency of the spiritualization of the physical, as cosmic awareness is transmitted to every physical, mental, emotional, and spiritual body cell and they are all fused to unity. "When Thine eye is single, then thy whole body is full of light." Light scatters darkness. The restless, anxious insecurity of duality gives way to the harmony, peace, and dynamic tranquillity of the eternal Now.

The other planets, so-called impersonal, and the principles they symbolically represent, are also important in the transformation of sexual energy, especially as they relate to the planetary energies already discussed.

Saturn is the letter of the law, time, ambition, the limitations or controls of the world of matter which must be respected and honored in building a secure identity simultaneously in many dimensions. In sexual perspective, it is the powerful environmental factors of enculturation and social endorsement which either block natural energy expression or provide the universal badge of recognized achievement, marking positive fulfillment in a material frame of reference. Aspects to Saturn always reveal how one has worked with Time and Law. Have they been used or abused?

Jupiter is the expansion of objective understanding which correct application of sexual energy ultimately brings. Individually, it is the enthusiasm and rewards earned through adhering to an ideal or goal held up by an organized religion, or a recognized societal grouping, or potential confusion in not doing so. Here the opinions and knowledge (or prejudices) come from interaction with human society.

Neptune symbolizes the devoted service to a transcendent universal ideal personally received. It is the unique individual creative vision which lures us on to worlds beyond the mundane illusion of "reality." We are, one and all, ultimately artists in a process of becoming, and this personal glimpse or voyage which Neptune symbolically affords us, into what is beyond the world of the five senses, is the image which gives ultimate direction to the enlightened application of the sexual urge to grand union with the All-in-All. Under challenge, some degree of addiction, promiscuity, or breakdown or neurosis is highly probable in Western cultures.

Uranus can signify an inventive direction of sexual tension which heightens individuality and challenges the enculturation factors signified by Saturn. The new, the daring, the shocking sexual expression can, in the extreme, lead to a so-called perversion or an imbalance which may delay or detour spiritual fulfillment if the energies become rebelliously channeled. In easy positive flow it denotes sparkle, magnetism, and a humanitarian bent of friendly interaction, the democratic lover.

All the astrological factors work to produce an ultimate transformation which proceeds in stages of growth. The greatest driving, underlying need which propels us from life to life through a million nights and days, from the depths of emotional bereavement in shadow and sorrow, to the apex of spiritual exultation in the sunshine of high fulfillment, *will be chiefly indicated in each life by the positive qualities of the rising sign in blend with any ascending planets, Ascendant ruler, and aspect network or other signs sharing the 1st House.* This underlying need is like the leitmotif of a symphony which weaves through a composition, subtly integrating in development all other variations and counterpoints.

The needs of the Moon seem more insistent in day-to-day growth, but the lunar needs should be positively fulfilled in orientation to fulfillment of the more deeply significant positive qualities of the rising sign. The Moon in reference to Houses rules one pole of the axis of material form and structure, Midheaven/Imum Coeli (MC/IC), while the Ascendant marks the eternal dawning point where we eventually, in exaltation, reverse the dark and become light.

Sexual Profile of America

Now that we have a macrocosmic overview of how astrological symbolism relates to the embrace of sexual energy en route to high spiritual integration, let's take a microcosmic overview of how the management of sex energy by the United States of America is astrologically reflected in the traditional Gemini rising chart.

Human sexuality is a fact of life; it's a state of mind; it's the most natural and fundamental part of our personalities; one of the most joyous and troublesome parts of our lives, and pretty consistently, the most fascinating and controversial subject around today. Part of the confusion about our sexuality is that *as a nation we're so uncomfortable with sex, the act of sex itself.*

In the United States chart, we have Mars, the planet of sexual desire with particular reference to males, rising in Gemini, sign of diversity, duality, and communications. No nation in recorded history has been so saturated and virtually immersed in blatant sexual iconography and imagery on a mass scale as America has. One of the greatest challenges to the fulfillment of our national destiny, which is to herald the New Age ideals of brotherhood, freedom, equality, and the free circulation of truth (rising Uranus in Gemini), and prove in a responsible way that these ideals can work by and for the masses in a democratic society where the people rule (Moon in Aquarius in the 10th), is how we deal with our national guilt, our mass addictions, and our tendency to an unhealthy sublimation of the national sex drive (Mars square Neptune from 1st House to 5th) in the addictive phallic culture of an exploding industrial technology.

Mars square Neptune also shows a distortion of natural understanding about how to use the sex act to convey love. This is compounded by the square of the Sun to Saturn, 2nd to 5th House, our national puritanical guilt about having fun and radiating love and light!

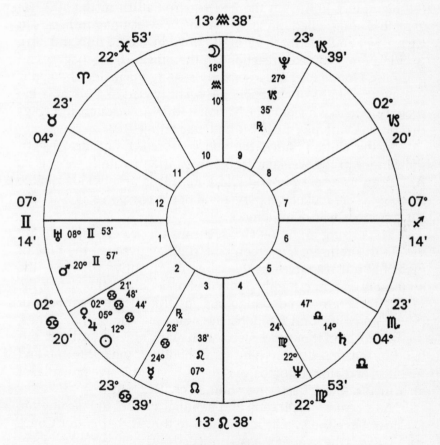

United States of America
July 4, 1776, 2:13 A.M. LMT
Philadelphia, PA
39N57 75W10
Koch Houses

Neptune, when challenged, can be subtle, but pervasive, like termites eating away at a foundation. Under tension in the U.S. chart (square Mars), it depicts a distortion and sublimation of sexual energy which is appalling, and a tendency to addiction which is currently built into our society. Our celebrated technological expertise (Grand Air Trine with Mars rising in Gemini) realizes great human possibilities, but we are paying a great price for them, and with every year the price keeps going up.

We are literally sick of and sick with the culture of industrial technology. It is a subtle virus. For years, a rampaging capitalism (Sun conjunct Jupiter in the 2nd square Saturn in the 5th) has exploited and excited the sexual selling of everything from cars to cigars. Sex and death are naturally linked (Mars, Pluto and 8th). Exciting one provokes reactions in the other. The teenager who bought a Honda because a sexually teasing magazine showed it parting the thighs of a shapely girl scantily clad in a bikini is the grown-up man who joins the National Rifle Association and vows that no one will take away his bullet-spurting guns.

In the United States, the gun is sacred. From the Western gunslinger to the weekend sportsman, the private firearm is as American as apple pie and Old Glory. It is an obvious phallic symbol (as are rockets), a perversion of sex energy as a result of a subconscious fear of impotence.

Mars rising in the 1st House means the sex energy is highly visible in subliminal, overcompensating aggression: the rape of great natural resources in the name of inventive progress, the seemingly endemic, highly publicized national racial violence, the mania for high speed dangerous automobiles as symbols of power, mobility, and freedom, the notorious motorcycle gangs, the covert adulation and fascination with brazen outlaws and bandits, the senseless drive-by gang shootings, the fighter jets and missiles, and atomic bombs, and the always explosive potential of an armed military beast on a strained civilian tether.

As a central inspiration and national symbol in Washington, D.C., we have the phallic monument to the "Father of our Country." There is the over-emphasis on speed and engineering achievement; faster, farther, higher in a nervous, restless rush (again Mars rising in Gemini, Sun conjunct Jupiter square Saturn) to assuage national self-esteem within the tensions building from the emphasis of economic values at the expense of human consideration.

Although there is a potential high awareness in our public media and educational systems (Mercury ruler of 1st and 5th, dispositor of Mars, opposing Pluto, 3rd House to 9th), it is in our contacts with our children (Neptune and Saturn in the 5th) that we tend to confuse the issue, because of the need to produce programmed automatons as replacement parts for our capitalistic, assembly-line, throw-away waste culture (Sun conjunct Jupiter in 2nd square Saturn in 5th).

With Saturn in the 5th squaring the Sun, Americans tend to feel guilty if they are enjoying themselves. The Saturnian Puritan work ethic is a strongly pervasive and persistent value. Heart attacks are the number one killer: repressed flow of love energy (Saturn in the 5th square Sun), sublimated distortion of sexual energy (Mars square Neptune) in the 5th.

As the stress of accelerating tension accumulates, the intensity, frequency, and impersonal destructiveness of our wars mount. They become but great national orgasmic rites to relieve the tensions of an attempted sublimation of natural healthy sex expression and the rageaholic outbursts of a society which has become an addict.

Women have long retained an exceptionally strong hold on the national consciousness, first through their scarcity, then for utilitarian purposes as a source of babies who could be of help on the farm in a rapidly expanding agricultural growing phase, and finally as status symbols: All-American beauty queens and Mom.

Phillip Wylie (*Generation of Vipers*) was raging against the tyranny of American "momism" over five decades ago: mother, home, and apple pie. Women have also long controlled, in a passive way like queen bees, most of the privately owned wealth in the country, while paradoxically being formally denied equal status in the bureaucratic power structure. (Elevated Moon is conjunct the MC, dispositor of the Cancer Sun in the 2nd).

The instant nostalgia, the obsessive sentimental infatuation, and the worrying with the past (Mercury in Cancer in the 3rd opposing Pluto), and, of course, our national fixation on the female breast is a legendary oral sublimation (Sun in Cancer square Saturn), as is the nervous, restless consumption of cigarettes in the face of overwhelming statistical evidence linking smoking with deadly forms of cancer (Mercury in the 3rd disposits Ascendant, Uranus, Mars in Gemini, and opposes Pluto).

"And the beat goes on," with Saturn in the 5th, ruling the 8th House of sexual intercourse as a potential refocusing of creative love expression (the 8th is the fourth of the 5th). It is small wonder that national confusion and guilt about love and sex are rampant; and need I add, abortion!

Actual spontaneous love and play with these energies, gaining secure expression through sexual intercourse, are tragically foreign to most American adults. The concept of original sin and the influence of the Puritan ethic have combined to insinuate subtly an undertone that man is inherently evil. Most of us feel worthless if we are only living from day to day. We *feel* that we must do something to justify our existence. To like oneself just for being human and alive almost seems un-American.

We are warned by subtle social cues that spontaneous impulse must be controlled in conformity to social norms. "Control yourself," we are told from the earliest age, with the implication that letting go would unlock Pandora's box with ghastly results.

Institutional dictators are established from the cradle to the grave to ensure conformity and squelch spontaneous creative self-expression: family, school, military, athletics, corporations, keeping up with the Joneses, and overshadowing all the gargantuan federal bureaucracy with its incredible waste of material and human resources.

In cultural scholar Riane Eisler's perspective (note later reference to this perspective), the United States is a classic dominator society—ruling predominantly male hierarchies with authority backed up by force or the threat of force. The result, as Anne Wilson Schaef has perceptively and clearly demonstrated (note later reference to this perspective), is that our entire society functions as an addict, and that practically each and every one of us is involved in one addiction or another to a greater or lesser degree (Mars square Neptune, Saturn contraparallel Neptune).

Controls are necessary for social living and constructive channeling of energies, but the control mechanism in this nation is out of balance. So we experience the extremes of over-control and under-control. Dependence on exterior authority breeds outer conformity and rigidity in expression, and inner lack of self-discipline, with consequent low frustration tolerance and need of immediate gratification, the aforementioned rampant addiction, and escalating random violence. The enforced competitiveness upon which our capitalistic society breeds, in the name of technological progress—bigger, better, faster, "Progress is our most important product," "What's good for General Motors is good for the country,"—is a mighty detriment to creative, individual development and sane living.

Also as reflected by the Sun-Jupiter conjunction in the 2nd square Saturn in the 5th, America has become a bureaucratized and oligopolized country. Through mergers and acquisitions, a handful of giant companies dominate key industries. We instituted anti-monopoly laws but not anti-oligopoly laws, so we have shoddy goods, catastrophic poor service, economic disparity, environmental crisis and government as the nation's largest employer.

With Jupiter conjunct the Sun square Saturn from the 1st to 5th, our organized religions have emphasized repression, restriction, and penance rather than benediction, expression, celebration, and love. Instead of helping us love this magic God coursing through our being, we have been taught to distrust ourselves and our physical existence.

Our nation has many virtues and an impact on world affairs that have altered men's and women's minds. The imbalance of our control factors, the strong Saturn, can be offset by emphasizing the rising Uranus, the enlightened free circulation of truth, freedom, and equality within and without, *but time is running out.* As with individuals, the positive qualities of the rising sign blended with the positive qualities of any rising planets point the way to integration and spiritual growth.

An enlightened astrologer's greatest gift to a client is to help him or her be themselves, accept themselves, trust themselves, love themselves, and develop naturally as they would if they were not, in Bob Dylan's apt phrase, "bent out of shape from society's pliers." Society today on the whole is sick, inhuman, out of balance, insane. That is why we have the great cleansings in progress in every area, to readjust our balance—the keynote of all health.

With regard to sex energy, national conscious understanding must be developed for the need for sexual desire, for its use to express love creatively and constructively, not focused hysterically and obsessively on war, pornography, random violence, racial disturbances, etc. Mass American culture is not yet filled with masters to lead a great raising and redirection of the sexual energy to open the crown chakra, although the continuing focus on oral sex from *Deep Throat* to Madonna, etc., seems to be an hysterically anxious, but crude, inchoate attempt to heal the split between mind and body by getting semen back into the head, by trying literally to swallow the phallus whole. As always, profane pornography reflects an exoteric reversal or mirror-image of a sacred, esoteric truth.

Education is the key problem and the key answer; to bring constructive awareness rather than anxious schizoid obsession (Mercury disposits Mars, Uranus, and Ascendant opposing Pluto from the 3rd to the 9th House).

Pluto, symbolic of the higher spiritual will, is in the 9th House. This placement's potential is that striving to attain a deeper, higher understanding of the underlying mysteries of existence will lift the applied energy and sex drive in service to shared goals, with expansion in higher consciousness toward a practical fulfillment of a grand, shared transcendent ideal which will in turn liberate individual expression of creative love-sharing (Pluto trine Neptune in the 5th exactly bi-quintile to rising Mars).

Healing the Emotional Body

Modern civilization has reached a breaking point! This is the end result of what cultural historian and scholar Riane Eisler in her breakthrough 1987 book, *The Chalice and The Blade,* has called the dominator model of social organization which has been prevalent for the last 5,000 years. This model is characterized by the ranking of one half of humanity over the other—male over female—and involves the power to take rather than give life. In more recent years, this same model has been called the White Male or Addictive System by Anne Wilson Schaef in her books *When Society Becomes An Addict* and *Beyond Therapy, Beyond Science.*

This addictive system has wreaked havoc on Western civilization and reached its destructive climax in the 20th Century with the explosion of the atom bombs. Psychologically the effect has been equally as devastating on the mental and emotional health of individuals. The resulting widespread varieties of addiction, from alcoholism to drug abuse to overeating and the supporting infrastructures which involve drug lords, gangs, modern mass advertising, etc., are all too familiar modern maladies. This has led to the breakdown of the family and other traditional political, social, and economic institutions. Clearly, we are a culture in crisis.

This addictive system places the greatest stress on the individual's emotional body, making emotional healing essential for those raised in a Western culture. Emotional healing involves clearing complexes created by perhaps more than one lifetime, and reinforced in the current childhood by addicted parents operating in an addicted culture. There may be abandonment or abuse issues along with the usual multiple addictions, etc. Read *Codependent No More* and *Beyond Codependency* by Melody Beattie, and John Bradshaw's *Bradshaw on: The Family*, for starters.

The degree of addictive behavior is almost always indicated astrologically by a prominent Neptune, often angular and highly aspected or challenged. There may be a heavy 12th House or many Pisces planets as we shall see in our case studies. A prominent Pluto is also often featured.

Just as an addict's major defense mechanism is denial, so is our addictive society in deep denial from the national government on down through all the various institutional and corporate bureaucracies.

One of the most encouraging developments over the last few decades has been the emergence of group-healing systems based on the original Twelve-Step Model of Alcoholics Anonymous. As an instrument for mass healing, it has proven to be a Godsend.

Before an individual can truly begin to move seriously toward total spiritual liberation he/she *must* undergo emotional healing. Intellectual understanding is a great first step, and here astrology can play an important role by identifying the potential areas of dysfunction as well as the strengths, but no intellectual awareness or knowledge can ever substitute for direct emotional cleansing and healing therapy.

Currently, the Twelve Step program called Codependents Anonymous offers the most available and inexpensive opportunity for this healing. Other helpful approaches are Past Life Therapy, Rebirthing, Reiki, Mari-El, Deep Process, Jungian Active Imagination, and others. Any therapy will do that encourages or facilitates *direct* emotional experience with a therapist who ideally is also in recovery. You cannot really advance far without it. Otherwise, your life, health, and efforts will fall apart somewhere on the spiritual path.

It is a case of pay me now or pay me later. Until we change the crazy-making structure of our society and educate our citizens about addiction and the necessity for emotional healing before true spiritual growth can be achieved, this kind of tragedy will continue. The good news is that the process of healing and recovery is gaining strength throughout our society, and the awareness of the need to change the basic structure of society is slowly dawning. Let us do what we can to be part of the solution and not part of the problem.

Some Case Studies of Addiction

Elton John

Elton John, the talented British superstar and rock icon, whose career already spans over two decades, is also a classic example of multiple addictions. In a recent interview with biographer Philip Norman, author of *Elton John*, John admitted, "I was cocaine-addicted. I was an alcoholic. I had a sexual addiction. I was bulimic for six years." Note the classic addictive indicators in his horoscope: Sun in the 8th House ruling the 12th House in opposition to Neptune in the 2nd House of self-esteem and Venus, ruler of the Midheaven and most of the 2nd House, exactly sesquiquadrates Neptune in the 2nd; both Mercury in Pisces in the 7th House and the Moon in Taurus in the 9th are inconjunct Neptune.

His childhood was strongly emotionally repressed (Moon exactly square Pluto in the 12th House, co-ruler of the 4th House and Moon inconjunct Neptune in the 2nd House). "My father never showed me any affection, and that made me keep everything in," John now understands. Mars (male energy indicator), co-ruler of the 4th House of home and parental figure, exactly sesquares Saturn (father indicator) in Leo in the 11th, and squares Uranus in the 10th House of parental figure. John goes on, "I was always held up by my family as a paragon of what a child should be, which, I think, never left me. I wish I'd had the courage to really express my feelings—like not going on-stage and performing when I felt I couldn't face it. But, I always made myself do it. I was too afraid of letting people down."

The rebellion against this childhood shows most obviously in the over-the-top fancy-dress, outrageous absurdity of his stage costumes and weird spectacles, hats, and multi-colored, dyed hair. As John himself has candidly admitted, "It's a reaction against everything I wasn't allowed to do as a kid." Uranus (shocking, inventive, unusual), primary ruler of the 7th House of public presentation, is in the 10th House of career.

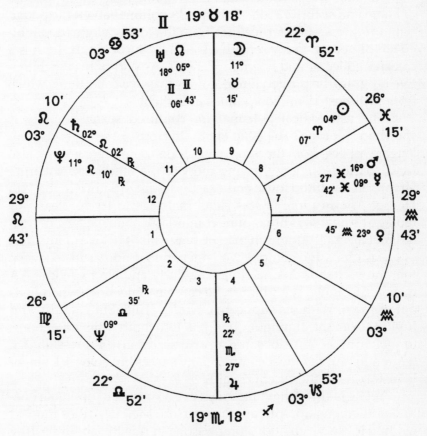

Elton John
Mar. 25, 1947, 4:00 P.M. GMD
Pinner, England
51N36 00W23
Koch Houses

His parents' marriage was a hollow sham with the military officer father away for long periods. (Venus ruler of the 10th House exactly sesquare Neptune in the 2nd.) "I grew up with inanimate objects as my friends, and I still believe they have feelings. That's why I keep hold of all my possessions. I'll look at them and remember when they gave me a bit of happiness, which is more than human beings have given me."

The Moon in Taurus (need for possession) rules the 11th House of friends and expected affection and is exactly square Pluto in the 12th House of fantasy and imagination ruling most of the 3rd (substitute brothers and companions) and the 4th House of home and security roots. This speaks volumes about the potential for repressed, bitter feelings from the lonely, slighted, blighted childhood of a very sensitive soul. Not surprisingly, John is a massive collector and hoarder of things. As part of his rehabilitative program, he purged himself of his massive collections, which fetched almost 15 million pounds at Sotheby's.

The astrological potential for confused sexual identity is shown in Neptune's rulership of the 8th House of sex with its challenging aspects from the Sun, Venus, Moon, and Mercury, and also Mars (basic sex energy) ruling most of the 8th House squaring Uranus in the 10th House and exactly sesquare Saturn in the 11th House. After a more or less sham marriage to try to please his mother, he now says he is "quite comfortable about being gay" and has met a young American man he now calls "the love of my life."

An obsessive-compulsive codependent addict in recovery, John now attends AA meetings regularly and asks a fellow AA member to travel with him so he can have meetings when he is out of town. With his supportive Grand Trine (Sun, Saturn, and Jupiter, over the signline), John has transmuted his addictions, torments, and confusions into an artistic, creative expression that has made him the most commercially successful solo rock singer in history, with the exception of Elvis Presley.

Yet he is still struggling to achieve a successful, intimate one-to-one relationship with another person. Mercury rules most of his 1st House Virgo, indicating lessons in this life about healthy discrimination, especially in relationships (7th House placement), will be challenging; Mercury conjuncts Mars in Pisces and inconjuncts Neptune and Pluto. Relationship challenges are also indicated by the square from Mars in the 7th to Uranus co-ruler of the

7th as well as by the exact sesquiquadrate from Mars to Saturn co-ruler of the 7th in addition to all the challenges to Neptune, primary ruler of most of the 7th House.

Although he remains rock music's highest grossing performer and is "respected throughout the rock industry as a musician's musician," John declares he has no idea of what he will "be doing over the next few years" other than staying in recovery and working on building a healthy relationship.

Madonna

Madonna Louise Ciccone (see p. 257), singer, dancer, and superstar celebrity, known worldwide simply by her first name, has the chart of a classic addict, and her compulsive bisexuality and tireless obsessive workaholic self-promotion are public knowledge. Mars (sex drive and applied energy) in Taurus (stubborn, persistent) in the 9th House (promotion) ruling the 8th House (sex) squares Uranus in the 12th (explosive, shocking, rebellious, unusual desires and fantasy potential under challenge) and the Sun in Leo in the 12th, showing high energy and anger potential especially directed against men.

Just before Madonna's 7th birthday, her mother, for whom she is named, died of breast cancer. Using degree for a year [generalized Solar Arc.—Ed.] progression, Pluto (death, major change of life perspective) was conjunct the Ascendant and the progressed MC/IC parental axis was square the Moon (mother) and the progressed IC (mother) was exactly conjunct the IC/Saturn midpoint and the progressed Moon advanced to partile in the natal Moon/Saturn square.

Her father, grief-stricken and unable to cope with both job and children, sent Madonna and her five siblings to live with relatives. According to Marie Cahill, author of *Madonna*, "As soon as possible the family was reunited, but much to the children's surprise their 'housekeeper' was to become their new mother." Madonna was deeply affected by it all, and still is years later. "I had to deal with the loss of my mother, then I had to deal with the guilt of her being gone, and then I had to deal with the loss of my father when he married my stepmother. So I was just one angry, abandoned little girl. I'm still angry." Note the retrograde Saturn in the 4th House (psychological or physical absence of father) semisquare Neptune in Scorpio in the 2nd (confusion and abandonment by father) and Pluto exactly conjunct the Sun/Moon midpoint in the 12th House and, of course, also conjunct the Sun, Moon, Mercury, and the Ascendant and square MC/IC axis.

As the oldest girl, Madonna was responsible for taking care of the younger siblings and doing many household tasks. Looking back, Madonna said, "I really saw myself as the quintessential Cinderella. You know, I have this stepmother and I have all this work to do and it's awful and I never go out and I don't have any pretty dresses" (natal Moon in Virgo conjunct the Asc. in the 1st House square Saturn in the 4th).

The urge to transform the emotional pain of abandonment, guilt, loss of parents, and the other insecurities and burdens of childhood and the sexual ambivalence and the rebellion against the Catholic school uniforms and upbringing are all too familiar in Madonna's public stage shows, which are a kind of artistic, stylized acting out. She has become famous for rebelliously and outrageously wearing lacy underwear and stage costumes and simulating unusual sex acts on stage in settings adorned with religious symbolism. Neptune (potential for spiritual confusion when challenged) ruler of the 7th House of public presentation is square Venus semisquare Saturn. The MC ruler and chart co-dispositor Mercury is in the 12th conjunct the Ascendant and Pluto and square the MC. She has also gained wide notoriety for blatant bisexual promiscuity and for promoting a book filled with sexually explicit photos of herself.

Moon in Virgo is a classic symbol of potential emotional immaturity and the tendency to intellectualize feelings and medicate oneself emotionally through busyness or distractions, especially when challenged, as is Madonna's by Pluto, Saturn, and Uranus.

Madonna's life mission, as suggested astrologically, involves getting emotional healing (Moon conjunct Ascendant in Virgo) so she can enjoy real emotional intimacy and security, and consciously learn a healthy, non-obsessed discrimination, a direct communication of emotions within a belief system that nurtures and sustains, instead of oppresses and suppresses. She needs to work a recovery program around her addiction issues. Her chart suggests that she needs to deal with and heal the past so she can fully enjoy the present.

In her determination not to become a victim, she risks victimizing herself by the potential self-destructiveness of her own tireless promotion of an outrageous sex symbol image. From all indications, she needs a real program of emotional healing and recovery. She obviously has a very intense desire to find something to really believe in. So far she feels disillusioned by the lack of childhood nurturing.

She already has had one stormy marriage in which she was apparently physically abused and, from all indications, there could be some very bumpy times ahead personally which she should defuse through getting off the media merry-go-round and getting healing. Her basic thrust is toward health and happiness

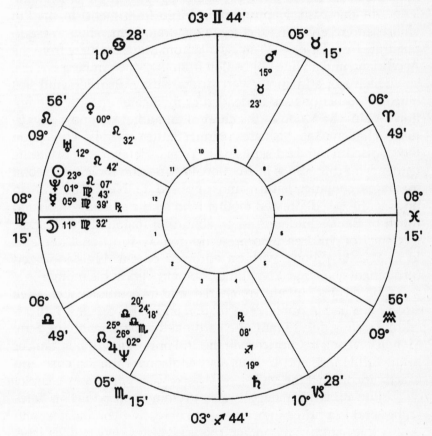

Madonna L Ciccone
Aug. 16, 1958, 7:05 A.M. EST
Bay City, MI
43N36 83W53
Koch Houses

through getting her betrayal and anger out and getting belief in through transformation (Pluto in Virgo in the 12th House conjunct Ascendant ruler Mercury).

Elvis Presley

Elvis Presley is another classic case of self-destructive addiction. The most successful rock star of all, and a national icon and sex symbol, he is still selling over a million records a year, and his home and place of death, Graceland Mansion, Memphis, Tennessee, is one of the most visited tourist attractions in America. We have the usual classic addictive indicator of Neptune under challenge. In this case, Neptune is in Virgo (detriment) in the 9th House, and receives an exact sesquiquadrate from Venus, a sesquiquadrate from Uranus, a semisextile from Mars, a square from the Ascendant, and a wide opposition from the Moon in Pisces.

His major addictions were drugs, eating disorders and sex. Since all addictions are to deaden or medicate unresolved emotional pain, the Moon in the chart of an addict is almost always under challenge as it is here conjunct Saturn, exactly semisquare the Capricorn Sun and semisextile Venus. Here we see a definite tendency to difficulties in emotional expression indicated (Moon in Pisces conjunct Saturn and opposed to Neptune) and an unusual tie to a depressed mother who restricted and constricted much of Elvis' childhood to an abnormal degree. In the classic tendency of children who grow up in a dysfunctional home to form a fantasy bond with an addicted parent, Elvis idealized (prominent challenged Neptune, Moon in Pisces) his mother.

The electric, inventive, charismatic, revolutionary creative effect Elvis had in public presentation and in his career is indicated by Uranus, focal point of a cardinal T-square involving Sun, Mercury, Venus in Capricorn in the 2nd opposing Pluto in Cancer in the 8th House and Uranus also semisquare the 7th cusp and exactly inconjunct the MC.

Pluto under challenge is also prominent in addictive horoscopes and is a prime indicator of the obsessive, compulsive, self-destructive nature of the addict. This is highly evident in Elvis' case.

Despite great talent and wealth and unrivaled fame, there was no recovery from addiction despite evidence that Elvis had a much more than average interest in metaphysical spiritual growth and development (he studied the teachings of Yogananda), there was no one apparently to encourage the disciplined systematic positive transformation of the sex energy.

Instead there was the sad downward spiral of a great talent who sought escape through sex, food, and drugs. In the last 31 and a half months of his life, his doctor prescribed over 19,000 doses of a wide range of drugs. That works out to an average daily intake of over 20 doses.

Using degree for year progression, his natal Moon ruler of the 8th House of death had progressed to an exact inconjunct to

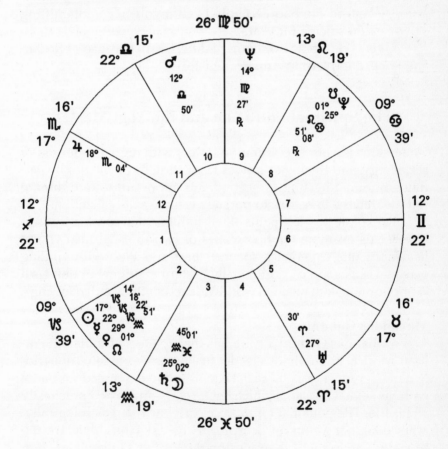

Elvis Aron Presley
Jan. 8, 1935, 4:35 A.M. CST
Tupelo, MS
34N15 88W42
Koch Houses

Neptune, and his Ascendant had progressed to an exact opposition to Pluto (death and rebirth) in the 8th House at death. Natal Uranus had progressed to an exact semisquare to Pluto in the 8th. Natal Mars ruling most of the 4th House of the end of life had progressed to an exact square to natal Saturn dispositor of the Capricorn Sun triggering the exact natal inconjunct between Saturn and Pluto.

Existing circumstantial evidence indicates that Elvis may have committed intentional suicide through drug overdose although controversy surrounds the validity of his existing public autopsy report. He had certainly been involved in committing slow-motion suicide for years.

Elvis is different from other addicts only because of his talent, fame, and place in American history.

The Spiritual Politician and the Yogi Master

Understanding our enculturation factors with regard to our use of sex energy, and freeing ourselves from addictive behavior by getting emotional healing as needed, are important to our gaining self-awareness, to be free to pursue personal self-realization.

To explore possible paths of self-fulfillment in constructive service, let us examine the horoscopes of two unusual men whose developmental experience spanned East and West with guiding personal philosophies, traditionally Eastern in origin but universal in application. Both attained worldwide recognition and followings.

Mohandas Gandhi

Mohandas Gandhi, revered as the architect of Indian liberation, political and religious leader to a nation, an ascetic, non-violent martyr for social and racial equality, had a tremendous battle with his sexual passions which began early and lasted practically all his life. The potential for this is clearly mirrored astrologically: Mars conjunct Venus in Scorpio in the 1st House, square the Moon in Leo in the 10th, opposing the Jupiter-Pluto conjunction in Taurus in the 7th. The lower will (Mars) is in exact opposition to the higher spiritual will (Pluto in detriment by both sign and house placement).

Gandhi has described his inner struggles with devastating

candor in his autobiography, beginning with his early marriage, his almost overwhelming sexual desire which led to an abortive, emotionally searing early pregnancy for his wife at age 14. His powerful sexual urge drove him to hurry from ministering to his dying father in order to have intercourse with his teenage wife just minutes before his father's death, an incident which self-admittedly pained his conscience for life.

The theme of sex is strong throughout Gandhi's life. In his autobiography, *The Story of My Experiments with Truth,* he contin-

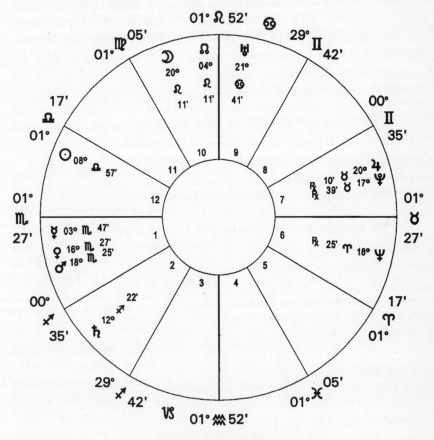

Mohandas Gandhi
Oct. 2, 1869, 7:33 A.M. LMT
Borbandar, India
21N38 69W36
Koch Houses

ually describes his carnal impulses and desires. As late as his 70th year, he says he has not completely conquered them. His first and greatest struggle for freedom from earthly attachments was in regard to sex. All his incredible experiments with diet and his final choice of goat's milk as his ideal food were caused by his determination to diminish sexual desire. For many years of his life amid intermittent controversy, he slept each evening in the same room with nude young girls to test his will. Obviously, despite his great will power, Gandhi could have used some *emotional* healing.

His brush with prostitution and the internal guilt conflicts with sheer sexual desire which Gandhi frankly describes are all clearly mirrored in his horoscope (rising Mars-Venus conjunction in Scorpio in the 1st House opposed Pluto, the axis squared by the Moon). After intense self-analysis (rising Mercury ruling the 8th House conjunct Ascendant in Scorpio) of his faults and virtues, he came from the depths of inner torment and self-doubt (Saturn in the 2nd House of self-value) literally to father modern India (Moon in Leo in the 10th House) and communicate profound spiritual truths to millions around the world (Mercury conjunct Ascendant in Scorpio).

As his self-perception (Mercury in Scorpio conjunct Ascendant) was transformed in service to a transcendent ideal (Sun in the 12th House), he was able to be a focal, transforming agent for an emerging nation (Moon in Leo, oriental, and in the 10th House) and a dramatic worldwide apostle of non-violence. In terms of soul growth, Gandhi's challenge is spelled out by his rising Scorpio and the need to purge past, deeply held habits and develop the tenacity and powerful strength of will to use sexual energy constructively.

It is now obvious that Gandhi's early home environment was highly dysfunctional. He was raised under rigid Hindu rules by an aloof, stern, temperamental father, a bureaucratic manager who married four times. Gandhi was the youngest child of the fourth wife, a very dominating individual. Today we would diagnose him as a codependent sex addict with eating disorders. Mercury rules his 8th House and conjuncts the Ascendant in the 1st House. Note also the classic addictive indicator of Sun in the 12th House opposing a challenged Neptune in the 6th (ruler of the 5th) which also receives inconjuncts from the Venus-Mars conjunction in Scorpio in the 1st House. Gandhi's own marriage was troubled and turbulent, as was his relationship with his own children.

After these early inner struggles, Gandhi devoted himself to celibacy for the rest of his life, and to a strict dietary regimen so that he could "turn sexual fluid into vital energy for the whole body." As Gandhi expressed it, "one must conquer the palate before he can control the procreative instinct." As a vegetarian, he counseled a "natural vegetarian diet with all necessary vitamins, minerals, calories, and so forth" as a necessity in maintaining the victory over an "inward greed for food."

Obviously, it was Gandhi's powerful desire to devote himself—body, mind, and soul—to the highest ideals to which he could attune. This powerful devotion helped him to transform himself, by dint of his high spirituality, from a slave to physical passion to a spiritual giant, revered and respected the world around.

With his elevated Moon in Leo in the 10th House of worldly honor and his Sun in Libra in the 12th House, Gandhi's mundane need was to shine regally in a position of control and authority; to serve in a practical fashion intensely held ideals of harmony, peace, and a just universal brotherhood, which he achieved through the practice of austere living and non-violence to all life.

The highly inspirational grand trine in fire (Moon, Saturn, Neptune) received a 10th house emphasis by virtue of the Moon's additional position as focal point of the fixed T-cross. *Emotional energy over-controlled in a turbulent personal and domestic life found inspirational self-motivated release on a grand world stage.* Universal love and compassion as a humanitarian counselor was easier to share than a one-to-one relationship. His wife remained illiterate her whole life and was forced by circumstance to adopt a role as disciple rather than equal partner.

His Moon as T-cross focal point discharges its potent emotional energies easily into the 4th House, which came to represent, in Gandhi's chart, his homeland of India.

On January 30, 1948, at age 78, Gandhi was assassinated. Apparently in this chart of high violence *potential*, there was for the apostle of non-violence a vestige of challenging karma still to be balanced, and he chose to do it in this way. Although there were several interesting progressions and transits, two will suffice for corroboration.

Transiting Saturn was exactly conjoining his natal Moon, indeed suggesting the completion of a karmic fulfillment from the past. Natal Saturn by Solar Arc direction had reached 0 degrees Pisces in the 4th House. The universal forces via Saturn were in a sense applauding his earthly attainment, and promising a new start elsewhere for his ambitious pattern of self-development as an example of a productive style of balanced discipline.

The untouchables of India, as did all the common people (elevated Moon), saw Gandhi as their champion. Upon him they bestowed the title (although he himself never used it) of Mahatma, which means "great soul." It seems he rightly deserved it, for, in his candor and his intense search for truth, he reached to his depths to transmute his baser energies. He thus shines forth in retrospect as an outstanding fulfillment, astrologically, of his Scorpio Ascendant.

Yogananda

The great Yogi, Paramahansa Yogananda, whose spiritual teachings were a beacon light to large followings, not only on two continents, but in many other countries, was a lifelong celibate. Mars, the indicator of sexual desire in the 8th House, is the dispositor of his chart and opposes Saturn in the 2nd House. Additionally, Neptune co-rules the 8th House and is conjunct Pluto, symbol of the higher spiritual will, in the 10th House. The discipline of sex energy for transformative spiritual purposes is clearly indicated. His worldly mission was to teach others a way of practical, gradual transformation and spiritualization of the physical through mental, physical, and spiritual discipline.

The Sun in the 5th House in Capricorn, focal point of a cardinal T-cross, disposits the Moon in Leo conjunct the Ascendant from the 12th House. The message of a practical spirituality applicable in the mundane world is easily conveyed with charm and grace by one at home both in the ashram and in public life.

Again, as with Gandhi, we have the dramatic public personality (Moon in Leo conjunct the Ascendant as part of a highly inspirational Grand Fire Trine, and the Sun in Capricorn in the 5th House) who needed a large stage in order to radiate the practical application of his idealistic teachings to a world awash in materialistic philosophy. [See Valentino (p. 25) and West (p. 135) for comparisons of manifestation levels for the Neptune-Pluto conjunction.—Ed.]

In his life mission to bring the spiritual wisdom of the East to feed the spiritual hunger of the West and create a closer tie between East and West, Yogananda appropriately employed the instrument of Yoga (union) as a means of redirecting the life energy and expanding the conscious awareness to a vision of universal wholeness.

Pluto, the higher transforming spiritual will, widely conjuncts the MC in the 10th House exactly conjunct Neptune in Gemini, reflecting Yogananda's desire to be a communicator, a

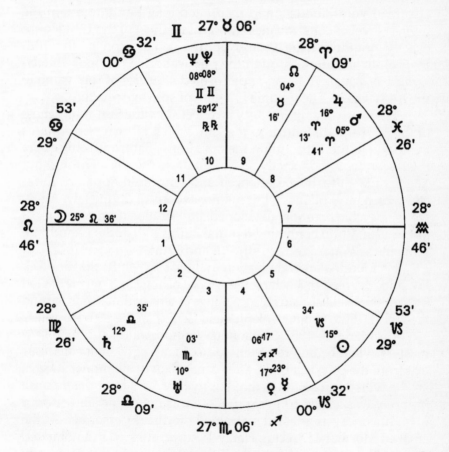

Paramahansa Yogananda
Jan. 5, 1893, 15:04 GMT
Gorakhpur, India
26N45 83E22
Koch Houses

teacher of transforming truths in accordance with a high ideal as the path to ultimate security and inner peace.

He was energetic and restless (Mars in Aries in the 8th House ruling the 9th House and most of the 3rd). He traveled constantly beginning at a very early age (Sun square Jupiter; Moon conjunct Asc. square Uranus in the 3rd; Venus, ruler of the 3rd and most of the 9th House conjunct Mercury in the 4th House). Everywhere, he sought examples of spiritual truths which he used in his thousands of lectures and classes all over the world to make these truths live in the hearts of his listeners. He also read voluminously and meditated long hours to attain the highest level of consciousness (Sun ruling most of the 12th House exactly bi-quintile the Pluto-Neptune conjunction in the 10th House). In addition, through the publication of his book *Autobiography of a Yogi*, Yogananda performed a service of rare value to the truth seeker. The volume is a gem of spiritual wisdom.

The sense of a divine duty is reflected by the Sun ruling most of the 12th square Saturn in the 2nd, which in turn semisquares the Moon in the 12th, ruling the 6th House; Saturn is semisquare the Ascendant and exactly sesquiquadrate the MC. Throughout Yogananda's life, he experienced and witnessed apparent miracles which he explains as but manifestations of divine law. Again we see psychic potential developed and fulfilled (Sun ruling most of the 12th; Pluto conjunct Neptune in the 10th and a Grand Fire Trine in the Water Houses, 4th, 8th and 12th).

He founded an organization in the West (Self Realization Fellowship) devoted to teaching the science of Yoga as a means of God realization. It still spreads his teachings to tens of thousands around the world (Pluto conjunct Neptune in Gemini in the 10th House).

On March 7, 1952, Yogananda demonstrated supreme self-mastery when he entered Mahasamadhi, a Yogi's final conscious exit from the physical body, after conclusion of a banquet speech; i.e., he willed himself to death. For twenty days after death, until his body was sealed from sight, there was no visible sign or odor of bodily decay as attested by trained mortuary personnel. As the amazed Mortuary Director, Harry T. Rowe, attested in a notarized letter: "The absence of any visual signs of decay in the dead body of Paramahansa Yogananda offers the most extraordinary case in our experience . . . No physical disintegration was visible . . . This state of perfect preservation of a body is, so far as we know from mortuary annals, an unparalleled one."

Among the many interesting progressed and transiting aspects in effect at this time, the following may be noted: transiting Saturn conjunct its natal position and thus also exactly semisquare the Ascendant and exactly semisquare the MC, suggesting triumphal fulfillment of his divine duty and his control and physical mastery of the laws of life and death in a very public setting. Also, transiting Jupiter was just completing its return to its natal position in the 8th House of death, transformation and rebirth which it co-rules and exactly trined natal Venus, ruler of the MC in Sagittarius in the 4th House of endings. This indicates the seemingly easy, almost effortless manner of his completion of physical life, and the way he transformed his death experience into an expanded public awareness of the possibilities of death and rebirth. He did everything but physically return from the dead.

Also, transiting Pluto, Venus, and the Moon exactly aspected natal Mars in the 8th House, and the transiting Sun exactly squared natal Venus in the 4th House. In one degree for a year progression, Neptune, the ruler of the 8th and in exact conjunction with Pluto natally in the 10th House, exactly squared the Mars/Neptune and Jupiter/MC midpoints. Again we have the public demonstration of the spirit triumphant over death by Yogananda's controlling not only his manner of dying but his body after death.

The Challenge of Growth

What deductions can we draw from the lives of these great spiritual leaders in light of the sexual energy transformation which they accomplished in service to a transcendent ideal?

There are those who merely avoid or renounce their sexual energies because they feel that by so doing they are *being* "spiritual." Alas, in many instances, they are not being spiritual at all *but only repressive.* Their frustration is highly evident as their anxious expressions and wide variety of vague but chronic health complaints bear witness. Mere repression is not spiritual, nor is denial. *Energy is to be used.* There must be an active, disciplined, balanced expression of the sexual energy in either a fulfilling total relationship with another or through a form of spiritual, mental, or physical discipline, such as many systems of Yoga involve, or both.

The life of a strict renunciant is not for everyone. We may achieve balance within by achieving balance in relationship without. All lives must be illuminated by a dream which orders a set of intermediate goals within the physical reality in which we function. Ideals are not dysfunctional in our times. In a time of visible moral bankruptcy, they are indeed more important to personal development than ever before.

There are no magic measurements either in astrology or in life. The magic lies in gaining direction and discipline from inner attunement. None of us gets something for nothing.

The Transforming Fire

In our brief glances into the lives of two remarkable men, we have traced an approach to the transmutation of sexual energy which is the extreme one of celibacy. This is one approach, but not the most appropriate one for every person in every situation.

Tragically, there are many, many people consciously on a spiritual path who believe that enjoying sexual intercourse is "sinful" or detrimental to spiritual growth, and is even somehow bestial. This is a misconception which is unfortunately propagated by many teachers who should know better.

As discussed earlier, *the urge to sexual union is a physical expression of an underlying drive to inner unity.* All unions, to be beneficial, must have one essential ingredient present and that ingredient is love. Life is flooding us at every instant. The radiance of people in love is something to behold. It is contagiously magnetic and we all respond. "Everybody loves a lover." There is an electromagnetic charge, a blooming that is beautiful and sacred.

Power is released, interchanged in any union. We *are* energy. What we interact with, we become. In the very powerful fusion of sexual interaction, we absorb and accept and are affected or infected psychologically, emotionally, spiritually, and mentally by those with whom we share energies.

In sex, there is a primal interchange of energies, the depths are plumbed or the heights are reached, or both. Understanding this, we can easily see why the proper mental, spiritual, emotional and physical setting is important. Harmonious attunements must exist on many levels for the interchange of energies to be transforming and uplifting: mutual love, respect, a sharing, a giving and a receiving.

Sexual desire aims at fusion. But the sheer primal desire as an energy-wave carrier can be stimulated by a variety of strong emotions such as loneliness, the wish to dominate or be dominated, by vanity or pride, by the urge to hurt or destroy as easily as it can be stimulated by love.

This is a point of confusion for many. Sexual desire can be the vehicle of many strong feelings of which love is only one. In many minds, sexual desire is practically synonymous with love, and mere physical attraction is confused with being *in* love. How often in how many backseat encounters has the word "love" been a magical "Open Sesame" to provide a way of release for a powerful "need press" built by strong physical attraction?

So, *there is chemistry and there is alchemistry.* If sexual union is not stimulated by the radiance, the light, the fire of love, it results in a coupling which is never more than merely transitory. There is never any real release from darkness.

Love is the light, powerfully inclusive, that leads to wholeness. Mere sexual desire from Adam onward is exclusive and leads us on to separation in a bewildering, frightening darkness. The light in the jungle of confusion is love, the magic transforming ingredient of light. When we convey love through sex then and only then do we have true sexual love.

Sexual love is a path of knowing the riddle of existence through an active illuminated penetration into an unknown future. In the true sharing of sexual love between two people, *each of them is reborn.*

In this prelude of alchemical sharing, the foundation for the union of each with the Creator is built in a brighter, fuller light. In this light, we rejoice like unself-conscious babes at play in the creative joy of sunshine. We need this light in which to grow, for in sexual love, as in spiritual growth, most of us *are* babes.

Jayj Jacobs

Jayj Jacobs has had a full-service astrological practice in San Francisco since 1972, counseling businesses, couples, individuals, and politicians, and has recently relocated to the nearby suburban community of Mill Valley. Jayj became interested in astrology in 1964, at age 15, and his initial training was with his father, Don "Moby Dick" Jacobs, with whom he developed an innovative approach known as "Experience Astrology." Jayj distributes his father's works, the 10 "Moby Dick Matrix Charts," *Astrology's Pew in Church*, and the Jesus biography, *Joshua.*,

Jayj has studied Human Sexuality at the University of Hawaii, More University, the Human Awareness Institute, San Francisco Sex Information, Landmark Education, and other institutions. He is also a Certified Awareness Counselor, and a Self-Expression and Leadership Coach.

Jayj has lectured throughout the country, and his articles have appeared in *Astrology Now, Aspects, Welcome to Planet Earth, The Sun-Sign Astrologer, Llewellyn's Sun Sign Book,* and others. This is his third contribution to Llewellyn's New World Astrology Series. Jayj is an AFAN co-founder, on the Steering Committee, and Chair of AFAN's Legal Information Committee. He received the AFAN's Service Award in 1992 for his contribution to Astrology as a profession.

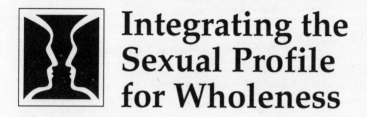

Integrating the Sexual Profile for Wholeness

Jayj Jacobs

mpowering clients to be more successful and more satisfied in *every* area of their lives is the legitimate aim of every astrologer. We might design a practice around a specialization in relationships or career concerns, but we can not ignore the rest of a client's life if we intend to enhance the whole person. We need to be willing and able to deal with the private and the often painful, the repressed as well as the blissful. We need to validate the spiritual, to accept the material, to recognize the disturbed, to confront the crisis of failure, and not blink at the possibility of death when it looks a client in the eye.

In short, we need to face all the challenges of our time as well as of life itself. The totality of human life, particularly since Pluto in transit has established its Scorpio message, necessarily includes "the *facts* of life."

Victorian astrologers, unable to confront the reality of sex (or at least unwilling to deal with it in print), effectively amputated sexuality from the horoscope. Contemporary astrology has yet to recuperate fully from that literary surgery. When sex began to be reintroduced, it was placed in the 5th House as merely the means for making babies, and it was left there as an expression of love. That denial of reality regarding the use, frequency, and importance of sexuality has left astrology disempowered. This volume, and this article, are a step toward recovery for astrologers and astrology.

What is Sex?

Sex is a biological drive with a chemical basis, physiological parameters, physical manifestations, emotional and psychological dimensions, and sociological implications.

At the most basic physical level, sexual activity is friction. At the most spiritual level, it is merging into a transcendental oneness. At all levels, healthy sexuality is presumed to be pleasurable, even designed to be delightful, for all the parts and parties involved.

Surely, ecstasy is its own reward; it needs no justification, no redeeming social value, no higher purpose, no additional personal payoff to grant it permission to be. Yet these "bonuses" for great sex do exist, and they affect us profoundly by their presence and by their absence. Great sex—maybe even merely good sex— regenerates and invigorates. It's not the only activity that empowers. It is one sure and valid way to tap a source of personal power and to support a process of empowerment, even transformation.

Let's be clear. I'm not crudely calling for more sex or promoting promiscuity. I'm neither suggesting nor dismissing sexual harassment. I'm not promoting unsafe sex or teen pregnancy. I *do* suggest strongly that we *face up to and use* Nature's own biological and astrological technology of transformation and regeneration, for our minds, bodies, and spirits.

Unhealthy sex, bad (or even mediocre) sex, unwelcome sexuality, repressed sexuality, and no sex (in the sense of reactive rather than temporary volitional celibacy), degenerates and debilitates. Blocked energy festers. I'm not claiming that more sex is always better: I do assert that better sex is better, and is beneficial for your clients. Almost all of them will say that that is what they want.

This article presents a guide to help us to counsel clients to ascend from okay sex to great sex, and to realize the rewards of an elevated, satisfying sexuality.

I propose to demonstrate that, when sexual energy is manifested at the higher levels of expression for the signs and planets involved (with the 8th House), the client's sexual activity and experience are more satisfying and more fulfilling. These elevated expressions of zodiacal orientation and planetary energy are then transferred to or shared with and applied to the other houses in the horoscope where equivalent indicators appear; the client then experiences greater freedom, facility, success, and satisfaction in these associated houses. The quality of life is enriched by this transference; the whole person is enhanced by the integration of these elevated expressions of sexuality.

This chapter is designed to be "how to" in orientation, and not merely a report on "what is." My approach should facilitate your being creative rather than repetitive in sharing the following interpretations, guidelines, and principles with your clients.

My Sign and Planet delineations, while valid, are not meant to be comprehensive, but, as catalytic seeds they will blossom in your mind and become food for thought. As you fertilize them with your own astrological philosophy, techniques, and experience, they will grow into a harvest which you can serve to your clients.

Maybe I'm stating the obvious, but some things aren't obvious at all until they *are* stated.

The primary operative principles upon which this thesis is based are Equivalence, Elevation, Reciprocity, and Transference.

The Principle of Equivalence

A Sign, its ruling Planet, and its Natural House constitute one complex unit which I call an Astrological Triad. They arise from and share a common essential energy or nature that establishes the similar, overlapping, and yet distinct meanings and manifestations of each facet of the Triad. Some of the interpretations of each component of the essential set are the same. Other meanings are similar to, and a few are different from, but still related to, the others.

While a planet is not *equal* to a sign, i.e., it doesn't have exactly the same energy, meaning or identifying effect, it is *equivalent* to a sign in that both *produce similar results*, operate in a similar manner, deal with similar issues, expressions and activities. Each may substitute for, or be taken for, the other. Mars, Aries, and the 1st House are three facets of the Expressive, Active, Immediacy Principle. Mercury, Gemini, and the 3rd House are the three varieties of the Sensory, Mental, Communicative Principle. There is only one principle; it manifests in three directions, or exists in three dimensions.

Since they combine equivalent energies, Aries on the 3rd House cusp will produce the same eager curiosity, sharp mind and sharp tongue that is generated by Mars in the 3rd House. Mars in Gemini indicates a similar degree of mental and verbal energy and eagerness. Mercury in Aries also shares some expressions, as does (to a lesser extent) Gemini on the 1st. None of these is exactly the same; a Sign on a House and its ruling Planet in a House are the most similar.

Additionally, people will take similar approaches to, and have similar experiences in, a house that is "cusped" by a sign and the house that holds its ruler. Of course, this is modified in many ways, but if Aries on the 5th is "competitive recreations," then Mars in the 3rd often is mental/verbal competitions.

It is not that Mars *is* Aries or that Aries *is* the 1st House. It's that Mars is *as if* Aries, which in turn is *as if* the 1st House.

As with synonyms, the denotations or essential meanings in an astrological Triad are shared; they converge to closeness if not to identicalness, but the connotations, the suggestive and associated *implications*, diverge. In the syntax of astrological language, planets are analogous to verbs, signs to modifiers, and houses to nouns. Thus Mars is *speed*, Aries is *speedy*, and the 1st House is *speeding*; or: competes, competitively, and competition.

The Principle of Elevation

The expression of any horoscopic indicator or any combination of factors is not static. The way in which people manifest their chart is not constant or permanently fixed. Every factor can be elevated to the point that clients experience more success and satisfaction, less frustration and anxiety, greater freedom and facility in their life through manifesting that component of their chart.

All attitudes are not created equal. While all of us progress at our own pace, some ways of being, like some actions, produce desired results more than others do. Responsibility, for example, produces more success than blame or guilt does. Issues and actions in life are not black and white. Neither are they shades of gray. Between black and white are all the colors of the rainbow.

It is possible to consider the collection of traits and actions associated with any sign or planet and judge which of a pair might be a more positive manifestation of the essential principle.

Think of the various expressions, meanings, or interpretations of any sign or planet on a *scale of possibility* from lowest to highest expression. This scale includes every expression of that principle from the common through the uncommon and to the rare states that people seldom reach as a peak or survive as a plunge into the depths.

Within such a scale there exists a range of probability which delineates where most people operate most of the time with that particular Sign or Planet. This denotes what people usually do with a planetary energy, or what they conventionally see from a zodiacal perspective.

The Principle of Reciprocity

Signs on Houses and Planets in Houses indicate a person's attitude or orientation toward the activities of that house—how they will conduct themselves in the affairs of that arena of life (and with whom). Equally, the indicators on or in a House show *the results of engagement in those activities.* You get out of a House (or of life) what you put into it. In addition to signs and planets affecting the houses they are connected with, the essential nature or principle that each sign or planet embodies is equally and reciprocally effected by the houses to which it is connected.

For example, if the Moon is in the 7th House, then the longing for a nurturing relationship draws the client into entanglements with emotional partners. If the partner is kind and considerate, the client feels cared for and is content. That state of contentment, of emotional fulfillment, exists in the person (not merely in the chart). It may be pervasive, adding a glow to the whole person, the whole chart, to all of life, but it shows-up predominately in this house area that hosts the Moon.

Contentment is a state of being, a dynamic orientation, that can be brought to or applied to a house's activities. If you enter a relationship already content, satisfied, and emotionally complete, the relationship has a much better chance of succeeding and of generating more happiness. Any House activity is *enhanced by what you bring to it,* like a potluck dinner.

If the client pursues and enters a relationship from a "needy" or emotionally deprived space, the perception and selection of partners will most likely be faulty. Even with a good choice of partner, *the grasping neediness will tend to vacuum the joy out of the relationship.* Less satisfaction will result; there may even be a great deal of emotional pain which will also drain the joy out of other Houses' experiences in the horoscope.

The three components of any Essential Triad (sign, planet, house) are linked together such that the level of expression of any one of them affects the level of expression of the others. If either the energy, the attitude, or the activity (the planet, sign, or house) is enhanced, *the other two components will be enhanced naturally and spontaneously.* There are three facets, but only one principle. Imagine lifting a triangle off a table by one of its points or sides. Whichever focal point you elevate, the other two rise with it. There are three sides, but only one triangle.

This is a principle of transference. It is actually an extension of the concept of rulership. Energy and expression flow not only from a ruling Planet to its Sign and into the House it is on, they travel simultaneously and concurrently across all the paths among the Sign, Planet and House in an Astrological Triad.

A complete horoscope also has three sides or dimensions: the Natural Chart, the Natal Chart, and the Solar Chart. The expression of a Triad—elevated or not—is transferred among, across and between these wheels.

The Natural Chart (from 0° Aries) is the basic chart of human nature: the Signs, or the Signs as Houses, or even interpreting the Signs as on the Houses, illuminate the orientations, drives, and desires that human beings have in common, perhaps as a reflection of our shared socio-biological heritage. In this dimension, *all of us* have Aries on the 1st House, Gemini on the 3rd, Scorpio on the 8th, Pisces on the 12th, etc. These interpretations are valid for all humans, even though they are somewhat disguised and modified by the overlay of individual Natal and Solar charts. These traits we share unite us and are as important as those that distinguish us as unique.

The planets in the signs at the moment of birth personalize the individual's Natural chart. We all have the territorial imperative, nesting instinct, and need for family bonding of Cancer on the 4th, but only some of us also have Jupiter in Cancer as benefic enhancement of home and family.

Note that since aspects between planets are computed from their angular separation in degrees of longitude—measured through the Signs—aspects are a function of and a factor in the

Natural Chart. Aspects are more truly between the Planets themselves, or between Planets in Signs, than they are between Planets in Houses. Their functioning may be channeled into the occupied houses, but that functioning is by no means limited to those houses. Aspects permeate the whole chart.

The Natal Chart, of course, is calculated from the date, time, and place of birth of an event, an individual, or some other entity. The Ascendant (the degree and minute of the Sign rising) is used as the cusp of the 1st House. The Houses are either Equal (which I recommend) or are calculated from the Midheaven in a variety of ways (take your choice) that make one-half of them more and less than equal. In most instances, the degrees on the cusps will vary, but the sign will be the same as in Equal Houses. The Ascendant Wheel for each Rising Sign places the Signs in order around the wheel, one per house, but isn't personalized by planets in houses or signs. It is what we can say about *all* Scorpio Ascendants, rather than a particular person with that Sign rising.

The Natal Chart or Ascendant Wheel is the Framework of Reality that arises from a certain self-image and manner of self-expression. The Ascendant is your view of yourself that you present to the world as you enter into life. Personality and Self-Expression generate a set of attitudes and orientations toward the activities that comprise living; the arenas for action that are the houses.

The Solar Chart is derived from the Sun's position, (calculated for the birthdate, place and time), *which is used as the 1st House cusp.* All of the houses are 30° in size, with the Sun's degree and minute in subsequent Signs as the house cusps. A complete personal Solar Chart contains Planets in Sign, and Houses. All of a Solar Chart's components have the same meaning, weight, and worth as they would have in a Natal Chart. A Solar Chart is the ordered set of Signs on Houses that follows from any Sun Sign being the cusp of the 1st House. The Sun, as the indicator of the core concept of Self, the true essential identity, the basic inherent character, and the point of view on life, *will also generate a congruent set of attitudes and orientations to the houses.* This set of perceptive and interpretive filters through which one views and experiences life is specific to a particular Sun-Sign.

Most of what astrologers have memorized as the delineation of Sun-Sign characteristics can be seen from the Signs on Houses in the Solar Chart. For example, Scorpio's secretiveness or verbal reticence is a function of Capricorn on the 3rd in the *Solar* Chart, while their willingness to talk about (and during) sex is shown by Gemini on the 8th.

Using the Solar Chart (or Wheel) along with and equal to the Natal (and the Natural) allows us to see another vector of transference: as the house that hosts Cancer in one wheel is enhanced, the house in the other wheel that has a Cancer cusp *will be enhanced simultaneously.* So, too, will both houses that hold the Moon. Thus, one elevation produces up to four other improvements. Each of these will generate feedback to the initiating house, and to the other houses as well. A complete horoscope

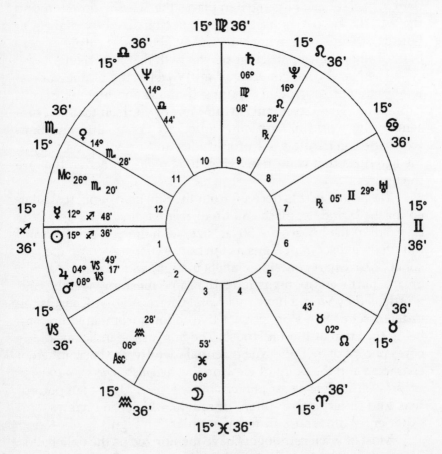

Solar Chart 1

being a synergistic system, rather than a mere collection of components, it can't be any other way. There are three wheels, but only one horoscope. A complete and whole chart is necessary to reflect, understand, or counsel the whole person.

As an example to illustrate the above, consider the Solar and Natal Charts of the same person, respectively shown here as: Solar Chart 1 and Natal Chart 1: in the Solar Chart, Cancer is on the 8th with the Pisces Moon in the 3rd; in the Natal Chart, Cancer is on the 6th (from the Aquarius Ascendant) with the Moon in the 2nd. The 8th House Cancer suggests great sex, fulfilled through a nurturing of needs resulting in a permanent emotional bond, obviously making the client happy, if not delirious. The

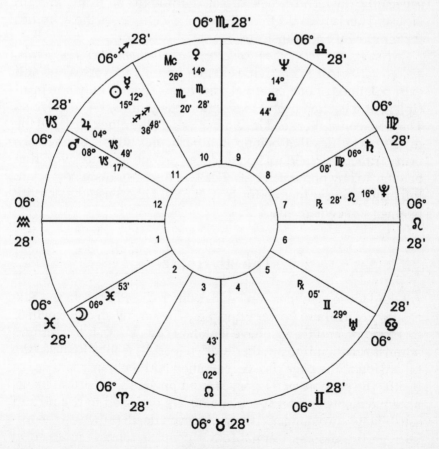

Natal Chart 1

improvement in mood enhances the mental acuity, the listening ability, the willingness to verbalize and the writing talent (Moon 3rd). These vitalized functions from the Solar Chart *are transferred to* the 6th House in Natal Chart 1, through the Cancer cusp (as is the original elevated mood). This generates both an enjoyment of work (the 6th) and a need to produce effectively with enhanced (interpersonal) skills. The wish to be—and sense of being—resourceful is also fed by this transference when it reaches the 2nd House Moon. Every satisfaction reflects back to the other Lunar/Cancer houses.

"What's This Got to Do With Sex?" The principles of Equivalence, Elevation, Reciprocation, and Elevation operate everywhere throughout the horoscope, adding rich dimension, but are especially powerful when directed through, or from, the 8th House. This is because the 8th House encompasses the activities that empower and transform.

Houses are not random collections of functions, faculties, forms, and activities. All the activities in any house are expressions and extrapolations of one essential principle. (There is only one principle, but it is often useful to describe it with three related terms.) This core concept or seed idea generates all the other ideas, all the diverse activities that belong in a particular house. Conversely, every function, field of experience, or line of endeavor that belongs to any house can be logically reduced or distilled back to the originating principle for that House. Otherwise the activity belongs somewhere else.

The 8th House

All 8th House activities can be logically reduced back to the Sex, Death/Rebirth, and Power Principles. They are all an outgrowth of this concept, and they all have it at their core. Death is a crisis and a transformation into another hidden (occult) reality. Rebirth (the other side of the page) is a regeneration and the transcendence of death. The purpose of a legacy is to empower the inheritor. Insurance payments and legal settlements are designed to restore and rehabilitate after danger, damage, or even death (to which the former are precursors). Capital (other people's money) invested in you is also intended to empower you and your endeavors.

Power is the ability to move people or particles; overpowering is the state of moving them too far, too fast, or in a direction against their choice. A crisis is too many things coming together too rapidly, including all of them at any same time. A "catalytic experience" takes you from crisis through breakdown to breakthrough, and leaves you empowered.

Proximity, friction, tension, release, breakthrough, a new state of being, relaxation; crisis and resolution? Or sexual activity and orgasm? Sexual activity follows the same course, moves through the same process as a catalytic crisis. Sex *is* catalytic.

Sex sells, and gets sold. Sex drives, and gets driven out. Sex motivates, and intimidates. Sex magnetizes, and terrorizes. Sex invigorates, and degenerates.

Manipulation, suppression, repression, dominance, domination, debilitation, and destruction are neighboring ideas within this housing development. They all misuse power and take it away.

Power, *ki, chi, (or Ch'i), prana, kundalini, élan vitale,* life force, sexual energy; different names from different frames of reference for the same force that moves you and allows you to move the world. Life force, life direction, life design, destiny, purpose; they are all extensions of the 8th House, the Scorpionic, Plutonian essence.

Healthy sexuality; sexual energy that entices and pleases, that excites and satisfies; sexual activity that neither demeans nor harms anyone, that is invited and shared stimulates, activates, and exercises the energy that empowers and transforms. It is all the same energy. Sexuality, sexual activity, is but one access to the regenerative energy. Access is almost immediate, it is right at hand.

Some systems of thought say progress on "the path" presupposes ignoring the sex drive, others require repression, and still others recommend redirection. Ignoring sex doesn't work any better than trying to not think of pink elephants; especially when all media are plastering pink pachyderms on everything. Every psychologist (not just Freud and Reich) warns of the danger of repression.

You can't miss seeing the potholes in people's lives where they've tried to bury crises, or re-bury the complexes they've discovered. As for redirection, it's awfully hard to get energy to flow through one-half of a wire, or water to go up only one side of a hose. *How do "they" expect us to raise the Kundalini to the pineal and crown chakras, with a knot tied in the hose at the 2nd chakra?* It's better to open up and manage, than to close down and repress.

People are told to curb their appetite for food, but not to stop eating permanently. We suggest they watch what they eat, but rarely do we ask them to wait till they're eighteen before indulging. We say slow down, even stop, and look where you're going, but almost never do we say you can't ever drive again. We ask people to be quiet, but not to never speak again. Some say you should drink water when you're hungry, but we don't tell people to eat when they're thirsty. Why do people suggest taking a shower, or meditating, when they are aroused?

Neither money, nor *maya*, nor love, nor lust is evil or even the root of evil. Evil results from frustrated, festering *unresolved desire*. Desires fulfilled are no problem.

- If you want what you don't have, you have a problem.
- If you don't want what you do have, you have a problem.
- If you do have what you want, you're fine.
- If you don't have what you don't want, you're fine, too.

From the birth of understanding, the idea of sex is magnetic, it attracts your notice. Sex is gripping, it grabs your attention. Sex is striking, it penetrates your consciousness. Sex is absorbing, it holds your awareness. Sex has power, sex is power. If the power isn't directed responsibly, effectively, and positively, it *will* manifest negatively: as overpowering or disempowering, or through fixations and compulsions. Perhaps any activity with that much power must be managed. Like a car with no brakes, since it can't be stopped, it must be steered. But, truly, there are brakes, a steering wheel, an accelerator, and all manner of modifying controls. They need to be handled properly.

If we followed standard astrological procedures and precepts, we'd use the Signs and Planets associated with any particular House to get a handle on that life issue, so we could use it, or manage it, or move it to where or how we wanted it to be. *Management is a much higher expression than deflection or denial.*

To manage sexuality you have to use the 8th House and/or Scorpio and/or Pluto together with the Signs, Planets, and Houses with which they are connected.

If you want to use astrology to empower someone, to enhance their experience of living, to direct them toward being the best person they can be, to further their twin quests for satisfaction and success, put them centered in time, knowing when to inquire, when to reflect, and when to take affirmative action so they and their life are more the way they want them to be . . . then look, (if not last, then first) to the 8th House, the arena of empowerment. Since sex is a valid integral component of that House, and since it is also a catalytic, transformative energy, a client can use sexuality as a tool of empowerment to enhance the whole person.

Elevating a Sexual Profile

Principles are more valuable than the examples which serve to illustrate them. As Copernicus advised, rely on sure principles, leaving out nothing essential, nor adding in anything inappropriate. Counsel your clients to express the higher levels of the Sign(s) on and Planets in the 8th House in their sexual activity to enhance their sex life. Besides being more satisfying, this reinforces those higher expressions and generates their integration. The elevated energies will then be transferred to the other Houses that network through those Signs and Planets.

Planets produce the same effects as the Signs they are equivalent to—except for the results that are *directly* related to the construction of the Natal and Solar Wheels and the inherent characteristics of those Signs. Don't be too specific in maintaining the same assignment of qualities to Signs rather than Planets that I use in the following section. Be careful, but be creative.

Note: Given the ponderous pace of the Outer Planets, they will be in Signs and in the 8th House of certain Signs for several years. Dates for each Outer Planet involved with the particular 8th House are given at the end of each segment. During the whole period, one-half of all the people born with this Sign on the cusp will have the Outer Planet in the 8th. This is a function of the planet's position being earlier or later than the degree on the House cusp.

Mars in the 8th (or) Aries on the cusp, the Virgo wheel (Solar Chart). From impatience to accomplishment, from challenge to leadership.

Mars is eager for nearly instant gratification. Courtship is inconvenient (although the challenge is exciting); consummation is the immediate concern. The sexual desire is impulsive; Mars just wants to jump, it doesn't much care if there's water in the pool. Martian lust for immediate action leads to intercourse without pre-play or (much) foreplay, in women as well as men. Its impatience for whatever is next allows but little time to enjoy the afterglow.

When Mars learns to entice and excite, to lead the partner to a new plateau, and from there to another peak, then it experiences the rewards of aiming for a higher goal. Aries' short attention span can be transcended if the client will stop part-way to the desired destination on the path of pleasure (perhaps to let the partner take a turn, as in a game of chase and tag) and then re-start. Virgo's inherent ability to perceive what will produce the desired result supports the 8th House Aries in pursuing the pin-nacle of pleasure. Direct the action to gain one first-down (after another?) before driving for a touchdown.

Great sex fills 8th House Mars/Aries clients with energy. They are invigorated (rather than drained and depleted) and ready for the next challenge. But the release has taken the edge off; latent anger and combativeness are elevated to dynamic assertiveness and cooperative competitiveness. The successful completion of this pleasure project validates the Virgo client's positive self-concept and dissipates much of their self-criticism. The exercise in leadership primes them to take the initiative in their other Mars/Aries Houses. Fresh from victory, having con-quered desire with passion, the client is eager for the next chal-lenge. Sex has generated energy which is aimed at the next target—the other Mars/Houses.

Note: Look for Uranus in the 8th in Aries or Taurus (1927–1942).

Venus in the 8th (or) Taurus on the cusp—The Libra Wheel. From indolence to sensuality, from possessive to resourceful.

Since Venus has dual rulership over Taurus and Libra, it may manifest in the 8th with either a Taurus or a Libra flavor—or even with facets of both. (Check the Pisces Wheel section for the Libra style of Venusian sexuality.)

Clients with Venus in the 8th are turned on by the apprecia-tion of their partners and the luxuriant sensuality they are gifted with. They revel in tactile experience and savor sensory overload. Those with a Venus/Taurus 8th are much more responsive to touch than to looks. Taurus cusp clients may be indolent, not exactly selfish, but more apt to partake of sensory delights than to produce them. The sentiment is "love me and linger over me."

Librans who discover the stimulating sensuality of using the whole body to caress with enter a new realm of pleasure. Being the source of their partners' response is rewarding and validating, especially for the Libra client. Sharing sensation and providing pleasure stimulate the Libra self-concept and the generous Taurus 8th to a higher expression.

Fostering a highly tactile, intimate partnership strengthens and vitalizes the Libran client in more ways than the physical. Taurus, transferred from this house of empowerment, transformation, and commitment, produces a result-oriented approach to the other Taurus/Venus Houses.

Satisfaction generates a grounded sense of stability that gives Libra a solid base of consistent practicality upon which to weigh their options and the optimum use of their resources. Taurus helps anchor the Libran tendency to waffle and re-decide. Elevating Taurus (or Venus) clarifies values and sharpens the sense of what's worthwhile. The Taurean 8th gathers energy and focuses intent, giving the Libran more power to foster intimacy, or to enhance their performance in other arenas of life.

Note: Look for Uranus in the 8th in Taurus or Gemini (1934–1949).

Mercury in the 8th, Gemini on the cusp—The Scorpio Wheel. From frivolousness to versatility, from crassness to communication.

Since Mercury has dual rulership over Gemini and Virgo it may manifest in the 8th with either a Gemini or a Virgo flavor— or even with facets of both. (Check the Aquarius Wheel section for the Virgo style of Mercurial sexuality.)

Clients with an 8th House Mercury may spend so much time talking about sex and trying to decide if they want to bother with it, that the time lost and mind-tripping interfere with just doing it or with fully enjoying it. If you try to do two, or too many things at once, make sure both (or all) directly pertain to the matter at hand.

These clients can be gently informed that a prurient mind is a terrible thing to waste; read a book or get a tutor and discover what you didn't know you didn't know. Inquiry, education, and mostly experience raise the level of Mercury from chatter to true communication. The Gemini cusp clients' telling tall tales of past times changes to a play-by-play commentary on the current action and metamorphosizes into inquiry, invitation, and negotiation over what comes next.

When the clients' thoughts and touches are in sync with their partners', there is a synergy that sends them beyond rationality. Scorpio clients, now recognizing that communication is an effective, constructive, powerful action, become willing to say what's on their mind in a way that produces the results they desire. Now that they can enroll people (by presenting a possibility and its outcome), they no longer need to manipulate them.

A new acuity in the senses, aiding a fresh clarity of consciousness, and a nimble agility of thought, deliver new answers to the prior puzzles of the other Mercury/Gemini Houses.

Note: Look for Pluto in the 8th in Cancer (1912–1939). Look for Uranus in the 8th in Gemini or Cancer (1942–1956). With Mercury, since the Sun is within 28°, check if the Sun is also in the 8th.

Moon in the 8th, Cancer on the cusp—The Sagittarius Wheel. From craving to fulfillment, from coveting to care-giving, from caution to contentment.

Lunar desires wax and wane, the sexual appetite comes in and goes out like the tides. The recurring cravings are felt like hunger and the client may substitute caloric satiation for sexual satisfaction in a Pyrrhic transaction. Moon/Cancer clients feel a compelling need to couple, consummate, and connect their hearts to another. Careless choices leave a bad taste in the heart.

Caring and feeling cared for helps to transcend the twin hurdles of hormonal immediacy and selfish neediness. Learning to care for another's needs as much as their own guides them to the gatepost marked "Forever Yours." A true-blue Moon/Cancer client adopts lovers into the family clan, neither forgetting nor relinquishing the connection that was made. The sex act may never be repeated, but sexual adoption is permanent.

Satisfied Sagittarians develop a new sense of family and of roots; a rationale for staying or a reason to return. They recognize that they explored this uncharted territory and tamed the wild beasts they discovered by being perceptive of and sensitive to the cares, concerns, and sensitivities of another. They'll be less blunt and brusque for it. They might even have a cure for the fear of commitment.

Sexual contentment then transfers to the other Cancer/Moon houses as *joie de vivre*, the precursor to the perception of opportunity and benefit, especially for Sagittarius, and to the happiness that heals, for the Moon.

Note: Look for Pluto in the 8th in Cancer or Leo (1912–1958). Look for Uranus in the 8th in Cancer or Leo (1948–1962).

Sun in the 8th, Leo on the 8th—The Capricorn Wheel. Leo/Sun from pride to playfulness, from arrogance to re-integration.

The 8th House Sun client may have flipped over from too much personal sexual energy, or too much sexual attention from others (especially the wrong kind of attention—or the wrong others), into an asexual limbo or an anti-sexual purgatory. Double Capricorn Linda Lovelace, former porn star (of *Deep Throat*) is now an Evangelical Christian and an anti-porn activist. Anita Bryant, the anti-gay crusader, has an 8th House Sun in Aries. Those who reinterpret experiences are trying to reinvent themselves. Leo on the 8th is such a powerful sexual identity that it seems a Capricorn is just a Scorpio in a suit. Growing beyond the unearned arrogance of being God's gift to the other sex and learning how to play sexually (the creativity is inherent) and how to perform (to please rather than show-off), earns a gold star for the Capricorn client. Satisfaction and sexual success are the antidotes for Capricorn self-abasement. It also produces the romance they desire.

Confidence is an immediate consequence of consummate connubial bliss. Great sex takes the stiffness out of Capricorns and fills them with self-validation, more so than accomplishing any other goal. Proud and pleased Capricorns apply their recharged vitality to problem solving and to creative solutions in the other Sun/Leo Houses. Often, they just have fun in those Houses, for awhile.

Note: Look for Pluto in the 8th in Leo or Virgo (1937–1972). Look for Uranus in the 8th in Leo or Virgo (1955–1969) or both!

Mercury in the 8th, Virgo on the 8th—The Aquarius Wheel. Virgo/Mercury from negation to refinement, from mechanics (tinkering) to virtuoso mastery.

Since Mercury has dual rulership over Gemini and Virgo it may manifest in the 8th with either a Gemini or a Virgo flavor—or even with facets of both. Check the Scorpio Wheel section for the Gemini style of Mercurial sexuality.

An 8th House Mercury client has analyzed all positives and negatives of sexual energy and all the ups and downs of the ins and outs of sexual activity. The critical recognition of the accompanying absurdities may produce a pseudo-intellectual disdain for such awkward (animalistic) behavior. Some Aquarians (like Geminis) often forget they are physical beings.

Aquarian clients bring their scientific curiosity and a mechanistic approach to the Virgo cusp. These sexual technicians know where all the buttons, dials, and switches are, and exactly how to turn them on, but if the client doesn't have some softening water placements their partner may conclude they're in bed (or somewhere) with a robot. A true Virgo-on-the-8th virtuoso manufactures the human tenderness that their partner might otherwise miss.

Discovering what's actually and currently needed and wanted takes Aquarian clients out of their heads, brings them back from the future, and plants them in reality, rather than in the science-fiction world of their aspirations.

The Virgoan qualities and traits of attention to detail, discrimination, clarity of analysis and choice of project are transferred to the other Mercury/Virgo Houses in the Aquarian clients' chart. There they produce concrete results in the present.

Note: Look for Neptune in the 8th in Virgo or Libra (1928–1957). Look for Pluto in the 8th in Virgo or Libra (1956–1984). Look for Uranus in the 8th in Virgo or Libra (1961–1975) or both!

Venus in the 8th, Libra on the 8th—The Pisces Wheel. Libra/Venus from charming (conning) to cherishing, from doting to dedicated.

Since Venus has dual rulership over Taurus and Libra in may manifest in the 8th with either a Taurus or a Libra flavor—or even with facets of both. Check the Libra Wheel section for the Taurus style of Venusian sexuality.

Clients with Venus in the 8th are as much in love with beauty and charm as they are in love with love. They associate love with sex (even more than most), and sometimes they can't tell the difference. Falling for looks and a good line is as much a Pisces

Wheel/Libra 8th problem as it is a Venus vexation; when the client misses the substance which may be lacking in their partner they're left with a movie, rather than real memories.

Being kind and compassionate, receptive and affectionate—without turning off the judgment—while appreciating the affection and responding appropriately, elevates the cooperation to partnership.

Pisces clients need to know someone is on their side. They need to see they are accepted as is, now, with their faults as a part of the equation, and not just for what they will be later whenever their 7th House Virgo mate says they're done.

The cataclysmic translation to another dimension lets Pisces be more effective in this one since they recognize that someone else didn't do it to them. They cooperated and co-created this.

They can do the same in their other Venus/Libra Houses. Now that they know what spice conditional love adds to consummate bliss, they can refine their approach to Venus/Libra Houses. They now, post-passion, diplomatically balance acceptance and surrender with ethical standards for co-operation and legalistic standards for fair treatment. They cancel capitulation; trading it for enrollment. The affairs of the other Venus/Libra House find a resolution in balance and harmony.

Note: Look for Pluto in the 8th in Libra (1971–1984). Look for Neptune in the 8th in Libra or Scorpio (1942–1970). Look for Uranus in the 8th in Libra (1968–1975) and soon Scorpio (1974–1981). Look for Pluto currently transiting the 8th to emphasize the sexuality and empower the transformation. Be wary of Passion to Puritan flips; great sex is an effective vaccine against bad piety.

Pluto in the 8th, Scorpio on the 8th—The Aries Wheel. Scorpio/Pluto from depravity to empowerment, from obsession to commitment. (As this Sign on a House is a reflection of the Natural Chart, all people will have this component in their make-up, perhaps hidden behind their Natal and Solar Charts. Clients who also have Scorpio on the 8th in their Natal or Solar chart get a double-whammy, as will those with an 8th House Pluto.

A client with Pluto in the 8th may be obsessed with sex, although some are merely preoccupied with the subject. Nothing may loom larger in the life, nor fill the consciousness so completely as the passionate desire for sexual engagement and temporary release from this worldly coil. If Pluto (or Scorpio) also expresses as an interest in reincarnation, salvation, and/or transformation, these other avenues may compete for the client's attention but will more likely complement (and be integrated with) the fascination with sexuality.

The Pluto/Scorpio 8th client radiates the electricity of sexual energy and interest, whatever they may be involved in, unless they have been recently discharged. The intensity of the driving desires may unintentionally intimidate others with less passion or less sense of personal power. They aren't necessarily dangerous, just don't cross them.

Clients who have partners who can stand the heat, or better, who thrive near the inferno, will build a bonfire worthy of the mythical Phoenix. They will be born anew, explosively, from the ashes of passion, totally refreshed and strengthened, even if not completely reconstituted. Clarity of purpose comes with them.

It was the clients' intention to generate the result, to produce maximum impact, without attachment to the particular form it would take, that drove the process. Physically sated, for the time being, they search for the next powerful action to further their commitments. Aries gain consistency and maintain a sense of purpose that's bigger than they are.

Note: Look for Neptune in the 8th in Scorpio and Sagittarius. (1956–1984). Look for Pluto currently transiting the 8th to emphasize the sexuality and empower the transformation. Here too: be wary of Passion to Puritan flips; great sex is an effective vaccine against bad piety.

Jupiter in the 8th, Sagittarius on the 8th—The Taurus Wheel, from excess to enhancement, from plethora to perfection, from avoidance to abundance, and waste to wisdom.

Jupiter in the 8th House is almost totally uninhibited, and quite often indiscriminate as well. So many men and/or women, so little time. So much enthusiasm, so little opportunity (but only by comparison to what they'd like to think they could handle). Jupiter here produces *a love of excess.* These clients think too much of a good thing is wonderful. The great outdoors may beckon to Jupiterians, but Sagittarius, arising from the Taurus wheel, prefers to be comfortable under the trees; there'll be no bed of leaves without a down comforter.

Getting beyond the blind optimism and terminal arrogance of the 8th House Sagittarius cusp, the sensual Taurus discovers the freedom and insight to transform quantity into quality in sexual matters. More is better, but better is best. Taurus clients learn their lessons well. They'll put the maxim to work everywhere, eventually.

Some see shooting stars and rockets, Taurus clients see new possibilities, and sense their best move, when the doors of perception are cleansed. Taureans become unstuck from their habits and traditions when they feel the Earth move. Perhaps a whole new world awaits discovery. They'll start by looking into their other Jupiter/Sagittarius Houses with a new-found flexibility and willingness to take reasonable chances.

Note: Look for Neptune and/or Uranus in Capricorn transiting the 8th and creating confusion to mask the chaos, or inspiration to guide the experimentation. Note that Pluto is on its way.

Saturn in the 8th, Capricorn on the 8th—The Gemini Wheel, from inconsequence to significance, from denial to mastery.

Clients with Saturn in the 8th House deny the importance of sexuality to themselves, to you, and to the world. Many discredit all forms of sexual experience or expression. Repression and rigidity are symbiotic, but not healthful. Some 8th House Saturn clients merely want to keep sex "in perspective," to restrict it to its proper place and function.

Gemini Wheel clients often over intellectualize, and some would prefer not to experience life from the neck down. This can limit sex but not eliminate it. Some Geminians begin by satisfying their curiosity about this activity that involves all five physical senses, and intrigues so many other people. If they take responsibility for their own responses (and connect with a partner who has slow hands), they become very accomplished lovers.

A few Geminis (or clients with Saturn here), will dedicate themselves to mastering sexuality and sexual techniques, since that is so useful in relationships. The squeaky wheel, having gotten the oil, now runs smoother and goes farther than the uncomplaining ones that were left to their own devices.

Satisfied Saturn/Capricorn 8th clients have learned dedication, perseverance and personal responsibility. They've had to learn to concentrate and focus. They manifest these qualities successfully in their other Saturn and Capricorn Houses.

Note: Look for Neptune and/or Uranus in Capricorn transiting the 8th and creating confusion to mask the chaos, or inspiration to guide the experimentation.

Uranus in the 8th, Aquarius on the 8th—The Cancer Wheel. Aquarius/Uranus from indifference to altruism, from perverse (kinky) to ingenious.

Rarely are clients with Uranus in the 8th House indifferent to sexuality. Some are mildly curious, but dispassionate. The norm is that they are much more likely to be intrigued, or even perplexed, but still willing to participate. Atypical preferences, of all sorts, are common among those with Uranus in the 8th.

Cancer clients, with Aquarius on the 8th House, share the preference for the unusual in people, places, poses, and playthings. They are drawn to unique, independent individualists or at least to people who are different from them in age, race, religion, background, or outlook.

Uranus in the 8th clients are always trying on new things to see if they fit, or can be tailored. Cancers will eagerly experiment sexually when they feel secure personally. Successful explorations lead to more innovations and additional pleasurable discoveries. Cancers' sexual preferences change with time and experience. Their erogenous zones wander, but a persistent partner will find where they are and bring them home, or feed them sensation on the spot.

Security becomes less a matter of belonging to a group, and more a function of individual initiative. Cancers learn to break with other traditions, when it suits them, beginning by cooking up innovations in their other Uranus/Aquarius Houses.

Neptune in the 8th, Pisces on the 8th—The Leo Wheel, from martyrdom to mysticism, from self-sacrifice to union.

Clients with Neptune in the 8th House may come to you as a victim, complaining of misuse (if not actual abuse), and bemoaning the sacrifices they've been coerced into making. Pisces on the cusp, given by Leo on the 1st, is less likely to produce a whiner, but will still show disappointment with their sex life.

Leos may get trapped in either unconsciously, or resentfully accepting whatever is offered, or in the flip side of Pisces, expecting to be worshiped as a god/dess. For those who transcend these levels, a creative sexual artistry develops, through intuition and listening, which entertains and delights their partner. There is no taking away from in true giving and receiving. The generosity of "this one's for you, dear" (especially from both partners) creates mutual delight through empathy and often reciprocation.

Pisces/Neptune on the 8th prepares the way for a blending of beings, a transcendental oneness, that furthers enlightenment with or without tantric techniques. The creative and/or psychic founts of inspiration are opened, turned on, and flowing. Leo clients, having learned how to give love, attention, and support sexually and emperingly, now transfer the art of contribution to their other Pisces/Neptune houses. Magic manifestation produces an enjoyable show.

The Afterglow

After the rockets have been launched in consuming fire, after whirlpools have drained the swirling oceans, after the Earth has moved in quaking shudders, after Suns have been born in cosmic coalescence, now that the Hurricane has subsided and its deluge has soaked into the cells of body, mind, heart, and spirit, a new reality is being born under the rainbow of promise fulfilled.

Ecstasy is still its own sufficient reward, but its concomitant benefits are readily available and already active. The Pleasure Principle is still the bond between people, but *its reach extends through and far beyond the physical and emotional.*

Enhancement of the whole person is still realizable through direct transformation and empowerment, but Elevation, Equivalence, Reciprocity, and Transference are expanding and accelerating the regenerative process. What *goes* around, *comes* around. The enhancement of the whole person will inevitably result in more positive sexual energy, more successful sexual activity, and a more satisfying sex life, and the Wheel keeps turning.

But for some, fear and resentment will still keep them apart (from their Self and from others) and less than fully empowered, less than completely whole. If we let them walk their walk, will they let us dance our dance?

LEVELS OF PLANETARY EXPRESSION:
A Concise Scale of Possibility

SUN
Vitalizes
Creates
Awakens
Strengthens
Takes Pride in
Identifies with
Adds Awareness
Glories in
Is Arrogant about

MERCURY (Virgo)
Expertise
Skill
Analyzes
Discriminates
Criticizes
Figures
Routine
Menial

MARS
Leadership
Strengthens
Activates
Instigates
Energizes
Desires
Competes
Angers
Attacks

MOON
Nurtures
Cares for
Enjoys
Responds to
Sensitizes
Emotionalizes
Wants and Needs
Hungers for
Covets

VENUS (Taurus)
Excellence
Quality
Appreciates
Comforts
Stabilizes
Possesses
Placid
Indulgent
Indolent

JUPITER
Wisdom
Knowledge
Perception
Exploration
Enhances
Elevates
Expands
Excesses
Wastes

MERCURY (Gemini)
Educates
Inquires
Communicates
Listens
Thinks
Verbalizes
Changes
Scatters

VENUS (Libra)
Loves
Relates thru
Beautifies
Appreciates
Values
Eases
Softens
Charms
Pacifies

Levels of Planetary Expression (cont'd)

SATURN	**URANUS**	**NEPTUNE**
Masters	Makes Unique	Unifies
Manages	Individualizes	Serves
Manifests	Innovates	Inspires
Focuses	Experiments	Spiritualizes
Structures	Aspires	Intuits
Limits	Objectifies	Accepts
Delays	Alters	Confuses
Denies	Rebels	Sacrifices
Invalidates	Shocks	Dissipates
		Deceives

PLUTO
Transforms
Empowers
Commits
Sexualizes
Intensifies
Controls
Dominates
Obsesses
Damages
Destroys

Anthony Louis

Anthony Louis is a psychiatrist with a strong interest in astrology. He has a private office practice of psychiatry, and serves as medical director at a community mental health center. As an astrologer, he specializes in horary and electional astrology, and has written a highly acclaimed book, *Horary Astrology: The History and Practice of Astro-Divination* (Llewellyn, 1991). He has also written an introduction to horary astrology that accompanies the Matrix Software BlueStar horary module.

Anthony Louis is a regular contributor to the *Llewellyn Sun Sign Book,* and his articles have appeared in *American Astrology Magazine, Aspects Magazine, The Mountain Astrologer, The Ascendant,* and numerous other astrological periods. Dr. Louis has lectured internationally on horary and electional astrology.

Issues of Sexual Repression: The Interface Between Astrology and Psychology

Anthony Louis

P sychotherapists say that the two most difficult topics for clients to discuss are sex and money, the latter being the more difficult of the two. Astrologers will not be surprised at the linkage between sex and money because both are 2nd House (Taurus, Venus) and 8th House (Scorpio, Mars, Pluto) issues. Clinically, we can often glean clues about a client's sexual life by observing how they handle their money; that is, by attending to the Taurus-Scorpio axis in the natural distribution of signs.

The idea of a specific sexual therapy is relatively recent in the history of modern medicine. It was only with the pioneering work of Masters and Johnson beginning in the 1960s that sexual problems came out of the closet. Unfortunately, the story of the treatment of sexual disorders in Western civilization is replete with hushed tones, superstitions, taboos, old wives' tales, and the meddling influence of religious zealots.

There is perhaps no better example of the religious influence on sexual behavior than in the story of Onan in the Old Testament (Genesis 38: 8-10). Apparently Onan spilled his seed on the ground rather than impregnate his dead brother's wife. The

Hebrew god looked askance at Onan's contraceptive efforts and killed him good and dead for voluntarily spilling that valuable seed. Five thousand years later, Western boys still feel guilt and dread for spilling their seed in masturbation. Some authorities have speculated that Onan might have been a premature ejaculator who was unable to control his orgasms voluntarily, prior to penetrating the vagina. If so, Onan was struck dead for what we now would regard as a treatable sexual dysfunction.

Since the time of Christ, the Roman Catholic Church has had a major influence on Western attitudes toward sexuality. In the thirteenth century, the brilliant thinker St. Thomas Aquinas espoused the classical theory of Natural Law. According to this theory, the natural goal of sexual activity is to impregnate the woman so that she can bear children and produce more good Catholics to love and serve God. Any pleasurable aspects of sex are secondary to the primary purpose of procreation. To engage in sex primarily as recreation is to pervert its natural and true purpose of procreation.

Of course, the devil (Satan, Saturn) is always around tempting us to seek sexual pleasure first, and worry about having babies later—such is the corrupt and concupiscent aspect of human nature. In addition, sexual behavior between members of the same sex is corrupt and immoral because in homosexual acts there is no chance of producing a baby. Today, some fundamentalist religious thinkers blame the AIDS epidemic on the flagrant violations of the Natural Law in our society.

As recently as a century ago, there was still little enlightenment about sexual matters. In the mid-nineteenthth century, the medical profession believed that over-indulgence in sexual intercourse could cause barrenness and that masturbation (then referred to as "self-pollution") could cause a host of maladies.

A book entitled Light and Life, published in the 1800s by C. H. Robinson and Company of Charlotte, North Carolina, advised its readers about the typical appearance of a self-polluter as someone who has "hot, dry skin with something of a hectic appearance." Other symptoms caused by masturbation in the nineteenth century included poor sleep, restlessness, night sweats, disturbing dreams, discharge from the urethra, headache, giddiness, ringing in the ears, stiff neck, darting pains in the forehead, and poor vision. (We all know the joke about the little boy caught masturbating by his mother who warned that such behavior would lead to blindness. "Don't worry," he told her, "I'll stop as soon as I need glasses.")

Fortunately there was treatment for the nineteenth-century self-polluter. The patient suffering from masturbation was instructed to "sleep in a hard bed, and rise early and take a sponge bath in cold water every morning." Additional measures included eating only light suppers, emptying the bladder thoroughly before bedtime, avoiding spicy foods as well as caffeine and alcohol, vigorous exercise, taking iron tonic, and reading good wholesome books. Above all else, "never sleep lying on your back."

Kevin

No doubt the case of "Kevin" would have received radically different treatment in the nineteenth century than he receives today. This troubled young man was considered mildly autistic in childhood. Kevin never developed peer relationships and lived in a private fantasy world. Because of his high intelligence, he did well academically and managed to go away to college. Unfortunately his college education was interrupted when he suffered a paranoid psychotic breakdown.

Because of his schizoid existence, Kevin has never been involved sexually with another person. His sexual life consists entirely of fantasies which accompany his masturbation, often several times daily. The fantasies consist of seducing attractive young boys and entering into a sexual relationship with them. Kevin is quite troubled by such fantasies and has never acted on them. He lives alone and as much as possible avoids human contact.

In Kevin's natal chart (p. 301), we discover the closest aspect be-tween planets to be Mercury in Gemini in the 11th House square Uranus in Virgo in the 2nd House. Uranus rules the 8th House cusp (sexuality) and Mercury rules the 3rd (mind, communication) and is in the 11th (friends, hopes). Mercury square Uranus is probably a signature of his childhood autism and later psychotic disorder. Because Uranus governs the 8th House (sex), this square aspect tells us something about his troubled sexual life and his conflicted (square aspect) attraction to boys (Mercury).

Furthermore, Venus (love) conjoins Mercury (youths) in Gemini in the 11th (friends). Consider the formula here: Venus conjunct Mercury = I love boys. In Kevin's fantasies, the boys he makes love to *are the friends he never had in childhood*. Note also the retrograde Saturn in Aquarius. In the 8th House, Saturn brings frustrations, restrictions, and delays. Acting through Aquarius in the 8th, Saturn here suggests *highly unusual or eccentric inhibitions in the sex life.*

The two planets closely involved with human instinct, Mars and Pluto, are conjunct in Virgo (celibacy) in the 2nd and form a powerful focus with Uranus. Mars conjunct Pluto usually shows a potent sexual instinct which Kevin expresses through compulsive masturbation. You will see this same stellium in the case of "Felipe" (later, on page 307). Venus, the goddess of love, squares the Uranus-Mars-Pluto stellium early in the mental 3rd House, from the 11th House. Kevin's other prominent fantasy is to become a wealthy powerful executive in charge of a major corporation and receive the respect and admiration of all for his brilliant intellect.

Kevin's case would have lent credence to the prevailing views about masturbation during the previous century. An American medical textbook by W. Paine, M.D., in 1866 lumped together masturbation, spermatorrhoea, nymphomania, and satyriasis with gonorrhea, balanitis, and syphilis as sexual pathologies needing treatment.

Dr. Paine believed that spermatorrhoea (involuntary loss of semen) was most often caused by "self-abuse" (a.k.a, masturbation or self-pollution). According to Dr. Paine, the pernicious habit of self-abuse could lead to insanity "besides so enfeebling the general forces of the body as to predispose the sufferer to many other maladies." In women, masturbation could lead to nymphomania, "a disease of females, consisting of an irresistible desire for sexual intercourse." Dr. Paine reports that he cured many cases of nymphomania with a combination of two grains of Senecin to one tenth of a grain of Gelsemin two or three times a day. In cases where masturbation was driving the nymphomania, he recommended cauterizing the clitoris with argenti nitras. Being a man himself, Dr. Paine did not recommend cauterizing the penis of male masturbators.

Such was the state of enlightenment about sexuality into which Sigmund Freud was born in 1856. Freud trained in neurology, but he turned to psychology and psychiatry, partly to earn a living and partly because he realized that many of the symptoms his patients exhibited were rooted in sexual conflict and sexual repression. Through his clinical work, Freud came to realize that sexual drives have a developmental history beginning in infancy. Sexual interest does not spring forth fully blown at puberty like Venus on a half-shell.

We all know Freud's stages of psychosexual development: oral, anal, phallic, latent, and genital. We know that sexual interest can be arrested at any stage of development due to psychological conflict or trauma. We know that what was repressed at an early age lives on in the unconscious and continues to affect adult behavior outside of our awareness. The effects of repressed feelings and desires often lead us to seek counseling or psychotherapy as adults. Repressed sexual desires can also be sublimated into productive aspects of personality function.

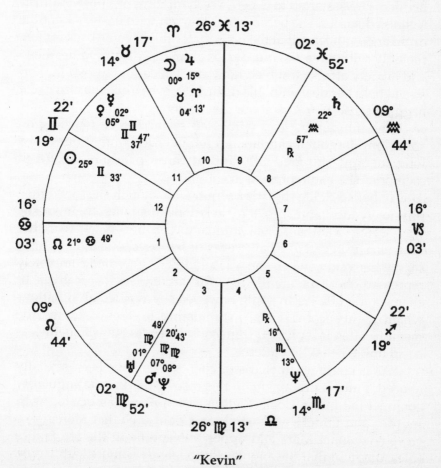

"Kevin"

Grace

The next case ("Grace") illustrates the lasting effects of childhood trauma on sexual development. Grace, born out of wedlock, is the only daughter of a psychotic mother. Her alcoholic father abandoned the mother when she became pregnant with Grace. To cover its embarrassment, the family pretended that Grace's father was killed in a car accident before Grace was born. The truth about the father became a well-guarded family secret. Grace learned only in adulthood that her father was still living.

Grace entered psychotherapy because of severe anxiety and panic attacks. Her symptoms began after she witnessed from her kitchen window a man fatally assaulting a woman in the parking lot of her apartment building. The perpetrator was not apprehended. Grace started to experience symptoms of a post-traumatic stress disorder. She became preoccupied with flashbacks of the event and with fears that the perpetrator might come back for her, the only witness to the murder. Nightmares disturbed her sleep and anxiety attacks troubled her days. Grace sought psychotherapy to help her deal with this disturbing event, but she also had a nagging sense of *déjà vu* about the incident.

The murder she had witnessed seemed to be touching on some long-forgotten childhood reminiscences. In the course of a long therapy, she gradually and at times painfully recovered memories she had repressed in childhood.

In her adult life she was a virgin who, though she found men physically attractive, broke off relationships when the man she was seeing wanted sexual intimacy. Through work with her dreams, she began to recall scenes of her psychotic mother massaging her vagina when she was a toddler. Grace had completely repressed these memories and the accompanying feelings of shame and guilt. As an adult, however, she avoided all situations which might become sexually stimulating. In cases of trauma, the memory often is repressed from consciousness but is nonetheless acted out in behavior patterns.

As is common in charts of clients who have been sexually abused, Pluto is prominent, in this case by its extreme angularity conjunct the Imum Coeli. Pluto is also a planet associated with murder and underworld activities. Could it be that Mercury so closely conjunct Mars and opposite Neptune in the 5th House (pleasure) and that the angular Pluto loosely conjunct 8th House

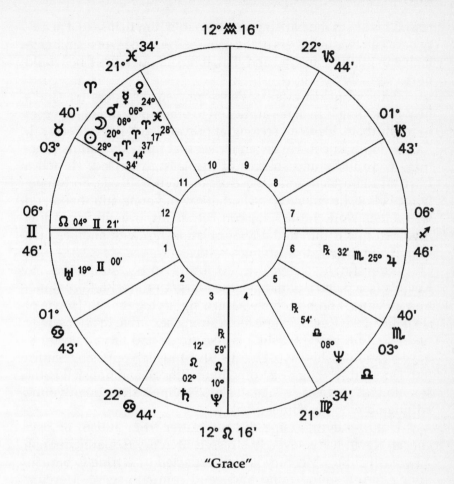

"Grace"

(death) ruler Saturn in the 3rd house (conscious mind, local environment) are astrological indicators of being witness to an assault and murder? Could these same factors also be astrological markers of the sexual abuse Grace underwent in childhood?

Felipe

"Felipe" is another example of the effects of sexual repression in childhood. Born on an island in the Caribbean, Felipe grew up in a staunchly Roman Catholic household. As a boy, he gradually began to realize that he was attracted more to men than to women. At age 14, he engaged in mutual masturbation with another boy in his neighborhood. Ridden with guilt, Felipe confessed his sin to the parish priest who told him that sexual activity between two members of the same sex was the worst sin imaginable in the sight of God and that, if he did not repent, he would burn eternally in hell.

Being a good Catholic, Felipe prayed for hours for God's help in ridding him of his attraction to other men and of his urges to masturbate. He knelt so long in prayer that he developed callouses on his knees. He began to feel that his body and its functions were filthy and sources of displeasure to God. He felt a lowered self-esteem and a sense of nothingness inside. Fortunately for Felipe, he entered psychotherapy in young adulthood and was able to work through the conflicts about sexuality. He is now involved in a committed, loving relationship with another man with whom he has a satisfying sex life.

Interestingly, Felipe's chart bears many similarities to Kevin's (see p. 301). Both have the Mars/Uranus/Pluto conjunction in Virgo, and both have Saturn signifying the 8th House of sexuality. Like Kevin, Felipe has a strong sex drive that for a long time went unfulfilled. Felipe is also single and has no desire to have a family of his own. Uranus (the unusual) opposing Saturn (8th House ruler) suggests something difficult and unusual in the sex life and serves as a signature for Felipe's struggle in young adulthood with his homosexuality.

Unlike Kevin, Felipe did not suffer from autism or psychosis. Kevin has a severely stressed Mercury (square Uranus), whereas Felipe's Mercury is well-aspected by a trine to Saturn, giving him a sound mind and good common sense. Mercury (the mind) trine Saturn (8th ruler) has allowed Felipe to think through his issues around sexual identity and to reach a satisfactory conclusion.

As in the case of Grace (p. 303), Felipe has an angular Pluto conjunct the Imum Coeli. Unlike Grace, as far as Felipe can recall, he was not sexually abused in childhood. He was, however, subject to a moderate amount of physical abuse at the hands of his siblings, as well as his parents, while growing up.

With an Aquarius 9th House cusp (the church, religion), both Saturn (traditional ruler of Aquarius) and Uranus (modern ruler of Aquarius) rule the 9th. Saturn here rules both Felipe's 8th House of sexuality and 9th House of religion. Saturn opposing Uranus shows the conflict Felipe experienced between his religious upbringing and his sexual orientation. The Saturn-Uranus opposition takes place across the 4th House-10th House axis, showing the arena of family and community traditions where the conflict was most acutely experienced. Fortunately, Felipe has several close favorable aspects (Moon sextile Jupiter, Sun trine Jupiter, Venus sextile Sun) which he has utilized to develop a charming personality and many strong positive friendships and loving relationships.

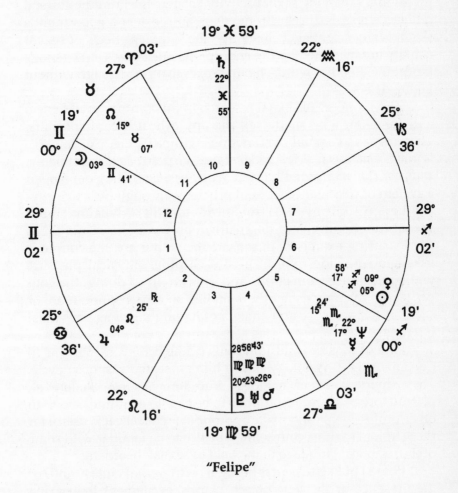

"Felipe"

These cases illustrate the negative aspects of childhood trauma and repression on personality development and adult sexuality. In contrast, modern researches have been documenting the positive effects of a satisfying sex life on our general health and well-being. The Institute for Advanced Study of Human Sexuality in San Francisco has studied 37,500 adults and found that those with a fulfilling sex life are calmer, less anxious, less hostile, and less blaming of others for their own problems. Other studies reveal that satisfying sexual activity bolsters the immune system, relieves stress, reduces chronic pain, and fosters a good night's sleep. Many scientists believe that the salutary effects of sexual activity are mediated by the endorphins, the body's endogenous morphine. In other words, having sex is like getting high without taking drugs.

The pioneers of sexual research in this century are Masters and Johnson, who made sex therapy a health care specialty. They regarded sexual dysfunctions without a medical cause *as learned behaviors fostered by ignorance, anxiety about performance, and poor communication between sexual partners.* They developed a system of treatment of sexual problems through directive psychotherapy, improved communication skills, education about sexual functioning, and desensitization through sensate focus or pleasuring exercises. In sensate focus therapy, the couple is asked to set aside time to give each other physical pleasure while refraining from coitus and orgasm. In so doing, the couple learns to enjoy each others bodies' in an accepting manner without the pressure and anxiety of having to engage in sexual intercourse.

One of Masters and Johnson's prime achievements was to document the physiology of the human sexual response cycle. They divided sexual response into four stages: excitement, plateau, orgasm, and resolution. To be able to communicate with other professionals and make appropriate referrals, it is useful for the astrologer with a counseling practice to be familiar with some of the technical language in the field of sexual disorders.

Phase I of Excitement is brought on by sexual fantasy and/or the presence of the love object. During excitement the vagina becomes lubricated and the penis becomes erect. The nipples of both partners also become erect. The clitoris gets hard and turgid, and the labia minora thicken as its veins become engorged.

Excitement may last minutes to hours and is followed by a plateau stage.

Phase II, or Plateau, is characterized by a 50-percent enlargement and elevation of the man's testes and, for the woman, by constriction along the outer third of the vagina, the so-called "orgasmic platform." The woman's breasts enlarge by 25 percent. The clitoris elevates and retracts. Both the penis and vagina change in color, large muscle groups begin to contract, the heart rate and respirations increase, and the blood pressure rises. The plateau phase lasts from about 30 seconds to several minutes and culminates in the next stage of orgasm.

Phase III, or Orgasm, lasts from 3 to 15 seconds and is accompanied by a mild clouding of consciousness. In men, there is a sense of ejaculatory inevitability, followed by the forceful ejection of about a teaspoon of semen containing 120 million sperm cells. In women, orgasm consists of three to fifteen contractions of the lower third of the vagina and potent sustained contractions of the uterus. Orgasm leads to a sense of well-being. After orgasm, men have a refractory period which can last from minutes to several hours in which they are physiologically incapable of having another orgasm. Women have no refractory stage and are capable of multiple successive orgasms.

During Phase IV, or Resolution, there is a detumescence or disgorgement of blood from the genitalia, and the body returns to its resting or pre-excitement state. The resolution stage is brief following orgasm, but if there is no orgasm, it can take several hours to achieve resolution, and the person often feels irritable and uncomfortable during this period.

The current third revised edition of the *Diagnostic and Statistical Manual of the American Psychiatric Association* (DSM-III-R) has modified the four stages of sexual response described by Masters and Johnson, and defines seven syndromes of sexual dysfunction based on its revision of Masters and Johnson's phases of sexual response.

The DSM-III-R inserts an appetitive phase before the excitement and plateau phases of Masters and Johnson, which DSM-III-R combines into a single excitement phase. The orgasm and resolution phases are identical in both systems.

DSM-III-R Phase I (Appetitive) refers to sexual fantasies and the desire for sex based on inner motivations, drives, and personality factors. The sexual desire disorders of this appetitive phase include *hypoactive sexual desire disorder and sexual aversion disorder.*

Among couples presenting themselves to sex therapy clinics, lack of sexual desire is the most common complaint. Causes of such lack of interest include unconscious fears about sex, depression, stress, medical illness, anxiety, drug or alcohol use, and marital disharmony. Sometimes suppressed homosexual wishes in a marriage partner cause decreased heterosexual desire in the marriage. Often, the withholding of sex is an expression of hostility between partners.

Freud attributed diminished sexual desire to inhibitions arising during the phallic phase of sexual development as a result of castration anxiety. Some men experience *vagina dentata* fantasies of the woman's genitals possessing teeth that can bite off the penis during intercourse. A college student whom I saw in consultation had a bad trip after ingesting LSD, in which he hallucinated a vagina with sharp teeth and became flooded with panic. Following this horrifying experience, he ceased dating women and began to wonder if he might be homosexual.

In one study of the reasons young married couples ceased having sexual intercourse for a significant period of time, there was a difference found between men and women. Men lost interest in sex under social pressures like job stress, immigration, religious factors, and their wives' employment status. Women cited factors like dominance in the relationship, the amount of affection they received from their husbands, the decision-making process in the marriage, and threats by the husband to leave home. Both partners felt that lack of privacy inhibited their desire for sexual activity.

DSM-III-R Phase II (Excitement) consists of all the physiological changes of the Masters and Johnson excitement and plateau phases, plus the subjective sense of sexual pleasure. The disorders of this phase are *female sexual arousal disorder and male erectile disorder (impotence).* Such disorders may be caused by medical problems, drug or alcohol abuse, or psychological factors as described under Phase I (Appetitive Disorder), or by a combination of all three.

For example, one client became distressed to learn that his father, who was approaching retirement age, was laid off unexpectedly by his factory after 30 years of service. Shortly thereafter, the client's own boss at his job was suddenly transferred to another department because of the company's dissatisfaction with his performance. The client became preoccupied that his own job security might be in jeopardy. The very day his boss was transferred, the client was unable to achieve an erection with his wife. "My wife doesn't understand why this is happening," he said, "it has to do with being a man." His impotence lasted three weeks, until he came to terms with his worries about his job.

Freud found among his patients that impotence was often caused by the man's inability to reconcile feelings of affection toward a woman with feelings of carnal desire, the so-called madonna/putana (mother/whore) complex. The next case of "Jim" illustrates a variation of the madonna/putana complex.

Jim

Jim is a man with numerous sexual difficulties (see p. 310). His sexuality 8th House ruler Mercury also rules his 5th House of pleasure and recreation. Mercury is the most stressed planet in the chart with its semisquare (octile) to the MC, opposition to Saturn in Cancer in the 6th, square to Neptune in Libra in the 8th, and quincunx to Uranus in Gemini in the 4th. Mercury also conjoins Mars in the 12th House.

Jim grew up in a dysfunctional family. His father was a violent alcoholic. His mother had always wanted a girl and, when Jim was young, dressed him in girl's clothing to make up for her lack of a daughter. The Moon (mother) is semisquare Uranus (the unusual) in the 4th (early home environment).

In such a family matrix, Jim came to feel *that male sexual activity consisted of violence toward women.* After witnessing his father's constant aggression, Jim felt anxious about any kind of male assertive behavior and found relief by dressing in women's clothing. In adulthood, he became a devout Roman Catholic to help himself deal with his conflicts about assertiveness and male sexuality.

Jim's conflicts are clearly reflected in his chart. The 8th ruler Mercury (sexuality) conjoins Mars, the planet of assertion and male sexuality, in the 12th House of psychological conflict, victimization, sacrifice, and self-undoing. Jim views normal male sexuality as the man violently subjugating the woman for his own selfish ends. Mercury ruling the 8th (sexuality) opposes Saturn ruling the 1st (personal identity) and both square Neptune (victimization, Christianity) in the 8th, forming a close and very stressful T-square formation. Mars (self-assertion, male sexuality) conjoins Mercury and becomes part of the T-square.

With Neptune so prominent, it is no surprise that Jim, for a while, drank heavily like his father. His strong faith in God and his devout Catholicism has since enabled him to remain sober for many years. Jim eventually married a needy woman with whom he has a stressful relationship devoid of any sexual intimacy. The 7th ruler, the Moon (his wife), is almost exactly semisquare Uranus (the unusual) in the 4th of the domestic life.

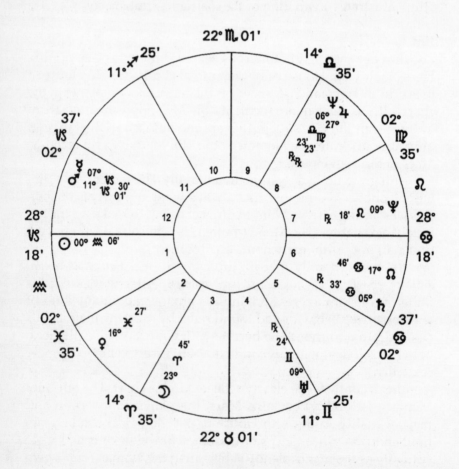

"Jim"

Continuing with DSM-III-R Phase III (Orgasm): consists of a peak of sexual pleasure and the release of sexual tension, accompanied by rhythmic contractions of the perineal musculature and the pelvic reproductive organs. The disorders of orgasm include *anorgasmia (inhibited female orgasm), retarded ejaculation (inhibited male orgasm), and premature ejaculation in the male.*

Psychological factors are usually associated with inhibited female orgasm. Often there is a fear of damage to the vagina, a concern about getting pregnant, or a fear of rejection by the partner. The woman may view orgasm as a loss of control or, as in the case of Jim above, may view sexual intercourse as a violent or brutal victimization. Cultural and religious precepts may also play a role. The overall nature of the relationship between the partners will affect the orgiastic phase of sexual activity.

Inhibited male orgasm that is not caused by a medical problem usually indicates significant psychological difficulties. Such men usually come from strict puritanical backgrounds and regard sex as filthy and sinful. They tend to have problems getting close in any kind of relationship.

In premature ejaculation, the man reaches orgasm and ejaculation before he wants to and is unable to keep his penis inside the vagina long enough to satisfy his female partner during sexual intercourse. This condition is more common among better-educated men and may be related to concerns or anxiety about being able to satisfy the partner. Stress in the marriage tends to worsen the problem. The same conflicts that underlie male impotence often play a role in premature ejaculation.

There are no dysfunctions associated with the final DSM-III-R Phase IV of Resolution. As mentioned earlier, *sexual suppression or repression does not necessarily lead to disorder.* Freud described the defense mechanism of sublimation in which an unacceptable impulse in channeled into socially acceptable behaviors. Let me conclude this chapter with such a case.

Mother Teresa is a good example of Freudian sublimation of instinctual sexuality. By becoming a nun, she publicly renounced a personal orgasmic sex life. While following her vocation or divine calling as a nun to serve the poor, she has become a twentieth-century symbol of caring, self-sacrifice, religious idealism, and compassion for the needy. Having no single sexual partner for personal orgiastic satisfaction, Mother Teresa has been able to spread her sublimated love to a large segment of humanity. Mother Teresa's sex life is her vocation as a nun.

There is disagreement in the literature about Mother Teresa's time of birth. According to Richard Nolle in *Horoscope Magazine* (August 1989, page 41), Mother Teresa was born of peasant stock in Skopje, Yugoslavia on August 27, 1910 at 2:25 P.M. (TZ: -1) into a devoutly religious Roman Catholic family. On the other hand, Sara Corbin Looms, in Llewellyn's *The Houses, Power Places of the Horoscope* (page 315), gives the birth time as 1:25 P.M. CET, an hour earlier than Nolle's data, and cites as her source Auskunftsbogen, 8/23/83 via *Astrologue*, "A."

In rectification, it is often difficult to decide between two charts that are exactly sixty minutes apart, because they resonate so strongly with one another. However, after studying the relocation and local space charts for Calcutta, I felt that the 1:25 P.M. birth time better described Mother Teresa. In Calcutta her natal Sun in Virgo conjoins the Descendant and describes the light she brought to the suffering people of that city, as well as the prominence she achieved for her efforts. Mars is the prominent planet in her local space (azimuth) chart for Calcutta and reflects the tremendous energy she put into helping the poor. Her relocated chart for Calcutta has a Pisces Ascendant and a Sagittarius Midheaven; in Calcutta she personally identifies with Christ (Pisces rising) and pursues publicly a religious ideal (Sagittarius MC). Her chart for 1:25 P.M. is shown on the opposite page.

What does Mother Teresa's chart tell us about her vocational potential? How will she make her mark upon the world? Each astrologer has his or her own method of chart interpretation. I like to read a chart by noting its most salient features and its repeated themes. Then I integrate these factors into a coherent picture.

The most important points in a chart are the Angles. The signs on the Ascendant and Midheaven give key information about the identity, both personal (Ascendant) and social (Midheaven), of the native. Mother Teresa has Sagittarius rising, the natural sign of the 9th House ruled by the planet Jupiter. Sagittarius is traditionally associated with the Law, the Church, universities, foreign interests, distant travel, different cultures, religion, and philosophy. The Sagittarius theme is repeated by Jupiter, ruling the Ascendant, posited in the 10th House of career. Her personal identity is bound up with Sagittarian issues.

Mother Teresa has the potential to excel in the religious life, but she could also be a successful lawyer, philosopher, university professor, import-export merchant, broadcaster, etc. It is not the specific occupation that matters; rather, it is that she expresses her sense of self (Ascending Sign) in a Sagittarian way through a particular ideology, a systemized set of ideas, or through religious ideals. That she expressed her identity through organized religion has more to do with her cultural and familial heritage than with her natal chart.

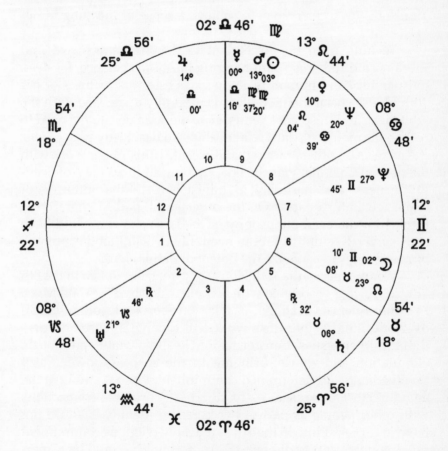

Mother Teresa
Aug. 27, 1910, 1:25 P.M. LMT
Skopje, Yugoslavia
41N59 21E26
Koch Houses

The Sagittarius/9th House/Jupiter emphasis is focused by a striking stellium of planets in the 9th House. She has the Sun (core identity), Mars (self-assertion), and Mercury (thought, communication) in the 9th House. Jupiter, natural ruler of the 9th House, is angular in the 10th. Furthermore, the closest aspect in this chart (within 23 seconds of being exact) is Mars (self-assertion, energy, drive) semi-sextile Jupiter (religious interests, philosophy), again stressing that her identity is bound up with Jupiter, Sagittarius, and 9th House matters. See how the 9th House theme repeats over and over in this chart! She must express her Sagittarian 9th House drives to feel alive, to achieve a sense of meaning in her existence.

Turning from the Ascendant to the Midheaven, we find Libra on the 10th cusp, emphasizing harmony, balance, fairness, partnership, and human relatedness as essential features of her 10th House social identity. Libra is naturally associated with the 7th House and the planet Venus. Here we see a vocational need to restore harmony, to adjust relationships, to deal justly with others; the focus is on others rather than the self. Think of her work with the poor in Calcutta. Was she not pursuing a Libran ideal of beauty, fairness, and harmony in ministering to the suffering of neglected unfortunates? On the other hand, had Mother Teresa pursued a career in philosophy or the Law, she also could have constructively met this Libran need. Living sainthood is but one of many ways to actualize the potential in this chart.

Venus, ruler of the 10th House of career, lies in Leo in the 8th House which is associated with Scorpio, ruled by Pluto and Mars. Her 10th ruler of vocation thus takes on Scorpionic (often sexual) overtones; that is, her life's work will involve intense and profound human issues, transformation, healing, death and rebirth, elimination and refuse, bringing to the surface, power, deep involvement, and determined commitment. Pluto is strong in the angular 7th House, again stressing her Scorpionic connections with other people as part of her personal identity. She did not have to express Pluto in the 7th as a deeply religious commitment to bring peace and harmony to the suffering. She could have married (7th House) an abusive spouse (Pluto in the 7th) and lived a life of personal suffering and self-sacrifice. Instead, by becoming a nun, she "married" God (Mercury, 7th ruler, in the 9th conjunct the Aries point axis) and, through her work, wedded herself to the most profound abuse and human suffering (Pluto in the 7th). The world is a better place because she made her vocational choices as she did.

The theme of self-sacrifice comes up repeatedly in the chart. Neptune in the 8th forms a close parallel of declination with the Moon, ruler of the 8th House of sexuality. Neptune is also in Cancer where many astrologers feel it is exalted and expresses itself most naturally. In addition, Neptune in the 8th House opposes Uranus (the unusual), a singleton planet in the 2nd House. Uranus opposing Neptune in the 8th suggests something unique or different about the sexual life. The chart forms a bucket pattern with Uranus (concern for humanity) as the handle. The bucket pattern highlights the tension between Uranus (humanitarian ideals) and Neptune (self-sacrifice, compassion, religious idealism) which must find an outlet.

The theme of self-sacrifice is also shown by the square between the 10th ruler Venus (love, pleasure, attachments) and 2nd ruler Saturn (duty, restriction, limitation). When Venus squares Saturn, love becomes a duty, an obligation to perform. Furthermore, her Moon (feminine identity) lies precisely at the midpoint of Saturn/Pluto, which Ebertin associates with "the pursuit of difficult work" and with "the process of growing spiritually."

That Mother Teresa would dedicate her life to service is also suggested in the chart. Her Sun (core identity) and Mars (self-assertion, sexual expression) both lie in Virgo (service) in the 9th House (religion). Furthermore, her Gemini Moon (emotional life, 8th ruler of sexuality) occupies the 6th House, whose natural sign is Virgo (service). The Moon in the 6th closely squares her 9th House Sun in Virgo and trines her 9th House Mercury in Libra, again emphasizing the theme of religious service. Through sublimation, Mother Teresa expresses her repressed sexuality by serving humanity and being a handmaiden of God.

Some Clinical Guidelines

Many astrologers will feel uncomfortable dealing with client-issues of sexual repression and sexual abuse. It is important to remember that repression is a defense mechanism we all employ to keep at bay thoughts, feelings, and memories we feel we can not deal with in our everyday lives. We have seen in the examples in this chapter how such repressed material eventually makes its way to consciousness through our behavior patterns, our dreams, and various symptoms like anxiety and depression.

What is the astrologer to do when he or she suspects that sexual repression is an issue for the client? Perhaps the best advice is that given by Hippocrates to new physicians: "Above all else, do no harm!"

Discuss such issues gently and in a tentative manner with your client. For example, if a client has an angular Pluto square Mars and opposite Saturn, you might say, "I have seen such a pattern in charts of other clients who have experienced some kind of sexual difficulty or trauma. I don't know if this is the case for you but I wanted to bring it to your attention." Then drop the subject and let the client decide whether he or she wants to discuss the matter further. If you as the astrologer are not comfortable with such material (and it's O.K. not to be!), you should develop a referral list of competent therapists to whom you can refer your client for further consultation and possible treatment.

Never force the issue. Repressed material is powerful and deserves respect. It needs to come to light slowly and in measured doses; otherwise, there is a risk of overwhelming the client and precipitating a state of panic or disorganization. I have seen cases of inexperienced therapists causing their clients to need hospitalization by digging too deep, too fast into memories of childhood trauma and abuse. Remember that Pluto is our astrological symbol for issues of sexual repression. Pluto can erupt with volcanic force if not treated with tact and respect. The astrologer who counsels victims of sexual abuse needs to work through Pluto in his or her own chart before being able to serve clients with such difficulties. My final word of advice is to give Pluto his due in your own life before trying to help others deal with Pluto in theirs.

Bibliography

Diagnostic and Statistical Manual, Third Revised Edition. Washington, DC: American Psychiatric Association, 1987.

Ebertin, Reinhold. *The Combination of Stellar Influences*. Wurttemberg: Ebertin-Verlag, 1972.

Kaplan and Sadock. *Clinical Psychiatry*. Baltimore: Williams & Wilkins, 1988.

Kaplan, H.S. *The New Sex Therapy*. New York: Brunner/Mazel, 1974.

Krohne, Eric C. *Sex Therapy Handbook*. Lancaster, England: MTP Press Limited, 1982.

Light and Life. Charlotte, NC: C. H. Robinson and Co., no date (1800s).

Louis, Anthony. *Horary Astrology*. St. Paul: Llewellyn, 1991.

Masters and Johnson. *Human Sexual Response*. Boston: Little, Brown & Co., 1966.

Paine, W. A. *Treatise on the Principles and Practice of Medicine and Pathology, Diseases of Women and Children, and Surgery*. Philadelphia: Pub. Soc., 1866.

Tyl, Noel. *Holistic Astrology*. McLean, VA: TAI Books, 1980.

von Kreisler, Kristin. "The Healing Powers of Sex." *Redbook Magazine*, April, 1993.

Bruce Hammerslough

Bruce holds a B.A. in Biology and an M.Ed. in Science. Certified as a professional astrologer in 1983, he has served two terms each as President for the Metropolitan Atlanta and Washington State Astrological Associations, and four years as a Steering Committee member of AFAN. Bruce's many articles on astrology have been published nationally and internationally, and he has appeared on various radio and television shows. He is also the author of *The I Ching Manual* and *Forecasting Backward & Forward: Modern Techniques of Timing and Rectification*.

A co-founder (with Dennis Flaherty) of Greenlake Metaphysical Center, Bruce teaches and offers a broad range of services, from general counseling, forecasting, and relationship analysis, to such specialized techniques as Astro*Carto*Graphy™ and Relocation, Rectification, Horary, and Electional Astrology. Bruce is also certified in Alchemical Hypnotherapy.

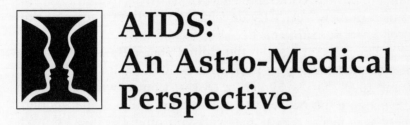

AIDS:
An Astro-Medical
Perspective

B. F. Hammerslough

> Life is a sexually transmitted disease which is
> invariably fatal.
>
> —Anonymous

One cannot discuss sex in these Pluto-in-Scorpio times without also discussing AIDS. It seems that every generation has its own major health threat which challenges the medical skill and spiritual strength of society. Cancer is still a terrible concern, while the generational disease before that was polio, and before that, influenza, and before that, tuberculosis. It is obvious that the disease of this present time is Acquired Immune Deficiency Syndrome: AIDS.

As astrologers, we are in a unique position to help put situations into perspective and imbue life events with deeper meaning. What insights, advice, and perhaps even inspiration can we provide our clients who suffer from AIDS, and indeed *any* life-threatening disease? In order to answer this question we must first understand the nature of the disease itself. It should be said right at the beginning that I do not ascribe AIDS to astrological causes, nor do I intend to dispute the various medical models of the disease. Astrology is a language of symbols that reflects the synchronicity of our experience and lets us realize that life can be interpreted at more than one level. It is to obtain this different, and often broader perspective, after all, that our clients come to us.

Since we are discussing perspective, perhaps it is appropriate first to put AIDS into some historical perspective. In 1977, two gay men in New York City developed a fairly rare form of skin cancer, Karposi's sarcoma. Looking back, these were probably the first AIDS cases, at least in the United States. By 1980, the incidence of such cases were numerous enough (estimated between 500 and 1000) that the Center for Disease Control was called upon to investigate the matter, and it was soon realized that modern society was facing a new medical syndrome. Because approximately nine out of ten cases involved homosexual males, the disease was initially dubbed GRID: Gay Related Immune Disorder. Before too long however, the disease also appeared among hemophiliacs, Haitian refugees, intravenous drug users and female prostitutes. As a result, on June 5, 1981, the name GRID was changed to AIDS: Acquired Immune Deficiency Syndrome.

By 1983, awareness of AIDS was becoming pronounced within the gay male subculture as well as within the medical community. It was not until 1985 however, when famous film star Rock Hudson finally admitted that he had AIDS, that the disease truly established itself within the consciousness of the general public. Since then, the disease has continued to spread, both within the original specific vector populations, as well as into the more general population in Europe and the United States. AIDS is currently an increasingly serious epidemic in central Africa, Southeast Asia, and Indonesia, where it primarily effects the heterosexual population. In some of these countries, the epidemic is so severe that up to 70 percent of the hospital beds are taken up by AIDS patients, and worker production has fallen to points where the economy has begun seriously to falter, and, of course, this pandemic is spreading to other regions of the world as well.

In retrospect, it is generally believed that the AIDS virus was transmitted to humans by the green monkey, which is indigenous to the jungles of central Africa. This monkey, which is itself essentially immune to the virus, is both eaten and sold as pets by some natives of the central African nations, and one theory is that bites and scratches by these monkeys infected humans with the virus. Another hypothesis is that green monkey organs were used to create vaccines for humans, and the virus entered the human population through administration of the vaccine. A third conjecture is that some sicko in a germ warfare laboratory purposely created the virus.

In any case, the virus probably spread from central Africa to Cuba and the Caribbean islands through military and cultural exchanges in the 1960s and 1970s, and from there spread into the United States and the rest of the world. Since most "new" diseases are actually either mutations of already familiar pathogens or else their introduction into a new region or population, it is probable that AIDS *is not really new.* Indeed, it bears a striking similarity to what in the mid-1800s was called "the thinning disease." This illness was experienced by European explorers of the "Dark Continent" and was typified by a wasting away and severe lassitude. The belief that the AIDS virus is thought to mutate fairly readily, creating various strains, some of which are more aggressive than others, can also fit this theory.

AIDS is generally thought to be caused by a retrovirus. Discovered at about the same time in France and the United States (in the midst of intense competition to isolate the AIDS causing pathogen), the virus was named LAV and HTLV-3 respectively, and is now known as HIV-1 (Human Immunodeficiency Virus 1). Retroviruses are a recently discovered type of virus which contain single strands of RNA as opposed to the double helixed DNA found in other viruses and all other biological organisms. Retro viruses become double-stranded by stealing genetic material from the host cell and then inserting their genetic material into the cell's chromosomes, essentially hiding until the chromosome is activated.

The HIV virus presents two horrendous medical challenges. Because the viral genetic material becomes so intimately integrated into the host's chromosomes, it is probably impossible to eliminate the cell without also killing it. Also, unlike other viruses which have to wait until a cell is replicating in order to enter it, the HIV virus can enter a host cell at any time. Given our present stage of medical technology, all that can be reasonably hoped for is to find some way to keep the virus under control until a cure is found. Current expectations are that it will probably take the better part of a decade to develop such a cure.

The HIV-1 virus is transmitted via body fluids: essentially blood and semen. Although the virus is quite fragile and short-lived outside of its biological environment, it also takes a very small amount of body fluid to infect another individual. For example, residue blood traces in a shared syringe are enough to transmit the disease from one drug addict to another. This shared IV needle mode and anal intercourse are the most common means of infection in the United States and Europe, although infection through heterosexual vaginal intercourse without a condom is increasing in percentage. Initially, people were also infected through tainted blood supplies, and about a third of infants born to infected women also develop the disease.

Fortunately, the HIV virus is not passed on casually. One does not get it from shaking hands, even sweaty ones, using the same glass, towel or water fountain. Nor is it transmitted by mosquito bites or to or by pets. If this were otherwise, the epidemic would be far more wide-spread. As stated above, only a third of the children born to HIV positive mothers develop the syndrome. (This is pretty amazing, considering the intimate biological connections between mother and child.) At the same time, it is wise not to share tooth brushes, razors, or other implements which might transmit body fluids with those known to be infected with the AIDS virus.

Once it enters the body, the HIV virus is thought to infect T-4 cells. The thymus gland helps produce three kinds of T (for thymus) cells. Killer T-cells (also called CD8 cells) actively destroy infected cells. Suppressor T-cells suppress B-cell (white blood cells produced in bone tissue) production of antibodies after an infection has diminished. Helper or T-4 cells (also termed CD4 cells) chemically identify pathogens, stimulate the Bcells to produce antibodies to attack the infection, and activate the killer T-cells. Once the virus enters the T-4 cells, it copies itself into parts of the cell's chromosomes, where it then hijacks the cell's genetic material to reproduce more HIV viruses, eventually destroying the cell and releasing more viruses into the bloodstream, infecting more T-4 cells until the immune system begins to collapse. The virus is also believed to infect other cells which have receptors for the T-4 cells. Such cells include B-cells, monocytes, nerve and brain cells and perhaps killer T-cells. The infected person never dies from the AIDS virus, but rather from numerous infections, many of which are caused by innocuous organisms which most people can easily fight off.

Although AIDS can strike some individuals soon after their infection by the virus, it often has a long more or less active incubation period of up to eight or more years. Technically, AIDS is only the last stage of progressive immune system break-down, wherein the body is so weakened that the person becomes vulnerable to both rare diseases and common pathogens to which most people are immune. The intervening stages before full-blown AIDS is reached (originally named ARC, for AIDS Related Complex) is now simply termed HIV infection.

HIV infection usually starts off with night sweats, swollen lymph glands, unexplained weight loss, loss of energy, candidiasis or thrush (yeast infection, especially in the mouth), persistent coughing (often an early sign of Pneumocystis pneumonia), and various skin rashes and irritations. These conditions generally ebb and flow in their severity over several years, until the person develops full-blown AIDS. According to the Center for Disease Control, a person is diagnosed as having AIDS once they develop Pneumocystis pneumonia, Karposi's sarcoma (a rare skin cancer generally seen in gay men but, interestingly, not in IV users or Hemophiliacs, thus leading to the idea that the organism which causes it is sexually transmitted) or other such opportunistic diseases as Toxoplasmosis, or when an individual's T-4 cell count drops below 200, (for the average person the T-4 counts run around 400–1500, but usually hovers around 1000 cells per mm).

Once the stage of AIDS is reached, the general prognosis used to be two or three years. However, doctors and researchers are increasingly finding individuals diagnosed with both HIV infection and even AIDS who have lived ten years or more.[1] In addition to having to deal with painful, debilitating, and often frightening diseases (often several at once), one of the worst manifestations of the last stages is AIDS dementia, where damage to brain tissue causes the person to lose not only touch with reality, but also emotional control and even the loss of physical coordination. At the present time, there is no known cure for or vaccine against the HIV virus. All modern medicine can do is try to prolong the life of the patient and keep the quality of life as high as possible.

---

1   Nielsen, Robert. *Long-Term Survival Skills*. Seattle: STEP Perspective, vol. 5, no. 1, Feb., 1993, p. 7.

An Astrological Perspective

In order to understand AIDS from a correspondent astrological point of view, it is helpful first to understand the nature of Pluto, Neptune, and the planetoid Chiron. For reasons which will soon become apparent, let us start with Neptune.

Neptune and AIDS

Neptune, god of the oceans, has perhaps the broadest range of behavior of any of the planets. The nature of the oceans, seas, lakes and rivers is that they all merge together. What might have been an individual raindrop loses its individuality once it hits water. This is how Neptune works. On its highest level, Neptune represents pure universal love; a total lack of discrimination or differentiation, with all connected to the totally loving Godhead.

After the Pluto initiation of conception, the commingling of cellular nuclear material, Neptune is experienced as the state of gestation, where the fetus is intimately and inextricably bound with the maternal environment, and existence is experienced as a psychic, dream-like, gentle rocking in a warm amniotic ocean where there is no differentiation between self and the rest of the universe. This translates into human behavior later in life as a remembrance and yearning of this sense of one-ness and this feeling is acted upon as empathy, compassion, charity, self sacrifice and a searching for the highest spiritual meaning in life.

Dissolution is another important theme of Neptune. Neptune represents the oceans, and water is the universal solvent. It is the dissolution and dissipation of the separate for which Neptune strives. On a psycho-spiritual level, this means viewing the situation from a sense of understanding and compassion, which enables one to forgive and let the issue go. In its negative aspect, Neptune can dissolve form, destroying order and structure and creating chaos.

Of course most people find it difficult to function at the most exalted levels of Neptune, and we often see its energy stepped down in the forms of intuition, imagination, vision, romantic idealism. At the next lower quantum level, we observe or experience escapism, lying and scamming, guilt, substance abuse, being a victim and finally becoming self-destructive. Most germane to our discussion of AIDS is the notion that Neptune deals *with a sense of vulnerability and victimization.*

When I first studied AIDS several years ago,[2] I was struck by the strong Neptune component in the charts of those who developed the disease. Indeed, I have since come to the conclusion that AIDS is a singularly Neptunian disease. All the groups initially associated with the disease are well represented by Neptune's energy. First, of course, are gay men. It's hard to think of a group more historically rejected and discriminated against. At the very least, most other minority members can depend upon the love and support of their own families, but many gays are not so lucky. Gay men are also linked to Neptune through the stereotype of creative imagination and sensitivity and the myth of exaggerated femininity. Actually, I see gay men as falling into three archetypal categories: the sensitive, creative Neptunians, the sexually intense clone Plutonians, and the politically, socially or personally radical Uranians.

Historically, however, the general heterosexual population has tended to see gay men as Neptunian. This is especially true in western cultures, which intellectually tend to dichotomize everything, seeking to fit experience into the scientific mode of binomial classification; i.e. it's either black or white, good or bad, male or female, heterosexual or homosexual, etc. Primitive and simplistic logic thus suggests that since most men are attracted to women, and most women to men, then if a man is attracted to another man he must be more like a woman. Neptune thus becomes a symbol for this misperception of male homosexuals, as it is among the most feminine of planetary energies, and also incorporates the concepts of deception, illusion (the closet), and confusion (not being able to identify readily the person's sexual orientation).

It is my belief that this kind of crude either-or approach to life is the basis of homophobia, the irrational fear of homosexuals. In the late 1940's, Alfred Kinsey and co-researchers found convincing evidence that human sexuality forms a broad spectrum of behavior, with many predominantly heterosexual people experiencing occasional homosexual fantasies or urges, (and

---

2 "AIDS in the Horoscope," B. F. Hammerslough, *Aspects*, Spring, 1987, Encino, CA.

vise versa).[3] But since most people are taught that one is *either* male or female, gay or straight, then those heterosexuals who have these inconsistent desires are thrown into a panic because "logic" tells them that they must be homosexual, and if this is discovered, they will be relegated to a generally despised social classification. The result is often a classically Freudian "reaction formation," where one actively hates the external image of one's own internal fear.

Ironic evidence of this type of thinking shows up in our society's treatment of bisexuals. Since they are neither exclusively heterosexual nor homosexual, bisexuals are generally castigated by both groups. Heterosexuals usually say that the bisexual is afraid of commitment; homosexuals say they are really gay and don't have the courage to confront that.

Another Neptunian AIDS-related group is Haitians, who were associated with the disease early on. The Neptune theme fits here in that many of the HIV+ Haitians in the United States were politically disenfranchised, cast away, literally, on the sea as boat people, and totally vulnerable both politically and economically. The association with the tropics, and especially tropical islands, is also Neptunian.

Hemophiliacs also fall under Neptune's rule. The very image of blood, flowing like the ocean and refusing to clot, is quite Neptunian. Even more significant to our hypothesis however, is the fact that hemophiliacs spend their lives constantly aware of their vulnerability; any bump or cut can be life-threatening. Hemophiliacs were quite vulnerable to the HIV virus early in the epidemic, because the clotting agent so necessary to their well-being is derived from literally hundreds of thousands of blood donations which could not be heated, as that would destroy the clotting agent. Fortunately, once the blood supply was sufficiently purified, this threat was essentially removed for hemophiliacs.

Intravenous drug users are perhaps the most Neptunian group of all in their self-destructive quest for escape, for beneath the behavior is perhaps an over-sensitivity and vulnerability to the world as they perceive it, and beneath that there is, I strongly suspect, a deep, unconscious desire to merge once again with the

3   Kinsey, A. C., Pomery, W. B., and Martin, C. E. *Sexual Behavior in the Human Male.* Philadelphia: W.B. Saunders, 1948.

Source of Being, the Prime Cause. The HIV virus is spread among IV users through the practice of sharing the same needle. Sharing, especially indiscriminate sharing, is typically Neptunian behavior. Needle exchange programs in some areas are having a significantly positive impact on the spread of the disease among IV drug users.

Central Africa can also be seen as being associated with the planet Neptune. This pertains particularly to the great Congo basin, whose immense, dark, and often impenetrable jungle creates a very other worldly experience. It is believed that the mutated HIV-1 virus had its origins here through the green monkey, and of course it is in sub-Sahara Africa where AIDS has taken its most devastating toll. On a more contemporary level, the poverty, suffering, and political confusion of this region also suggests Neptune. Indonesia, which has also been terribly hard hit by the spread of AIDS, is primarily a nation of tropical islands, and thus fits the Neptunian theme as well.

Now of course not every member of these groups discussed above develops HIV infection or AIDS, and some members outside these groups do manifest the disease. We are dealing here with archetypal groups, and I certainly don't have the answers as to why certain people, especially those outside of the so-called "high risk" groups, contract AIDS. I suspect that on an individual level, those who get AIDS are in some way very connected with Neptune. They are often people who feel cut off, vulnerable, or perhaps conversely, so empathic that their identification with others' suffering draws in the disease.

Even the symptoms of HIV infection and AIDS are often strikingly Neptunian. On a cellular level, it is thought that the HIV virus *confuses* the immune system to such an extent that it attacks itself. On the symptomatic level, many people with HIV infection experience a debilitating and often chronic fatigue. These people do not usually have the luxury of enjoying a good book or watching a show on TV. Energy levels are often so low and the people are so tired and weak, that all they can do is drift in and out of sleep. One begins to feel quite helpless, and this of course becomes quite depressing. Local and systemic yeast infections (candidiasis) are also typical in HIV infection, and yeast is certainly a Neptunian organism, not only through its association with the production of wine, but also because the presence of the organism, *Candida albicans*, is essentially universal in humans; it is just those with impaired immune systems who can not keep the organism in check.

In addition, the symptoms of systemic yeast infection are often confusing and hard to diagnose, disrupting the metabolism in unexpected ways, and often creating irrational emotional fluctuations. Pneumonia, of course, creates a drowning feeling as the lungs fill up with fluid. Karposi's sarcoma creates embarrassing lesions which not only make the sufferers self-conscious, but also stigmatize them for ostracism and thus further alienation. Dementia, another Neptunian phenomenon, leads to emotional irrationality and loss of control.

The roller coaster of expectations in terms of both survival and cures is also quite Neptunian. Often patients become so ill that they and loved ones believe that death is imminent, and then they improve, often dramatically, so that long-term hopes are again raised, only to be dashed weeks or months later when severe illness again strikes, often with the patient recovering, again triggering the cycle of hope versus resignation. In addition, the media and the AIDS health communities, both traditional and alternative, have repeatedly announced hopeful cures, only to have them later disproved, discredited, or drastically reduced in significance. People with AIDS and their loved ones are constantly wondering: maybe ozone is the cure, maybe Compound Q, perhaps it's bitter melon extract, or interferon, or AZT, or AZT and DDI or DDC. One thing is certain, when an effective cure or controlling agent is finally found, it won't be surrounded by vague wonderings. It will work, and word will spread like a wild fire, not like a nebulous, drifting, questioning fog.

The very uncertainties within the scientific community about various aspects of AIDS is quite Neptunian as well. Confusion swirls around such issues as: the disease's origins; does the virus enter latency periods or does it remain continuously active within the lymphatic system; is it really transmitted by oral sex or not; methods of viral activation and approaches to a cure; all typical of Neptune's fuzzy, confusing energy. All of the many factors discussed above demonstrate clearly that AIDS is a Neptunian disease.

Pluto and AIDS

Even though AIDS is a disease primarily ruled by Neptune, many people also associate the disease with Pluto. Pluto is a small but intensely powerful planet at the edge, so far as we now know, of our solar system. It is actually a double-bodied system, having a moon, Charon, which was discovered by James Christy on June 22, 1978, in Washington, D.C. Charon, named after the ferryman who carries the dead across the black rivers of the underworld, is almost as large as Pluto itself. Pluto and Charon orbit around each other, keeping the same parts of their surfaces facing each other, as if in a perpetual staring contest.[4] Pluto is associated with power and tenacity, and while it is lined up between Earth and Charon, perhaps it is a time to resist external factors and test our will against the forces of fate. Charon, on the other hand, might well be linked with the principle of letting go and opening to the changes that must be faced for meaningful growth and evolution. Charon, the ferryman, is the agent who helps us cross the established currents within us so that we can enter into another realm of experience. It represents our acceptance of the necessity and growth inherent in evolution. As Charon occults Pluto from Earth's perspective, he offers us passage on his ferry to a deeper realm. I would like to suggest here a glyph for Charon incorporating the traditional elements of the circle, crescent, and cross: ⚓

Along with the sign Scorpio, which it rules, Pluto symbolizes the process of evolution through death, transformation, and rebirth. It is as if Pluto is the demarcator between normal and paranormal experience. It is the null-point between death and conception, the entrance and exit of life as we know it. Later in life, it represents the point at which we turn from outward experience to examine our deepest inner nature. Pluto is the planet which challenges us with extreme conditions and makes us say "Who the hell's life IS this, anyway?" The inevitable answer calls upon us to find ways to bring about greater control and self-empowerment in our lives. Pluto thus demands that we take the reins of our own destiny.

As with all the outer planets, Pluto especially functions on a transpersonal level. Thus it rules social and biological evolution

---

4   Sobe, David. "The Last World." *Discovery Magazine*, May 1993, p. 75.

as well as change on the personal level. It is appropriate that Pluto was discovered in 1930, as several super-powerful people began to shape their countries into super powers. Hitler, Stalin, and Roosevelt all had tremendous influence in shaping and evolving their societies. It was as if evolution were testing the competitive and survival abilities of three different socioeconomic and political systems. It was not too long after the discovery of Pluto that humanity suddenly had the means to make itself and the rest of the world extinct.

For astrologers, it transcends coincidence that AIDS became part of the general public's consciousness when Pluto entered the sign of Scorpio in late 1983. In 1740, the last time Pluto was in Scorpio, a typhus epidemic swept Europe, killing 30,000 in France in that year alone, and lasting for thirty years in Italy. Typhus is a disease caused by the *rickettsia* microorganism, and is spread to humans through the feces of the human body louse when a bite is contaminated by scratching. Humans are actually the natural host of the rickettsia, and human body lice simply spread the typhus infection from human to human via their bites. The body louse lives in the seams of clothing and in bed clothing, and is associated with overcrowding and unsanitary conditions. The disease is characterized by high fever, intense headache, and a few days later, pink spots which darken and become raised, and spread from the armpits and upper trunk over the rest of the body. Interestingly, typhus is rarely fatal in children less than ten years old, but mortality increases up to 60 percent over the age of 50.[5]

The Pluto ingress into Scorpio before that of 1740 was in 1495, and marked Europe's first Syphilis epidemic, which lasted 25 years. It is important to realize that at that time syphilis was far more virulent than it is now, and was every bit as terrifying as AIDS seems presently. It is believed to have been brought to Europe by the recently returned crews of Columbus, who picked up the disease in the New World. (Realize, of course, that diseases brought to the New World by Europeans wreaked even greater havoc upon the native American populations.) Camp followers of the Spanish defenders of Naples against France's Charles VIII are thought to have infected French soldiers, who then carried the disease to the rest of Europe. Of course, Frenchmen called syphilis the

---

5 *The Merk Manual*, 14th Ed., Robert Berkow, editor. Rachway, NJ, 1982, p. 160.

Neapolitan disease, while the Italians called it the French disease. Another theory is that in the same way that AIDS may not really be a "new" disease, syphilis may have been around for some time before 1495, but was mistaken for leprosy.[6&7]

Syphilis is a sexually transmitted disease caused by the spirochete bacteria *Treponema pallidum*. Within hours of infection, the spirochetes invade the lymph nodes, and from there spread rapidly throughout the rest of the body. Usually within four weeks after infection, a painless ulcer or chancre appears at the primary site of infection and heals within one or two months if untreated. Six to twelve weeks after untreated infection, rashes turning into lesions appear on the skin, especially around mucous membranes. These sores may come and go, and some can persist for months. (It is these lesions, especially on the face, which led to the fashionable false mole in Europe.)

During the first two years, the person is particularly infectious as the spirochete is widely disseminated throughout the body. At this stage, it is very easy for an untreated mother to infect the fetus through the placenta. The more active the infection, the greater the chance of congenital syphilis in the infant. Nowadays, congenital syphilis is easily preventable and treatable with proper prenatal care.[8]

After the first two years, the bacteria usually enter a latent period, which can last for a few years or for the rest of the patient's life, and gradually the person becomes non-infectious. About one-third of those infected go on to develop late or tertiary syphilis, often leading to blindness, dementia and death through destruction of cardiac tissue.[9]

There are several interesting similarities between syphilis and AIDS, and to a lesser degree typhus. Syphilis and AIDS are both primarily sexually transmitted, and even typhus, spread by the body louse which inhabits bed clothing, takes on a somewhat sexual connotation. Both diseases tend to last many years and bring about a slow, steady deterioration of the body. The purple bruise-like spots of Karposi's sarcoma remind one of the chancre

---

6   Hellemans, Alexander and Brunch, Bryan. *The Timetables of Science.* New York: Simon & Schuster, 1988, p. 98.
7   Trager, James. *The People's Chronology.* New York: Henry Holt & Co., 1992, p. 160.
8   *Merck Manual*, p. 1623.
9   *Merck Manual*, p. 116–117.

sores of syphilis and even the rash of typhus. Both diseases often lead to dementia in their later stages. It is also interesting that children are less likely to be infected or affected by all three diseases. Syphilis is transferred to the infant only when the mother is very actively infected. Only one-third of infants born to mothers with HIV infection contract the virus, and fatality of children under ten years old from typhus is rare.

In Roman mythology, Pluto was the god of the underworld, and this is apt considering the themes of death, transformation, and rebirth. In order to change, we have to let an old, no-longer useful part of ourselves die, and yet nothing dies unless it is first allowed to live. (Recall still again that two-thirds of infants exposed to AIDS do not contract it, and that most children infected with typhus do not die from it.) In dealing with Pluto psychologically, we are dragged down to our own subconscious hell and forced to deal with our personal demons. This is a process which takes time, and perhaps this is a clue to the long-term infections of syphilis and AIDS. Unlike typhus, the Black Plague or cholera, which often bring death fairly quickly, AIDS and syphilis usually grant several years of life at the very least. This avails one the opportunity to grow, put one's affairs, both worldly and spiritual, in order, and coincides with the slow evolutionary nature of Pluto. Once we have fought our way from hell back to the surface world, hauling our struggling and resistant demons with us, we can then expose them to the light of rationality, in which they dissolve like vampires, leaving us cleansed and stronger and more profound than when we started our journey.

Pluto, being the god of death, is also, of course, the ruler of vermin, plagues, and viruses, and through the theme of transformation is also associated with mutation, a problematic characteristic of the AIDS virus. Interestingly, Pluto is also said to be the god of riches. As James Burke pointed out in his excellent book and TV series *Connections*, after the period of the Black Plague in Europe, fashions and luxury blossomed and more money flowed as the survivors inherited the wealth of those who succumbed.[10] On a deeper level, perhaps the real wealth lies in the profound truth about ourselves that Pluto reveals in times of crisis, because such truth enlightens and empowers us to control and regenerate our lives.

---

10 Burke, James. *Connections*. Boston: Little, Brown & Co., 1978, p. 98

Chiron and AIDS

Finally, we come to Chiron. Chiron is a very new body, discovered on November 1, 1977 by astronomer Charles Kowal, who also gave it its mythological name. This new player in the astrological field is by nature a bit confusing. It has been variously described as a planetoid, an asteroid, and a cometary nucleus; and its highly elliptical 50-year trajectory carries it within the orbits of both Saturn and Uranus.

In Greek mythology, Chiron was the immortal king of the centaurs; beings half horse, half human. Most of the centaurs were dominated by their animal side, and as a result were bad news on the social level. They were always crashing parties, fighting, pillaging and raping, as in the notorious case of the Sabine women, but Chiron, their king, was the exception. By integrating the instinctive and intuitive wisdom of the animal side with the rational attributes of the human side, *he became a role model for philosophical diplomacy*, not just to the centaurs, but to the gods as well. Because of these attributes, Zeus made Chiron tutor to several of the Greek demi-gods such as Perseus, Hercules, Achilles, and his own foster son, Aesclepius. He was most noted for teaching herbology and healing, but also taught sports, philosophy, and music, and is credited with naming the constellations.

One day, while entertaining a visit from one of his students, most likely Perseus, Chiron accidentally backed into an arrow that had been dipped in the blood of the slain gorgon, Medusa. Now the blood of Medusa was so venomous that if a drop hit the ground, scorpions would spring forth. Naturally it was fatal to any mortal. However, Chiron was immortal, and had to endure the chronic agony of his wound. It is typical of the Greek love of irony that one of their greatest mythic healers was unable to heal himself. He finally petitioned Zeus to let him take the place of Prometheus (who had disobeyed the gods by bringing fire and language to humanity and as punishment was chained to a rock and had his liver devoured daily by an eagle). Inspired by Chiron's selfless offer, Zeus freed Prometheus and let Chiron enter heaven as the constellation Centaurus.

Chiron has several archetypes, and has been ascribed as the ruler of several different signs. Canadian astrologer Sandy Hughes has suggested, most correctly I feel, that Chiron rules the mutable cross. Chiron was a teacher (Gemini), philosopher, diplomat, and teacher of sports (Sagittarius), healer (Virgo), and wounded healer and martyr (Pisces). These are all themes that can be activated by Chiron through or by transits. Astrologer Al H. Morrison also has pointed out that because Chiron connects Saturn to Uranus through its orbit, it enables one to function as a maverick, working within conventional boundaries (Saturn) while maintaining one's individuality (Uranus). The difficulty in categorizing Chiron as an astrophysical body (part asteroid and part comet), reflects not only its maverick identity but also its centaur attributes.

When Chiron is involved in transits, issues such as trusting one's intuitive wisdom, ability to impart knowledge, and sense of authority to teach and heal (either others or oneself) frequently arise. Often Chiron transits will make us aware of an illness, physical or emotional, in order to bring about a healing. We are often challenged in terms of our intellectual authority, and find ourselves saying: "Hey, I've been around the block; I have a right to say what I think and to be listened to!"

Essentially concurrent with Chiron's discovery, traditional western medical paradigms have begun to be challenged by researchers, laymen, and even doctors. Healing techniques such as acupuncture, biofeedback, and visualization, and the realization that one's emotional status has a profound effect upon one's health, are becoming increasingly appreciated as society has come to realize that modern medicine does not have all the answers, especially to such difficult diseases as cancer and AIDS. Medical patients are beginning to question their doctors and to take a more assertive role in their healing process, and this is generally being recognized as a healthy development rather than a merely rebellious one.

In 1977,[11] scientists found that most neurons contained several neuro-transmitters and not just one as they had previously thought. Around the same time, researchers were surprised to discover nerve tissue in and around the human immune system. It had previously been assumed that the immune system functioned independently from other body systems, but this finding strongly implied that the immune and nervous systems were interactive. This has led to a slowly growing understanding of the connection between not just the brain, but the mind, and human health.

---

11 *Timetables of Science*, p. 580.

Many astrologers believe that planets are "discovered" when humanity's collective consciousness is ready to assimilate their energy. *Thus Chiron's recent detection may be seen as ushering in a new age of medical understanding, wherein learning becomes an integral part of the healing process.* Indeed, this certainly seems to be the case with not only AIDS, but with cancer and other gradually developing diseases which generally give us adequate time to process many of our issues. We are seeing increasing numbers of people who are successfully combating cancer and the AIDS virus in medically *non*traditional ways. There is also a growing appreciation for the connection between symptoms and the inner emotional and spiritual root causes of disease. Healers are now starting to place a stronger emphasis on supplementing traditional western scientific medical techniques with proper diet, psychological healing, and spiritual faith. It is especially these last two that should interest us here, because they relate to Pluto and Neptune respectively.

The Pluto-Chiron Connection

While researching the astro-history of medical breakthroughs, it became quite apparent to me that there is a strong connection between Chiron and Pluto and advancements in medical understanding. It is especially when these two bodies make hard aspects *to each other* that society can expect innovations in healing. A few examples from the vast array of medical discoveries heralded by this potent celestial combination are: an explanation for scurvy (1752), the first treatise on pathological anatomy (1760), Philippe Pinel's book on mental illness advocates more humane treatment (1791), hypnosis (1795), Jenner's Smallpox vaccine (1797), quinine sulfate discovered as a cure for malaria (1819), beginning of experimental psychology by William Wundt (1856), Robert Koch demonstrates germ theory of disease, starting a landslide of pathogen identifications (1883), P. E. Smith discovers that the pituitary gland controls the endocrine system (1884), Louis Pasteur developed the rabies vaccine (1885), Sigmund Freud founds psychoanalysis (1896), first use of X-rays for diagnosis (1896), Gregor Mendel's work on the genetics of the garden pea rediscovered independently by three different researchers (1899), first blood transfusion (1905), syphilis pathogen identified (1905), hormones described (1906), first IQ test (1906), psychological behaviorism developed (1919), penicillin developed (1940), first "wonder drug," a sulfa drug created by Gerhard Domagk, Streptomycin discovered and the term antibiotic created (1941), Salk creates polio vaccine, Christine Jorgenson undergoes first sex-change operation and the first tranquilizer is created (1952), recognition that cancer is caused by changes in DNA (1961), and genetic engineering for medical cures (1987).

As you can see, these Chiron-Pluto discoveries concern not only germ-initiated diseases, but also involve psychology and genetics. This makes perfect sense when one considers the nature of the two bodies involved. Of course, Chiron deals with healing in general, and Pluto deals with death and plagues as well as genetics, but Pluto also deals with our need to empower ourselves through transformation, especially utilizing psychological insights, and Chiron insists that we be true to our own uniqueness in order to heal, and that we learn in order to grow. When we combine these two planets on a personal level, we can understand their powerful potential for psychological and spiritual healing from a very personal perspective. This is the realm of mind over matter.

My favorite example of the potent psychogenic effects of Chiron and Pluto occurred in 1892, with Chiron entering a waxing square to Pluto. *The Timetables of Science* reports that "Max Joseph von Pettenkofer (b. Lichtenheim, Germany, Dec 3, 1818) miraculously fails to get sick after swallowing cholera-causing bacteria in an effort *to disprove* the germ theory of disease."[12] Why didn't he get sick and die? Because, in essence, we all create our own reality.

This is a philosophy which has become particularly popular since the discovery of Chiron. To those who feel a bit more grounded in reality (actually ground down by their perception of reality), the concept that we consciously alter our lives through such modes as "positive thinking" and unconscious thought patterns is simply nonsense, but those who have experienced such transformations believe with a certainty that this is a truism.

This discrepancy can best be explained using an analogy involving physics. Shortly after that apocryphal apple fell on his head, Newton's description of how the physical universe worked

---

12 *Timetables of Science*, p. 375.

sufficed quite nicely for just about all of us. However, when science started to investigate *extremes:* extreme speed, or heat, or temperatures—then Newton's laws started to break down, and only the theory of relativity could explain the more exotic phenomena. And yet, for most everyday experiences, Einsteinian relativity is still subsumed within Newtonian physics. And it is just so with our everyday emotional experience of reality. It is only when conditions in our life become extreme that we can actually observe a higher law, where we do create our own reality. Normally, however, we are oblivious to these psychospiritual mechanics. Pluto, of course, brings about just such life-and-death extremes, and it is only by using our own unique wisdom and resources that we can face such tests. At such radical times, we cannot depend upon what someone else thinks; we have to rely upon our own knowing.

While Chiron formed a semi-square to Pluto from the fall of 1992 through July of 1993, promising some advances in healing, *it seems more likely that a cure will be found for AIDS, and perhaps even cancer, in the year 2000, when Chiron again conjoins with Pluto.* This makes sense, given the time expectations for developing a cure, and also fits the 25- to 30-year duration of the Syphilis and Typhus epidemics experienced when Pluto was in Scorpio.

AIDS: An Astrological Synthesis

Sometime around 1979, Pluto's highly elliptical orbit brought it inside the orbit of Neptune, *combining the symbolic energy of the two planets.* Usually, when Pluto makes some contact with Neptune, he ruthlessly rips away any pretty illusions we may have. The process can be devastating, but if we open our eyes to the profound truth Pluto offers, we end up understanding Neptune far better, and realize how naive our romantic ideas may have been compared to Neptune's truest radiant depths. When Pluto came closer to Earth than Neptune, this energy became manifest. Neptune rules our immune systems, both through water (body fluids, especially lymph) and through vulnerability (the opposite of immunity). *So Pluto's crossing of Neptune's orbit manifested a virus to challenge the immune system, our spirituality, sense of compassion, and global love and tolerance.*

Pluto is forcing us to look at the functioning of Neptune, within ourselves as individuals, and as communities, nations, and a biosphere. (It is no coincidence that the first global environmental treaty was conceived during Pluto's perigee.) Let's take a look at what Pluto is trying to tell us about Neptune, and how our personal and social demons may have misused its energy.

Remember that Neptune's highest form is universal, nondiscriminating love. However, most of us are taught to believe that none but God and the Avatars can act at that level. At least we certainly aren't given many day-to-day role models. (Jesus is a perfect example, but look at how His teachings of compassion, forgiveness, and unconditional love have been qualified and distorted!) More importantly, many of us have been told, in one way or another, that *we do not deserve unconditional love.* If we are under the illusion that we are not a part of the Universal Source of Love, we feel cut off, vulnerable, potential victims, perhaps unworthy of such love. This is classic Neptunian alienation.

Another theme of both Neptune and Pluto is that of pollution. In an effort to enhance the standard of living through technology, industrial societies are increasingly removing us from our originally intimate connection with nature and natural cycles. Although we have succeeded in reducing biological contaminants in most of our food and water, we are being subjected increasingly to an overwhelming barrage of chemicals, primarily from industry and agriculture, which are totally alien to our bodies. As well, we face a dramatic concentration of wastes in our urban and suburban ecosystems as humanity's population continues to increase.

Homeopathy tells us that the body's first line of defense against disease occurs at the cellular level, and that our immune system is more of a secondary system. As long as our cells are healthy, they can resist infective agents, which the immune system then destroys and removes. If the Neptunian water which composes the bulk of our cells becomes polluted, cellular health becomes impaired and we become infected. It does not seem farfetched to speculate that the intense sweating and weight loss associated with AIDS may be the body's Plutonian attempt to purge these toxins.

Chiron, as the wounded healer, makes us aware of our need for healing on various levels, usually through illness. In my research on the charts of people with AIDS, I found Chiron to be extremely active in triggering initial symptoms, *with the most common aspect being a square to the person's natal Pluto.* Saturn was the only planet more active than Chiron in producing symptoms, and its most frequent aspects were *to the person's Moon (ruler of the body and emotions) and Neptune.*

With Chiron's help, we can see that AIDS is not merely a disease, but also an opportunity for healing. This healing is not just physical, but operates primarily on a psycho-spiritual level. On a personal level, impelled by Pluto's ruthless "change or die" influence, many people are getting much more deeply in touch with their true selves. Pluto both necessitates and facilitates the difficult process of introspection, transformation, and regeneration, and finally shows us our true power. Once we own our power, we no longer see ourselves as victims, and can start to relate to Neptune's universally loving nature. Both processes are necessary for healing.

Chiron, Neptune, and Pluto are all slow-moving, transpersonal, generation-altering planets, and it is important to realize that the opportunity for healing is not reserved exclusively for those who have AIDS. On a broad social level, AIDS is an opportunity *for all people to get in touch with their Neptunian, nondiscriminating compassion and willingness to be of service to others.* It seems beyond coincidence that the vast majority of those who have contracted AIDS are those whom our culture has rejected: gay men, IV drug users, and the poor and politically disenfranchised, (represented by the people with AIDS in "Third World" countries). While the political administrations of the previous 12 years failed miserably in showing compassion by transcending prejudice in this crisis, many other people did not. This disease is a great spiritual opportunity. Pluto has pressed upon us a terrible and awesome gift. How we use it is up to each one of us.

Looking for Trouble

One of the most important services we can provide as astrologers is to forecast potential up-coming trends. While it is always nice to peer into a rose-colored future, it is equally important that the astrologer actively search for trouble spots, whether they be in health, love, career, or finance. How else can the person know what lurks around the corner of time? Of course some clients may worry and fret excessively once they have been told of a potentially difficult time, but the wise ones will not squander their energy in such a negative way, and instead prepare for the possibility of the event. Perhaps it is important that we remember to remind our clients how to use constructively the information we provide them.

When on the look-out for potential health problems, three factors are important. The first is the timing and the type of energy activating the natal chart. The second thing to look for is the possible underlying psychological issues which might be triggering the disorder. By understanding such issues, we can help clients correctly focus on and streamline their approach to well-being. Finally, we must examine the chart to see how the person will most likely stand up to crisis. Do they have the courage, grit, and tenacity to deal with what seems to be a catastrophe? For if AIDS, cancer, and other long-term diseases are going to teach us anything, it is that *we must search within ourselves for the strength and wisdom to heal.*

In the following sections, we will deal with the first and third factors: the indicators or disease and the person's resources in coping with it. The second category, the possible underlying causes of a particular health crisis, whether psychological, dietary or environmental, is more germane to the individual horoscope and is quite beyond the scope of this chapter.

In looking for potential health problems, we generally look for transits, directions, and progressions to the Sun, Moon, Ascendant, Midheaven, 6th House, and the ruler of the 6th. The planets from Saturn on out are the most likely generators, including the lunar nodes. In a 1987 study of AIDS,[13] it was found that both by

---

13 Hammerslough, B. F., *AIDS in the Horoscope.*

transits and Solar Arc Direction, *Saturn was by far the most active triggering planet, especially contacting natal Moon and Neptune.* Chiron was the second most active stimulus, with a predominance of transiting squares to Pluto. The Lunar North Node, Neptune, and Pluto were also significant activators of health issues.

At the onset of HIV symptoms, the most frequently observed aspects to the natal chart from both transiting and directed planets were, in descending order: Chiron to Pluto, Saturn to Moon, Saturn to Neptune, Saturn to Pluto, Neptune to Jupiter, and North Node to Mars. Of course there are many possibilities and variations in triggering a health crisis besides the few mentioned here, and astrologers must rely upon their experience in judging such matters.

Surviving the Plague

Researchers are now finding that almost 40 percent of those diagnosed with AIDS have survived for at least a 10-year period. The reasonable question is, why do some people contract a disease and die, while others survive and even thrive? Indeed, in the pathology of everyday life, why do some people remain healthy during outbreaks of the flu or common cold, while others find themselves constantly susceptible? Most likely *it is their state of mind.* Recall the example of Max von Pettenkofer, who swallowed a flask of cholera bacteria to no apparent ill effect. After all, the polar opposite of the 6th House of health is the 12th House of the unconscious mind. Our physical health is merely the final manifestation of our awareness and willingness to illuminate and deal with certain emotional patterns, or our lack of awareness and refusal to do so.

In order to examine the problem of who gets sick and who stays healthy, I requested a respected physician with a large AIDS case-load to provide me with the birth dates of patients who were either doing very well or very poorly. He provided me with fifty birth dates and the approximate dates of either infection or the onset of symptoms. Because no birth times or places were provided, it was necessary to omit the Moon, angles, and other sensitive points. Nevertheless, the results of dividing the charts into two extreme groups were quite illuminating.

The following tables show five groups: (+) denotes those who are doing well, (-) indicates those who have a poor prognosis, HIV indicates a control group of 91 men with HIV spanning the spectrum from being asymptomatic to having died; GAY indicates a control group of 319 gay men, some of whom are presumably HIV positive, and HET represents an 861 data base of heterosexual men and women. This is an appropriate time to thank Alphee Lavoie and William Weber for creating the ARP research program, as I can now accomplish in a matter of minutes what took me months to piece together five years ago.

Research Tables

Table 1
Lunar Phase Percentages

	New	Crescent	1st Qtr	Gibbous	Full	Disseminating	3rd Qtr	Balsamic
+	10.5	15.8	15.8	10.5	10.5	26.3	10.5	0.0
−	13.0	17.4	13.0	17.4	17.4	4.3	8.7	8.7
HIV	17.6	12.1	14.3	14.3	12.1	11.0	11.0	7.7
GAY	11.3	13.2	11.3	12.5	10.7	13.2	12.2	15.7
HET	11.4	13.0	13.0	12.5	12.9	11.8	13.1	12.2

Table 2
Retrograde Planet Percentages

	☿	♀	♂	♃	♄	♅	♆	♇
+	26.3	5.3	15.8	31.6	42.1	52.6	57.9	36.8
−	17.4	13.0	4.3	47.8	26.1	43.5	43.5	47.8
HIV	18.7	8.8	7.7	33.0	28.6	40.7	41.8	39.6
GAY	24.5	6.6	11.9	27.6	36.4	37.0	41.4	39.5
HET	20 1	7.9	9.9	27.3	32.5	33.8	33.3	31.9

Table 3
Planets Rising Before Sun (Oriental) (Promethean)

	☽	☿	♀	♂	♃	♄	♅	♆	♇
+	0.0	42.1	26.3	10.5	0.0	10.5	5.3	5.3	0.0
−	4.3	43.5	13.0	8.7	0.0	8.7	0.0	13.0	8.7
HIV	4.4	30.8	19.8	12.1	5.5	9.9	5.5	5.5	6.6
GAY	6.6	30.7	17.2	10.7	6.6	6.9	5.6	6.9	8.8
HET	6.6	33.8	17.2	8.8	7.4	7.4	4.5	7.4	6.7

Table 4

	% Elements				% Modalities		
	Fire	Earth	Air	Water	Cardinal	Fixed	Mutable
+	36.8	31.6	31.6	47.4	21.1	52.6	36.8
–	47.8	17.4	26.1	21.7	39.1	60.9	13.0
HIV	42.9	30.8	34.1	29.7	33.0	53.8	33.0
GAY	35.1	41.1	30.7	28.5	34.2	53.0	33.5
HET	34.4	32.9	36.5	33.4	41.0	43.2	32.6

Table 5

☉

	♈	♉	♊	♋	♌	♍	♎	♏	♐	♑	♒	♓
+	5.3	21.1	10.5	10.5	0.0	5.3	5.3	15.8	5.3	5.3	0.0	15.8
–	8.7	17.4	4.3	13.0	13.0	4.3	4.3	13.0	8.7	4.3	8.7	0.0
HIV	6.6	8.8	7.7	6.6	15.4	7.7	6.6	9.9	9.9	4.4	7.7	8.8
GAY	6.6	8.8	10.7	8.8	9.1	9.1	7.2	10.7	6.9	6.6	9.4	6.3
HET	6.6	8.9	9.2	8.8	10.3	8.4	7.4	9.3	6.5	7.5	8.1	8.8

☽

	♈	♉	♊	♋	♌	♍	♎	♏	♐	♑	♒	♓
+	5.3	10.5	0.0	15.8	10.5	5.3	5.3	5.3	5.3	10.5	5.3	26.3
–	8.7	17.4	4.3	13.0	13.0	4.3	4.3	13.0	8.7	4.3	8.7	0.0
HIV	9.9	12.1	9.9	9.9	8.8	5.5	3.3	8.8	5.5	9.9	9.9	6.6
GAY	7.5	10.2	7.2	7.5	8.5	8.2	6.6	11.6	8.2	7.5	7.8	9.4
HET	9.1	7.5	7.0	7.4	6.9	10.2	8.7	8.6	10.3	8.1	6.2	10.0

☿

	♈	♉	♊	♋	♌	♍	♎	♏	♐	♑	♒	♓
+	21.1	15.8	5.3	5.3	5.3	10.5	5.3	15.8	5.3	0.0	5.3	5.3
–	21.7	4.3	0.0	8.7	13.0	4.3	8.7	13.0	8.7	0.0	17.4	0.0
HIV	6.6	6.6	6.6	5.5	16.5	5.5	8.8	13.2	6.6	4.4	11.0	8.8
GAY	7.8	7.2	7.5	11.0	7.8	6.9	10.7	9.7	6.9	9.1	8.8	6.6
HET	7.0	7.3	8.4	8.5	9.2	8.1	10.0	7.5	9.1	6.9	10.2	7.9

♀

	♈	♉	♊	♋	♌	♍	♎	♏	♐	♑	♒	♓
+	10.5	15.8	10.5	15.8	0.0	15.8	5.3	5.3	10.5	0.0	5.3	5.3
–	17.4	4.3	0.0	21.7	4.3	13.0	4.3	8.7	0.0	13.0	13.0	0.0
HIV	6.6	0.0	7.7	16.5	6.6	14.3	11.0	6.6	3.3	11.0	9.9	6.6
GAY	10.3	7.2	10.0	7.8	7.5	8.8	9.7	10.3	8.2	5.6	8.5	6.0
HET	8.2	8.0	8.6	10.2	6.0	9.8	8.8	9.4	5.9	7.3	10.3	7.3

♂

	♈	♉	♊	♋	♌	♍	♎	♏	♐	♑	♒	♓
+	10.5	10.5	0.0	15.8	0.0	5.3	10.5	10.5	5;3	10.5	21.1	0.0
–	4.3	8.7	0.0	17.4	13.0	13.0	4.3	8.7	8.7	4.3	8.7	8.7
HIV	2.2	9.9	7.7	6.6	14.3	8.8	7.7	11.0	8.8	6.6	5.5	11.0
GAY	4.7	7.2	8.5	10.7	9.7	15.0	5.0	9.4	9.7	6.9	7.5	5.6
HET	5.9	8.4	8.1	10.2	8.7	10.8	9.3	8.4	8.2	6.3	7.4	8.2

♃

	♈	♉	♊	♋	♌	♍	♎	♏	♐	♑	♒	♓
+	10.5	15.8	15.8	10.5	10.5	10.5	5.3	0.0	10.5	0.0	10.5	0.0
–	8.7	8.7	17.4	8.7	8.7	8.7	13.0	13.0	0.0	8.7	0.0	4.3
HIV	7.7	6.6	7.7	7.7	6.6	11.0	6.6	15.4	11.0	11.0	4.4	4.4
GAY	8.2	11.6	7.2	5.0	6.0	7.2	7.8	9.1	12.2	10.7	9.7	5.3
HET	9.1	8.7	8.6	8.8	7.4	7.5	9.4	9.9	8.1	7.2	7.5	7.7

♄

	♈	♉	♊	♋	♌	♍	♎	♏	♐	♑	♒	♓
+	0.0	15.8	5.3	5.3	0.0	10.5	10.5	26.3	10.5	10.5	0.0	5.3
–	0.0	4.3	4.3	4.3	8.7	4.3	17.4	17.4	21.7	4.3	13.0	0.0
HIV	2.2	5.5	5.5	4.4	13.2	15.4	9.9	13.2	15.4	7.7	5.5	2.2
GAY	0.9	2.5	2.5	3.1	5.3	7.8	11.3	11.0	11.3	23.8	13.5	6.9
HET	4.6	4.9	6.4	5.5	9.6	10.0	11.7	11.6	11.7	10.5	7.8	5.7

Table 6
Strongest Signs ☉ - ♄

	♈	♉	♊	♋	♌	♍	♎	♏	♐	♑	♒	♓
+	10.5	21.1	10.5	10.5	15.8	10.5	10.5	26.3	21.1	0.0	21.1	10.5
–	8.7	4.3	0.0	8.7	39.1	4.3	17.4	13.0	8.7	13.0	8.7	0.0
HIV	12.1	14.3	12.1	9.9	24.2	9.9	15.4	17.6	13.2	13.2	11.0	7.7
GAY	11.0	18.8	11.0	10.7	22.6	17.2	10.7	14.4	10.7	13.5	14.7	8.5
HET	14.9	14.8	12.8	14.4	16.6	12.3	17.0	13.8	9.5	11.0	12.8	10.2

Table 7
Significant Midpoint Combinations

+	%	(–) %	–	%	(+) %
☉/♃ =♇	36.8	21.7	☿/♀ =⚷	34.8	10.5
♂/♅ =♀	36.8	13.0	♀/♅ =☉	34.8	21.1
♃/♇ =☉	36.8	13.0	♃/♄ =☊	34.8	15.8
♅/♇ =♂	36.8	13.0	♄/☿ =♄	34.8	10.5
♆/⚷ =♆	42.1	30.4	♄/⚷ =♆	39.1	15.8
♇/☊ =♅	36.8	13.0	♅/♆ =♆	47.8	36.8
			♅/☊ =☿	34.8	10.5
			♅/⚷ =☿	30.4	21.1
			☊/⚷ =☿	43.5	10.5

Table 8
Significant Midpoint Percentages

	☉ = ♀/♅	☉ = ♃/♇	☉ = ♅/☊	☉ = ♆/♇	☉ = ♂/♅	☉ = ♅/♇
+	21.1	36.8	10.5	26.3	36.8	36.8
–	34.8	13.0	17.4	26.1	13.0	13.0
HIV	16.5	22.0	14.4	19.8	13.2	18.7
GAY	16.9	19.1	30.7	36.1	15.0	12.5
HET	15.6	14.8	12.5	15.3	14.4	12.3

	♃ = ♂/♄	♃ = ♆/♇	♄ = ♀/♂	♄ = ♄/♇	♅ = ♂/♄	♅ = ♇/☊
+	36.8	5.3	0.0	10.5	36.8	36.8
–	0.0	34.8	34.8	34.8	0.0	13.0
HIV	14.3	16.5	11.0	13.2	11.0	11.0
GAY	13.8	15.7	12.2	16.9	13.8	18.8
HET	12.1	15.8	13.0	14.2	12.8	18.7

	♆ = ♄/⚷	♆ = ♅/♆	♆ = ♅/⚷	♆ = ♆/⚷	♇ = ☉/♃	♇ = ♅/♆
+	15.8	36.8	26.3	42.1	36.8	36.8
–	39.1	47.8	26.1	30.4	21.7	47.8
HIV	23.1	23.1	19.8	30.8	14.3	23.1
GAY	12.2	21.9	36.1	31.3	15.0	21.9
HET	18.6	20.3	15.3	12.0	10.7	20.3

	♇ = ♅/☊	♇ = ♅/⚷	♇ = ♆/☊	♇ = ☊/⚷	☊ = ♃/♄	⚷ = ☿/♀	⚷ = ♆/☊
+	10.5	21.1	26.3	10.5	15.8	10.5	26.3
–	34.8	30.4	30.4	43.5	34.8	34.8	30.4
HIV	12.9	16.5	15.4	23.1	22.0	14.3	15.4
GAY	12.1	11.6	14.1	14.7	14.7	14.7	14.7
HET	13.2	0.1	13.0	15.1	17.7	13.7	13.0

A thorough analysis of the above data is beyond the scope of this chapter, but I hope that these tables will provide the readers with much to investigate and ponder on their own. This information not only sheds light on the astrological influences of coping with disease, but can also illuminate some of the dynamics of gay versus "straight" horoscopes. Here are a few of the observations that can be drawn from the data.

Natal Lunar Phases

Even though the lack of birth times prevented examining aspects of the Moon, by having the birthday *we can still determine the Lunar Phase* (Table 1, p. 342). It is significant that the Moon was in the Disseminating phase at birth for 26.3 percent of those who are doing well with HIV, and only 4.3 percent for those doing poorly. The control groups fell in-between these values, ranging from 11 to 13.1 percent. In *The Lunation Process in Astrological Guidance*, Leyla Rael calls this phase "Demonstration," and explains:

> The Disseminating phase can entail a struggle, but it is now a struggle to understand, to let go of mere forms and begin to see what is underlying them. A wider social participation should begin under this phase; what has been learned in the first hemicycle can begin to be shared with others and be made useful within the context of a growing vision.[14]

> Linking with others to generalize one's experience is often an important feature of this period. The desire to demonstrate one's now-realized capacities, to make one's efforts meaningful in terms of a larger social frame of reference, can be an important step in coming to understand and assimilate what has (previously) been "revealed". . . If one is shocked or disappointed by what one has seen (or experienced), a period of reforming or even revolutionary activity may follow. The soli-lunar trine occurs early in this phase, and it provides the challenge and opportunity to begin to integrate what has happened in the first hemicycle and what has been "seen' at the Full Moon into a workable philosophy of life.[15]

The implication here is that those who do better with HIV infection *tend to look for meaning from their experience*, and are also more likely to share what they've learned with others. As we shall see, this element of sharing is vitally important. Conversely, notice that *none* of the long-term survival group had the Balsamic phase Moon, which is more introverted and withdrawing by nature.

Retrograde Planets (Table 2, p. 342)

Those doing well with HIV infection have a strong tendency to have a retrograde Mars, 15.8 percent, as opposed to only 4.3 percent for those who are doing poorly, and between 7.7 and 11.9 percent in the control groups. This implies a more conscious, deliberate, and less spontaneous use of energy, making the person more of a concentrated fighter.

---

14 Rael, Leyla. *The Lunation Process in Astrological Guidance*. Self-Published Pamphlet, 1979?, p. 10.
15 Rael, p. 24 & 25.

Those doing poorly with HIV tend to be more likely to have Venus retrograde (13 percent) as opposed to those who do well (5.3 percent) or the control groups (6.6 percent–7.9 percent). This finding implies a greater reserve in affection and perhaps a tendency to be less demonstrative. The group having greater difficulty with HIV also tended to have Jupiter and Pluto more frequently retrograde, and Mercury and Saturn more frequently direct, while long-term survivors were more inclined to have Saturn, Uranus and Neptune retrograde.

Promethean Planets (Table 3, p. 342)

Promethean planets are those which rise before the Sun in clockwise rotation. (The term "oriental" is often used interchangeably, but oriental is also used to refer simply to planets on the East side of the chart.) The traditional belief is that the planet rising before the Sun strongly lends its energy to the person's sense of self. Notice the relatively high percentage of Neptune rising before the Sun in the group dealing poorly with HIV. This fits well with the general Neptunian theme of AIDS, and implies an excessive sensitivity and thus potential vulnerability in those individuals. Conversely, for those doing well with the virus, Promethean Venus had very high values while those doing least successfully had the lowest percentages of Venus before the Sun. This reinforces the thesis that those who are more overtly social and affectionate are able to create more love and support, which thus help them cope with crisis.

What is surprising is that Pluto did not rise before the Sun for any of those doing well (+). One might have expected such a Pluto to impart a deep sense of tenacity for survival, but apparently it seems to lend a darker tone.

Aspects

Along the same lines, the problem group had Sun semisquare Venus 39.1 percent of the time (this table is not included here), while in the more successful group Venus semisquared the Sun by only 15.8 percent. The control groups ranged from 29.7 percent to 34.8 percent, showing the more successful group to be exceptional. Similarly, while 15.8 percent of the group doing well had Venus trining Mars in their chart, *not one of the group having difficulty had this aspect*, while the control groups ranged from 1.1

to 4.4 percent. Again, this shows demonstrativeness and strong affections to be powerful traits for improving chances of survival.

Optimism and the desire to learn are of course essential in maintaining good health during a crisis. 15.8 percent of the more successful group had Mercury trining Jupiter, while none of the more problematic group did, and the control groups only ranged from 3.4 to 6.6 percent.

Other interesting trends show up in the aspect data, but frankly, some of it is confusing, and may be influenced by the nature of the clientele the doctor attracts.

Elements, Modalities, and Signs

The Elements, Modalities, and Signs were investigated for the Sun through Saturn. The trans-Saturnian planets were omitted because their slow movements through the zodiac would distort the data. The Moon was included in this count because that's how the research program handled things, but this data is not completely accurate for the first two groups, those doing very well or very poorly with HIV infection, as birth times and places were not provided. The information is valid for the last three groups, where the birth times and places, and thus accurate lunar positions, were known.

In examining the elements, the long-term group had a significantly higher percentage of Water, perhaps indicating a group more in tune with or expressive of their emotions. This, of course, can be a very healthy trait. The (-) group, on the other hand, scored low in Earth, implying a less grounded and practical nature. This same group also scored noticeably higher in Fixed signs and lower in Mutable, evidence of more rigid, less adaptable personalities, who might therefore have greater problems dealing with crisis and change.

An examination of the planets in the signs is also illuminating. Perhaps most striking is the high percentage in Scorpio among the long-term survival group. The sign Scorpio is noted for its powerful regenerative and survival powers. The signs Sagittarius and Aquarius were also more pronounced in this group, possibly indicating a more extroverted, social and perhaps even idealistic nature. Surprisingly, this same (+) group showed 0% for the sign Capricorn. While Capricorn can be depressive, which this finding apparently indicates, it can also add practicality and responsibility—traits essential for survival.

Another surprising finding is that the group having more difficulty dealing with HIV infection had a very high percentage of planets in Leo (39.1 percent). One might think of Leo as providing the fire of optimism, but it can also become self-indulgent in excess drama, which is my suspicion in this case. This same group also showed 0 percent for the signs Gemini and Pisces, again indicating a potential lack of adaptability, and significantly low values for the practical signs of Taurus and Virgo.

Midpoints

An analysis of hard aspects to midpoints (8th harmonic) in the natal charts also proves quite revealing in terms of one's ability to cope with crisis. Most striking is the observation that 36.8 percent of the group doing well with their HIV infection have *either Jupiter or Uranus in aspect to the midpoint of Mars-Saturn*, while 0 percent of those not doing well had this midpoint combination, and the control groups ranged about half way in between. Reinhold Ebertin describes Jupiter = Mars/Saturn as "The complete concentration of energy upon a particular objective to the entire exclusion of other interests, the ability to render quick work (satisfactorily). The ability to destroy or eliminate something thoroughly."[16] Correlating nicely with this last statement is the finding that long-term survivors tend to have high Killer T-Cell counts.[17]

Uranus = Mars/Saturn is explained as "Extraordinary and unusual powers of resistance, the ability to give as well as to take under provocation, the inclination to apply brute force."[18]

Also of major significance was the fact that while none of those doing well had Saturn = Venus/Mars, 34.8 percent of those having more difficulty did, and again the control groups fell at the half-way point. Ebertin defines this midpoint as: "Inhibitions in love-life, an inclination to adultery, an abnormal and pathological sex-expression.—A separation in love."[19] All of this shows a degree of strain in the expression of love and affection.

---

16 Ebertin, Reinhold. *The Combination of Stellar Influences*. Tempe, AZ: American Federation of Astrologers, 1972, p. 157.
17 Nielsen, Robert, p. 7.
18 Ebertin, Reinhold, p. 157.
19 Ebertin, p. 137.

Another interesting finding which might tempt one to modify the traditional definition of the midpoint Jupiter = Neptune/Pluto, was that those doing poorly with HIV scored a significantly high 34.8 percent for this midpoint, while those doing well only had 5.3 percent, and the control groups fell between both extremes. Ebertin categorizes this midpoint as: "A general love of humanity, universal and all-embracing love, a peace-loving disposition, religiousness, a high degree of inner cognition and perception."[20] One would think that these would be excellent survival traits. Perhaps one can rationalize that being too peace-loving might reduce one's desire to fight the virus, and being too religious might backfire into feelings of guilt. On a more esoteric level, perhaps those with Jupiter = Neptune/Pluto have chosen to suffer more profoundly in order to attract society's attention to the AIDS epidemic, thus affording others the opportunity to express compassion and universal love.

A full examination and explanation of this data is, unfortunately, beyond the scope of this chapter. Some of the significant percentages are shown in darker print to facilitate the reader's own examination, which is encouraged. Sun = Uranus/N. Node at 30.7 percent for gays speaks eloquently of the karmic nature of sexual orientation, as does the 0.1 percent Pluto = Uranus/Chiron for heterosexuals. Several of these findings challenge the traditional interpretation of Ebertin's midpoint descriptions, and might well lead to some interesting further research.

Concerning all of the data, it is important to realize that these are just *trends and percentages*. A retrograde Venus or Saturn in hard aspect to a Venus/Mars midpoint are no more a death sentence than having Mercury trine Jupiter or Uranus in hard aspect to a Mars/Saturn midpoint guarantees survival. Such astrological configurations show our tendencies, but each of us has the ability and free will to grow beyond our challenges.

Survival Tips

From the above discussion, it seems as though the key to why some people fare better than others in the face of HIV infection is *a combination of hope, sharing, and tenacity*. Following is a list of common survival traits observed not only in those with HIV

20 Ebertin, p. 207.

infection, but also in those with cancer, injury from combat, or extensive burns. The list was gathered from various sources and collated by the Seattle Treatment Education Project.[21]

1) Survivors are optimistic for the future; they feel that good times are ahead.

2) They feel personally responsible for their health; believe they can influence their own wellness.

3) Are satisfied with the quality of their lives.

4) Believe life is meaningful.

5) Believe that life has become more meaningful as a result of HIV infection.

6) Have dealt with or healed their own emotional wounds; they have good coping mechanisms; don't allow difficult people or situations to get them down.

7) Are involved in life and activities meaningful to them (career, hobby, volunteer work, politics).

8) Participate in fitness or exercise programs.

9) Pragmatic and realistic; take each day as it comes.

10) Don't give in to disease—seek treatment.

11) Verbal, talkative; especially when discussing their condition with doctors; good communicators.

12) Want doctors they can trust and expect to be treated as equals, collaborators; will change doctors if not satisfied.

13) Good medical consumers; they stay informed about medical developments and assertively demand excellent treatment.

14) Generally not obsessed by CD4 counts.

15) Some have survived other life-threatening or psychologically disturbing circumstances (serious auto accident, loss of parent as a child, etc.).

---

21 Nielsen, Robert, p. 7.

On Writing this Chapter

When Noel Tyl asked me to write this chapter, I thought to myself: "Who better to write an article on AIDS than a 6th House Scorpio Sun with Pluto right on the IC and conjoined the Moon?" But even more appropriate is the fact that as I am writing this paragraph, I am also celebrating, to the very day, my eighth anniversary with HIV. I have been incredibly lucky in that I have remained, for the most part, quite healthy and have usually only suffered from symptoms which have assaulted my vanity—mostly rashes, the heart-break of psoriasis, and such. I was also lucky in being forced to face my situation immediately, and was not given the luxury of denial.

Near the end of 1984, it finally dawned on me that Pluto was really going to transit my natal Sun and that there was no way that even I could stop it. So I did the next best thing and purchased, for the first time in my life, health insurance. (Oh, the benefits of astrology!) In July of the following year, I developed about 20 or more very painful ulcers in my mouth and throat. Between not being able to eat or drink without severe pain, antibiotics allowing a massive systemic yeast flareup, and especially because my pharmacist misread a prescription for pain killer and instead gave me a very potent high-blood-pressure medicine, I was soon brought to the razor's edge of death. Fortunately, I was dating another pharmacist who caught the prescription mistake, and while I obviously survived, I remained quite weak and ill for two weeks, until I demanded that my doctor put me in the hospital before I wasted away from malnutrition. Scorpionic constitutions and hospital bills being what they are, my recuperation was remarkably swift. Of course I figured I had AIDS. So did everyone else, and we were all correct.

One of the wonderful things a potentially fatal disease does is to make us examine our life from a new perspective. Essentially, assuming that we don't just give up, diseases like AIDS and cancer can scare the life *into* us! So I worked hard on facing my issues, and tried to create a life I thoroughly enjoyed.

Much of astrology is applied synchronicity, and the universe is amazingly obliging in steering us in the right direction. Soon after I began to write this article, I fell ill, probably the sickest I've been since my first onset. My usually abundant energy plummeted to hibernation levels; I got depressed (especially because of some of the information I read while researching this chapter), stopped dancing and exercising, and everything generally spiraled down hill. However, as I continued to research for this piece, I started to stumble increasingly onto more hopeful reports, until the universe was aiming more and more positive information in my direction. It turned me around, and I finally realized that my symptoms were a reaction to a medication I was taking. I stopped taking it, and was improving within 24 hours.

The double-edged blessing here is that I had been so healthy for so long that I had forgotten what it was like to feel so miserable. I might have ended up writing some glib drivel about just keeping your spirits up. The brutal truth is that there are absolutely no guarantees. I have seen pass on several spiritual warriors who I would have bet would beat the virus. What is more important is that they fought like heroes, not just to survive, but to maintain a high quality of life. I was reminded how important it is to fight and to take charge of one's condition, and to embrace the Pluto-Chiron phenomenon of the spirit-mind-body connection of trusting one's own inner wisdom. In that light, I would like to add a few survival do's and don'ts of my own to the excellent list above, which you, as an astrologer, may wish to pass on to your HIV+ clients.

1) Work on your Neptune! Do your best to convert alienation, victimization, and vulnerability into compassionate understanding, forgiveness, and letting go. Cultivate truth, spiritual faith, and unconditional love, which do not grow easily in the arid soil of fear and despair. Don't isolate yourself—you deserve love, and sex(!), as much as anyone else, and it is probably the most important medicine there is. Lovers, friends, and family are essential to share life with and don't get bogged down in self pity (although just a little is judicious and justified).

2) If you don't know your HIV status, have it checked. Many people are afraid to know, and yet they may not have the virus. Conversely, the earlier you find out, the sooner you can start the healing process which might prolong and even save your life. This is part of the Pluto work, to face our fears and conquer them.

3) If you test HIV+, don't assume you're going to die. Plan realistically and work for the future, even retirement. Otherwise you may end up in embarrassing and even dire financial straits, adding undue stress which can adversely effect your health.

4) Don't buy into religious or moralistic guilt trips. I think I got angriest when heterosexual Kimberly Bergales, who apparently contracted AIDS from her dentist, lamented to Congress "I didn't do anything wrong!" Oh, and the rest of us DID? The best purpose of religion is to give us faith and remind us of our ties with the rest of creation. Those using religion to separate or diminish are simply wrong. Period.

5) Don't obsess over the disease! Monitoring your health is important, but don't mistake test results for the ultimate reality. A healthy diet is essential, but there's nothing like a good chocolate sundae! Group support, such as healing groups, is important, but not if it becomes the primary focus, so that all you're doing is talking about AIDS.

6) Do work that you love. It's no coincidence that the 6th House rules both work and health. If you don't like your work, you get sick! Of course it's not always possible for us to leave a disliked job, especially with the potential medical costs of HIV infection, but if you can at least change conditions for the better, strive to do so.

7) Give of yourself to others or to some higher cause. As Benjamin Franklin said: "We make a living by what we get. We make a life by what we give."

8) Pets are a great blessing for their companionship and because of their ability to love unconditionally. There used to be some concern about cats transmitting toxoplasmosis, but studies have shown that this disease in a person with HIV is usually a reactivation of a prior exposure. Cats only shed the toxoplasma virus for about two weeks after the initial infection. Clean the stool out of your cat's litter box every day, as it takes 24 hours for the toxoplasmo virus to become infectious.[22]

---

22 Downing, Dyer. *HIV and Pet Ownership.* Seattle, WA: STEP Perspective, Feb. 1993, p. 16.

9) Make sure you can get enough rest. Protestant work ethic not withstanding, there's absolutely nothing wrong with stopping and smelling the roses, or just kicking back and relaxing or "vegging out."

10) Conversely, get enough aerobic exercise, but make sure it's something you enjoy. Exercise will not only get your blood flowing and keep you healthier, it will also energize you, especially if your energy level is low. Also, exercise builds up lean muscle, which is exactly the tissue that becomes depleted through HIV-associated weight loss.

11) Don't just survive, THRIVE!!! You will be happier living your life, rather than living your disease. None of us knows how long we have. One of my best friends has been HIV+ since 1980 and is still quite vigorously healthy. Two years ago his mother was diagnosed with cancer, and she struggled with her issues and is now in remission. Both were shocked when my friend's 30-year-old brother suddenly died of a heart attack. It simply wasn't expected. Life is precious *because* it is so precarious. We could get hit by a bus while crossing the street tomorrow. What ultimately counts, more than anything else, is the caliber of the life we create, and the quality in which we share ourselves with others.

Bibliography

Asistent, Niro Markoff. *Why I Survive AIDS*. New York: Simon & Schuster, 1991.

Badgley, Laurence, M.D. *Healing AIDS Naturally*. Foster City, CA: Human Energy Press, 1987.

Bramforth, Nick. *AIDS and the Healer Within*. Emeryville, CA: Amethyst Press, 1987.

Bramforth, Nick. *Trusting the Healer Within*. Emeryville, CA: Amethyst Press, 1989.

Bartlett, John & Finkbeiner, Ann K. *A Guide to Living With HIV Infection*. Baltimore: John Hopkins University Press, 1991.

Bing-shan, Huang, et al. *AIDS and its Treatment by Traditional Chinese Medicine*. Boulder, CO: Blue Poppy Press, 1991.

Eidson, Ted. *The AIDS Caregiver's Handbook*. New York: St. Martin's Press, 1993.

Granbard, Stephen R. *Living With AIDS*. Cambridge, MA: MIT Press, 1990.

Gregory, Scott J., O.M.D. *A Holistic Protocol for the Immune System*. Joshua Tree, CA: Tree of Life Publications, 1989.

Hay, Louise. *The AIDS Book*. Santa Monica, CA: Hay House, 1988.

_____. *Love Yourself, Heal Your Life Workbook*. Carson, CA: Hay House, 1990.

_____. *The Power is Within You*. Carson, CA: Hay House, 1991.

_____. *You Can Heal Your Life*. Carson, CA: Hay House, 1984.

Henderickson, Peter A. *Alive and Well: A Path for Living in a Time of HIV*. New York: Irvington Publishers, 1990.

Jarvis, Debra. *The Journey Through AIDS: A Guide for Loved Ones and Caregivers*. Batavia, IL: Lion Press, 1992.

Kaiser, Jon D., M.D. *Immune Power—A Comprehensive Treatment Program for HIV*. New York: St. Martin's Press, 1993.

Kidd, Parris, Ph.D. & Huber, Wolfgang, PhD. *Living With the AIDS Virus*. Berkeley, CA: HK Biomedical, 1991.

Martelli, Lennoard J., & Peltz, Messina & Petrow. *When Someone You Know Has AIDS*. New York: Crown Books, 1993.

McCormack, Thomas P. *The AIDS Benefit Handbook*. New Haven, CT: Yale University Press, 1990.

McKenzie, Nancy F., editor. *The AIDS Reader*. New York: Penguin Books, 1991.

Monette, Paul. *Borrowed Time: An AIDS Memoir*. New York: Avon Books, 1988.

Monte, Tom. *The Way of Hope: Michio Kushi's Anti-AIDS Program* (Macrobiotics). New York: Warner Books, 1989.

Pinsky, Laura, and Harding, Paul D. *The Essential HIV Treatment Fact Book*. New York: Pocket Books, 1992.

Rimer, Robert A. and Connolly, Michael A. *HIV+: Working the System*. Boston: Alyson Publishers, 1993.

Shelby, R. Dennis. *If a Partner Has AIDS*. Binghamton, NY: Harrington Park Press, 1992.

Shilts, Randy. *And the Band Played On*. New York: Penguin Books, 1987.

Siano, Nick. *No Time to Wait*. New York: Bantam Books, 1993.

Sontag, Susan. *Illness as Metaphor & AIDS and its Metaphors*. New York: Anchor Books, 1988.

STAY IN TOUCH

On the following pages you will find some of the books now available on related subjects. Your book dealer stocks most of these and will stock new titles in the Llewellyn series as they become available. We urge your patronage.

To obtain our full catalog, to keep informed about new titles as they are released, and to benefit from informative articles and helpful news, you are invited to write for our bimonthly news magazine/catalog, *Llewellyn's New Worlds of Mind and Spirit*. A sample copy is free, and it will continue coming to you at no cost as long as you are an active mail customer. Or you may subscribe for just $10.00 in the U.S.A. and Canada ($20.00 overseas, first class mail). Many bookstores also have *New Worlds* available to their customers. Ask for it.

Llewellyn's New Worlds of Mind and Spirit
P.O. Box 64383-K865, St. Paul, MN 55164-0383, U.S.A.

* * *

TO ORDER BOOKS AND TAPES

If your book dealer does not have the books described, you may order them directly from the publisher by sending the full price in U.S. funds, plus $3.00 for postage and handling for orders *under* $10.00; $4.00 for orders *over* $10.00. There are no postage and handling charges for orders over $50.00. Postage and handling rates are subject to change. We ship UPS whenever possible. Delivery guaranteed. Provide your street address as UPS does not deliver to P.O. boxes. Allow 4-6 weeks for delivery. UPS to Canada requires a $50.00 minimum order. Orders outside the U.S.A. and Canada: Airmail— add retail price of book; add $5.00 for each non-book item (tapes, etc.); add $1.00 per item for surface mail.

FOR GROUP STUDY AND PURCHASE

Because there is a great deal of interest in group discussion and study of the subject matter of this book, we offer a special quantity price to group leaders or agents. Our special quantity price for a minimum order of five copies of *Sexuality in the Horoscope* is $44.85 cash-with-order. This price includes postage and handling within the United States. Minnesota residents must add 6.5% sales tax. For additional quantities, please order in multiples of five. For Canadian and foreign orders, add postage and handling charges as above. Credit card (VISA, MasterCard, American Express) orders are accepted. Charge card orders only ($15.00 minimum order) may be phoned in free within the U.S.A. or Canada by dialing 1-800-THE-MOON. For customer service, call 1-612-291-1970. Mail orders to:

LLEWELLYN PUBLICATIONS
P.O. Box 64383-K865, St. Paul, MN 55164-0383, U.S.A.

Prices subject to change without notice.

SYNTHESIS & COUNSELING IN ASTROLOGY
The Professional Manual
by Noel Tyl

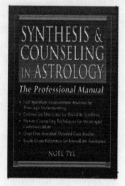

One of the keys to a vital, comprehensive astrology is the art of synthesis, the capacity to take the parts of our knowledge and combine them into a coherent whole. Many times, the parts may be contradictory (the relationship between Mars and Saturn, for example), but the art of synthesis manages the unification of opposites. Now Noel Tyl presents ways astrological measurements—through creative synthesis—can be used to effectively counsel individuals. Discussion of these complex topics is grounded in concrete examples and in-depth analyses of the 122 horoscopes of celebrities, politicians, and private clients.

Tyl's objective in providing this vitally important material was to present everything he has learned and practiced over his distinguished career to provide a useful source to astrologers. He has succeeded in creating a landmark text destined to become a classic reference for professional astrologers.

1-56718-734-X, 924 pgs., 7 x 10, 115 charts, softcover　　　　**$29.95**

HORARY ASTROLOGY
The History and Practice of Astro-Divination
by Anthony Louis

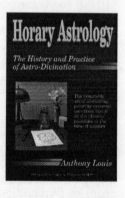

Here is a how-to guide for the intermediate astrologer on the art of astrological divination. It's the best method for getting answers to questions of pressing personal concern based on the planets' positions at the time of inquiry. Delves deeply into the heritage and the modern applicability of the horary art. Author Anthony Louis is a practicing psychiatrist, and he brings the compassion and erudition associated with his field to this scholarly textbook.

Written beautifully and reverently in the tradition of William Lilly, the book translates Lilly's meaning into modern terms. Other features include numerous case studies; tables; diagrams; and more than 100 pages of appendices, including an exhaustive planetary rulership list, planetary key words and a lengthy astrological/horary glossary. Dignities and debilities, aspects and orbs, derivative houses, Arabic parts, fixed stars, critical degrees and more are explored in relation to the science of horary astrology. Worksheets supplement the text.

0-87542-394-9, 592 pgs., 6 x 9, illus., softcover　　　　**$19.95**

Prices subject to change without notice.

PREDICTION IN ASTROLOGY
A Master Volume of Technique and Practice
by Noel Tyl

No matter how much you know about astrology already, no matter how much experience you've had to date, you'll be fascinated by *Prediction in Astrology,* and you'll grow as an astrologer. Using the Solar Arc theory and methods he describes in this book, the author was able to accurately predict the Gulf War, including the actual date it would begin and the timetable of tactics, two months *before* it began. He also predicted the overturning of Communist rule in the Eastern bloc nations nine months in advance of its actual occurrence.

Tyl teaches through example. You learn by doing astrology, not just thinking about it. Tyl introduces Solar Arc theory in terms of "rapport" measurements, which you begin to do immediately, without paper, pencil, or computer, dials, or wheels. Just with your eyes! You will never look at a horoscope the same way again!

Tyl, in his well-known, very special way, also gets personal. He presents 30 Aphorisms, the keenest of maxims, the most practical of techniques, to create predictions from any horoscope. And as if this were not enough, Tyl then presents 20 Aphorisms for Counseling. Look for Tyl's "Quick-Glance" Transit Table, 1940-2040, to which you can refer more quickly than a computer. The busy astrologer will use this Appendix every day for many years to come.

0-87542-814-2, 360 pgs., 6 x 9, softcover **$14.95**

THE MISSING MOON
by Noel Tyl

This delightful collection of ten short stories illustrates principles of astrological counsel and practice with deliciously absurd wit. Read about the mysterious man whose horoscope has no Moon, and learn what the famous poem "Casey at the Bat" really means!

Follow Tyl's hero-astrologer, Michael Mercury, through a series of trials and misadventures on his journey around the horoscope. This is exact astrology presented through exhorbitant humor. You'll enjoy so much while you check your techniques as you solve mysteries, locate Plutonium, follow heroine Atlantia Lemuria into hypnosis . . .

0-87542-797-9, 180 pgs., 5 1/4 x 8, illus., softcover **$4.95**

HOW TO USE VOCATIONAL ASTROLOGY FOR SUCCESS IN THE WORKPLACE
edited by Noel Tyl

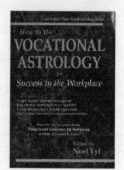

Announcing the most practical examination of Vocational Astrology in five decades! Improve your astrological skills with these revolutionary NEW tools for vocational and business analysis! Now, in *How to Use Vocational Astrology for Success in the Workplace*, edited by Noel Tyl, seven respected astrologers provide their well-seasoned modern views on that great issue of personal life—Work. Their expert advice will prepare you well for those tricky questions clients often ask: "Am I in the right job?" "Will I get promoted?" or "When is the best time to make a career move?" With an introduction by Noel Tyl in which he discusses the startling research of the Gauquelins, this ninth volume in Llewellyn's New World Astrology Series features enlightening counsel from the following experts: Jayj Jacobs, Gina Ceaglio, Donna Cunningham, Anthony Louis, Noel Tyl, Henry Weingarten, and Bob Mulligan. Read *How to Use Vocational Astrology* today, and add "Vocational Counselor" to *your* resume tomorrow! Includes the complete 1942 classic by Charles E. Luntz *Vocational Guidance by Astrology*.

0-87542-387-6, 384 pgs., 6 x 9, illus., softcover $14.95

ASTROLOGY'S SPECIAL MEASUREMENTS
How to Expand the Meaning of the Horoscope
edited by Noel Tyl

Every new student of astrology looks with bewilderment at that first horoscope and asks, "What's it mean when there's nothing in my 7th house? Won't I ever get married?" The student feels the strong need to *measure*. He needs something to define the space in the house and give meaning to the picture. Measurements are the lenses that help us see nearer, farther, and with greater contrast and clarity. In the process of analysis, measurement becomes diagnosis.

In this volume, ten experts discuss the finer points of measurement and meaning, analysis and diagnosis. How many measurements do you need? How many should fortify you for meaningful conversations with clients? Not all measurements work in every horoscope or for every astrologer—and too many can present so much data that you lose confidence within the multiplicity of options. Furthermore, no matter how precise the measurements, they still rely on the astrologer to adapt them to the human condition. *Astrology's Special Measurements* will be a tremendous resource for putting those special measurements to work easily and without fear.

ISBN: 1-56718-864-8, 6 x 9, 352 pgs., charts, tables, softbound $12.00

HOW TO PERSONALIZE THE OUTER PLANETS
The Astrology of Uranus, Neptune & Pluto
Edited by Noel Tyl

Since their discoveries, the three outer planets have been symbols of the modern era. Representing great social change on a global scale, they also take us as individuals to higher levels of consciousness and new possibilities of experience. Explored individually, each outer planet offers tremendous promise for growth. But when taken as a group, as they are in *Personalizing the Outer Planets*, the potential exists to recognize *accelerated* development.

As never done before, the seven prominent astrologers in *Personalizing the Outer Planets* bring these revolutionary forces down to earth in practical ways.

- Jeff Jawer: Learn how the discoveries of the outer planets rocked the world
- Noel Tyl: Project into the future with outer planet Solar Arcs
- Jeff Green: See how the outer planets are tied to personal trauma
- Jeff Jawer: Give perspective to your inner spirit through outer planet symbolisms
- Jayj Jacobs: Explore interpersonal relationships and sex through the outer planets
- Mary E. Shea: Make the right choices using outer planet transits
- Joanne Wickenburg: Realize your unconscious drives and urges through the outer planets
- Capel N. McCutcheon: Personalize the incredible archetypal significance of outer planet aspects

0-87542-389-2, 288 pgs., 6 x 9, illus., softcover $12.00

INTIMATE RELATIONSHIPS
the Astrology of Attraction
edited by Joan McEvers

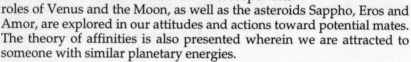

Explore the deeper meaning of intimate relationships with the knowledge and expertise of eight renowned astrologers. Dare to look into your own chart and confront your own vulnerabilities. Find the true meaning of love and its place in your life. Gain new insights into the astrology of marriage, dating, affairs and more!

In Intimate Relationships, eight astrologers discuss their views on romance and the horoscope. The roles of Venus and the Moon, as well as the asteroids Sappho, Eros and Amor, are explored in our attitudes and actions toward potential mates. The theory of affinities is also presented wherein we are attracted to someone with similar planetary energies.

Is it a love that will last a lifetime, or mere animal lust that will burn itself out in a few months? Read *Intimate Relationships* and discover your *natal* attractions as well as your *fatal* attractions.

0-87542-386-8, 240 pgs., 6 x 9, softcover   **$14.95**

HOW TO MANAGE THE
ASTROLOGY OF CRISIS
edited by Noel Tyl

More often than not, a person will consult an astrologer during those times when life has become difficult, uncertain or distressing. While crisis of any type is really a turning point, not a disaster, the client's crisis of growth becomes the astrologer's challenge. By coming to the astrologer, the client has come to an oracle. At the very best, there is hope for a miracle; at the very least, there is hope for reinforcement through companionship and information. How do you as an astrological counselor balance a sober discussion of the realities with enthusiastic efforts to leave the client feeling empowered and optimistic?

In this, the eleventh title in Llewellyn's New World Astrology Series, eight renowned astrologers provide answers this question as it applies to a variety of life crises. *How to Manage the Astrology of Crisis* begins with a discussion of the birth-crisis, the first major transition crisis in everybody's life—their confrontation with the world. It then discusses significant family crises in childhood and healing of the inner child . . . mental crises including head injuries, psychological breakdown, psychic experiences, multiple personalities . . . career turning points and crises of life direction and action . . . astrological triggers of financial crisis and recent advances in financial astrology . . . astrological maxims for relationship crises . . . and the mid-life crises of creative space, idealism, and consciousness.

0-87542-390-6, 224 pgs., 6 x 9, charts, softcover   **$12.00**

Prices subject to change without notice.

THE HOUSES
Power Places of the Horoscope
Edited by Joan McEvers

The Houses are the departments of experience. The planets energize these areas—giving life meaning. Understand why you attract and are attracted to certain people by your 7th House cusp. Go back in time to your 4th House, the history of your beginning. Joan McEvers has ingeniously arranged the chapters to show the Houses' relationships to each other and the whole. Various house systems are briefly described in Joan McEvers' introduction. Learn about house associations and planetary influences upon each house's activities with the following experts.

- Peter Damian: The First House and the Rising Sun
- Ken Negus: The Seventh House
- Noel Tyl: The Second House and The Eighth House
- Spencer Grendahl: The Third House
- Dona Shaw: The Ninth House
- Gloria Star: The Fourth House
- Marwayne Leipzig: The Tenth House
- Lina Accurso: Exploring Your Fifth House
- Sara Corbin Looms: The Eleventh: House of Tomorrow
- Michael Munkasey: The Sixth House
- Joan McEvers: The Twelfth House: Strength, Peace, Tranquillity

0-87542-383-3, 400 pgs., 5 1/4 x 8, illus., softcover $12.95

EXPLORING CONSCIOUSNESS IN THE HOROSCOPE
edited by Noel Tyl

When Llewellyn asked astrologers across the country which themes to include in its "New World Astrology Series," most specified at the top of their lists themes that explore consciousness! From shallow pipedreaming to ecstatic transcendence, "consciousness" has come to envelop realms of emotion, imagination, dreams, mystical experiences, previous lives and lives to come—aspects of the mind which defy scientific explanation. For most, consciousness means self-realization, the "having it all together" to function individualistically, freely, and confidently.

There are many ways to pursue consciousness, to "get it all together." Astrology is an exciting tool for finding the meaning of life and our part within it, to bring our inner selves together with our external realities, in appreciation of the spirit. Here, then, ten fine thinkers in astrology come together to share reflections on the elusive quicksilver of consciousness. They embrace the spiritual—and the practical. All are aware that consciousness feeds our awareness of existence; that, while it defies scientific method, it is vital for life.

0-87542-391-4, 256 pgs., 6 x 9, tables, charts, softcover $12.00

SPIRITUAL, METAPHYSICAL & NEW TRENDS IN MODERN ASTROLOGY
Edited by Joan McEvers

This is the first book in Llewellyn's New World Astrology Series. Edited by well-known astrologer, lecturer and writer Joan McEvers, this book pulls together the latest thoughts by the best astrologers in the field of Spiritual Astrology.

- Gray Keen: Perspective: The Ethereal Conclusion
- Marion D. March: Some Insights Into Esoteric Astrology
- Kimberly McSherry: The Feminine Element of Astrology: Reframing the Darkness
- Kathleen Burt: The Spiritual Rulers and Their Role in the Transformation
- Shirley Lyons Meier: The Secrets Behind Carl Payne Tobey's Secondary Chart
- Jeff Jawer: Astrodrama
- Donna Van Toen: Alice Bailey Revisited
- Philip Sedgwick: Galactic Studies
- Myrna Lofthus: The Spiritual Programming Within a Natal Chart
- Angel Thompson: Transformational Astrology

0-87542-380-9, 264 pgs., 5 1/4 x 8, softcover   **$9.95**

THE ASTROLOGY OF THE MACROCOSM
New Directions in Mundane Astrology
Edited by Joan McEvers

Explains various mundane, transpersonal and worldly events through astrology. The perfect introduction to understanding the fate of nations, weather patterns and other global movements.

- Jimm Erickson: A Philosophy of Mundane Astrology
- Judy Johns: The Ingress Chart
- Jim Lewis: Astro*Carto*Graphy—Bringing Mundane Astrology Down to Earth
- Richard Nolle: The SuperMoon Alignment
- Chris McRae: The Geodetic Equivalent Method of Prediction
- Nicholas Campion: The Age of Aquarius—A Modern Myth
- Nancy Soller: Weather Watching with an Ephemeris
- Marc Penfield: The Mystery of the Romanovs
- Steve Cozzi: The Astrological Quatrains of Michel Nostradamus
- Diana K. Rosenberg: Stalking the Wild Earthquake
- Caroline W. Casey: Dreams and Disasters—Patterns of Cultural and Mythological Evolution into the 21st Century

0-87542-384-1, 420 pgs., 5 1/4 x 8, charts, softcover   **$19.95**

WEB OF RELATIONSHIPS
Spiritual, Karmic & Psychological Bonds
edited by Joan McEvers

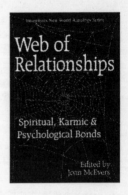

The astrology of intimacy has long been a popular subject among professional astrologers and psychologists. Many have sought the answer to what makes some people have successful relationships with one another, while others struggle. *Web of Relationships* examines this topic not only in intimate affiliations, but also in families and friendships, in this eighth volume of the Llewellyn New World Astrology Series.

Editor Joan McEvers has brought together the wisdom and experience of eight astrology experts. Listen to what one author says about the mythological background of planets as they pertain to relationships. Discover how past life regression is illustrated in the chart. Consider the relationship of astrology and transactional analysis. *Web of Relationships* explores the karmic and mystical connections between child and parent, how friends support and understand each other, the significance of the horoscope as it pertains to connections and much more. Each chapter will bring you closer to your own web of relationships and the astrology of intimacy.

0-87542-388-4, 240 pgs., 6 x 9, softcover **$14.95**

ASTROLOGICAL COUNSELING
The Path to Self-Actualization
Edited by Joan McEvers

This book explores the challenges for today's counselors and gives guidance to those interested in seeking an astrological counselor to help them win their own personal challenges. Includes articles by 10 well-known astrologers:

- David Pond: Astrological Counseling
- Maritha Pottenger: Potent, Personal Astrological Counseling
- Bill Herbst: Astrology and Psychotherapy: A Comparison for Astrologers
- Gray Keen: Plato Sat on a Rock
- Ginger Chalford, Ph.D.: Healing Wounded Spirits: An Astrological Counseling Guide to Releasing Life Issues
- Donald L. Weston, Ph.D.: Astrology and Therapy/Counseling
- Susan Dearborn Jackson: Reading the Body, Reading the Chart
- Doris A. Hebel: Business Counseling
- Donna Cunningham: The Adult Child Syndrome, Codependency, and Their Implications for Astrologers
- Eileen Nauman: Medical Astrology Counseling

0-87542-385-X, 304 pgs., 5 1/4 x 8, charts, softcover $14.95

PLANETS: The Astrological Tools
Edited by Joan McEvers

Explains various mundane, transpersonal and worldly events through astrology. The perfect introduction to understanding the fate of nations, weather patterns and other global movements.

- Jimm Erickson: A Philosophy of Mundane Astrology
- Judy Johns: The Ingress Chart
- Jim Lewis: Astro*Carto*Graphy—Bringing Mundane Astrology Down to Earth
- Richard Nolle: The SuperMoon Alignment
- Chris McRae: The Geodetic Equivalent Method of Prediction
- Nicholas Campion: The Age of Aquarius—A Modern Myth
- Nancy Soller: Weather Watching with an Ephemeris
- Marc Penfield: The Mystery of the Romanovs
- Steve Cozzi: The Astrological Quatrains of Michel Nostradamus
- Diana K. Rosenberg: Stalking the Wild Earthquake
- Caroline W. Casey: Dreams and Disasters—Patterns of Cultural and Mythological Evolution into the 21st Century

0-87542-381-7, 384 pgs., 5-1/4 x 8, softcover $12.95

SIGNS OF LOVE
**Your Personal Guide to Romantic
and Sexual Compatibility
by Jeraldine Saunders**

Unlimited love power can be yours through an intimate knowledge of your horoscope, your numerical birth path, and other vitally important signs and signals that lead the way to loving relationships.

Now in an irresistible approach to the human heart, Jeraldine Saunders, a noted authority on the mystic arts, shows you how to look for love, how to find it, and how to be sure of it. With the aid of astrology, graphology, numerology, palmistry, and face reading, you will discover everything you need to know about your prospects with a given individual. You will learn the two enemies of love and how to eliminate them; the characteristics of all twelve zodiacal signs; the signs that are compatible with yours; the secrets behind your lover's facial features.

Signs of Love is the ultimate guide for gaining a better understanding of yourself and others in order to create a meaningful love life and attain lasting happiness.

0-87542-706-5, 320 pgs., 6 x 9, illus., softcover   **$9.95**

NAVIGATING BY THE STARS
**Astrology and the Art of Decision-Making
by Edith Hathaway**

This book is chock full of convenient shortcuts to mapping out one's life. It presents the decision-maker's astrology, with the full range of astrological techniques.

No other one source presents all these cutting edge methods: Uranian astrology, the 90° dial, astromapping, Saturn quarters, hard aspects, angular relationships, the Meridian House System, secondary progressions, solar arc directions, eclipses, solstice and equinox charts, transiting lunation cycles, monthly kinetic mundascope graphs, among others.

To illustrate the immediate applications of the techniques, the author examines many charts in depth, focussing on study of character, destiny, timing cycles, and geographical location. She draws form 45 wide-ranging personal stories, including famous figures from history, politics, show business, the annals of crime, even corporations.

0-87542-366-3, 320 pgs., 6 x 9, softcover   **$14.95**

THE BOOK OF LOVERS
Men Who Excite Women,
Women Who Excite Men
by Carolyn Reynolds

What are you looking for in a lover or potential mate? If it's money, set your sights on a Pisces/Taurus. Is exercise and health food your passion? Then a Virgo/Cancer will share it with you.

Where do you find these people? They're all here, in *The Book of Lovers*. Astrologer Carolyn Reynolds introduces a new and accurate way to determine romantic compatibility through the use of Sun and Moon sign combinations. And best of all, you don't have to know a single thing about astrology to use this book!

Here you will find descriptions of every man and woman born between the years 1900 and 2000. To see whether that certain someone could be "the one," simply locate his or her birthdata in the chart and flip to the relevant pages to read about your person's strengths and weaknesses, sex appeal, personality and most importantly, how they will treat you!

0-87542-289-0, 464 pgs., 6 x 9, softcover **$12.95**

IN DEFENSE OF ASTROLOGY
Astrology's Answers to Its Critics
by Robert Parry

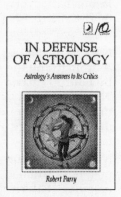

Enthusiasts of astrology often find themselves confronted by others who are hostile to their cause. Now Robert Parry gives you the ammunition that astrologers have been waiting for in the form of real proof that astrology is a legitimate science.

Parry uncovers cautionary tales, lies and statistics and provides supportive examples, observations and illustrations that are a persuasive defense of late 20th century astrology in light of modern research. He provides quick-fire answers for common criticisms and gives the 12 types of critique usually levelled against astrology.

Learn about the mechanics of the birth chart, explore the history of astrology, find out how to select a reputable astrologer, discover why newspaper horoscopes are not accurate, and examine how personality can have an effect on astrology.

0-87542-596-8, 224 pgs., 6 x 9, softcover **$9.95**

FORECASTING BACKWARD AND FORWARD
Modern Techniques of Timing and Rectification
by B. F. Hammerslough

While it is a profound experience to understand the *meanings* of the symbols in the horoscope, astrology *really* comes alive when you can see how your chart's potentials unfold in *time*. This book will teach you the dynamics of specific time periods and instruct you in how to forecast the coming trends in your life.

The most difficult area for both the student and professional astrologer is in understanding and applying the various forecasting techniques. In clear, contemporary language, *Forecasting Backward and Forward* explains the classical methods of forecasting and introduces many powerful new techniques such as Uranian Astrology and Cosmobiology, Astro*Carto*Graphy and relocated charts, composite and Davison relationship charts, and planetary arc directions.

In order to forecast accurately, you need a precise time of birth. Because this is often not available, the second half of this book is dedicated to the craft of chart rectification. You will learn how to work backward from important life events to determine the exact moment of birth.
ISBN: 0-87542-396-5, 288 pgs., 6 x 9, 110 charts, softbound $14.95

OPTIMUM CHILD
Developing Your Child's Fullest Potential Through Astrology
by Gloria Star

This is a brand new approach to the subject of astrology as applied to children. Not much has been written on developmental astrology, and this book fills a gap that has needed filling for years. There is enough basic material for the novice astrologer to easily determine the needs of his or her child (or children) All it takes is the natal chart. A brief table of where the planets were when your child was born is included in the book so that even if you don't have a chart on your child, you can find out enough to fully develop his or her potentials.

In *Optimum Child*, you will find a thorough look at the planets, houses, rising signs, aspects and transits. Each section includes physical, mental and emotional activities that your child would best respond to. It is the most comprehensive book yet on child astrology. This one is definitely not for children only. Every parent and professional astrologer should read it thoroughly. You should use it and help your child develop those talents and potentials inherent in what is shown within the natal chart.
0-87542-740-5, 352 pgs., 6 x 9, softcover $9.95

THE INSTANT HOROSCOPE READER
Planets by Sign, House and Aspect
Julia Lupton Skalka
Find out what was written in the planets at your
birth! Almost everyone enjoys reading the popular
Sun sign horoscopes in newspapers and maga-
zines; however, there is much more to astrology
than knowing what your Sun sign is. How do you
interpret your natal chart so that you know what it
means to have Gemini on your 8th house cusp?
What does astrology say about someone whose
Sun is conjoined with natal Jupiter?

The Instant Horoscope Reader was written to answer
such questions and to give beginners a fresh, thorough overview of the
natal chart. Here you will find the meaning of the placement of the Sun,
the Moon and each planet in the horoscope, including aspects between
the natal planets, the meaning of the houses in the horoscope and house
rulerships. Even if you have not had your chart cast, this book includes
simple tables that enable you to locate the approximate planetary and
house placements and figure the planetary aspects for your birthdate to
give you unique perspectives about yourself and others.
ISBN: 1-56718-669-6, 6 x 9, 272 pp., illus.   **$14.95**

TIME & MONEY
The Astrology of Wealth—How You Can
Anticipate the Changing Times and Turn
Them to Financial Advantage
by Barbara Koval
This book is about using a 2,000-year-old accumulation of knowledge to understand money, what it
does, where it's heading, and how to make it work
for you. *Time & Money* is based on the premise
that astrology and its symbols form a theoretical
model that contains almost everything you need
to know about economic principles and trends.
Using astrology, *Time & Money* demonstrates pat-

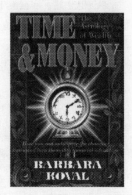

terns of economic activity that enable the average person to dig through
the hysteria that is seeping into our consciousness due to bank failures,
national debt and unemployment.

Time & Money is for everyone. Students of astrology will gain an understanding of financial and economic analysis as well as mundane astrology. Investors, market analysts and students of cycles will find much to
apply to their own knowledge of fundamental and technical analyses of
the financial markets—timings that can be enhanced by simple references to ephemerides and astrological charts.
0-87542-364-7, 352 pgs., 6 x 9, softcover   **$12.95**

YOUR PLANETARY PERSONALITY
**Everything You Need to Make Sense of
Your Horoscope
by Dennis Oakland**

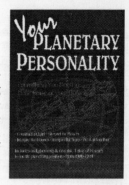

This book deepens the study of astrological interpretation for professional and beginning
astrologers alike. Dennis Oakland's interpretations of the planets in the houses and signs are the
result of years of study of psychology, sciences,
symbolism, Eastern philosophy plus the study of
birth charts from a psychotherapy group. Unlike
the interpretations in other books, these emphasize the life processes involved and facilitate a
greater understanding of the chart. Includes 100-year ephemeris.

Even if you now know *nothing* about astrology, Dennis Oakland's clear
instructions will teach you how to construct a complete and accurate
birth chart for anyone born between 1900 to 1999. After you have built
your chart, he will lead you through the steps of reading it, giving you
indepth interpretations of each of your planets. When done, you will
have the satisfaction that comes from increased self-awareness *and* from
being your *own* astrologer!

This book is also an excellent exploration for psychologists and psychiatrists who use astrology in their practices.

0-87542-594-1, 580 pgs., 7 x 10, softcover **$19.95**

ASTRO-ECONOMICS
**A Study of Astrology and the Business Cycle
by David Williams**

This informative, comprehensive volume combines history, theory,
astrology, and finance to form a systematic predictive science of the
business cycle.

Following a review of economic thought pertaining to this cycle, the
author examines possible planetary causes of heavy sunspot activity and
its correlation to business cycles. Major economic turns and geocentric
planetary aspect data have been compiled with Jupiter-Uranus, Jupiter-
Saturn and Saturn-Uranus conjunctions coinciding with depressions or
low business activity in America. Uranus moving into the sign of Gemini, however, has come to be a predictor of a major liberating event.

An extensive discussion of the nullification of unfavorable aspects by
more powerful favorable aspects (and vice versa) is also presented.
Numerous tables, charts and wheels graphically represent such findings. A great introduction to financial astrology for the novice, as well as
a wonderful reference book for any financial analyst.

0-87542-882-7, 64 pgs., 8 1/2 x 11, charts, softcover **$3.00**

TRANSITS IN REVERSE
Astrological Planning for Success
by Edna Copeland Ryneveld

Have you wondered about whether you should take that trip or ask for that raise? Do you want to know when the best time is for a wedding? How about knowing in advance the times when you will be the most creative and dazzling?

This book is different from all others published on transits (those planets that are actually moving around in the heavens making aspects to our natal planets). It gives the subject area first—such as creativity, relationships, health—and then tells you what transits to look for. The introductory chapters are so thorough that you will be able to use this book with only an ephemeris or astrological calendar to tell you where the planets are. The author explains what transits are, how they affect your daily life, how to track them, how to make decisions based on transits and much more.

With the information in each section, you can combine as many factors as you like to get positive results. If you are going on a business trip you can look at the accidents section to avoid any trouble, the travel section to find out the best date, the relationship section to see how you will get along with the other person, the business section to see if it is a good time to do business, the communication section to see if things will flow smoothly, and more. In this way, you can choose the absolute best date for just about anything! Electional astrology as been used for centuries, but now it is being given in the most easily understood and practical format yet.

0-87542-674-3, 408 pgs., 6 x 9, softcover $12.95

THE ASTROLOGICAL THESAURUS, BOOK ONE
House Keywords
Michael Munkasey

Keywords are crucial for astrological work. They correctly translate astrological symbols into clear, everyday language—which is a never-ending pursuit of astrologers. For example, the Third House can be translated into the keywords "visitors," "early education" or "novelist."

The Astrological Thesaurus, Book One: House Keywords is a the first easy-to-use reference book and textbook on the houses, their psychologically rich meanings, and their keywords. This book also includes information on astrological quadrants and hemispheres, how to choose a house system, and the mathematical formulations for many described house systems.

Astrologer Michael Munkasey compiled almost 14,000 keywords from more than 600 sources over a 23-year period. He has organized them into 17 commonplace categories (e.g., things, occupations and psychological qualities), and cross-referenced them three ways for ease of use: alphabetically, by house, and by category. Horary users, in particular, will find this book extremely useful.

0-87542-579-8, 434 pgs., 7 x 10, illus., softcover **$19.95**

ASTROLOGY AND THE GAMES PEOPLE PLAY
A Tool for Self-Understanding
in Work & Relationships
by Spencer Grendahl

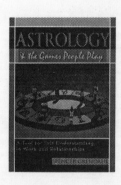

Expand your self-awareness and facilitate personal growth with the Astro-analysis approach to astrology! Astro-analysis is a completely new and unique system that enables you to combine simple astrological information with the three-ring model of basic ego states—Parent, Adult and Child—used in popular psychology. This easy-to-follow technique makes available to the average person psychological insights that are generally available only to astrologers. Not only is it easy to transcribe your horoscope onto Astro-analysis' three-sphere diagram, but you will find that this symbolic picture provides accurate and meaningful perceptions into the energy patterns of your personality, clearly delineating the areas that may be "overweighted" or most in need of balance. This material is enhanced by examples and explanations of horoscopes of actual people.

Astro-analysis is a powerful self-help tool that will quickly make you aware of the basis for your behavior patterns and attitudes, so you can get a new perspective on your relationships with others and determine the most promising strategies for personal growth.

1-56718-338-7, 224 pgs., 7 x 10, softcover **$12.95**